AD INFINITUM

AD INFINITUM

A Biography of Latin

NICHOLAS OSTLER

WALKER & COMPANY
New York

Published by Walker Publishing Company, Inc., New York
Distributed to the trade by Holtzbrinck Publishers

All papers used by Walker & Company are natural, recyclable products
made from wood grown in well-managed forests. The manufacturing processes
conform to the environmental regulations of the country of origin.

LIBRARY OF CONGRESS CATALOGING-IN-PUBLICATION DATA HAS BEEN APPLIED FOR.

Art credits Page 8: Universidad de Navarra. Pages 19, 22, 28, 33, 48, 125, 129, 186, and 310: University of
Saskatchewan Museum of Antiquities. Pages 27 and 28: Katholische Universitat Ingolstadt. Pages 33, 35,
45, 72, 74, 76, 84, 153, 169, 176, 200, 225, 241, 256, 280, 282, and 305: Bridgeman Art Library. Pages
275 and 298: Science Photo Library. Pages 288 and 312: National Archives. Page 102: Getty Images
(both images). Page 50: University of East Anglia. Maps on pages 31, 52, 88, and 311 by Jeffrey Ward.

ISBN-10: 0-8027-1515-X
ISBN-13: 978-0-8027-1515-9

Visit Walker & Company's Web site at www.walkerbooks.com

First U.S. edition 2007

1 3 5 7 9 10 8 6 4 2

Designed by Sara Stemen
Typeset by Westchester Book Group
Printed in the United States of America by Quebecor World Fairfield

To the memory of my parents

Kenneth MacLachlan Ostler
Yvonne Louise Ostler, née Jolly

HISTORIAM VERO, QVA TOT SIMVL RERVM LONGA ET
CONTINVATA RATIO SIT HABENDA CAVSAEQVE FACTORVM
OMNIVM SINGVLATIM EXPLICANDAE ET DE QVACVMQVE RE
IVDICIVM IN MEDIO PROFERENDVM, EAM QVIDEM VELVT
INFINITA MOLE CALAMVM OBRVENTE TAM PROFITERI
PERICVLOSVM EST QVAM PRAESTARE DIFFICILE.

But a history, in which a long, continuous account must be given of
so many things at once, and the causes of all the events explained singly,
and a judgment offered on each, with its infinite-seeming mass bearing
down on the pen, is as dangerous to propose as it is difficult to deliver.

Leonardo Bruni, *Historia Populi Florentini,* preface

❖

IDEO AVTEM PRIVS DE LINGVIS, AC DEINDE
DE GENTIBVS POSVIMVS, QVIA EX LINGVIS GENTES,
NON EX GENTIBVS LINGVAE EXORTAE SVNT.

Therefore we have first discussed languages, and only then peoples,
because peoples have arisen from languages, not languages from peoples.

Isidore, *Etymologiae,* ix.i.14

❖

LECTOR INTENDE: LAETABERIS.

Reader, pay attention. You will enjoy yourself.

Apuleius, *Metamorphoseon,* i.i

Contents

PART III: WORLDS BUILT ON LATIN

PART IV: LATIN IN A VERNACULAR WORLD

Praefatio

NOWADAYS LATIN SEEMS A comical language. Its antiquity over-whelms us and we are embarrassed. The thing to do with it is make laconic remarks (*mea culpa* 'my fault', *carpe diem* 'pluck the day', *veni vidi vici* 'I came, I saw, I conquered', *tu quoque* 'you too'), cast spells (*reparo* 'I repair (my spectacles), *expecto patronum* 'I await the master'), or translate children's classics (*Winnie Ille Pu, Alicia in Terra Mirabili, Harrius Potter*). Modern English students of Latin receive their lessons by courtesy of a Roman mouse, *Minimus Mus*. The sheer ponderosity of the Latin word-endings calls forth guffaws in English speakers, whether it is Monty Python's Pontius Pilate defending the honor of his friends Biggus Dickus and wife Incontinentia Buttox, or anonymous macaronic punsters, providing Anglo-Latin non-sense:

> *boyibus kissibus priti girlorum*
> *girlibus likibus wanti somorum.*

And then there are the associations with anatomy and sex, where Latin seems a whole language provided for purposes of euphemism: *fellatio, coitus interrup-tus, eiaculatio praecox*. When Queen Elizabeth II rather poignantly called 1992 her *annus horribilis*, the *Sun* newspaper immediately had the vulgar wit to translate it as 'one's bum year'.

Latin is often happy to be ridiculous. Plautus' twenty-one comedies from the third century BC are the first substantial set of texts that have sur-vived in it; and faced with current events, as Juvenal pointed out in the second century AD, DIFFICILE EST SATVRAM NON SCRIBERE 'it is difficult not to write a satire'.

But it was not always frivolous: for more than two thousand years written

Latin was the preeminent mode of serious expression in Europe. That is a long time, and time for a lot of business. Even so, one of its first recorded poets, Naevius, was coyly doubtful of its future:

> ITAQVE POSTQVAM EST ORCHI TRADITVS THESAVRO,
> OBLITI SVNT ROMAI LOQVIER LINGVA LATINA.
> And so after he passed to the vault of Orchus [the Underworld],
> the Romans forgot how to speak the Latin language. (Naevius, 204 BC)

Naevius' jocular prediction was not borne out. Yet at the other end of its history, there was just as little comprehension of what the future held in store for Latin. Eighteen centuries later and shortly before it was at long last to go out of active use, a disgraced former chancellor of England, expressing relief at the final publication of his work in Latin, had roundly stated his faith in its durability among languages: "For these modern languages will at one time or another play the bank-rowtes [bankrupts] with books; and since I have lost much time with this age, I would be glad as God shall give me leave to recover it with posterity" (Francis Bacon, 1623 AD). Those who lived with and in Latin clearly could not see the full trajectory of its history, the strengths and ultimately the weaknesses revealed during these two millennia. But that trajectory is what this book sets out to reveal.

Ad Infinitum tells the story of how Latin spread, first as the speech of an unremittingly aggressive and expansive city-state, Rome, then as the lingua franca of the barracks, farming estates, and urban trading centers that its empire established across the lands of the whole western Mediterranean; and of how much later it would spread as the medium of a Christian church that went even farther, seeking converts out to the Atlantic coast of Ireland, the fjords of Norway, and the plains of eastern Poland. Latin was a language spread by force of arms, colonial settlement, trading networks, cultural diffusion, military recruitment, and religious conversion. The character of the civilization expressed in this language changed over time, but there were elements—associated with Latin—that did not change.

This common thread of Latin, once the sound of Europe's distinctive view of the world, is now a universal academic code, but also a thing of nostalgia. Latin, having been the no-nonsense, hectoring voice of Roman power, and then the soaring mood-music of the Catholic Church, has ended up being used above all to provide the scientific formulas that characterize every life-form on earth. But it is also a language of the heart: the foundation for

romance—in all its senses—and a common cultural basis for Europe, the ultimate classic of education.

After the fall of the Roman Empire, Latin came to be a schoolmaster's
language, passed on exclusively in the classroom by the inculcation—literally
'trampling in'—of rules of grammar. (Not that this limited its prospects, or its
utility in the wider world of power and propaganda: its influence was undi-
minished even a millennium later.) The popularity of favorite textbooks could
be amazingly long-lasting: the record must be held by one of the first, Martianus Capella's *Marriage of Philology and Mercury*, still being given to pupils
twelve hundred years after it was first written in the fifth century AD, but
honorable mention is due also to Alexander's *Doctrinale* (279 editions all over
Europe from the thirteenth to the sixteenth centuries), and William Lily's
Short Introduction of Grammar, which was still regularly being used by English
speakers everywhere two centuries after its first edition in 1511. By these standards, Benjamin H. Kennedy's *Latin Primer* (first issued in 1866 but still in
use today) is a mere latecomer. I was brought up on Kennedy, as was my father
before me, and very likely my grandfather too (though I never asked him).

We were latecomers to Latin, then; but also at a turning point. The British
Empire, which my father and grandfather had fought to defend, in India and in
Africa, was dissolved into the Commonwealth while I was growing up in the
1960s. Right on cue, elementary Latin had ceased to be a requirement for entry
to any British university by the end of the same decade. British imperialists of
the nineteenth and twentieth centuries had modeled themselves on the Romans,
just as Spanish imperialists had in the sixteenth, and indeed American consti-
tutionalists in the eighteenth. Europeans have in fact been enthralled by the
memory of Latin ever since it ceased to be our working language. But in the
1960s the world was turning its back on it.

This Latin winter was sharp. Yet new and rather different institutions
were already establishing themselves as the last of the European empires were
passing to the vault of Orcus. The new world status of the United States of
America after the Second World War was widely characterized with the Latin
phrase *Pax Americana*; here was a new imperial order, but one declaredly without colonies. Could the Roman model apply to it—whether of Empire or
Church? And a Europe newly determined to abolish war among its nations has
transformed itself into a European Union, choosing for itself a new Latin
motto, *In varietate concordia*. In the twenty-first century, breakdowns in good
governance in countries all over the world have tempted foreign-policy mak-
ers to reexamine the virtues of imperial-style intervention. The Roman model

remains implicit, and that is one reason why Latin's importance remains controversial to this day. It is time to examine the character of an empire, of a church, of a civilization, whose life was in Latin.

The language itself remained curiously unchanged throughout its long active career. Naevius' and Bacon's works are written in a common code, whose stable rules were transmitted intact through eighty generations of grammar school classes: contrast English, which has only existed at all for sixty generations, and which in its modern form has only lasted for twenty. What has changed has been in the handwriting, epigraphy and typefaces that have represented the eternal words on the page. The SQVARE CAPITALS* of the Roman Republic and Empire,

INMORTALES MORTALES SI FORET FAS FLERE,
FLERENT DIVAE CAMENAE NAEVIVM POETAM.

which are represented straightforwardly in the first nine chapters, yielded to a variety of rounder and more cursive scripts beginning in the fourth century. First there is rustic:

ECCE OMNIS TERRA AD POTENTISSIMAE GENTIS FREMITVM CONTREMISCIT,
ET TAMEN ROMANO AD TE ANIMO VENIT, QVI BARBARVS PVTABATVR

In the fifth century this was largely replaced by uncial, in the main a Christian innovation:

---

*Latin had a consonantal i and v (pronounced as English *y* and *w*), and a vocalic i and v (pronounced as in *hit, Evita; put, lunar*); but in spelling *J* was not distinguished from *I*, nor *U* from *V* (therefore, VT VOVI 'as I vowed', EIVS IVSTI 'of that just man'). Such distinctions were not made until well after the advent of printing, although both forms of each letter had long been used stylistically in handwriting, e.g., *v* at the beginning of a word, *j* at the end, regardless of whether a vowel or consonant is meant (*vt voui, eius iustj*). *J* began to represent a consonantal sound in Spain in the fifteenth century, *V* in France in the seventeenth, and this fashion spread across the European languages. They were still, however, seen as variants of the vowel letters. Only with Noah Webster's *American Dictionary of the English Language* (1828) did *J* and *V* become established as letters independent of *I* and *U*.

This development of new letters had nothing to do with change in Latin, or its pronunciation; yet irrationally, the usual convention in writing Latin nowadays is to distinguish consonantal *V* from vocalic *U*, but to leave consonantal and vocalic *I* undistinguished: *ut vovi, eius iusti*.

lingua latinorum, quae meditatione scripturarum
ceteris omnibus est facta communis

Then, in the late eighth century, Carolingian style took over, and this lasted
for more than four centuries:

Me legat antiquas vult qui proferre loquelas;
Me qui non sequitur vult sine lege loqui.

But in the thirteenth century this in turn was succeeded by the new Gothic, or
Blackletter, style:

Dicebat Bernardus Carnotensis nos esse quasi nanos, gigantium humeris incidentes, ut
possimus plura eis et remotiora videre

Gothic was still in place when the Germans of the fifteenth century invented
the first typefaces for printing, and it became the model for them (e.g., for
Gutenberg's Bible). Italians, however, soon attempted to reinstate the old
styles that they found in old (uncial and Carolingian) manuscripts and attributed to their beloved Ancients, inventing for the purpose the italic and Roman
styles, which have remained characteristic of western European (and hence
American) printing to this day.

> *An grammaticorum, quorum propositum videtur fuisse ut linguam latinam dedo-*
> *cerent? An denique rhetoricorum, qui ad hanc usque aetatem plurimi circumfere-*
> *bantur, nihil aliud docentes nisi gothice dicere?*
>
> Italice loquentem soli Itali intelligent; qui tantum Hispanice loquatur inter
> Germanos pro muto habebitur; Germanus inter Italos nutu ac manibus pro
> lingua uti cogetur; qui Gallico sermone peritissime ac scientissime utatur, ubi
> e Gallia exierit, saepe ultro irridebitur; qui Graece Latineque sciat, is, quo-
> cunque terrarum venerit, apud plerosque admirationi erit.

Aside from the square capitals of Rome's Republican and Imperial language,
this book systematically represents Latin in italics. Other languages that crop
up—such as Etruscan, Greek, German, Hebrew, and the many varieties of
Romance that have culminated in modern western European languages—are
also set down in an italic transcription, but where a text is quoted in extenso at
the head of a chapter, the authentic script is occasionally used.

Although plenty of Latin is cited in the text—and even more in the endnotes—the book does not aim to give you the rudiments of the language. For that—in default of a serious Latin course—you must consult Tore Janson's *Natural History of Latin*, Harry Mount's *Amo, Amas, Amat . . . and all that*, or indeed dear old Benjamin Kennedy himself. What this book aims to do, rather than to give a halting competence in the language, or re-create an echo of the experience in a grammar-school classroom, is to show what the career of Latin amounted to; and wherever possible, to infer the character, the respected ideal, that grew up within the tradition of the Latin language. This is partly an inspiration to us, but also a warning.

For although it claimed to be universal, Latin always indicated Rome as the fixed point of reference for its world. Latin knew no boundaries because it was looking inward, back toward the Eternal City. Perhaps the effort to understand a language and a civilization that were so polarized may reorient our own sense of direction.

⟡

I owe thanks to my agent, Natasha Fairweather of A. P. Watt, for assurance that now is the time for a book about Latin, and to my publishers, George Gibson of Walker & Company and Richard Johnson of HarperCollins, for encouragement to see it through. To Natasha I have looked for SEMINA RERVM, discussing themes, to George for the LABOR IMPROBVS of detailed criticism, to Richard for AEQVVS ANIMVS in grand strategy. My background resources have been the London Library of St James' Square (as ever, my flexible friend), the Sackler and Bodleian libraries of Oxford, and the unexpected riches of the Hitotsubashi University Library in Kunitachi, west of Tokyo. I depend here on all I learned from Latin teachers over the 1960s and early 1970s: Michael†, Eric†, and Maurice† Bickmore, Geoffrey Allibone, James Howarth†, Jack Ind, Michael McCrum†, Robert Ogilvie†, Eric Smalman-Smith, Jasper Griffin, Anthony Kenny, Oliver Lyne†, Anna Morpurgo Davies, John Penney, Harald Reiche†, and Jochen Schindler†. Friends too over the years have injected and interjected much wit: I think especially of David W. Bradley†, Charles and Francis Montagu, Jeremy Lawrance, David Nash, Harald Haarmann, and Jonathan Lewis. My wife, Jane, and daughter, Sophia, have endured, inspired, and sweetened all my necessary absences.

HOC ILLVD EST PRAECIPVE IN COGNITIONE RERVM SALVBRE
AC FRVGIFERVM, OMNIS TE EXEMPLI DOCVMENTA IN
INLVSTRI POSITA MONVMENTO INTVERI; INDE TIBI
TVAEQVE REI PVBLICAE QVOD IMITERE CAPIAS, INDE FOEDVM
INCEPTV FOEDVM EXITV QVOD VITES.

This is what is beneficial and good for you in history, to be able to examine
the record of every kind of event set down vividly. Here you can find
for yourself and your country examples to follow, and here too ugly
enterprises with ugly outcomes to avoid.

Livy, *Ab Urbe Condita*, preface

PART I

A LATIN WORLD

✧⊶✦⊷✧

CHAPTER I

Ad infinitum—
An Empire Lived in Latin

. . . HVMANITAS VOCABATVR, CVM PARS SERVITVTIS ESSET.

. . . called "civilization," when it was just part of being a slave.

Tacitus, *Agricola*, xxi

T HE HISTORY OF LATIN is the history of the development of western Europe, right up to the point when Europe made its shattering impact on the rest of the world. In fact, only seen from the perspective of Latin does Europe really show itself as a single story: nothing else was there all the way through and involved in so many aspects, not Rome, not the Empire, not the Catholic Church, not even Christianity itself.

For the people who spoke and wrote it, the language was their constant companion; learning it was the universal key for entry into their culture; and expression in it was the unchanging means for taking social action. And this relationship with Latin, for its speakers and writers, lasted for two and a half thousand years from 750 BC. There was a single tradition through those millennia, and it was expressed—almost exclusively until 1250, and predominantly and influentially for another five hundred years thereafter—in Latin. Romans' and Europeans' thoughts were formed in Latin; and so the history of Latin, however clearly or vaguely we may discern it, is utterly and pervasively bound up with the thinking behind the history of western Europe.

Latin, properly understood, is something like the soul of Europe's civilization. But the European unity that the Romans achieved and organized was something very different from the consensual model of the modern European Union. It was far closer in spirit to the kind of unity that Hitler and Mussolini were aiming at. No one ever voted to join the Roman Empire, even if the empire itself was run through elected officials, and LIBERTAS remained a Roman ideal. ROMANITAS—the Roman way as such—was never something voluntarily adopted by non-Roman communities.* Conquest by a Roman army was almost always required before outsiders would come to see its virtues, and knowledge of Latin spread within a new province.

At the outset, the Latin language was something imposed on a largely unwilling populace, if arguably—in the Roman mind, and that of later generations—for their greater good. There was no sense of charm or seduction about the spread of Latin, and in this it differs from some other widespread languages: consider the pervasive image of Sanskrit as a luxuriant growth across the expanse of India and Southeast Asia, or indeed the purported attractions of French in the nineteenth century as an alluring mistress. Speakers of Latin, even the most eloquent and illustrious, saw it as a serious and overbearing vehicle for communication. In the famous words of Virgil:

TV REGERE IMPERIO POPVLOS, ROMANE, MEMENTO	you, Roman, mind to rule peoples at your command
—HAE TIBI ERVNT ARTES— PACISQVE IMPONERE MOREM	(these arts will be yours), to impose the way of peace,
PARCERE SVBIECTIS ET DEBELLARE SVPERBOS	to spare the conquered, and to battle down the proud.[1]

EXPOLIA, "Strip him."

The most excellent Flavius Leontius Beronicianus, governor of the Thebaid in southern Egypt in the early 400s AD,† ruled a Greek-speaking province. Greek had been the language of power there since the days of the Ptolemies more than seven centuries before, but the judicial system over which he presided was Roman. Its official records were kept in Latin, even of proceedings that actually took place largely in Greek and perhaps marginally (and through Greek interpreters) in Egyptian. The record we have, apparently verbatim, is in a mixture of Latin and Greek. Fifteen centuries later, it turned up on an Egyptian rubbish dump.

---

*Probably the closest to such a voluntary annexation happened in 133 BC, when the king of the Asian city of Pergamum died and bequeathed his whole kingdom to the Roman people.
†FL(AVIVS) LEONTIVS BERONICIANV(S) V(IR) C(LARISSIMVS) PR(AESES) TEBAEI(DIS)

Slaves called to witness in Roman trials had always been routinely beaten, in theory as a guarantee of honesty; but on this day Beronicianus seems to have been in two minds. EXPOLIA. The governor was speaking Latin, and so the first the witness would have known of what was to happen was when his shirt was taken off him. The governor went on in Greek, "For what reason did you enter proceedings against the councillor?" remarking to the staff officer (also in Greek), "Have him beaten." The record states that the witness was thrashed with ox sinews, and then the governor said in Greek, "Don't beat free men." And turning to the staff, PARCE, "Leave off."²

What was it like having your life run for you in Latin? Even after three centuries of Roman rule, Latin stood as a potent symbol of irresistible, and sometimes arbitrary, power, especially to those who did not know the language.

By the nature of things, we do not have many direct accounts of being on the receiving end of government administered in Latin. Our sources are writings that have survived, whether on papyrus and parchment through two millennia of recopying, or on scraps of masonry that have directly defied erosion and decay. And where Latin was dominant, Latin users largely monopolized literacy. We seek almost in vain for non-Latin attitudes to the advent of Latin.

In fact, some of the most vividly subjective statements of the impact of Roman rule and the advent of Latin come from the pen of a man who had held the highest elective office in the Roman state, the historian Cornelius Tacitus. He described the British in the second century as ready to tolerate military service, tribute, and other impositions of empire, up to but not including abuse, "being already schooled to obey, but not yet to accept slavery."* He also articulated the anti-Roman arguments of those who backed the British queen Boudicca's revolt, after a first generation of Roman rule: "Once we used to have one king at a time, but now we get two imposed, the legate to ravage our lifeblood, and the procurator our goods, one served by centurions, the other by slaves, all combining violence with insolence . . . and look at how few the invaders are, compared with our numbers."³

Clearly, the major inconveniences of life under the Empire were taxes and military conscription, and neither was helped by the manifestly arbitrary way that those in charge could abuse their offices. But for many in the first

---

*IAM DOMITI VT PAREANT, NONDVM VT SERVIANT. Tacitus, *Agricola*, xiii.

generation to be conquered, the far greater threats were of personal enslavement and deportation, a life made up of all duties and no rights, next to which
this "moral slavery" that exercised Tacitus was no slavery at all. This very real
prospect, aggravated by the thought that the new recruits would always be the
worst treated, was something else that he imagined looming large in the
minds of Calgacus and his army of North Britons about to make their last
stand against Rome.[4]

On the other hand, once the immovability of the Roman yoke had become established, there were compensations, if only for those nearer the top in
their societies.* Tacitus also commented cynically on the efforts made by the
British elite to accommodate themselves to Roman control (PAX ROMANA).
The governor Agricola, he said, in a deliberate policy of flattery, "instructed
the sons of the chiefs in liberal arts, and expressed a preference for the native
wit of the British over the studies of the Gauls, so as to plant a desire for eloquence in people who had previously rejected the Roman language altogether.
So they took to our dress, and wearing the toga. Gradually they were drawn
off into decadence, with colonnades and baths and chic parties. This these in-
nocents called civilized life [HVMANITAS], whereas it was really part of their
enslavement."[5]

So language was early seen as one of the benefits of the new dispensation.
Later, this enthusiasm threatened to get out of hand: Juvenal, a contemporary
of Tacitus' at Rome, commented on the Empire-wide popularity of the Romans' traditional education in rhetoric:

> Today the whole world has its Greek and Roman Athens;
> the eloquent Gauls have taught the British to be advocates,
> and Thule is talking of hiring an oratory teacher.[6]

In the early days, even some Romans bore the linguistic brunt when the
spreading PAX ROMANA temporarily outran the sphere of Latin's currency.
Ovid was the very model of Roman urbanity, a leading poet and wit in the
time of Augustus, HOMO EMVNCTAE NARIS as they would have put it, 'a man
with an unblocked nose'. With a divine irony, if not poetic justice, he was

---

*Until all free men in the Empire were made citizens in AD 212, Rome recognized the
workings of provinces' preexisting local laws among the majority who lacked Roman
status. But as we have seen in Egypt, in the criminal courts everyone was subject to
Roman law and the governor's assizes.

exiled in AD 8 to Tomi, a town on the western coast of the Black Sea (modern Constantsa) with less than a generation of Romanization behind it. Evidently, he suffered from the lack of Latin there. There was so little of it that his reputation counted for nothing. Instead, he described rather vividly the typical problems of a visitor who "does not speak the language": "They deal in their own friendly language: I have to get things across through gestures. I'm the barbarian here, uncomprehended by anyone, while the Getans laugh witlessly at words of Latin. They openly insult me to my face in safety, perhaps even twitting me for being an exile. And all too often they believe the stories made up about me, however much I shake my head or nod at their words."[7]

But these were just transitional difficulties for Latin speakers in the empire's borderlands. Over the long centuries of Roman domination, the language, even in its written form, came to be used at all levels, perhaps even among building workers. At Newgate in London, a tile has turned up with the graffito AVSTALIS DIBVS XIII VAGATVR SIB COTIDIM 'Gus has been wandering off every day for thirteen days'.[8] One hundred and fifty miles away, in the health resort and holiday center that Romans developed at Bath, a hundred ritual curses and oath tokens have emerged from the waters, written in Latin (sometimes backward): DOCIMEDIS PERDIDIT MANICILIA DVA QVI ILLAS INVOLAVI VT MENTES SVA PERDET OCVLOS SVS IN FANO VBI DESTINA 'Docimedis has lost a pair of gloves. May whoever has made off with them lose his wits and his eyes in the temple where (the goddess) decides'. Although the British language was never fully replaced in Britain (as the modern survival of Welsh and Cornish show), the rulers' language, Latin, clearly came to penetrate deeply into the days and ways of ordinary life.

All over the empire, from Britain to Africa, and from Spain to Asia, men were joining the army, acquiring a command of Latin, and when they settled at the end of their service—sometimes in colonies far from their origins—planting it there. The new Latin speakers made their mark permanently all over the Empire in the spread of their inscriptions. They are typically on tombstones, but the Mediterranean civic life that the Roman veterans brought to their new homes across Europe left written memorials of many kinds. And from these, it is clear that the language spread from military fathers to other members of the family.

In Isca Silurium (Caerleon in south Wales), for example, a daughter, Tadia Exuperata, erected beside her father's grave a memorial to her mother, Tadia Vallaunius, and her brother Tadius Exuperatus, "dead on the German expedition at thirty-seven."[9] At the spa of Aquae Sulis (Bath), where Romans

Memorial to Annia Buturra. Although the legend is in Latin, the imagery is Basque: the red heifer of Mari and the thistle-head 'flower of the sun' eguzki-lorea.

tried to re-create a little luxury to remind them of home, the armorers' craft guild recorded the life of "Julius Vitalis, armorer of the twentieth legion recruited in Belgium, with nine years' service, dead at twenty-nine."[10] Some inscriptions give glimpses of domestic sagas: Rusonia Aventina, visiting from Mediomatrici (Metz) in Gaul (perhaps to take the waters?), was buried at the age of fifty-eight by her heir L. Ulpius Sestius.[11] Some read more like statements by the proverbial "disgusted of Tunbridge Wells": "C. Severinus, Regional Centurion (retd), restored with virtue and the spirit of the emperor the purity of this holy place wrecked through insolence."[12]

In Gastiain, Navarra, Spain, a memorial to a daughter reads, "To the Gods and Spirits (DIIS MANIBVS). Annia Buturra, daughter of Viriatus, thirty years old, placed here." The opening phrase is classic for a Latin epitaph, but the effigies of a young woman seated on a ledge above, and a heifer looking out mournfully below, all surrounded by a frieze of vine leaves and grapes, show belief in a Basque underworld.[13]

Across Europe in Liburnia, modern Croatia, fragments of a sarcophagus no older than the second century AD have been found, this time recording a highly distinguished military career. The inscription reads:

> To the spirits of the departed: Lucius Artorius Castus, centurion of the III Legion *Gallica*, also centurion of the VI Legion *Ferrata*, also centurion of the

II Legion *Adiutrix*, also centurion of the V Legion *Macedonica*, also *primus pilus* of the same, *praepositus* of the Fleet at Misenum, *praefectus* of the VI Legion *Victrix*, *dux* of the legions of cohorts of cavalry from Britain against the Armoricans, *procurator centenarius* of the province of Liburnia, with the power to issue death sentences. In his lifetime he himself had this made for himself and his family.[14]

This sums up the life of an officer who evidently served right across the Empire: He had tours of duty with increasing seniority in five regular legions, as well as a naval command at Rome's prime naval base near Naples, and active service as leader of British native troops in a campaign in Brittany. His last military command had been as *praefectus* in Britain, commanding the VI *Victrix* Legion at York, south of Hadrian's Wall. But the final post of his career, in the area where his sarcophagus was found and where he presumably retired, was a high civil appointment (reserved for EQVITES—Roman 'knights') on the northerly coast of the Adriatic.

And in the great theater of Lepcis, in Libya, an inscription was placed in AD 1–2 by the theater's local patron: "Annobal Rufus, son of Himilcho Tapap, adorner of the fatherland, lover of concord, *flamen*, *suffete*, captain of ritual, had it built at his own expense, and dedicated the same." (It was dedicated to the honor of "the god's son Augustus," a nice touch that dates it, since Julius Caesar's deification had by then been achieved, but not yet that of his adopted son, the emperor Augustus.) Its bicultural credentials were advertised in two ways. He took both Roman and Phoenician priestly titles (*flamen* like the Roman priests of Jupiter and other major gods, and *suffete*, no different from the Hebrew *shophet*, the title of Israel's 'judges'). And the Latin inscription was immediately followed by a Punic equivalent, which actually omitted the loyal references to Augustus. Lepcis had been a relatively free ally of Rome since 111 BC.[15]

By the reign of Augustus, then, which bridged the millennium divide BC–AD, use of Latin was already a natural symbol of allegiance to Rome. And Latin's association with sinews of Roman power—with the army, the courts, and the organs of provincial administration, especially taxation—meant that it remained a highly politically charged language throughout the centuries of Roman rule, and especially so in those parts of the empire—Greece, Asia Minor, Egypt, Africa, and perhaps even Britain—where ordinary people continued to speak something else at home.

HIS EGO NEC METAS RERVM NEC TEMPORA PONO:
IMPERIVM SINE FINE DEDI . . .

On them I place neither bounds to their possessions nor limits in time:
empire without end I have granted . . .

Jupiter's promise to the Romans: Virgil, *Aeneid*, i.279

The Roman Empire was a mighty accomplishment, and it affected—as all empires do—the self-esteem of its citizens, its rulers, and above all its creators. They needed an answer as to what their unreasonable military success really meant. The only answer the Romans found seems to have been that they were fated to dominate the world. This consciousness, inseparable from Latin, is the sense of our title: AD INFINITVM.

When Julius Caesar was in his mid-thirties, serving as governor of Further Spain, he fell to brooding on the career of Alexander the Great. This man had conquered the greatest empire of his day before he was thirty-three, while he himself had not yet done anything memorable. Caesar wept.

In Latin, Suetonius wrote, IAM ALEXANDER ORBEM TERRARVM SVBEGISSET 'Alexander had already subdued the world'. Alexander's conquests had gone from Egypt to modern Pakistan, but on every border there were still neighbors who had not been conquered, Celts, Italians, Ethiopians, Arabs, Armenians, Sogdians, and above all the vast mass of Indians. Exaggerating the scale of mighty conquests came easily in that age. But the striking thing is how they saw their world as existing only as far as they knew it. Caesar went on to do his bit for conquest (he spent his forties subduing most of what is now France and Belgium—and so in a single decade laid the basis for the existence of French). He then enforced his personal rule over the whole Roman republic, a dominion that in his day included every land with a shore on the Mediterranean Sea. Twenty years after those bitter tears in Spain, he had made himself more famous, and more victorious, even than Alexander. And so, duly, when the dust cleared from the civil wars that followed Caesar's death in 44 BC, Rome was soon minting coins with the legend PAX ORBIS TERRARVM 'Control of the World'.

The very scale of the Empire, and the fact that its borders largely ceased to expand in the first century AD, laid the basis for a collective delusion that came to be shared by the whole Latin-speaking world. The distance that separated Rome from any outsiders, and the virtual absence of any dealings with them, whether to fight or (knowingly) to trade, spread the underlying sense that they were insignificant, almost nonexistent. The Latin word VNIVERSVM shows this idea built into the language. It means 'all', but is literally 'turned into one'. The Romans in their empire undertook to do just that to the whole world.

They liked to tell themselves that they had succeeded. Certainly, from the defeat of their rival city Carthage in the third century BC until the influx of Germans in the fifth century AD, the Romans had no neighbor that was a serious military threat and within the Mediterranean world were able to subdue utterly any power that they challenged. Wars with the Romans seemed to have only one outcome in the long term, the subjugation and control of the adversary, to the extent that its territory passed permanently under Roman control. The political environment that the Romans knew was unipolar in a way that has scarcely been conceivable since its empire was broken up. In the second century AD the emperor Antoninus Pius had affected in all seriousness the title DOMINVS TOTIVS ORBIS 'Lord of the Whole World'.

Aelius Aristides, a sophist from Greece, is famous for his encomium of Roman greatness, which he delivered when he visited Rome in 155 AD. He formulated the official self-deception rather well: for him, the boundary of the Empire was not so much nonexistent as irrelevant. What lay beyond it was insignificant, and the boundary itself was perfect both in its form (notionally a circle) and in the ordered zone it defined:

> Nothing gets away from you, no city, no people, no port, no fortress, unless— naturally—you have condemned it as useless: the Indian Ocean and the Nile cataracts and the Sea of Azov, called the ends of the earth in the past, are now just "the courtyard fences" for this city . . . Great and large in extent as is the Empire, it is much greater in its strictness than in its area encompassed . . . so the whole inhabited world speaks more strictly as one than a chorus does, praying that this empire will last forever: so brilliantly it is conducted by this maestro.

This last metaphor is the closest he came to hinting that Latin was the glue that held the Empire's peoples in place: he was a Greek, writing in Greek, after all. The "courtyard fences" were an allusion to the *Iliad*, ix.476, where a hero describes breaking out of a palace where he is held under guard: Aelius was implying that Rome could go beyond any of her boundaries if she so chose. Later, he wishfully strayed even further from the strict truth, addressing the Romans, rather than their city:

You have made factually true that saying from Homer "the earth is common to all" (*Iliad*, xv. 193), having measured out the whole inhabited world, yoking rivers with bridges of every design, cutting through mountains to make bridleways, filling the deserts with staging points, and taming everything with settled ways and discipline . . . There is no need to write geographical descriptions or to enumerate each nation's laws, since you have become common guides for all, swinging wide the gates to the whole inhabited world and allowing anyone so minded to see places for themselves, setting the same laws for all . . . organizing as a single household the whole inhabited world.[16]

Again Aelius quoted Homer; but the words were from a speech of the god Poseidon, explaining that the earth (unlike the sea, sky, and underworld) was shared between himself and his two brothers Zeus and Hades. The implication, for the learned reader, was to put Rome on an Olympian level.

Yet when they thought about it, educated Romans always knew that they had not quite pulled it off. Even as Augustus was putting PAX ORBIS TERRARVM on the coinage, the historian Pompeius Trogus was writing that Rome shared the world with Parthia, the power in what is now Iran. In the north—after a humiliating defeat in AD 9 in the Teutoburger Wald, which Augustus could never forgive or forget—it was official policy not even to try to conquer Germany. Practical discretion could cap pugnacious patriotism. And Romans had heard of many more peoples, Hibernians, Scythians, Sarmatians, Aethiopians, Indians, all well beyond their control. In the time of Christ, Pliny wrote of Taprobane (Ceylon), a whole new world across the ocean itself. And where, after all, did silk come from, that mystifying commodity in the luxury markets of Rome?

A generation later, in the prelude to his epic on the civil war that had brought Julius Caesar to power, the poet Lucan pointed out that there had been plenty more foreign enemies for Rome to conquer, before turning on itself for a good fight:

The Chinese should have gone beneath the yoke, and barbarous (dwellers by the) Aras, and any sentient people at the head of the Nile.

If you have such a passion for unspeakable war, Rome, turn your hand against yourself only when you have put the whole world under Latin laws: you have not yet run out of enemies.*

---

*Lucan, *On the Civil War*, i.19–23. (Continued on next page.)

The readiness of the Romans to overlook the actual limits on their power was more than overweening pride. It showed that although their empire's borders were far-flung, their consciousness was not. Rather, it stayed concentrated at its traditional center, in Rome, Italy, and MARE NOSTRVM 'our sea'. Tellingly, their word for *world* is actually an expression, ORBIS TERRARVM 'circle of lands'. Circles have centers. The Roman state did not identify with its provinces as the provinces were made to identify with Rome. Rome was mistress of the world; lands that she did not rule were hardly considered part of the real world at all.

❧

In the three centuries from 238 BC Rome's territory had expanded beyond Italy to include the whole Mediterranean basin, and with it had always come use of the Latin language. While its use was never officially required when these lands were added as provinces to the Empire, use of the original languages tended to dry up in the following centuries. Sicily, Corsica and Sardinia, Spain, North Africa, Southern Gaul, Northern Gaul, and Britain, the Alps, and—despite Ovid's early problems—the Balkans all found that Latin became the currency of power in the early centuries AD and was then taken up much more widely in general use.

Latin's expansion across Europe had happened by discrete stages, always after successful campaigns by the Romans' highly organized army. This language expansion through centrally planned campaigns is unique in Europe's history. It contrasts sharply with the progress of Gaulish, say, which filled the western lands and North Italy in the centuries up to 300 BC, or Slavonic, which was to spread into the Balkans after AD 450. For them, the engine of language spread was the incursion of large-scale raiding parties followed by settlement,

---

SVB IVGA IAM SERES, IAM BARBARVS ISSET ARAXES | ET GENS SIQVA IACET NASCENTI CONSCIA NILO. TVM, SI TANTVS AMOR BELLI TIBI, ROMA, NEFANDI, | TOTVM SVB LATIAS LEGES CVM MISERIS ORBEM, IN TE VERTE MANVS: NONDVM TIBI DEFVIT HOSTIS.

This work was published in AD 62–63, and with its regretful view of the lost republic was not only geographically, but politically, strangely out of keeping with the age of Nero. The word *silk*, from Latin SERICA, is named after the Sēres (here the word translated 'Chinese'). The Aras (Araxes) runs eastward into the Caspian: in Lucan's day, it was the boundary between Armenia and Parthia. Armenia was a buffer state and disputed between Rome and Parthia.

which in the extreme became full-scale migration with bag and baggage, *Völker-wanderung*. This more traditional way was how Gaulish had reached Galatia in Asia Minor in 278 BC; and indeed this was how the Sabellian tribes had spread Latin's southern neighbor language Oscan southward across most of Italy's Mezzogiorno in the early first millennium BC. But when Latin spread, it was as the result of a war waged at the behest of the Senate in Rome; it brought with it a civic culture, based on cities linked by roads, and a much wider use of literacy (in Roman script) than had been known before, even where the newly conquered peoples had long experience of contact with literate outsiders.

The displacement effect of this orderly advance of Latin on the previous languages of what was becoming Europe was devastating. It is calculated that in the five centuries from 100 BC to AD 400 the count of known languages in lands under Roman administration fell from sixty to twelve, and outside Africa and the Greek-dominant east, from thirty to just five: Latin, Welsh, Basque, Albanian, and Gaulish—among which Gaulish was already marginal and doomed soon to die out totally. The very names of the lost languages, crossing southern Europe from west to east, sing an elegy of vanished potential: Lusitanian, Celtiberian, Tartessian, Iberian, Ligurian, Lepontic, Rhaetic, Venetic, Etruscan, Picene, Oscan, Messapian, Sicel, Sardinian, Dacian, Getic, Paeonian.[17]

Although the spread of Latin was never an object of Roman policy, there was a certain triumphalism about it in some quarters, even early on. Pliny the Elder was writing in the mid-first century AD that Rome had been elected by divine providence "to unite in conversation the wild, quarrelsome tongues of all their many peoples through common use of its language, to give culture to mankind, and in short to become the one fatherland of every nation in the world."[18] And even if this attitude was not often made so explicit, there can be no doubt that de facto all Romans presumed that their language, if any, would be the standard for communication in their domains. The first emperor Augustus left a declaration of his achievements (INDEX RERVM GESTARVM) with the vestal virgins to be read in the Senate after his death; copies were likely placed in temples all across the Empire, although there is only direct evidence for four, all in the East. Its text is always in Latin, in the Greek-speaking cities of Antioch, Apollonia, and Ancyra in Asia Minor, as in the nearby major Roman city of Colonia Caesarea, though in Ancyra at least it appeared with a full Greek translation.

Anecdotes show the early emperors concern to assert the status of Latin. In the first century AD, Augustus' successor Tiberius is on record as having required, during a trial, a soldier who was questioned in Greek to answer in Latin; and his successor Claudius deprived a notable Greek of his judgeship, and even his citizenship, on the grounds that he did not know Latin.[19] Clearly the only language whose status could contend with Latin for official purposes was Greek; but even the cultural prestige of Greek, and its practical usefulness as a lingua franca, had to yield for the highest government purposes to Latin. As Cicero put it, "It is not so much creditable to know Latin as it is a disgrace not to."[20]

Romans' attitudes to others' languages and traditions as spoken in the provinces were always dismissive. The popular dramatist Plautus, writing in the generation after Rome had subdued and incorporated Carthage, introduced a Carthaginian character with the words "He knows every language and knowingly pretends he doesn't: a typical Carthaginian, you know what I mean?"[21] Occasionally we can see the kind of condescending attitudes that nonliterary Romans felt for the populations into which Latin was projected. "The Britons have all too many mounted troops. Their riders do not use swords, and these Brits don't sit back to discharge their javelins."[22] This is from a note made at the Roman garrison at Vindolanda on Hadrian's Wall, established in the first century AD on the boundaries of Scotland, perhaps speculating why these Brits were less effective as soldiers than the Romans.*

But war was not the only way that scope was created for the spread of Latin. People who were to be incorporated into the Empire might well have encountered Latin well before it became the language in which they were governed, most likely on the lips of NEGOTIATORES, Roman businessmen. Cicero in a defense speech in 69 BC, stressed how full Gaul already was of these operators: "Gaul is packed with businessmen, chock-full of Roman citizens. Not a Gaul does the slightest business without the involvement of a Roman citizen; not a coin changes hands without the involvement of Roman citizens' accounting."[23]

And in another speech, delivered a few years later, Cicero took for granted—even with an audience of Romans—the fact of Romans' abysmal behavior as governors and exploitative businessmen in the provinces: "Words fail me, Romans, to express how much hatred is felt for us among foreign peoples because of the lusts and depredations of those that we have sent out to govern them over these years. Do you think there has been a temple left honored by our

---

*Ironically, the Latin of the writer himself is substandard: the correct word for *javelins* is IACVLA.

magistrates, a community inviolate, a home adequately locked and defended? Nowadays cities are sought out for their wealth and resources so that war can be waged on them, just for greed to despoil them."[24]

The increasing presence of influential Romans, welcome or not to the host communities, would have given many a motive to learn Latin simply to get on in the world. Everyone must sooner or later have observed that Roman domination, once established, was permanent: indeed it was to last unbroken for five centuries, twenty generations, in western Europe. Except among the Basques, and in the wilder recesses of Britain and Dalmatia, every community in that vast territory came to abandon their own traditional culture and adopt Roman ways.

Latin, whether its use was spread by positive encouragement or contempt for any alternative, came to represent the universal aspirations of PAX RO-MANA. Although Roman domination came at a high continuing price in taxes and military service, once imposed, there was no resisting it. And once accepted, it did offer universal access to the Romans' own law, roads, and civic institutions, and beyond that to the wider pool of Western culture: Etruscan divination, Greek arts, commerce and engineering, Carthaginian agriculture and shipbuilding, Gaulish carriagework, Syrian and Egyptian mystery religions. And to the gastronome, besides an appreciation of OLEVM 'olive oil' and VINVM 'wine', it brought with it the culinary refinement of GARVM 'fish sauce'.

> You have made a single fatherland for peoples all over:
> With you in charge, for the lawless it paid to be defeated.
> And sharing your own justice with the conquered
> You have made a city of what was once the world.
>
> Rutilius Namatianus (fifth century AD)[25]

Latin was a factor unifying the Empire's elites, through a common education and literary culture. In literature, in the first and second centuries BC the greatest writers had tended to come from the provinces of Italy, not Rome. Virgil was from Mantua, Livy from Padua, Horace from Apulia, Catullus from Verona in Cisalpine Gaul. But after this, a large proportion of the greatest authors—essentially the creators of literary Latin in their ages—hailed from diverse regions outside Italy.

In the first century, Spain was preeminent. From Corduba (Cordova) came

L. Annaeus **Seneca**,* the tragedian and moralist (son of an equally literary father, who had concentrated on rhetorical declamations), and his nephew M. Annaeus **Lucan**us, the epic poet of the Roman civil war; from Bilbilis (Calatayud) came M. Valerius **Martial**is, writer of epigrammatic verse. L. Iunius Moderatus **Columella** from Gades (Cadiz) wrote the classic text on farming; and M. Fabius **Quintilian**us from Calagurris (Calahorra) was an orator, but even more famous as the classic authority on rhetorical theory.†

In the second century, the historian P. Cornelius **Tacitus** and the theorist of aqueducts and military strategy Sex. Iulius **Frontinus** came from southern Gaul. But the real competitor was Africa: C. **Suetonius** Tranquillus the biographer, M. Cornelius **Fronto** the orator, C. **Sulpicius Apollinaris** the grammarian, all came from there. Africa's cultural repute at the time was captured in a quip of Juvenal's: NVTRICVLA CAVSIDICORVM AFRICA 'Africa, that amah of advocates, suckler of solicitors'.[26] Meanwhile Greeks, and other residents of the eastern provinces, are absent from this roll, as they continued to write in Greek. Some famous literary westerners (notably the sophist Favorinus, hailing from Arelate in southern Gaul) even chose to be Greeks rather than Romans.

All these luminaries had felt they needed to travel to Rome to take part in the language's cultural life at the highest level. This changed in the later second century. Apuleius, after studying in Greece and Italy, returned to Africa to work and write his bawdy but devout novel *Metamorphoses* (better known as "The Golden Ass"). Thereafter it seemed no longer necessary to establish oneself at Rome to make a literary or philosophical reputation. The poet Nemesianus (around 250–300), and the Christian writers Tertullian (around 160–240), Lactantius (around 240–320), and Augustine (354–430) all stayed in North Africa; others, such as the Bible translator Jerome from Pannonia (347–420) and the historian Orosius (early fifth century) from Spain, were

---

*The full names of these men are given, with the usual shortening in English picked out in bold. The Roman citizen prided himself on his three names, a tradition that seems to have been derived from their Etruscan neighbors (pp. 40–41).

†Latin cognomina, worn with pride, were often surprisingly uncomplimentary. Here SENECA means 'gaffer', FRONTO 'beetle brow', COLVMELLA 'post', BASSVS 'low'. But some were geographical: LVCANVS 'from Lucania', APVLEIVS 'from Apulia', and some perhaps based on an ancestor's character: TACITVS 'silent', TRANQVILLVS 'quiet'. APOLLINARIS suggests an ancient link with the cult of Apollo, MARTIALIS of Mars. QVINTILIANVS points to an adoptive link with another family, the *gens Quintilia*.

happy to travel and work (in Latin) in different parts of the Empire.* The Empire was the basis for the creation of RESPVBLICA LITTERARIA, a Republic of (Latin) Letters, which was to be an aspect of western Europe for the next millennium and beyond, almost unaffected by political and economic collapse.

The army too, like the process of literary education, provided a motive for the spread of Latin within the Empire, but one that affected a different, and very much more numerous, class of people. We are best informed about the top flight of military men, drawn from ever wider circles: the most successful could ultimately even become emperor. Already in the last days of the Republic (to 44 BC) it had been possible for provincial Italian lads to ascend to high command: T. Labienus, Caesar's principal aide in Gaul, and P. Ventidius Bassus, who campaigned successfully on behalf of Mark Antony in Parthia, both seem to have come from modest backgrounds in Picenum.

A century later, after the Julio-Claudian and Flavian dynasties had run out of heirs, the Empire was forced to fall back on outstanding soldiers; and it became clear that such distinction was no longer restricted to men from the traditional elite in Rome and Italy. Two emperors from Spain (Trajan in 98, Hadrian in 117) were succeeded by one from Gaul (Antoninus Pius in 138). After a turbulent interregnum caused by an attempt to reinstate the dynastic principle, military candidates for emperor again started emerging from the provinces, and more and more distant ones: Africa (Septimius Severus in 193, Macrinus in 217), Syria (Philip 244), Thrace (Maximinus 235), Pannonia (Decius 249), Moesia (Aemilianus 253). Aurelian, acceding in 270, even came from outside the empire, in the lower Danube region.

⟡

The Latin language itself became a sort of repository of the languages of the peoples the Romans had subdued and brought into their great coalition. Many of the words are simple borrowings, but many more are harder to place, since they seem to be portmanteaux: Latin words clearly, but somehow dressed to look foreign. LYMPHA with its Y and its PH looks a clear borrowing from Greek, but it isn't. It is just a grandiose word for 'water', redolent of nymphs, limpid pools, and deliques-

---

*Despite any Christian associations, these were all very much Roman gentlemen, with (especially in the earlier centuries) the names to prove it: M. Aurelius Olympius Nemesianus, Q. Septimius Florens Tertullianus, L. Cae(ci)lius Firmianus Lactantius, Aurelius Augustinus, Eusebius Hieronymus, Paulus Orosius.

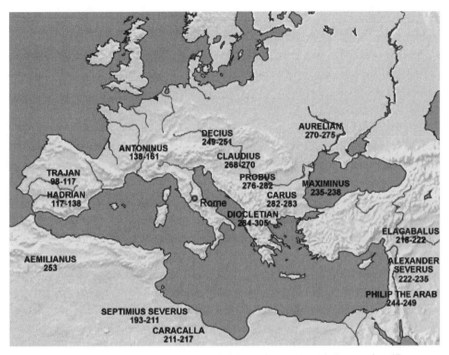

Home provinces of the Roman Emperors. From the first to the third centuries AD, emperors were chosen from ever farther afield.

cence. Sometimes it is matched with nymphs, as if it were the word for another kind of water fairy; sometimes it becomes the name of a goddess in her own right, as when Varro invokes her (along with the equally bogus 'Good Outcome') at the beginning of his treatise on agriculture.[27] It went on to be a pseudo-explanation for all kinds of frenzy, of the sort that the wild spirits of wood and water will send down on mortals: LYMPHATICVS was much the same as LVNATICVS.

ARRA is another such word, meaning a bond or surety, but this time shortened from a word taken from a Semitic language, probably Punic, the language of financial transactions par excellence. Pliny the Elder jokes that a doctor's fee is MORTIS ARRAM, a down payment on death.[28] Its original form ARRHABON represents the Semitic 'erabōn, but in ARRA it has been shortened to be like Latin ĀRA, an altar—but a more Roman-feeling security: as when Ovid says that a friend of his is "the only altar that he has found for his fortunes."[29]

To add a third cultural mixer, consider the word CARRICVM, unknown to Latin literature, but evidently universal in spoken Latin, since echoes of it are found in every modern Romance language (French *charge*, Spanish *cargo*, Rumanian *cârcă*, Catalan *carreg*, Italian *carico* . . .) as well as English *carry*. At the start, it evidently meant a wagonload, such as a CARRVS (a word borrowed from Gaulish, to mean four-wheeled cart) could hold. CARRVS has had a major career of its own (e.g., *car, chariot, career*), but CARRICVM is another example of a word borrowed into Latin that there found a new and extended life, first as the replacement for the ancient Latin word ONVS 'burden, load', later with a rich metaphorical life, ranging over duties, pick-a-back rides (in Romanian at least), accusations, attacks, and (much later) ammunition for firearms, and then explosives generally. Gaulish may have been the language of choice for words for wheeled vehicles, but Latin gave an opportunity for transfusion into Europe's future world-mind.

Languages create worlds to live in, not just in the minds of their speakers, but in their lives, and their descendants' lives, where those ideas become real. The world that Latin created is today called Europe. And as Latin formed Europe, it also inspired the Americas. Latin has in fact been the constant in the cultural history of the West, extending over two millennia. In a way, it has been too central to be noticed: like the air Europe breathed, it has pervaded everything.

It was the Empire that gave Latin its overarching status. But, like the Roman arches put up with the support of a wooden scaffold, the language was to prove far more enduring than its creator. As the common language of Europe, spoken and written unchanged by courtiers, clerics, and international merchants, its active use lasted three times as long as Rome's dominion. Even now, its use echoes on in the law codes of half the world, in the terminologies of biology and medicine, and until forty years ago in the liturgy of the Catholic Church, the most populous form of Christianity on earth. And through this last fifteen hundred years, Europe has remained a single arena, largely independent of outsiders, even as parts of it have sought to dominate the rest of the world.

Yet after the collapse of Rome's empire, Europe itself was never again to be organized as a single state. The Latin language, never forgotten, was left as a tantalizing symbol of Europe's lost unity. "Once upon a time the whole world spoke Latin." This mythical sense remained behind Europe, and its proud civilization. And so, more than Christianity, freedom, or the rule of law, it has in practice been the sense of a once-shared language, a language of great antiquity but straightforward clarity, that has bound Europe together.

CHAPTER 2

⟨⟩⊛⟨⟩

Fons et origo—Latin's Kin

MAIORES NOSTRI . . . VIRVM BONVM CVM LAVDABANT, ITA
LAVDABANT, BONVM AGRICOLAM BONVMQVE COLONVM. AM-
PLISSIME LAVDARI EXISTIMABATVR, QVI ITA LAVDABATVR.

Our ancestors . . . when they singled out a good man for praise, used these words:
"a good farmer and a good settler." Someone so praised was
thought to have received the highest esteem.

Cato, On the Country Life[1]

L ATIN OWES ITS NAME to its home region of Latium in west-central
Italy, the southern half of modern Lazio. With hindsight, it certainly
looks a good starting point for a future Italian, and then Mediterranean,
power. Its position is central in Italy, and it controls the ford on the river Tiber
(modern Tevere), which is the main divider of Italy's western coastal plains.
Italy, in turn, is central within the northern sector of the Mediterranean, equi-
distant from Spain in the west and Asia Minor (modern Turkey) in the east.

The first question that naturally arises is why the language is not known
as "Roman," for the power that spread the language far and wide was not Latium, but the city-state of Rome, and the result was the Roman, not the Latin,
Empire. But the Romans' influence was usually decisive, even with outsiders,
in setting the names of their institutions; and the Romans always referred to
their language as *lingua Latīna*, or *sermō Latīnus*. It shows that the language is
older, and its area, originally at least, wider than the Roman state.

Looking as far back as we can to the origins of Latin, we do not have the
convenience (as we do for English) of being able to give it a place and a period.
But it is discernibly an Indo-European language, a member of a highly diverse

Languages of ancient Italy. Until the third century BC, Latin was just one among many Italic languages.

family of related languages whose borders were set, before recorded history, between Bengal and Donegal (and indeed between Iberia and the edge of Siberia). Its speakers will have reached Latium along with the forerunners of most of the other language communities that largely surrounded Latin when we read their first traces in the written record. They are called Italic languages and included Faliscan, Umbrian, and Venetic to the north, Oscan to the south.* Sadly, there is no agreement on when these languages would have come to Italy (sometime between the sixth and the second millennia BC, but all as a group, or in separate events?), on what allowed their speakers to spread (prowess at farming? Copper, Bronze, or Iron Age weaponry?), or even on what their route would have been (over the sea from the Balkans? down the Adriatic or the Tyrrhenian coasts?). We can only say where in the Italian peninsula the Italic languages ended up, and what sort of languages they were.

As to where in Italy they settled, it is clear that there were two major groups or subfamilies: Latin-Faliscan-Venetic settled the north, whereas Oscan

---

*The written record in Italy comes by courtesy of the Greek colonists who brought the technique of writing to the peninsula in the eighth century BC. There were also many other languages, such as Aequian, Volscian, South Picene, Marrucinian, Marsian, Paelignian, and Vestinian, spoken in the area of Umbria and Le Marche to the east of Rome; but they were largely absorbed into the greater Latin community before they had much of an opportunity to leave many surviving inscriptions.

and the rest, usually known as the Sabellian languages, occupied most of the south of Italy. The main exception to this pattern is Umbrian, a dialect which is more similar to Oscan than northern Italic; so its position in north-central Italy suggests that the Umbrians migrated later from the south up into the Apennines. It is also significant that the very similar Latin and Faliscan—a dialect best known for its drinker's motto FOIED VINO PIPAFO CRA CAREFO "Today I shall drink wine; tomorrow I shall go without."[2]—were separated from their cousin Venetic by a large, and totally unrelated, Etruscan-speaking population. The geography suggests that the Etruscans moved in from the west, splitting the two wings of northern Italic apart.

The Italic languages were not mutually intelligible, at least not across their full range. An idea of how different they could be may be gained from looking at some very short texts in the two best known and farthest flung (Venetic and Oscan) with a word-for-word translation into Latin. (For comprehensibility, none of the languages is shown in its actual alphabet.)

First a Venetic inscription on a bronze nail, found at Este:

mego zontasto sainatei reitiai egeotora aimoi ke louzerobos [Venetic]
me dōnāvit sanātricī reitiae egetora aemō līberīsque [Latin]

i.e., word for word in English:
"me gave to-healer to-Reitia Egetora for Aemus and children"
or more clearly:
"Egetora gave me to Reitia the healer for Aemus and his children."

And then a clause of a Roman magistrate's arbitration (183 BC) between Nola and Avellino, written on a boundary stone:

avt púst feihúís pús fisnam amfret, eíseí tereí nep abellanús nep nuvlanús pídum tríbarakattins [Oscan]*
autem pōst murōs quī fānum ambiunt, in eā terrā neque avellānī neque nōlānī quicquam aedificāverint [Latin]

i.e., word for word in English:
"but behind walls which temple they-surround, on that land neither Avellani nor Nolani anything they-shall-have-built"
or more clearly:

---

*In Oscan spelling, using a restricted alphabet derived from the Etruscans, *ú* signals a sound written with *u* that is believed to be long *ō*, *í* one that is believed to be long *ē* or short *i*.

"but behind the walls which surround the temple, on that land neither the Avellani nor the Nolani may build anything."

Nevertheless, there are striking similarities among them, and features, from the most specific to the most general, that set Italic languages apart from the other Indo-European languages.

First of all, a distinctive sound in Italic is the consonant *f.* It is extremely common, cropping up mostly in words where the Indo-European parent language had once had either bʰ or dʰ. In Latin, the sound is mostly restricted to the beginning of words, but in Oscan and Umbrian it often occurs too in the middle: Latin *fūmus, facit, forēs, fingit*; Oscan *feihús, mefiú*; Umbrian *rufru*— meaning 'smoke, does, doors, makes'; 'walls, middle'; 'red'.*

With respect to meanings, the verb form 'I am' is *sum* or *esom*, with a vowel (*o* or *u*) in the middle and none at the end; there is no sign of such a vowel in Greek *eimí*, Sanskrit *asmi*, Gothic *im*, Hittite *ešmi*. There are also some distinctive nuances of words in the Italic vocabulary (asterisks show that forms are historical reconstructions): the common Indo-European root *deik- means 'say' here (Latin *dīcere*, Oscan *deíkum*), not 'show' as it does in the other languages (Greek <u>deíknumi</u>, Sanskrit <u>diśati</u>, English <u>token</u>); also, the root *dhē- means 'do' or 'make' (Latin *facere*, Oscan *fakiiad*, Umbrian *faςia*, Venetic *vhagsto* 'made') and not 'put' as it does in the other languages (Greek *-thēke*, Sanskrit *-dhā-*).

The pattern of verb forms is simplified and regularized from Indo-European in a distinctive way. As every schoolboy once knew, Latin had four different classes of verbs, each with slightly different endings, known as conjugations. The different sets of endings corresponded to the vowel that closes the stem and preceded the endings (as *amā-* 'love', *monē-* 'warn', *regī-* 'rule', *audī-*'hear'). This vowel then largely determined the precise forms of all the verb's endings, 106 choices in all.† Something similar is seen in Oscan and Venetic verbs. This is

---

*Otherwise [f] is unknown in ancient Indo-European languages. But it is frequent in the (unrelated but neighboring) Etruscan language. It can be considered the key sound of ancient Italy. The same change (from [θ], i.e., *th*, to [f]) has happened in cockney English: "fings ain't what they used to be."

†These express six tenses (present, imperfect, future, perfect, past perfect, future perfect), two voices (active and passive), and three moods (indicative, subjunctive, imperative), altogether a large set of combinations. Each of these combinations has up to six forms, to express person and number (I, you, one, he/she/it, we, you all, they). There are also infinitives (to do, to have done), participles (doing, done, about to do), a supine (in order to do), and a gerundive (which is to be done).

complex by comparison with English, but is in fact rather simpler than the fuller, differently organized systems seen in such distantly related languages as Greek, Sanskrit, or Gothic, where one can find more persons (dual as well as singular and plural), an extra tense (aorist), voice (middle), and moods (optative, benedictive).

The nouns, on the other hand, followed five patterns (declensions), choosing a set of endings on the basis of their stem vowel (-a, -o, none, or -i, -u, -e): the endings marked whether a noun was singular or plural (here too, in Italic languages, dual was not an option), and which case it was in, i.e., what its function was in the sentence; the cases were nominative (for subject), accusative (for object), genitive (for a noun dependent on another noun), dative (for a recipient), ablative (for a source), locative (for a place), and vocative (for an addressee), though the last two had become marginal in Latin. Hence analogously to a Latin noun like *hortus* 'garden', which had a pattern of endings

Sing. N. *hortus*, Ac. *hortum*, G. *hortī*, D. *hortō*, Ab. *hortō*, L. (*hortō*), V. *horte*
Plur. N. *hortī*, Ac. *hortōs*, G. *hortōrum*, D., Ab., L. *hortīs*

we find in Oscan (remembering that *ú* was probably pronounced just like *ō*)

Sing. N. *húrz*, Ac. *húrtúm*, G.*húrteis*, D. *húrtúí*, Ab. **húrtúd*, L. **húrtei*, V. ?
Plur. N. **húrtús*, Ac. **húrtúss*, G. **húrtúm*, D., Ab., L. **húrtúís*.

On this kind of evidence, one can say that Latin and Oscan in the second century BC were about as similar as Spanish and Portuguese are today.

⟡

Consciousness of Latin as a language with its own identity began in the words of the poet Gnaeus Naevius, one of the very first in the Latin canon, writing from 235 to 204 BC. He wrote his own epitaph, showing either a concern that the language was in danger of decay, or an inordinate pride in his own literary worth!

INMORTALES MORTALES SI FORET	If it were right for immortals to mourn
FAS FLERE, FLERENT DIVAE	mortals, the divine Camenae
CAMENAE NAEVIVM POETAM.	would mourn poet Naevius.

ITAQVE POSTQVAM EST ORCHI
    TRADITVS THESAVRO,
OBLITI SVNT ROMAI LOQVIER
    LINGVA LATINA.

And so after he passed to the vault
    of Orcus,
the Romans forgot how to speak the
    language.

Naevius is the earliest Latin poet whose works have survived. (He was actually a man of Campania and so probably grew up speaking Oscan.) But when these words were written, at the end of the third century BC, Rome already had three centuries of forthrightly independent existence behind her, and we know that Latin had been a written language for all of that time. Our earliest surviving inscriptions are from the sixth century BC.

Latin had been literate, then, but not literary: scribes will have noted down important utterances, but few will have consulted those records after the immediate need for which they had been made. One ancient historian recounted that important laws were stored on bronze pillars in the temple of Diana on Rome's Aventine Hill,[3] and at least one ancient inscribed stone has been found in the Roman Forum.[4] There was a tradition at Rome that the law was set down publicly on Twelve Tables in 450, but the fragments that survive, quoted in later literature, are all in suspiciously classical-looking Latin.[5] It seems unlikely that there was any canon of texts playing a part in Roman education in this early period.* Famously, the important written texts, such as the Sibylline Books, consulted at times of crisis by the Roman government, were not in Latin but in Greek. The absence of a literary tradition in Latin until the second century seems to have allowed speakers to lose touch with their own language's past, in a way that would have been unthinkable, say, for Greeks in the same period.

In fact, about three generations after Naevius, the historian Polybius managed to locate the text of a treaty that had been struck between Rome and Carthage, explicitly dating it to the first year of the Roman Republic, 508 BC ("under Lucius Junius Brutus and Marcus Horatius, the first consuls after the expulsion of the kings, twenty-eight years before Xerxes

---

*Yet Cicero (Leg. ii.59) reminisces that he was one of the last generation to learn the Twelve Tables by heart at school (in the early first century BC). Plutarch (QR 59=Mor. 278e) says that the first elementary school in Rome was opened in 234 BC; that is precisely when Naevius' generation (including Livius Andronicus and Ennius) were laying the foundations of Rome's literature.

The Duenos ceramic, a tripartite vase of uncertain, but perhaps erotic, use. It holds the earliest substantial inscription in Latin (sixth to fifth centuries BC).

crossed into Greece"). He commented, "We have transcribed this, interpreting it to the limits of accuracy possible. But such a great difference in dialect has arisen between modern and ancient that the most expert Romans can barely elucidate parts of it, even after careful study."[6]

He then quoted it in full, but tantalizingly only in Greek translation. However, one of the few inscribed survivals from earlier Latin may offer a hint at the kind of difficulties those Roman experts were encountering. Latin grammar had moved on quite smartly in those two hundred years; and many old inscriptions remain enduringly obscure, even though we now can approach them with a comparative knowledge of other Indo-European languages inconceivable to contemporaries.

Consider for example the oldest substantial example, on the famous DVENOS ceramic, a tripartite, interconnecting vase rather reminiscent of a Wankel engine. Found in Rome in 1880, it is dated to the sixth or early fifth century BC, the same period as that early treaty.

The inscription is in three lines, which may be transcribed as

IOVESATDEIVOSQOIMEDMITATNEITEDENDOCOSMISVIRCOSIED

ASTEDNOISIOPETOITESIAIPAKARIVOIS

DVENOSMEDFECEDENMANOMEINOMDUENOINEMEDMALOSTATOD

and which are conjectured to mean

> He who uses me to soften, swears by the gods.
> In case a maiden should not be kind in your case,
> but you wish her placated with delicacies for her favors.
> A good man made me for a happy outcome.
> Let no ill from me befall a good man.[7]

This is unlikely to be fully correct—some of the vocabulary may simply be beyond our ken because the words died out—but even if it is, it presupposes that the words here must have changed massively over three centuries to become part of a language that Naevius would have recognized. Here is a reconstruction into classical Latin, with the necessary changes underlined:

> *iurat diuos qui per me mitigat.*
> *ni in te comis virgo siet*
> *ast [cibis] [fututioni] ei pacari vis.*
> *bonus me fecit in manum munus. bono ne e me malum stato*

Virtually every word had changed its form, pronunciation, or at least its spelling between the sixth and the third centuries BC. This shows what rapid change for Latin occurred in these three centuries, comparable to what happened to English between the eleventh and the fourteenth centuries AD,

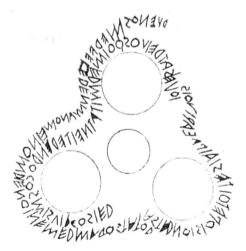

The inscription that circles the Duenos ceramic. Written in a highly archaic form of Latin, it appears to offer a love potion.

when Anglo-Saxon (typified by the *Beowulf* poem), totally unintelligible to modern speakers, gave way to Middle English (typified by Chaucer's writings), on the threshold of the modern language.

Yet (again like English), as reading and writing became more widespread, the pace of change in the language was to slow dramatically. Naevius' poetry of the third century remained comprehensible to Cicero in the first, and indeed Plautus' comedies, written in the early second century BC, were still being performed in the first century AD. Those plays are in fact written in a Latin close to the classical standard, canonized by Cicero and the Golden Age literature that followed him, a literary language that was simply not allowed to change after the first century BC, since every subsequent generation was taught not only to read it but to imitate it.

But why did this language, which only came to a painful self-awareness in the third century BC, go on to supplant not only all the other languages of Italy but almost all the other languages of western Europe as well? In the sixth century BC, a neutral observer could only have assumed that if Italy was destined to be unified, it would be under the Etruscans; and in the third century BC, Latin was still far less widely spoken than Oscan. Where did it all go right for Latin, and for Rome?

CHAPTER 3

Sub rosa—
Latin's Etruscan Stepmother

·MYƎM·MAꟼƎMIƎ·ᴎAMƎO·MᴎI†·ᴎAMƎO·
·)I†IꟼA8·I†IƎMƎO·ᴎƎOᴎVᴎ·XAJM·MVᴎV·
·ƎXAJM·)ƎᴎAJᶎV·ƎᴎAMƎO·MVᶎI)·IƎMA8·
·JOJI)·AJ)Iᴎ)AM·MIJƎOA·)Ǝᶾ·)IꟼƎᶾ·IꟼVJ·
·)MƎMVJOƎM·JAꟼVᴎM·

thesan tins, thesan eiseras seus, unus mlakh nunthen thesviti favitic fasei, cishum
thesane ushlanec mlakhe luri zeric, zec athelis sacnicla cilthl spural methlumesc

Dawn of the Day-god, Dawn of All the Gods, you in your goodness
I invoke in the east and in the west with a libation, and three times,
at dawn, at high noon, and by the serene brightness (of the stars), as written by
the ancestors, for the citizens of the tribe, the city, and the nation.

Etruscan prayer[1]

THE ETRUSCANS ARE FAMOUS for their attendant mystery. The puzzle of their origins goes back three thousand years; but when we first have evidence of which named people lived where in Italy, the Etruscans were already firmly ensconced in the northwest, richer and more powerful than any of the other residents. The identity of their language is at the heart of the mystery, since it was clearly unrelated to all the Indo-European languages, most of them Italic languages, that surrounded it on every side. Unlike them, it was an agglutinative language—which means that it was structurally more like Central Asian Turkish or Peruvian Quechua than Latin or Gaulish, or indeed other neighboring languages such as Greek (in Sicily) or Punic (in Sardinia). Any words that it shared with its neighbors are seen as individual cultural borrowings; they are not the kind of similarities, more distant yet more systematic, that could stand as evidence of a common origin.

Rome was to establish itself as the successor to the Etruscans, but before it could do so, it first had to extricate itself from their dominance. More permanently, this political transition would lead to the linguistic spread of Latin, as the successor language in Etruria.

The Etruscans were clearly the dominant power in Italy in the period when the Greeks, farther east, were establishing their classical culture. This raises the question why they were so much more outgoing and culturally influential than their local neighbors, who spoke Italic languages: for the Etruscans in their heyday were challenged only by the two seafaring powers, the Carthaginians (who were largely their allies), and the Greeks (who largely opposed them).

This period was largely documented through Greek sources: Greeks were literate and well-traveled in the middle of the first millennium BC. But it was also revealed through the discovery of inscriptions, and the Etruscans'

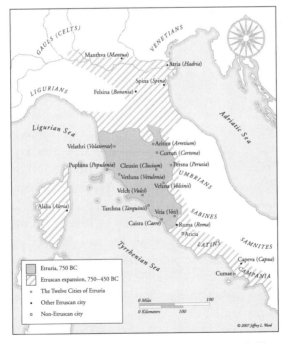

Etruscan "forward policy," 750–475 BC. Etruscan influence extended beyond the "Twelve Cities" of Etruria north into the valley of the Po and south along the Campanian coast.

distinctive black *bucchero* pottery. In it we can see evidence of the Etruscans expanding their power and commercial reach around what became known as the Tyrrhenian (i.e., Etruscan) Sea, as well as eastward overland from their famed "Twelve Cities." In the eighth century BC they were colonizing Campania in the southwest, but also northern Italy across to the Adriatic. With Greeks from Euboea they established a trading presence in Ischia. In 540 BC, in alliance with Carthage, they defeated the Phocaean Greeks at the Battle of the Sardinian Sea and established a foothold in Corsica.

They suffered a major reverse in 511 at Aricia, just south of Rome, when they lost to an alliance of Cumaean Greeks and Latins; two generations later in 474, they were defeated at Cumae itself by the combined naval forces of Cumae and Syracuse. Thereafter they rapidly lost their southern Italian bases and dependencies. It was the end of the Etruscan "forward policy," which had lasted for three hundred years. The next two centuries of Etruscan history were taken up with a long, drawn-out series of unsuccessful defenses, as one by one each of their cities yielded to the encroaching new power, Rome. The first city to engage Rome, in 477, was Veii, Rome's close neighbor north of the Tiber; but the struggle continued for eighty-one years, until Veii's annihilation in 396. The last one, Volsinii, fell in 264, 132 years later.

One clue to Etruscan identity lies in their various names for their nation. Their name for themselves was *rasna* or *rasenna*, but this turns out (like so many accepted ethnonyms all over the world) to be just their word for 'people'. The Greeks, however, were introduced to them as *tursānoi*.[2] In the Ionian Greek accent (which was characteristic of the Euboean and Phocaean colonists active in the area), this comes out as *tursēnoi*; and in Attic Greek (which, being Athenian, became the standard) as *turrēnoi*. (This was Romanized as 'Tyrrheni', still seen in the name of the Tyrrhenian Sea, modern Italian *Mare Tirreno*, which had once been the Etruscan lake.) Some Greeks knew them as *turranoi*, perhaps a compromise pronunciation; their own dedication plaque left at Delphi is marked in Greek TURRANO; and Hiero of Syracuse, on helmets taken at the battle of Cumae and dedicated at Olympia, wrote the name TURAN.[3] By contrast, the Latin name for them was *Etrusci* or *Tusci*. If the final consonant here is an adjectival ending (compare *Graii* vs. *Graeci* for Greeks, *Poeni* vs. *Punici* for Carthaginians), then the root looks like TRUS or TURS, also seen in *tursanoi*.[4]

Now, it is a remarkable fact that apparently this same root underlies the Greek words for Troy (*troia*) and Trojans (*trōes*), namely TRŌS.[5] So *Troia* and *Etrūria* would have the same origin: they are Greek and Etruscan-Latin developments, respectively, of the root TRŌS-IA.[6]

Coins showing Venus on one side with Aeneas carrying his father to safety on the reverse, and a votive statue of Aeneas and his father. Aeneas, the Trojan refugee to Italy, was a cultural hero of the Etruscans before the Romans.

For this, the cultural background turns out to fit pretty well. Not only is there a story in Herodotus[7] that the *Tyrsēnoi* migrated from Asia Minor (admittedly it is a story that they came from Lydia, about two hundred kilometers south of Troy),* but Hellanicus, a contemporary historian whose works have not survived, also apparently related that the Tyrrhenians were Pelasgians (i.e., pre-Greek inhabitants of the Aegean) who had migrated to Italy when driven out by the Greeks.[8] It was also a persistent theme of ancient folklore that some Trojans at least had escaped from the destruction of their city and headed west. Virgil, Rome's national poet, of course employed this as the basis for his *Aeneid*, with Aeneas leading a party of escaped Trojans ultimately to settle in Latium, there allying with the native Latini (specifically against the Etruscans) to found the race of Romans. And in the previous generation Julius Caesar himself had liked to trace his

---

*This conception of Etruscans as misplaced Lydians got deeply rooted in Roman culture. Even Virgil used *Lydian* as an elegant variation for 'Etruscan', and so did Cicero, at least when waxing poetic (LYDIVS EDIDERAT TYRRHENAE GENTIS HARVSPEX "a Lydian soothsayer of the Tyrrhenian race had spoken"). But one tantalizing piece of evidence tells for a Lydian-Etruscan link. Both Lydian and Etruscan used the western Greek alphabet, extending it with some new letters; one of them, *8*, their symbol for [f], otherwise unknown, is identical in both alphabets (Haarmann 2002: 129). And a recent study of the DNA in Tuscan cattle also suggests a Middle Eastern origin for the Etruscan herd (Pellecchia et al. 2006).

family's ancestry back to Aeneas' son Iulus: during his dictatorship he struck a coin that showed Venus on the front and Aeneas leaving Troy on the reverse.

But it is clear from votive statues found in the city of Veii (dated to 515–490 BC), and a score of vases (525–470) found farther north, especially in Vulci, all depicting Aeneas dutifully carrying his father to safety, that Aeneas the heroic Trojan survivor was already a cult figure, and a putative founding father, among the Etruscans themselves before the Romans appropriated him.[9]

Pursuing the origins of the Etruscans any further would not enhance an understanding of their impact on Latin. But the mystery remains, if anything, deeper today than ever before. Suffice it to say that trails of evidence lead in two apparently incompatible directions: one to the island of Lemnos, not far from Troy, where an epitaph from the late sixth century BC in a language closely related to Etruscan has been found, and even read; but the other to the eastern reaches of the Alps, where another language, clearly but more distantly related to Etruscan, and known as Rhaetic, survives in inscriptions from 500 to 50 BC. Clearly Etruscan had some link with the eastern Mediterranean; but rather than being an import from Asia Minor, the language may have been a remnant from Europe's pre-Indo-European past.[10]

❖

The Etruscans left abundant evidence of how luxurious a life their aristocrats were able to lead—and perhaps hoped to continue in the afterlife. Some of their tombs were decorated with exquisite, brightly colored wall paintings, which show much feasting, juggling, lyre and flute music and dancing, wrestling and game playing, enjoyment of gardens, hunting, and fishing. The coffins themselves were often elaborate statues, showing the deceased reclining as in life, occasionally as devoted couples lying down to dinner. Pottery and the engravings on the backs of mirrors show much of the same, but add more sober themes: sacrifice of animals, consultation of entrails, soldiers with crested helmets, warships, battle elephants, sea creatures including seals and octopuses.

The only work to match them at the time came from Greece or the Near East, and this again underlines how advanced the Etruscans were in the Italy of the sixth century BC. The city that was to become modern Bologna began as an Etruscan foundation of this period, Felsina. They had by then expanded

*Urn of the Spouses. This funerary image,
now in the Museo Guarnacci, shows an ideal
picture of Etruscan marital harmony.*

beyond their cities in Etruria to control the full extent of the Po's drainage in northeastern Italy and were also influential along the southwestern coast of Italy, well to the south of Rome. How was it that this political and cultural advantage did not translate into a permanent empire? And if this had happened, is there a chance that Etruscan might have supplanted all the Italic languages, including the then rather insignificant Latin?

Rome was the immediate neighbor to the south of their northern domains, which they seem to have dominated for a time, but then lost. The direct evidence that they *controlled* Rome was the Etruscan name (properly spelled *Tarchunies*) that was borne by two of Rome's latter kings, Tarquinius Priscus ('the Ancient') and Tarquinius Superbus ('the Proud'). The emperor Claudius (himself a serious Etruscologist, but writing six centuries after the events) added that according to Etruscan sources the intervening king Servius Tullius had also been an Etruscan, whose name in that language was Mastarna.[11] Yet a fourth example of an Etruscan ruler of Rome exists in the person of Lars Porsena of Clusium, who (according to a poorly kept secret)* conquered Rome and

---

*The historian Livy (first century BC) transmitted at length the patriotic story that Porsena was so impressed with Rome's heroic defenders that he spared the city (ii.9–15). But Pliny the Elder (xxxiv.139) and Tacitus (*Histories*, iii.72), writing in the the first and second centuries AD, both took it for granted, while their minds were on quite different matters, that the city was surrendered.

imposed disarmament on her, in the aftermath of the expulsion of Tarquinius Superbus.*

So Rome must have been dominated by Etruscan aristocrats or kings for at least a century. Whatever the precise political arrangement,† it was from Etruscans that they derived their tradition that kings, and hence magistrates, should wear purple. And from Etruscans came the symbol of their authority, the *fascēs*, a bundle of rods surrounding an ax, showing the right to give out corporal, and capital, punishment. Beyond politics, it is quite clear that the Etruscan language too had considerable influence on Latin.

Etymology and lexicography were not skills that flourished in the ancient world, so there is no full statement by Romans of the Latin vocabulary's debt to Etruscan. Nevertheless, it is possible to use modern methods on ancient materials. If we class together all the words that Roman authors tell us are of Etruscan origin, adding others whose origin is clear from their use in Etruscan inscriptions, a family resemblance emerges among them. Then, with an idea of what it is about a word that makes it look Etruscan, we can look for other such words.[12] The outcome is a substantial harvest, and we can see that the effect of Etruscan on Latin was quite comparable to the effects on medieval English of French after the Norman conquest of 1066—a major cultural infusion, essentially of an early urban culture on a more countrified society.‡

One first linguistic point of note—which has implications for the cultural history of the period—is that the words borrowed are overwhelmingly nouns. The only verbs we can find are, in fact, derived from nouns, and this is why they are all stems ending in ā-, referring to actions performed with some newfangled Etruscan item: *gubernāre* 'to steer' (a ship), from *guberna* 'steering oars'; *iduāre* 'to divide', from *idūs* 'the Ides, halfway through a month', *laniāre* 'to butcher' (meat), from *lanius* 'butcher', *triumphāre* 'to celebrate victory', from the Etruscan victory shout *triumphe*, and *fascināre* 'to charm', originally using a strange phallic object, the *fascinus*. This preference

---

*Both *Mastarna* and *Porsena* appear to be titles disguised by Etruscan phonology. "Mastarna" is *macstarna*, an Etruscan version of *magister (populi)*, an old equivalent of *dictator* (e.g., Varro, *de Lingua Latina*, v.14), with -*na* the adjectival ending added, as commonly with Etruscan clan names; whereas 'Porsena' is a shortening of *zilaθ purθne*, supreme Etruscan official, from *zil-* 'rule' combined with the Greek *prutaneus* 'president'. Ancient Tuscany was a multilingual place.

†It has indeed been suggested that the very phrase *res publica* is a translation of Etruscan *meχ rasnal* 'league of the people' (Rix 1984: 466).

‡A full list, organized by social domain, can be viewed at appendix II.

for nouns suggests that Etruscan words came in as names for unfamiliar objects; it does not show (as later, when Greek words flooded into Latin) that an important segment of the population was bilingual.* These are not the signs of a Roman elite who spoke (or thought) in Etruscan, but of Romans coming to terms with Etruscan practices, and (to some extent) Etruscan institutions.

The keynote is above all urban. It shows Etruscans leading the way in the architecture (*atrium* 'forecourt', *columna, fenestra* 'window', *fornix* 'arch', *grunda* 'gutter', *turris* 'tower', *mundus* 'crypt'), particularly temple architecture with attendant waterworks (*favisa* 'tank', *cisterna*). Domestic conveniences were often named from this source: *lanterna* 'lantern', *catēna* 'bracket' or 'chain', *verna*, a slave not bought but born and bred in the family. City trades tended to have Etruscan names: the word for a shop or tavern is *taberna*, the original currency unit was *as*, the people you dealt with *caupō* 'landlord, shopkeeper', *cociō* 'dealer', *mangō* 'slaver'.

Urban also meant urbane: Etruscans set fashions in clothing, including Greek-style *palla* for women and *pallium* for men,† as well as the warmer *laena* (from Greek *khlaina*). They even provided the light and practical *lacerna* cloak, which was to become so popular in Augustus' time that he tried to restrict its use: it seemed too informal. They provided the accessories, a belt (*balteus*) and cap (*cappa*), a cord (*cimussis*) to draw the cloak together, and a pair of stout shoes (*calcei*) on the feet. An early style of toga, the *tebenna*, is Etruscan. Even *tunica* itself, the standard Roman tunic, may be an Etruscan deformation of Greek *khitōn*, which is essentially the same garment. Etruscan also provided the dry-cleaning experts (*fullō, nacca*) to keep the clothes in good order. Cosmetics were naturally an Etruscan thing: *cērussa* 'white lead', *purpurissum* 'purple', *mundus* 'toiletries'. Even the word *pulcher* 'beautiful' may be an Etruscan loan.

The kind of urbanite who would wear this stuff was termed by an Etruscan word too, *scurra*. The characteristic Roman attitude to such people can still be felt in the derived adjective *scurrilous*: in Latin they were a by-

---

*Livy (ix.36.2–4) tells the story of a brother of a consul in 310 BC who had studied in Etruria and so was competent enough in both the spoken and written language to work undercover; Livy adds that he was informed that such studies in Etruria were common for Romans back then, just as studies in Greece were in his own time (first century AD). This is the only explicit account of Romans learning Etruscan.

†I conjecture that these are both derived from the Greek verb *ball-esthai* 'to throw on' (a garment).

word for tasteless—because disrespectful—humor. Insults to another's intelligence evidently tripped off the tongue in Etruscan: they could call an idiot *barginna*, *bargus*, *buccō*, or *barō* (and the last of these has become the standard word for a male in Spanish, *varón*, and a hereditary nobleman, a baron, in English). In general, the Etruscan type for the Roman was one who enjoyed the soft and easy things of life to excess: likely to be an *aleō* 'gambler', *ganeō* 'glutton', *helluō* 'splurger', *lurchō* 'guzzler', or *levenna* 'wimp', consorting with *lenōnēs* 'pimps' and *lenae* 'madams', *carisae* 'foxy ladies' and *paelicēs* 'tarts', in the *lustra* 'brothels' of Rome, and probably resorting to *calumnia* 'name-calling' and the services of a pettifogging *rabula* 'shyster' if ever you should cross him. At least his self-indulgent *madulsa* 'binge' would be likely to leave him suffering the torments of *crāpula* 'hangover' in the morning.

The only good thing about the type, Roman traditionalists might have felt, was that special virtues correlated with their vices: their mastery in the arts of the *culīna* 'kitchen' was second to none, with a heavy emphasis on meat from the *laniēna* 'butcher's', *arvīna* 'lard', *botulus* 'black pudding', *sagīna* 'fattening', and judicious addition of *mantisa* 'sauce' or 'trimmings'. *Lucuns* 'sweetmeat', *amurca* 'olive juice', and even *puls* 'porridge' were Greek words (*glukous*, *amorge*, *poltos*) deformed on the Etruscan tongue. Cooking utensils too tended to have Etruscan names, such as *calpar* 'wine jar', *clarnus* 'platter', *cortīna* 'cauldron', *crēterra* 'mixing bowl', *lagēna* 'bottle', *lepista* 'large cup', *orca* 'vessel with narrow neck', *situlus* 'bucket', *sporta* 'basket', *tīna/tīnium* 'wine jar', *urceus* 'pitcher', *urna* 'urn'.*

Much Roman shipping terminology is Etruscan, showing from whom these Italian farmers first learned to plow the waves (*saburra* 'ballast', *sentīna* 'bilge water', *carīna* 'keel'), but once again most of it seems to have come originally from Greek, showing who were the original naval tutors in this part of the world (*ancora* 'anchor', *antemna* 'yardarm', *aplustra* 'stern figurehead', *guberna* 'steering oars', *guberniō* 'helmsman', *prōra/prōris* 'prow').

---

*Etruscan vocabulary paints a pretty full picture of early Roman civilization in towns, but plant names were also represented, specifically *alaternus* 'buckthorn', *fusterna* 'knot wood', *genista* 'broom', *laburnum*, *malva* 'mallow', and *viburnum*. Even the *murtus* 'myrtle' and *rosa* 'rose' seem to have come into Latin through Etruscan. In the garden, a *nassiterna* 'sprinkle pot' would let you water them. *Curculiō* or *gurguliō* 'corn weevil' and *excetra* 'water snake' would be less welcome visitors.

The Etruscans also had some effect even on Roman military language. Some of the central terms appear to be Etruscan: *mīles* 'soldier', *vēles* 'light infantryman', *satelles* 'bodyguard', *clipeus* 'round shield', *tīrō* 'raw recruit'. But there are also loans for other realities of military life: *cācula* 'batman', *lixa* 'camp follower'. The *gruma* too (an Etruscan deformation of the Greek word *gnōmōn*) was the key tool for Roman surveyors, for roads and other developments.

The Etruscans were great purveyors of entertainment, whether onstage (*scaena*) or in the *arēna*. The Romans derived their taste both for comic theater and the spectacle of gladiatorial shows from them, though no doubt they took them to new heights, or depths.* Certainly many of the stock characters (*dossennus* 'hunchback', *miriō* 'ugly man', *mōriō* 'dolt') and some styles of gladiator (*murmillō* 'fish-crested') had Etruscan names; musicians too (*subulō* 'flautist') were typical of their arts.

The Etruscan roots of Rome's performing arts were recognized by the doyens of Roman literature. Livy, the historian of the city's early years, who wrote in the first century BC, recalled the story that stage peformances were first introduced around 365 BC, which would place them a century after the height of Etruscan influence. A pestilence was then racking the city, and one might have imagined the innovation would have been intended as a diversion. But no: according to Livy, they were introduced as CAELESTIS IRAE PLACAMINA 'appeasements of heaven's wrath'. Livy observed:

> They are said to have introduced stage plays [LVDI SCENICI], something of a revolution for this warlike people; before that, they had known only the spectacle of the circus.† But the plays were small, as is usual when something is new, and were in fact of foreign origin. Players who performed without songs or actions to mime them were called in from Etruria: they danced to the

---

*The favorite spectacles are given quite recent origins, gladiatorial combats in 264 BC, based on the rite at Etruscan warriors' funerals; *vēnātiōnēs* (battles with wild beasts)—possibly a Roman innovation—from 186 BC. The gratuitously bloodthirsty character of Roman entertainments seems new too, not reflected in Etruscan tomb art; but perhaps it developed out of crowd response to large-scale sacrifices, elementally showing life and death in the lap of the gods.

†The circus, as such, was for races. Horse rituals and sacrifices had been a common feature of Indo-European culture from time immemorial (e.g., Mallory 1989: 135–36), and Rome's ancient EQVVS OCTOBER sacrifice to Mars was preceded by a chariot race.

strains of a piper and performed quite decorously in the Etruscan manner. Later young people began to copy them, putting in funny business in rough verse; and their gestures were no better than the words suggested. So the practice was taken up and grew through frequent repetition. The country artistes were given the name *histriōnes*, because *ister* was the Tuscan word for 'player' [Latin *ludiō*]. They did not, as before, swap rough and ready Fescennine verses, but whole medleys [*saturae*] set to flute music, with movements timed to match.[13]

This even suggests an Etruscan source for the one known Latin literary form with no Greek model, namely the satire. But indeed early satires are called *sermōnes* 'talks', and some have suggested that this is the meaning of the Etruscan word *satri*. Their scurrilous content would certainly befit an Etruscan cultural import.

◈

Another aspect of Etruscan culture showing them to be city folk was their names.

The Indo-European system, found all over from Iceland to India, but notably retained by the Greeks despite their highly urban lifestyle, allotted each person an individual name, made more specific if necessary by referring to the name of the father: *Snorri Sturluson*, *Rāmo Dāśarathis* 'Rama son of Dasharatha', *Aineiās Ankhīsiadēs* 'Aeneas son of Anchises'. Powerful clans distinguished themselves from time to time, perhaps as royal or tyrannical dynasties such as the Greek *Atreidai* and *Peisistratidai*, but there were never enough of them—existing in parallel in the one society—nor did they last long enough, to become reflected in a naming system.

The Etruscan system, by contrast, gave an individual a first name (Latin *praenōmen* 'forename'), but added a distinct 'gentile' name (*nōmen* 'name' or *gentilicium*) for the clan to which he or she belonged: *Vel Tlesna*, *Thefarie Veliana*, *Marce Caliathe*; or in Latin, *Gaius Marius*, *Marcus Antonius*.* To this

---

*In Latin, this usually ended in -ius and so looks like the old pattern of an adjective derived from a father's name. It has been suggested that this Etruscan system was actually the result of their misinterpretation of such Indo-European patronymics, so in this sense the result of Etruscan and Italic coexistence (Solin 1999).

could be added a third, more specific name, referring to a family within a clan: *Aule Titi Nurziu, Vel Tutna Tumu*; or in Latin, *Marcus Tullius Cicerō*. The Romans called this last the *cognōmen*, translatable as 'eke-name' or 'nickname'. Both these latter names were soon inherited by birth, like a modern surname. Overall, this was a system designed for higher urban densities, where there were just too many people to distinguish by the traditional name and patronymic.

The Romans, or at least those who came from more distinguished families, adopted this system in the seventh century BC. Its bourgeois convenience was perhaps less significant than the snobbish implications that it made possible. As well as serving as a more discriminating name-pattern, the possession of a gentile name showed that an individual belonged to a free family of Roman citizens. (Slaves and provincials, such as Greeks, would have just one individual name.) And the possession of *tria nōmina* 'the three names' was in the early days a badge of coming from a clan that had been distinguished long enough for different branches to have been singled out.

Curiously, but presumably for reasons that made sense at the time, this system never applied to women of good family, each of whom had as her official name just the gentile *nōmen*, marked with the feminine ending -a. By this token, all women in a clan were interchangeable. Evidently this was impractical for everyday life, so pet names abounded. But these had no more status as badges of identity than the arbitrary name given to a slave.*

Romans adopted more than just the system. For *praenōmina*, they adopted pretty much the whole set of Etruscan names: in the table, we see the list of Etruscan forenames with their Roman equivalents. Most made no sense in Latin, but Tiberius clearly referred to the local river, and Marcus probably honored the god Mars.[14]

As the table on the next page shows, many other names too were of Etruscan origin, often of the most famous individuals in Roman history. But whereas anyone could be given an Etruscan *praenōmen*, the possession of an Etruscan-derived *nōmen* or *cognōmen* must actually have said something about

---

*In the early centuries AD, women begin to have serious *cognōmina* of their own: MESSA-LINA (daughter of Messala), AGRIPPINA (daughter of Agrippa), IVSTINA, MEDVLLINA, NIGRINA, PLANCINA. But again these were apparently derived from their fathers. They did not distinguish sisters, nor could they be passed on to another generation.

TABLE I

ETRUSCAN-DERIVED ROMAN NAMES

PRAENŌMINA* (ETRUSCAN = ROMAN = ABBREV.)	NŌMINA	COGNŌMINA	
Aule = Aulus = A.	Caecilius	Caecīna	Marō
Cae = Gaius = C.	Caelius	Caesar	Perperna
Cneve = Gnaeus = Cn.	Cassius	Catilīna	Pisō
Cuinte = Quintus = Q.	Papirius	Catō	Sisenna
Kaisie = Kaeso = K.	Petrōnius	Cethegus	Varrō
Laucie = Lucius = L.	Postumius	Cicerō	Vercēnās
Marce = Marcus = M.	Vettius	Coclēs	
Puplie = Publius = P.	Volumnius	Gracchus	
Spurie = Spurius = Sp.		Lucumō	
Thefarie = Tiberius = Ti.		Maecēnās	
Tite = Titus = T.			

the remote lineage of the man who bore it. The name Caesar, for example, suggests that some remote ancestor (possibly Lucius Julius, who fought in the First Punic War around 250 BC) had had a significant link with the Etruscan city of Caere (called in Etruscan *Caisr-*).[15]

This system was to die out in later antiquity, as social hierarchies changed. The ancient families lost power and influence (and their gentile names became widely diffused after 212 AD when all provincials became citizens). *Praenōmina* and *nōmina* were increasingly dropped for practical purposes: there were too few of them, so people too often had the same name. By contrast, *cognōmina* were more and more used as distinguishers, assigned to

---

*The only surviving Roman praenomen for a woman was *Gaia*. Quintilian says that the abbreviation for it was ɔ, *C* reversed (*Inst.*, i.7.28). It was only used at weddings, where the newlyweds were hailed as GAIVS ET GAIA. But GAIVSQVE LVCIVSQVE was the Latin equivalent of 'Tom, Dick, and Harry' (e.g., Martial, v.14.5).

individuals and no longer inherited. The upending of the social order in the German invasions of the fifth century AD would reinstate the prestige of the old Indo-European system, which the Germans had never lost, as well as break up the social world into smaller units. And by then the general scatter of *cognōmina* among individuals meant that there was little left of the traditional system.

Surnames (the equivalent of Roman *nōmina*) would only make their reappearance across Europe gradually from the tenth century (starting, as it happened, in northern Italy), as the growing fluidity of population in urban centers, and trade links among them, made unworkable the system of simple name and father's name, even when reinforced with a place of origin. But the fact that Latin had adopted, and sustained for a millennium, a form of the surname system fifteen hundred years ahead of its time speaks for the large-scale civic stability of Roman society from the seventh century BC to the third century AD, though—admittedly—no less for its conservatism and class consciousness.

But Etruria's most important influence on Latin, ultimately, lay in having shown the Romans how to make Latin a written language. This is amply attested in the technical vocabulary for writing that became established in Latin. *Scrībere* 'write' itself seems to be a native word originally meaning 'scratch' or 'incise' (cf Russian *skrebú*, Lithuanian *skrabu*, Old English *sćeorpan* 'scrape'), and *legere* 'read' originally meant just 'pick up'; but much of the rest has come through Etruscan. *Titulus* 'label', hence 'title' and *elementum* 'letter' (apparently derived from L-M-N) seem to be Etruscan innovations. Most often the ultimate source is (unsurprisingly) in Greek. The key word *littera* 'letter' seems to be a reworking of the Greek *diphthera* 'leather, parchment'. In *cēra* 'wax', the material on which many messages were scratched, the change of gender shows that the word was not borrowed directly from Greek *kēros*; an Etruscan intermediary is likely. Likewise, *stilus*, the implement for scratching, has no etymology and has also been proposed as a loan from Etruscan.[16]

The Etruscan and Latin alphabets show by their form that the Etruscans had acquired theirs from the (Euboean) Greeks of Italy, and the Romans from the Etruscans. The Euboean origin shows in the values of certain letters: notably *F* and *Q* survive, *H* represents [h] and *X* [ks] (although some early Latin inscriptions use Φ instead for this last). But the details of the transmission remain obscure: the earliest known Etruscan inscriptions are not found around the most likely point of contact, the island of Ischia, where

TABLE 2
EARLY ALPHABETS USED IN ITALY

EUBOEAN GREEK ALPHABET (8TH-4TH CENTURIES BC), AS WRITTEN RIGHT-TO-LEFT

Ψ Φ X Υ T Ƨ ꟼ Ϙ Ρ ᒋ 1 Ο ‡ Ꟁ Ϻ ᒑ Ӿ I ⊗ Β I ꓱ Ⅎ ꓷ) Ꝝ Ꝕ

Ψ Φ X V T S R Q Ꝺ P O Ξ N M L K I Θ H Z F E D C B A

ARCHAIC ETRUSCAN ALPHABET (7TH-5TH CENTURIES BC), AS WRITTEN LEFT-TO-RIGHT

A	⟨	E	F	I	⊟	⊗	I	K	L	ᛘ	ᛗ	⌐	M	Ϙ	P	Ɣ
a	g	e	v,f	dz	ch	th	I	k	l	m	n	p	sh	q	r	s

T	V	X	Φ	Υ	⊟F8
t	u	ks	ph	kh	f

EARLY ROMAN ALPHABET (6TH-3RD CENTURIES BC), WITH MIXED LEFT- AND RIGHT-FACING VARIANTS

AΛ	BƁ	()	Dꟼ	E∃	F∃	[GI]
a	b	c	d	e	v	z
HB	I	KX	Lꝶ	MMᛉ	NᛗꝐ	O
h	i	k	l	m	n	o
P1Ր	QQꝞ	RRRꝝ	SꟄ	T	V	Ϙ
p	q	r	s	t	u	ks

---

the Euboeans had their emporium; and they include some letters (*C* instead of Γ, Ϻ in addition to Σ to represent the [s] sound) that came from the Corinthian, not the Euboean, alphabet. (But Syracuse, the most powerful of the Greek colonies in Italy, had been founded by Corinth; so this is not wholly surprising.)

As in many cases of early literacy, the offer of writing to the Romans was not taken up as a chance to begin a literature; for them, as for their Etruscan

Mirror of Volterra. This picture, from the back of a lady's mirror, shows the goddess Juno formally accepting Hercules as her (adopted) son.

tutors, the first writing seems to have been a means of making spells or formulas effective by setting them down on a permanent medium. The word *zich*, meaning 'writing' or 'book', is common in the Etruscan religious or legal documents that have survived. The boundary stone known as Cippus Perusinus ends with the phrase *cecha zichuche* 'as has been written'. And likewise the Tabula Cortonensis, probably a land contract, contains the phrase *cen zic zichuche* 'this writ was written'. In the depiction on a bronze mirror, found at Volterra, of the goddess Uni (Juno) being formally reconciled with Hercle (Hercules) by suckling him, a written plaque is held up by an attendant character, who by his trident must be Neptune. The plaque reads in Etruscan, *eca sren tva ichnac hercle unial clan thrasce,* which would be translated (word for word): "this picture shows how Hercules Juno's son became."

It is another example of a written statement being used formally to characterize something, in this case the point of a mythical situation. Early writing, such as the Etruscans knew, and such as they transmitted to the Romans, was for records.

CHAPTER 4

❖❖❖

Cui bono?—Rome's Winning Ways

QVIS, QVID, VBI, QVIBVS AVXILIIS, CVR, QVOMODO, QVANDO?

Who, what, where, by what means, why, how, when?

Traditional hexameter line, setting out lines of analysis

IN THE FOURTH CENTURY BC the many cities of Greece's classical era yielded to the single dominating power of Macedon: Athens, Thebes, and Sparta were among them, but even they were powerless to organize resistance. In that same century, as we have seen, the many cultured cities of Etruria too lost their independence: one by one, they succumbed to the gathering might of Rome. The demolition of leagues of city-states by single, centralized powers—powers that had previously seemed rather backward—was a feature of this century in Italy as in Greece.

Before this happened, could the Latin language have been endangered? To the north and to the south, there were Etruscan-speaking communities; and as we know, in the fifth century Rome itself was heavily influenced, if not actually ruled, by noble Etruscan families. One can speculate that the situation, linguistically, might have been rather like that of England after the Norman conquests, a foreign-language ruling class living self-indulgently in the city while the indigenous farmers toiled in the fields to support them.

However, looking at the elite technical vocabulary of the period, there is little reason to believe that Latin speakers were being excluded. The names given to the tribes to which Romans were assigned for voting purposes are all, admittedly, words of Etruscan origin: *Luceres, Ramnes, Tities.* And it is argued—still inconclusively—that an important word such as *populus*, which came to mean 'the people', Rome's ultimate source of authority, was originally an Etruscan word for 'army'.[1] But besides these, all the mechanisms of government were couched in Latin terminology. Rome had a senate (*senātus*, literally 'elder-dom', related to *senex* 'old man'), whose members were addressed as *patrēs conscriptī* 'conscript fathers' and met in the *cūria* (< *co-viria* 'men together'). Its elected officers (*magistrātūs*) were *consulēs* 'advisers', *praetōrēs* < *prae-itōrēs* 'leaders', *aedilēs* 'buildings men', and *quaestōrēs* 'inquirers'. Its elections were called *comitia* 'goings-together', decided by *suffrāgia* 'votes'. In emergencies, the supreme power would be vested in a single *dictātor* 'prescriber', supported by a *magister equitum* 'master of cavalry'. From time to time *cēnsōrēs* 'assessors' would review the senatorial rolls. All these crucial terms are transparently native to Latin. Other ancient constitutional words existed, with more obscure etymology: *classis* 'levy' (an income-based electoral division), *tribus* 'tribe' (an electoral division based on lineage), *plēbs* or *plēbēs* 'masses, lower orders', *pūbēs* 'body of citizens that are of age'. These could have been borrowed, but they could just as well have been ancient Latin terms; in any case, they tended to apply to the opposite end of society from the aristocracy, where we may assume that Etruscan influence would have predominated.

Whatever the degree of intimacy between Etruscans and Romans, this period left Rome in a position to expand like no other Italian power: within 250 years of its independence, just ten generations, it had moved to dominate not only the rest of Latium and Etruria, but also the whole extent of the peninsula beyond, both northward and southward. Militarily and politically, by 400 BC Rome had secured alliances with all of Latium and defeated the surrounding hostile mountain peoples, the Aequi and the Volsci. The next century and a half saw a hardening of Roman control in Latium, and a simultaneous spread of Roman power in three directions: over Etruria in the northwest, completed by the conquest of Volsinii in 264; over Umbria and Picenum in the northeast, mostly by making defensive alliances against the Gauls, who repeatedly invaded from the north; and over the (Oscan-speaking) Samnite league, which had united most of the east and south, sealed by Roman victories at Sentinum in 295 and Lake Vadimo in 282.

The final military challenge to Rome's control of Italy came from an invading force of Greeks, under King Pyrrhus of Epirus (the Greek northwest), invited over by the leading Greek colonial city of south Italy, Tarentum. This war, coming so soon after Rome's victory over the Samnites, threw all Rome's previous gains into jeopardy; it lasted from 280 until 272 BC, and although the Romans did not defeat Pyrrhus, his "Pyrrhic" victories over them were so costly and indecisive that he eventually retired, leaving Rome in control of Italy as a whole, and indeed

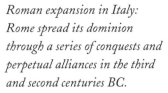

*Roman expansion in Italy:
Rome spread its dominion
through a series of conquests and
perpetual alliances in the third
and second centuries BC.*

unchallenged south of a line from Pisa to Rimini. Rome's grip within Italy was
not to be tested for another fifty years (during which time they had extended their
control as far as the Alps). But when Hannibal invaded the country in 218, at the
head of another foreign army (this one Carthaginian), the expected Italian revolt
in support of Hannibal never came. In those fifty years, then, Rome had established itself solidly as the ruling city of Italy.

Later on, when asked to explain their run of military success, the Romans
liked to claim a particular readiness to learn from their opponents. Sallust, a
historian of the first century BC, put the following words in the mouth of Julius Caesar:

> Our ancestors were never lacking in strategy or boldness, conscript fathers; nor
> were they prevented by pride from imitating others' institutions, if they were
> sound. They took arms and missiles from the Samnites, and most of their mag-
> istrates' insignia from the Etruscans. Above all, whenever anything apt was
> recognized among allies or enemies, they followed it up at home with the ut-
> most zeal; they preferred to imitate good things rather than envy them.[2]

In an unattributable fragment from a Greek historian, a Roman diplomat
gave the following lesson on Roman character to a Carthaginian, who was

claiming it could only be folly to challenge his own city at sea. (The dialogue is set in the 260s BC, between the departure of Pyrrhus and the outbreak of the First Punic War.)

> This is what we are like. (I shall tell you facts that are quite beyond dispute, for you to take back to your city.) When we face enemies, we take on their practices, and with those alien methods we surpass those with long experience in them. The Etruscans fought us with bronze shields, and in phalanx formation, not in maniples; we changed our weaponry and squared up to them; and in contest with those long-service veterans of phalanx warfare, we won. With the Samnites, the long "door" shields were not part of our tradition nor were javelins, since we had been fighting with spears and round shields; nor did we have much cavalry, practically all our strength lying in infantry. But we rearmed accordingly and forced ourselves into the saddle, and competing with these alien arms, we brought down those with high opinions of themselves. We did not know siege warfare; but we learned it from the Greeks, its masters, then went on to achieve more in it than those experts or anyone else. So men of Carthage, don't force the Romans to take up seafaring: if we need a fleet, we shall soon build one bigger and better than yours, and we'll fight better with it than long-hardened sailors.[3]

So much for Rome's military and political advance in these years, where the results show that Rome did have some long-term military, political, or perhaps even (as the Romans no doubt believed) moral advantage. Of greater interest, though, is how and why Rome was able to convert that into the permanent spread of Latin across Italy. The answers take us to the heart of why Latin ultimately expanded to be the majority language all around the western Mediterranean.

In fact, Latin tended to spread as a result of Roman conquests for three clear reasons.

First, and probably most important, when the Romans defeated an enemy, their usual practice was not to destroy its city and drive out or enslave its people, but rather to demand tracts of land from it. Even if a Roman treaty was not imposed at the end of a war, but struck as a defensive alliance, it would quite often involve permission for the establishment of a new Roman settlement or colony.* The land for this was methodically measured out and delimited

---

*Revealingly, whereas the Greek word for 'colony', *apoikía*, means a 'home from home', Latin *colōnia* means a settlement of *colōnī*, tillers of the land.

into rectangular plots by the land surveyors in a process called *centūriātiō*. Such regular land-plotting was to be practiced all over the Empire and is often still visible today.

Gradually, these tracts of farming land, or sites for new cities, were filled up with Romans and other Latin speakers from allied cities in Latium. It is estimated that in 260 BC there were approximately 292,000 Romans, and three quarters of a million other Latins; their joint population would have made up perhaps 35 percent of Italy's then population of 3 million souls.[4] And so, as the Romans and their allies gradually came to dominate the peninsula, the minority language Latin was seeded around Italy as a community language, and that of an increasingly high-prestige community.

Second, many treaties contained a condition giving Rome the right to levy young men for its army. (Military age for the Romans was from seventeen to forty-six years old.) As well as increasing the military strength of Rome, this too spread knowledge of Latin, since the Roman army was commanded in

Venta Icenorum, ca 4 AD. This impression shows the division of the land into square centuries.

Latin.* In the early centuries of Rome's wars, such levies would return to their homelands after service, mostly annually; but they remained available for enlistment for sixteen years. A famous example of a man who learned Latin in the army was Q. Ennius (239–169 BC), who went on to become a considerable tragic and epic poet in the language. Ennius had come from a noble family in Calabria but served in Sardinia, where he impressed M. Porcius Cato (later a consul) and so was taken to Rome.†

Later on, the latinizing effect of army service also reinforced indirectly the spread of Latin speakers in colonies: with the institution of a standing army by the general C. Marius at the end of the second century BC, it became usual for retiring soldiers, after their sixteen years' service or when armies were disbanded at the end of major campaigns, to be settled on the land, perhaps far away from the lands of their birth, but quite likely where they had seen service. This was a major reason for personal mobility through the war-filled periods of the late Republic and early Empire, from 100 BC until the emperor Hadrian ended the practice in the early second century AD. Thereafter soldiers tended to be recruited from home communities, so lifelong personal mobility was reduced. But in any case there were no more significant additions to the territories of the Empire; and by then, of course, the use of Latin had become dominant throughout the western Mediterranean provinces.

Looking back to Rome from his own (political) exile in the 40s AD, the philosopher and future statesman Seneca wrote, with some feeling, "The Roman Empire looks to an exile as its founder . . . [he meant Aeneas]. How many colonies has this nation since sent into every province! Wherever the Roman has conquered, he inhabits. Willingly they have given their names to this change of homes, and leaving their altars behind, the old would follow the settlers across the seas."[5]

The third reason that Latin spread so widely was the building of roads, a well-known feature of Roman civilization, which in fact extends back to 312 BC, with the first stretch of the Via Appia from Rome south to Capua. This also

---

*The army was perforce to become more multilingual in its practice when—after the second century BC—its recruits started to come from the eastern Mediterranean. Still Latin always remained the linguistic badge of Roman military identity. (Adams 2003: 760–61.)

†Ennius valued his knowledge of three languages, Oscan, Greek, and Latin, saying that they gave him three hearts. Aulus Gellius, *Noctes Atticae*, xvii.17: QVINTVS ENNIVS TRIA CORDA HABERE SESE DICEBAT, QVOD LOQVI GRAECE ET OSCE ET LATINE SCIRET. Probably he also knew Messapic, indigenous to his native Calabria. (Adams 2003: 116–17.)

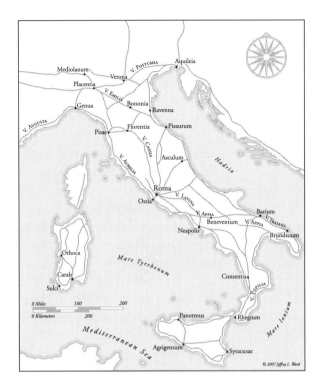

Roman roads.

tended to be a function of the army, since it required a mobile workforce, and was directly useful, above all, to the military. The whole of Italy, and later the whole world north of the Mediterranean, came to be linked by a network of roads that led back to Rome. This was especially true of the western provinces, where Latin became the dominant language. Like the postwar interstate highway system of the USA in our own time, the principal purpose of this government-financed road-building program was the easy movement of military forces and supplies to wherever they should be needed. But again as in twentieth-century America, the wider community received an immense social benefit, or at least an immense cohesive effect, in making their travel across longer distances more feasible. For all Rome's new dependencies, the costs of human contact beyond the immediate neighborhood, for whatever purpose, were lower within Roman domains than they had been before, in their independent past.

Such enhanced communications gave a differential advantage to Latin: its speakers were able to travel more easily, and farther, than speakers of any other single language. But the road network was also a vast contribution to the prestige of the growing Empire, ostentatiously measured out as it was by *mīliāria*, 'milestones', an extended symbol of *pāx Romāna*. That in itself acted as a further inducement to solidarity for those who lived within its bounds.

There is something of a paradox here. Rome's navy was to defeat every other naval power in the Mediterranean, and largely clear it of piracy as well. Its empire came to occupy the whole Mediterranean coastline and surrounding lands, so that from the second century BC onward the most direct route from Italy to most provinces would have been across the sea. The sheer cost of transporting goods by road must have meant that trade always favored shipping over wagon haulage: the cost difference was a factor greater than sixty.[6] Although some of the shorter roads near Rome had indeed had an economic origin (as the Via Salaria, which had supported Rome's ancient trade in salt with inland communities of Italy to its east, and the Via Latina, which ran southwest toward Campania), it appears that the road system was never primarily an economic infrastructure.

Yet despite these geographic and economic facts, Roman power, and hence Latin, was never spread by sea power. Rome remained a land-based power, and its roads remained as a highly durable trace of the route marches, *itinera*, of the Roman army. In a way, the fate of the Etruscans, as well as the limited political success in the long term of the Greek colonies in southern Italy, had demonstrated the lack of durability in what the Greeks would have called *thalassokratía* and *emporía*, an unchallenged navy and a trading network. What lasted was a centralized government, a large and mobile strike force, and a readiness to occupy territory permanently.

⟡

Although the long-term outcome is clear, the processes by which the various regions gave up their previous languages in favor of Latin are not well documented. Descendants of Latin are spoken to this day throughout the peninsula, as well as in the offshore islands of Sicily, Corsica, and Sardinia. Latin was already close to universal in Italy by the first century AD. But we can only find traces here and there of the changeover: late inscriptions in an inherited language, transitional effects as inscriptions in one language show the influence of another, the very occasional literary reference to language use.

What does emerge from this sparse evidence is how long the transition to Latin was delayed. Etruria in fact provides the richest source in Italy of such evidence of language shift, probably because it both had a history of literacy previous to any in Latin and was close to Latium. Epitaphs there have been traced by date, as Etruscan-language inscriptions yielded gradually to

Etruscan-Latin bilinguals and then to purely Latin inscriptions.[7] The
spreading wave of Latin-language use passed northward over two centuries,
from Caere (25 km from Rome) in the late second century BC, to Volaterrae
(200 km farther north) in the late first century AD.[8]

This means that the progress began as much as eleven generations after
Rome's first military inroad, the destruction of Veii in 396, and a good six generations after the conquest of the last independent Etruscan city, Volsinii, in
264. However, even after the Latin wave had passed, another four or five generations were needed before Roman burial customs were adopted by Etruscan
families.[9] People clearly went on feeling themselves culturally Etruscan long
after they had lost their own language, something one can see paralleled in
minority language communities to this day.[10]

In this delay, Etruria seems to have been quite typical. Cumae had been
the crucial bridgehead for Greek culture into Italy, founded jointly by the
Greek cities of Kyme, Khalkis, and Eretria around 750 BC (some 160 km to
the south of Rome, at the north end of what would be the Bay of Naples). It
had experienced an exciting history of its own before it came under the Roman
domination in 343 BC, together with its larger neighbor Capua. Despite being
a Greek foundation, its major language was the surrounding vernacular, Oscan.
An early and essentially voluntary adherent to Rome's league, whose citizens
had been awarded *civitas sine suffragio*, Roman citizenship without voting
rights, it was well integrated into the Roman system, governed from Rome by
annually elected officials (the four *praefecti Capuam Cumas*, 'officers for Capua
and Cumae'), a post that offered an early rung in Rome's *cursus honorum*, the
standard career path for a noble Roman. Nevertheless, only in 180 BC, after a
full six generations, did its burghers formally request permission of the Roman
government to use Latin in public business and for auctions.* And five generations later, in 54 BC, a letter from Cicero to a friend living there noted Oscan
farces still being performed in the local senate-house.[11]

The most significant inscriptions that have survived in the Umbrian and
Oscan languages were also dated long after Rome's domination in the region.

We know that Camerinum (Camerino) in Umbria had enjoyed what

---

*Livy, xl.42: CVMANIS EO ANNO PETEÑTIBVS PERMISSVM, VT PVBLICE LATINE
LOQVERENTVR ET PRAECONIBVS LATINE VENDENDI IVS ESSET. Livy mentioned it
apropos of nothing, in an incomplete sentence, which he did not explain. Indeed, it is not
clear why such permission should have been needed, and the request is without parallel
before or after. Politics was being played here, but we don't know whose, nor to what end.

Cicero termed "the holiest and fairest of all treaties"[12] with the Romans since the fourth century BC. Yet when the *Tabulae Iguvinae* from nearby Iguvium (Gubbio), mostly written in the Umbrian language and alphabet shortly after 300 BC, were updated between 100 and 50 BC, the language used was still Umbrian, even if the alphabet had changed from Umbrian to Roman.

The longest inscription in Oscan is the *Tabula Bantina*, from the Lucanian city of Bantia in southern Italy: it was written sometime between 133 and 118 BC. Lucania, as a previous hotbed of rebels loyal to the Samnite league, had sustained a fresh wave of Latin colonization from Romans, precisely in this period. The *tabula* is in fact the only Oscan inscription that has been found written in Roman letters, so changes were under way—and indeed there was a major inscription of a Roman law in Latin on the reverse; but this region had legally been under Roman control since the end of the Third Samnite War in 290. Old loyalties in the region continued to die hard; Venusia, just twenty kilometers northeast up the Via Appia, was the one Latin colony to side against Rome when the non-Latin peoples of central and southeastern Italy rose up to demand citizen rights in the so-called Social War of 90–89 BC.

This war, fought two centuries after Italy was supposedly subjected to Rome, actually used language to crystallize resistance. The belligerents characterized themselves on their coins as eight warriors, for the Marsi, Picentes, Paeligni, Marrucini, Vestini, Frentani, Hirpini, and Samnites. These all had originally spoken languages closely related to Oscan, though Latin seems by then to have penetrated the northerly regions (the Marsi and Picentes). They designated a new capital, the Paeligni's city of Corfinium, sited strategically to the north on the Via Valeria, but renamed it *Italia* or VÍTELIÚ, the name for the country in Oscan. Some coins hopefully showed the Italian bull (*vitulus*)* goring the Roman wolf or bore other legends in Oscan, such as the name of the commander in the south G.PAAPIÍ.G.MUTÍL (C. Papius Mutilus), or more generally EMBRATUR (*imperator*).[13]

Rome won the war, but its rulers had received a serious fright, and there came a total collapse of the Roman hard-liners' old theory of DIVIDE ET IMPERA, that Italy was best controlled by a policy of "separate development," encouraging its divisions and differences. The alternative, therefore, had to be pursued, of shared privileges and willing solidarity. Soon afterward the rights of Roman citizenship were made available to practically the whole of Italy.

---

*Borrowed from Greek *wetalos* 'yearling', and the ultimate source of the English word *veal*.

Oscan-language coins from the Social War, 90–89 BC. Eight warriors swear a pact against Rome, and the Italian bull gores the Roman wolf.

Although there is no concrete evidence of it, this strategy may also have extended into language policy, with the various communities actively encouraged to merge in the Roman identity and drop their languages in favor of Latin.[14] Certainly, it was in the period after the Social War, the first centuries BC and AD, that the diffusion of Latin, seeded through colonies, army service, and general mobility, accelerated and moved beyond the stage of bilingualism, so that it effectively supplanted all the other indigenous languages of Italy. And with this process, Italy was greatly homogenized.

As the Greek geographer Strabo put it, writing in the early first century AD, "But now, except for the cities of Tarentum, Rhegium, and Neapolis, all [of the Greek domain in southern Italy] has been flooded with foreigners, some parts taken by Lucanians and Bruttians, others by Campanians. But that is just in name; in fact by Romans—for that is what they have become."[15]

⟡

We have found the basis for an answer to our question: Where did it all go right, for Latin, and for Rome?

Latin had two main indigenous competitors in Italy, Etruscan and Oscan. All three languages had the potential for expansion and did indeed expand: Etruscan mostly to the northeast, Oscan to the south. Latin, with its central position, had nowhere to go but into the domains of Etruscan and Oscan. But unlike them, Latin combined three properties: it was a farmers' language, a soldiers' language, and a city language. Together, these gave it the victory.

Etruscan was certainly urban and cosmopolitan, and no doubt farmers used it in the country; but it was not linked with a constant military force, nor indeed a government strong enough to unite the various independent Etruscan-speaking cities behind a single policy. When the outposts that they had created for trade faced resistance, they could not project force to protect them; and when thrown back on the defense of their own homelands, they could not unite even for joint survival. Rome—and hence Latin—defeated and invaded them, one by one.

Rome was the heir to the Etruscan legacy of highly organized civic life; but, unlike the Etruscans themselves, Rome was able as a unified land-power to make its gains permanent. The Etruscans gathered wealth, enjoyed it, but ultimately lost it; the Romans acquired land and settled it for good. The Etruscans' sea power and federal politics meant that their links with their colonies remained rather light; they could not impose themselves on the Italian interior. The Romans not only came to live all over that interior, but they had control of an army that could range over it at will and increasingly made existence impossible for any city or tribe that wished to live independently of Rome.

Perhaps the Samnites, or Lucanians in southern Italy, might have achieved something similar; at the outset their social and military structures were much like Rome's. Oscan was a language of farmers and soldiers, like Latin; but unlike Latin, it was the language of a league of tribes, with no single centralized city that dominated it. Just such an urban core was Rome: this was the advantage Latin had derived from its centuries of contact with Etruria. Ironically, this single urban core turned out to be much more effective than the multiple urban cores that the Etruscans had developed for themselves. Rome's centralized control of Latium, and then of colonies that maintained its influence across Italy, meant it enjoyed a permanent hierarchical command structure that the Samnite league, or the other alliances of Italians, could never match. Ultimately, it expanded to absorb them all.

For the Romans had some winning ways that were all their own: after a victory they demanded not tribute, but land, which they would sooner or later settle with their own farmers; and they levied soldiers too from the defeated powers, who would add their strength to the Roman army. The Roman army too, with its compulsive program of road building, cumulatively and permanently improved ease of communication within the expanding empire. All these policies benefited not just the long-term strength of Rome but also sustained the growth of the Latin language.

◇•◇•◇

CHAPTER 5

Excelsior—Looking Up to Greek

τοὐμὸν ὄνειρον ἐμοί. EADEM OMNIA QVASI CONLOCVTI
ESSEMVS VIDIMVS.

You're telling me. [*Greek, literally*: (You're telling) me my own dream.]
We saw everything the same, just as if we had discussed it.

Cicero, *Letter to Atticus*, 6.9.3

E VEN AT THE END of the third century BC, when Rome already controlled Italy and had twice humbled its only serious rival in the west, the
city of Carthage, the Latin language was still to its users little more than a
practical convenience. Its speakers and learners did not yet conceive it as an
attribute of Roman greatness, a language to equal any in the world. To think
in such terms, the Romans would need to encounter Greek.

The discovery of Greek would give the Romans a new idea of what
skill in a language could do, for its speakers' attainments as well as for their
reputation. They would start to care about powers of expression, both their
own personal powers and whatever was connoted by the language itself.
They would begin to use Latin as a symbol of Roman power, for what it said
about them. Latin literature was consciously modeled on Greek, and techniques to use it effectively were laboriously abstracted from the best Greek
practice. In time—and this took more than three centuries—the new canon
of Latin classics became able to stand comparison with the best of Greek.
And when that happened, Greek had lost its one unchallengeable advantage: from the self-imagined center of the world in Italy, after all, there
could be no serious comparison between Romans and Greeks as ideals.
Thenceforth the temptation was to discard wholesale the old model, of

learning the best Latin through Greek: the best Latin could now be learned through Latin itself.

⟡

The Latins, and specifically the Romans, had always had the Greeks on the edge of their world. Indeed, the earliest known inscription in Greek letters anywhere is from Gabii, just outside Rome, and dates from the early eighth century BC, a generation or so before the traditional date of Rome's foundation in 753. The Greeks had the opportunity to pass on the technique of writing during this early period when the dominant regional power was still Etruscan; and in fact the story of Rome's legendary founders, the twins Romulus and Remus, has them learning their letters at Gabii.[1]

Greek visitors soon after this were establishing themselves as regular colonists farther south: Cumae (Greek *Kumē*), near the Bay of Naples, was founded around 750 BC, and some fifteen years later a clutch of colonies was established in eastern Sicily (Naxos, Syracuse, Catania, Zankle-Messina), followed a little later by more along the southern Italian coasts (Paestum, Rhegium, Sybaris, Crotona, Tarentum). The settlements grew, were reinforced, and sprouted others, until by 450 BC there were sixteen Greek cities in Sicily and twenty-two in Italy.

The south, however, was not the part of Italy that Romans or Latins frequented in these early years, so the early impact of Greek culture came to them indirectly, through Etruscan middlemen. Specifically—and despite what has turned up in Gabii—this included the technique of writing.

When the Greeks first used their alphabet, the direction of writing was rather fluid: right-to-left, left-to-right, or even alternating (which they called *boustrophēdon* 'as you turn an ox'). Etruscans—for reasons we can only speculate about—standardized on right-to-left; but the Latins, after a right-to-left period, finally settled on left-to-right, the same choice as the Greeks ultimately made. Etruscan speakers, who did not hear a difference between [g] and [k] (nor indeed [d] and [t], nor [b] and [p]) provided the reason why the letter Γ, Greek gamma, locally written (right-to-left) as ɔ, hence c, came to be pronounced unvoiced as [k], and to be distinguished from κ and ϙ only by the following vowel. (Their rule was, in the early days: κ before A, ϙ before v, otherwise c.)* The Etruscans also dropped (because it was useless to them) the

---

*Hence the Latin names of the letters (kā, cē, qū), regularly transformed in English into kay, sea, cue—[kei], [si:], [kyu:w]. This reinterpretation of Γ/C meant the Latins needed

letter o. Still, the Latins, unlike the Umbrians and Oscans, did manage to preserve or reinstate it, keeping it separate from v. They also retrieved the letters B and D (Greek β, Δ), which the Etruscans had discarded. These are all developments of the fourth century BC or before; but it was not until the first century BC that they reintroduced the letters Y and z, specifically to represent sounds in words borrowed from Greek.

In the fifth and fourth centuries BC, as their power grew in Italy, Romans were occasionally nudged to look to a wider Greek world. The Sibylline books, key to propitiation of the gods in time of crisis, were written in Greek; they are supposed to have been acquired in the reign of Tarquinius Priscus, in the early sixth century. In 433, in time of plague, the books enjoined the building of a temple to the Greek god Apollo Medicus; but apparently there was a site already dedicated to him at Rome. In the next generation, in 398 and 394, the Romans visited Apollo's oracle on the Greek mainland at Delphi, first to consult on their fortunes in the struggle with Veii, and then (after victory) to pay their vow to the god. (Understandably, during hostilities with Etruscan neighbors, the Romans' usual Etruscan soothsayers were not available or reliable.)² At some point in the Samnite Wars of the fourth century, Apollo also caused the erection in Rome of statues to two improbable Greek celebrities, Pythagoras of Crotona and Alcibiades of Athens.³ It was even said that Romans were among the embassies from all over the Mediterranean world who went to Babylon in 323 BC to congratulate Alexander.⁴ Anyway, after Rome had expelled from Italy the campaigning Greek dynast Pyrrhus in 273 BC, it is certain the equally Greek king Ptolemy II of Egypt offered a gratuitous treaty of friendship to this clearly important, rising city. By the early third century, Rome was impressing the Greek world in its own right.

Only when all the Greek cities had fallen under Roman political control did the idea form that something might be done with Latin at all comparable with what the Greeks did with their own language. Even in the late third century, Q. Fabius Pictor, the first known Roman to write Roman history, was writing only in Greek. In those days, the very idea of a written literature was inseparable from the Greek language.⁵ But in 240 BC the half-Greek freedman from Tarentum, L. Livius Andronicus, produced a comedy and a tragedy

---

to reinvent a symbol for [g], namely G. Amazingly, we are even told the inventor's name, one Sp. Carvilius Ruga (Plutarch, *Roman Questions*, 54). He only seems to have got around to this in the third century BC.

in Latin for performance at the Roman Games; in all, he is known to have written at least three comedies and ten tragedies, as well as a translation of the *Odyssey*. These new, literary forms of entertainment caught on at Rome, and the stories from Greek drama and epic dominated Latin literature for the next century. Among the early greats of Latin literature are Cn. **Naevius** (around 265–204), T. Maccius **Plautus** (around 250–184), Q. **Ennius** (239–169), M. **Terentius** Afer (around 190–159), M. **Pacuvius** (220–around 130) and L. **Accius** (170–around 86).* Among them, Ennius stands out for the variety of what he wrote, not only comedies, tragedies, and an epic of Roman history (*Annales*), but also epitaphs, theology, satire, and even the *Hedyphagetica* 'sweet eatings', a gourmet's review, with such deathless lines as:

BRVNDISII SARGVS BONVS EST; HVNC, MAGNVS SI ERIT, SVME.

The sar fish of Brindisi is good; if it is a big one, take it.[†6]

Among these writers—all still taken seriously by the critics of the first centuries BC–AD, when the classical canon was being laid down—only the comedy writers Plautus and Terence have been preserved with complete long works to their names. Hence early Latin literature comes down to us with a strong emphasis on a fantasy of Greek life, its situations and characters based in Greek plays. In this world, a universe away from Roman ideals, young men are hopelessly in love, whores have hearts of gold, old men are miserly and dirty-minded, and slaves—realistically, their only resource being their trickery—are more resourceful than their masters. Old women are largely unknown. No one has much on their minds but sex, money, food, mischief, and occasionally concern for their children, especially if long lost: there is not a whiff of military service, farming, or civic piety. Writers thought it worth

---

*The nomen *Livius* shows that he had been a slave in the gens Livia, while the cognomen *Andro-nicus* is pure Greek: 'man-winning'. The nomen *Naevius* seems to derive from *naevus* 'mole, birthmark'. The cognomen *Plautus* means 'flatfoot'. Cognomen *Afer* means 'African'.

†Ennius was the first writer of hexameters in Latin, and this seems a good moment to introduce this verse form, which will shape most of the snatches of Latin verse to come (as well as the lines of Virgil already quoted). The rhythm used to be taught to English schoolboys as:

"Dówn in a déep, dárk dítch ‖ lay an óldców, múnching a béanstálk" where ‖ marks the necessary word break (or *caesura* [pronounced "seize-youra"]) found in every line. More details will be found in the endnote.

telling the audience of their Greek sourcing. In the prologue to one play, Terence wrote, "As for the rumors put about by some grouches that the author has spoiled a lot of Greek plays to make just a few Latin ones: he does not deny that's what he's done—no worries—and he says he'll do it again."[7]

In his prologues, Plautus sometimes gave the name of the Greek author of the original version, but added that it was he who VORTIT BARBARE 'turned it into foreign'.[8] Either his tongue was firmly in his cheek, or Roman audiences were amazingly ready in the early second century to take their laughs from a Greek standpoint. Perhaps the explicitly Greek settings kept the feckless content at a safe distance from what would be accepted in real life at Rome, much as Indian Bollywood films in the twentieth century long played out ideas of romantic love in luxurious surroundings for the delight of orthodox Hindu and Muslim audiences who had no place for it in their actual lives.

Comedy may have been king for the Roman in the street, but serious statesmen and intellectuals, as they increasingly looked beyond Italy, were also coming to notice and value the Greek heritage. In 228 BC, when the Romans had cleared the Adriatic of Illyrian piracy, gaining themselves a coastal strip (the coast of modern Albania) as a first base in the east, they sent embassies to Greek cities, notably the trading centers Corinth and Athens, pointing out that the new Roman policing of the seas was very much in their interests. Symbolically, Romans were then invited for the first time to compete in the Isthmian Games, held every other year near Corinth.

Much of the third century was taken up with fighting Carthage at sea or overseas (264–241), and later surviving and then retaliating against the Carthaginian invasion of Italy under Hannibal (218–203); but even interactions with this age-old and non-Greek empire (founded around 900 BC, with a maritime empire since the seventh century) would increasingly have impressed on the Romans that Greek was the language of the wider Mediterranean. Amazingly, the Carthaginian senate had once in an earlier era legislated to outlaw knowledge of Greek at home, to prevent private contacts with the enemy.[9] Nonetheless, in Rome's day Carthage's troops, largely mercenaries, were commanded not in Punic but in Greek.* Hannibal himself had been educated in Greek and

---

*This seems to be Gustave Flaubert's inference (*Salammbô*, ch. 2, *A Sicca*, midpoint) from Polybius' remark (i.32.7) that the redoubtable Spartan Xanthippus, who in the first Punic War restored the fortunes of the Carthaginians' mercenary army, "began the giving of commands according to rules" (*paraggéllein katà nomous érxato*). Certainly when in 241–238 Carthage's unpaid troops had mutinied after the end of the First Punic War, some of

was an author in it, and in fact his old tutor Sosylus of Sparta accompanied him on his campaigns and wrote up their history in the language. Other Greeks, Silenus and Chaereas, also were involved as chroniclers.[10] Phoenicians, like those who founded Carthage, might have been the ones to give the Greeks their original letters (*tá phoinikéia grámmata*, as the Greeks still called them); but Carthage's nobility had nevertheless been drawn into the cultural force-field created by the application of those letters to Greek, recognizing it as the international language par excellence—or more authentically, in Greek, *kat'exokhén*. When, during a lull in his campaign in 205, Hannibal set an altar inscribed with his achievements in the temple of Juno at Lacinia, on the point of Italy's instep that faced the Ionian Sea, he used both Punic and Greek, but not Latin or Oscan.[11]

In 202 BC, with Carthage defeated, Rome can with hindsight be seen to have stood at a crossroads. It held, in principle, a score still to be settled with Philip V of Macedon, who had allied with Carthage against Rome; and Antiochus III, widely victorious Seleucid king of Asia, might have been seen as a very long-term threat to Italy—but only if he chose to pursue his conquests in a direction, and to an extent, that no Greek successor of Alexander's ever had before. Essentially, sleeping dogs here could have been left to lie—and would probably have been so left by a less aggressive, less military society. These major Greek kingdoms of the eastern Mediterranean made up a system four generations old, with endemic political problems and rivalries quite unfamiliar to Rome. To choose to enter this was an unprecedented step, whose long-term consequences were quite unpredictable. And it cannot have been popular with everyone to enter into such a new theater, with no end in sight, two years after the deliverance from Carthage.

Furthermore, foreign wars, without any casus belli in Italy, were strictly illegal. By Rome's IVS FETIALE, the law of the college of priests charged with opening and closing states of war, the relevant rites could only be performed if Rome was acting in defense of itself or its oath-bound SOCII 'allies'. Rome had no such SOCII east of the Adriatic. It had treaties of AMICITIA 'friendship'

---

the coins they struck were denominated in Greek (ΛΙΒΥΩΝ 'Libyans'). This army included Balearic slingers, Celtiberians (from northern Spain), Numidian cavalry (from western North Africa), and Libyan light infantry (from farther east). This said, it is clear (again from coinage) that Punic was used at home in Carthage, and in Numidia and the neighboring coastal kingdoms of Massylia and Massaesylia. Coins from Carthaginian colonies in Sicily since 410 had also carried Punic legends. (Cribb et al. 1999: 224–25; Lancel 1997: 357.)

(Greek *philía*) with some of the states there, notably Egypt, but this relationship was unprecedented as a basis for a war of solidarity, and not in any case
very relevant to the immediate choice of adversary, Philip of Macedon.

Nevertheless the Senate did resolve to act against the great powers of the
east. There is little in the written record to justify this momentous decision.*
Polybius, the main near-contemporary historian and a Greek himself, placed
the initiative with the Greeks. Of the conference of Naupactus in 217, which
brought Philip V of Macedon and sundry Greeks into ineffectual alliance with
Carthage, he wrote:

> This was the time and the conference which first brought into interplay
> Greek, Italian, and Libyan (i.e. Carthaginian) affairs: no longer would Philip
> or the leading Greek statesmen, when dealing with affairs in Greece, make
> reference to, war on, or agreements with, each other: from now on they would
> all look to their aims in Italy . . . those disaffected with Philip and some with
> differences with Attalus (king of Pergamum) would no longer turn east to
> Antiochus (of Asia) or south to Ptolemy (of Egypt), but send missions west,
> either to the Carthaginians or the Romans. Similarly, the Romans sent to the
> Greeks, for fear of Philip's audacity and to forestall any advantage he might
> take of their current predicament.[12]

But this merely marked the turning point as a Greek might have seen it.
Rome chose to keep raising the stakes and extending its involvement until all
the Greek regimes, big and small, had been deposed or incorporated into sub-
servient alliances.

Whatever the arguments presented in the Senate, the war—if it could be
decisively won—must have been financially tempting. In crude financial terms,
the Punic Wars had shown Rome what the benefits of victory over a major
foreign power could be: the war reparations adjudged against Carthage were
two hundred talents per annum for fifty years, a grand total of ten thousand
talents or 240 million sesterces ('MHS').†

---

*Livy (xxxi.7) reconstructed P. Sulpicius' speech in the Senate: in a way curiously familiar
to those who lived through 2003, he laid great weight (citing recent history) on the need
to nip enemy threats in the bud, and the need to carry the war abroad before the enemy
autocrat can bring it closer to home.

†*HS*, a graphic variant of *IIS*, is the received abbreviation for sesterce, or in Latin SESTER-
TIVS. This is itself an abbreviation of SEMIS TERTIVS 'the third half', i.e., not ½, nor 1½,
but 2½ (hence IIS, i.e., DVO SEMIS-QVE). A sesterce was originally 2½ ASSES, or a quarter

The lesson did not go amiss, and the rewards for conquest of Greek powers turned out to be quite comparable. The 24 MHS exacted from Philip V by T. Quinctius Flamininus* in 197 (half at once, half over ten years) were a mere first fruit of what was to come. When Antiochus was forced to surrender western Asia Minor by the brothers P. and L. Cornelius Scipio[†] in 189, he settled for a record indemnity of fifteen thousand talents, or 360 MHS. Annual revenues to Rome at this time were running at 30 MHS. When L. Aemilius Paullus[‡] returned victorious from his war against Philip's son Perseus in 167, he brought with him at least another 120 MHS in booty. Revenues from Macedon thereafter ran at 2.4 MHS per annum. In all, in the fifty years after 201, Rome would actually receive 648 MHS in indemnity payments, principally from Carthage, Macedon, and Asia, equivalent to 13 MHS annually.[13]

To put this in proportion, the property qualification for a senator was a landed fortune valued at more than 0.4 MHS. Pliny observed that Rome's treasury coffers in 157 BC held a credit balance of 100.3 MHS.[14] And this sum was to be doubled in 130 BC, when the northeast Asian kingdom of Pergamum was bequeathed to Rome. Then in 63 BC, after Pompey's conquest of Syria, the level leapt to 340 MHS.[15]

Flush with these windfalls of militarism, Rome was to go on a hundred-year spree. The indemnity paid by Antiochus in 189 sufficed to pay off the crippling national debt that Rome had incurred to its citizens during the war with Hannibal, equivalent to 25½ years of tax revenues (TRIBVTVM SIMPLEX).[16] At the same time Livy said that the return of the army from Asia at this time saw the "first influx of foreign luxury" into Rome.[17] In 167, with access to the loot from Perseus' kingdom in Macedon, Rome ceased to levy taxes on its own citizens, a kind of "war dividend." Meanwhile, there was a surge in public works spending: in 184, 24 MHS was spent on sewers; in 144–140 a new

---

of a DENARIVS, which was literally 'a tenner'. In this period, a talent of silver (25.86 kg at the Attic/Euboic standard) was worth HS 24,000. Using the 1879 valuation in Lewis and Short's *Latin Dictionary*, and applying inflation rates since, one MHS would equate in 2006 to just under £500,000 or US$868,500. Latin also used a different style, with superscript lines, to abbreviate large numbers, especially in cash sums: HSV would be 5 sesterces (SESTERTII QVINQVE); HSV̄ 5 thousand sesterces (SESTERTIA QVINA [MILIA]), and H̄S̄V̄ would have been 5 million sesterces (SESTERTIVM QVINGENTIES)—for us 5 MHS.

*The cognomen is derived from FLAMEN, a priest of a specific deity.
[†]The cognomen *Scīpiō* means 'staff, scepter'.
[‡]The cognomen *Paullus* means 'shorty'.

aqueduct, the Aqua Marcia, was built at a cost of 180 MHS; in 142 the first stone bridge across the Tiber, the Pons Aemilius, went up. Most of the major routes in Italy were built in this same century.[18] Politicians began to see the potential for applying Rome's wealth in unprecedented ways, directly for the benefit of the poor.

In 122 C. Gracchus involved the state in subsidizing the price of grain; in 58 BC P. Clodius began the policy of a free grain ration for citizens, an extravagant policy that once instituted could never be dropped.*

These eastern wars were certainly profitable, indeed life-transforming for the citizen populace back home. For a state that had always emphasized the glory of conquest, the new eastern-Mediterranean focus of Rome's unending willingness to pursue wars far from home needs little special explanation: that was, after all, where the world's wealth was to be found, and to be plucked.

There is controversy on how money-minded Roman strategy really was, from those who emphasized motives that were more publicly acceptable to the Romans, the preemption of dangerous rivals, and the aspiration for glory from a string of victories.† These motives were no doubt also present and are not incompatible. And evidently, Roman victories against the greatest and oldest powers then known—for that is what the Greek kingdoms were—may not have seemed so inevitable before the wars were waged. But the Roman attitude can perhaps best be gauged from an anecdote that Cicero put into the approving mouth of even an archconservative, Cato the Censor.‡ The great national hero M'. Curius Dentatus,§ sitting at his hearth in his latter years, was brought a great weight of gold by the Samnites, but declined it: it did not seem to him as glorious, he said, to have gold himself, as to rule over those that had it.[19]

Whatever the ambivalence about the tangible rewards, Rome's new enthusiasm for Greek culture provided an effective, and widely acceptable, justification for these interventions. When Romans made policy pronouncements

---

*Cyprus, another Greek territory, was annexed to meet the cost of this.

†As usual, the most eloquent testimony against Rome was provided by a Roman. The historian Sallust wrote an eloquent imaginary letter from Rome's enemy King Mithridates VI of Pontus (120–63 BC) to a king of Parthia. "The fact is that the Romans have one ancient motive for making war on all nations, peoples, and kings, the depth of their greed for empire and riches; this drove them to start a war against King Philip of Macedon, when they were hard-pressed by Carthage and pretending to be his friends." (*Epistula in Mithridatem*, v.)

‡M. Porcius Cato Censorius. The cognomen *Catō* is from CATVS 'sharp, crafty'.

§The cognomen *Dentātus* means 'toothy'.

during the wars with Philip, Antiochus, and Perseus, they consistently took the line that Rome's interest was in the freedom of the Greeks. Their declaration of war in 200 had the effrontery to require Philip to abstain from war against any Greek state.[20] In an inconsequential conference with Philip in 198, the Roman general T. Quinctius Flamininus declared that Philip must withdraw totally from Greece. After winning the battle of Cynoscephalae in 197,* Flamininus announced at the Isthmian Games in 196 that all the Greeks in Asia and in Europe were to be free and enjoy their own laws, a statement that apparently surprised with joy most of his audience, since they had been assuming that Rome would simply take over the control of Philip's possessions. In 193 he went on to declare that Rome would next liberate the Greeks of Asia from Antiochus. This promise was fulfilled in 188 in the Treaty of Apamea, concluded by the brothers Scipio,[†] who had just defeated Antiochus at Magnesia. Again Rome had scored a total victory, but not exacted control of the conquered, or even tranches of their land for settlement. Unlike the previously gained overseas territories in Sicily, Sardinia, Corsica, and Spain, no *prōvincia* was created in Greece with a Roman magistrate in command. Taxes were not exacted. It looked as if the Romans, faced with the Greeks, had found a new—and more restrained—model of empire.

Things began to change immediately afterward. The kingdom of Macedon under Philip's son Perseus rebelled and after a three-year war was crushed at the battle of Pydna (168) by L. Aemilius Paullus. Epirus, to its southwest, which had given some aid to the rebels, he also sacked, selling 150,000 of its inhabitants into slavery. In both Macedon and Epirus, land taxes were henceforth payable to the Roman treasury. But the power vacuum so created in the territories was judged to lay them open to unrest. Thus, in 148, Macedonia was annexed as a regular province.

---

*For ancient historians (e.g., Polybius, xviii.28–32), the main interest of this battle was that it established the tactical superiority of the Roman legion (combining a clear formation with disciplined flexibility) over the Greek phalanx (which had seemed for three centuries to show the invincibility of serried ranks of spearmen, but turned out to be crucially dependent on level terrain). This moral was underlined by further Roman victories over the phalanx at Magnesia (190) and Pydna (168).

†Lucius was officially in command. His brother Publius, once triumphant against Hannibal but unable to hold a command now for procedural reasons, served as legate. He was still the most influential man at Rome and had long been famous for his philhellene enthusiasms. But he proved less effective at political intrigue after his return, when he was prosecuted for bribery and spent his last years in exile.

Central Greece too became (for Rome) worryingly unstable in the two generations after Flamininus' declaration of its freedom. Political dissension continued to fizz in the free cities, which frequently appealed to Rome against one another and were felt to harbor undesirable elements on the run from Macedonia. Rome had attempted to eliminate troublemakers by interning one thousand prominent citizens in Italy from 164 to 151, but an anti-Roman rebellion occurred after they returned. It was based in Corinth, at the time the preeminent Greek center of trade and culture.

In 146 the new governor of Macedonia (Q. Caecilius Metellus* Macedonicus) crushed the revolt, and his successor, L. Mummius, reorganized Greece into an unstructured but unthreatening mass of unallied city-states, all under Macedonian command. Roman tax gatherers moved in. Mummius is most famous, though, for razing the ancient city of Corinth. Roman punitive action was not light, and not forgotten. Corinth never recovered, but one effect of the action was a sudden appearance of Greek artworks in the Italian mansions of Mummius' friends and associates. After fifty years of "freedom," the logic, or rather the accounting,† of Roman imperium had asserted itself over Greece.

◈

An immediate effect of Rome's annexation of mainland Greece was a surge of Greek immigrants to Italy. Supply was available to meet the increasingly sophisticated, and urbanized, demand from all levels of Roman society for entertainers, prostitutes, tailors, couturiers, grocers, vintners, cooks, importers, trainers, slave traders, farm laborers, gardeners, nursemaids, butlers, lady's maids, secretaries, accountants, doctors, architects, tutors, professors.‡ Greek words in Plautus' plays, our fullest record of early colloquial Latin, do occur mostly in the speech of lower-class characters, but this reflects the era 205–184

---

*The cognomen METELLVS means 'paid servant' or 'mercenary'.

†RATIO, literally 'thinking', is the Latin word, suitably ambiguous between a financial reckoning and a ruling principle. It is the origin of the English word *reason*.

‡The sheer omnicompetence of Greeks never ceased to amaze the Romans. As Juvenal (iii.76–78) put it, three centuries later, GRAMMATICVS, RHETOR, GEOMETRES, PICTOR, ALIPTES, | AVGVR, SCHOENOBATES, MEDICVS, MAGVS, OMNIA NOVIT | GRAECVLVS ESVRIENS: IN CAELVM IVSSERIS IBIT 'Schoolmaster, lecturer, geometer, painter, trainer, fortune-teller, tightrope walker, doctor, magician, a hungry Greek knows every trade: tell him to go to the sky and he will'.

BC, the generation when the Greek wars were still being fought. Many of the newcomers would indeed have been slaves resulting from Roman clearances, but increasingly there were volunteer adventurers from free families seeking their fortunes in the households of the newly dominant "barbarians" across the Adriatic. In an autobiographical incident datable to 167, Polybius, recently brought to Rome as a Greek political internee, said to his new friend, the young aristocrat Scipio, "As for these studies, which you and your brother seem to find more and more enthralling as well as promising for your careers, you will find plenty of people to help both of you: there are masses of scholars whom I can see flooding from Greece into Italy nowadays."[21]

"These studies" were in grammar and rhetoric, Greek specialties curiously ripe for transplantation, now that significant careers based on public persuasion in the courts and assemblies were less and less possible in a Greece under foreign masters. But such skills were precisely the ones needed to make a mark in Rome's republican institutions, which in the last two centuries BC were to be increasingly open to talent (if suitably well-heeled), and somewhat less dominated by scions of the old families with distinguished military traditions.*

Despite the masses of scholars recognized by Polybius as descending on Italy, no noted Greek grammarian or rhetorician taught at Rome until 159. Then one Crates of Mallos, who lived and taught in Pergamum in Asia Minor, came to Rome on an embassy from the king. It does not seem that these inaugural sessions were by invitation, or even deliberate: the story goes that Crates had broken his leg in a street culvert on the Palatine Hill and had to prolong his stay, profiting from the time by giving lectures.[22] But many high-class Romans had already had Greek classes in their education for a hundred years: Livius Andronicus and Ennius were famous early family tutors in the later third century (called by Suetonius "semi-Greeks"), and references to a PAEDA-GOGVS, a Greek slave who accompanied children to school (and often acted as 'pedagogue') go back to the early second century, for example, this jokey line from the comedian Pacuvius:

---

*As of this same early second century, the structure of a political career path (CVRSVS HONORVM) was actually established in law, with the highest elective offices, praetor and consul, restricted to those who had previously been elected quaestor (financial officer), and minimum ages set (e.g., thirty for quaestors, forty-two for consuls). Thereafter, the aim for the ambitious was naturally to achieve each office SVO ANNO 'in one's own year', i.e., at the lowest legal age.

DEPVLSVM MAMMA PAEDAGOGANDVM ACCIPIT REPOTIALIS LIBER

untimely weaned, he was taken up by the wine god of all-nighters for special
"schooling"

Upper-class education was to retain this early exposure to Greek, to the
extent that some believed that Roman children's schooling should start with
Greek, not Latin: children would learn Latin anyway, they felt, and the origins of education were after all Greek. (Quintilian, the consummate rhetorician of the first century AD, was one who shared this view—but in
moderation: it would not do to make a fetish of it [SVPERSTITIOSE], in case
the children's Latin should suffer from excess Greek.)[23] From the second
century BC it was also increasingly common for the elite to travel to some
Greek academic center in their twenties to complete their education: Athens
was supreme, but Pergamum, Smyrna, and Rhodes in Asia, and even Mas-
silia (Marseille) in southern Gaul, attracted many Roman students.

Beyond the elementary level, education without Greek was in fact inconceivable in republican Rome: classes were conducted in it from an early age,
and few Greek tutors showed any inclination to learn Latin, so that educated
Romans' competence in Greek, spoken as well as written, was seemingly
taken for granted whenever use of languages came up in surviving literature.
From 81 BC, it was apparently acceptable to address the Roman Senate in
Greek, "to deafen the House's ears with Greek proceedings," as the unsympathetic Valerius Maximus put it. Cicero's professor from Rhodes, Apollonius
Molon, established the precedent.[24] The pair of Greek and Latin came to be
expressed by the clichés VTRAQUE LINGVA or VTERQVE SERMO 'both languages': no other language came into consideration.

The unthinking respect for Greek as the common mark of learning is
proved, perversely enough, by the way Greek learning was often dismissed or
played down for rhetorical effect. Where Greek was concerned, Romans always felt they had something to prove. The historian Sallust made C. Marius,
a populist general in the second and first centuries BC, stress his lack of book-
learning, hence Greek: "My words are not refined: I don't care. True character
displays itself quite well enough; those others will be needing technical finesse,
as a way for words to disguise their chicanery. Nor did I learn to read and write
Greek: there was no point in learning it, since it did no good to the prowess of
the people who teach it."[25]

And before there was any Latin literature to speak of, Marcus Cato the

Censor had set the tone for Helleno-skeptic Romans. Though on a diplomatic mission of some delicacy—when in 191 he needed to persuade his audience to support Rome rather than the Greek emperor Antiochus—he deliberately chose to address the Athenians in Latin, speaking in tandem with an interpreter although he knew Greek himself: "The Athenians, he says, admired the quickness and vehemence of his speech; for an interpreter would be very long in repeating what he had expressed with a great deal of brevity; on the whole he professed to believe that the words of the Greeks came only from their lips, whilst those of the Romans came from their hearts."[26]

Yet this was the same man who, while on campaign in Sardinia, had discovered the poet Ennius; by bringing him back to teach and write at Rome as its first "national" poet, Cato did as much as anyone to set Latin literature into its Greek tracks. Cato, however, also went on personally to found Latin prose literature, with a treatise on running a farm (DE AGRI CVLTVRA), and another—his masterwork, though unfinished and now lost—on Roman history (ORIGINES), which was composed from 168 to his death in 149.

A century later, in summing up the early Greek-bound history of Latin literature, Cicero—who was to become its prose master—liked to emphasize the role of the circle of intellectuals who congregated at the house of Cato's younger friend P. Cornelius Scipio Aemilianus.* Cicero, in his dialogues *The Republic* and *Laelius on Friendship*, imagines conversations among Scipio's "flock," which besides aristocratic politicians included Roman poets such as the satirist Lucilius[†] and the dramatist Terence, and Greek scholars such as the historian Polybius, and the open-minded Stoic philosopher Panaetius, who apparently commuted between Rome and Athens. But here is a typical remark of Scipio: "And so I ask you to listen to me: not as a complete expert on things Greek, nor as someone who prefers them to ours especially in this field, but as one of the political class with a decent education thanks to his father's generosity, and one who has been burning with intellectual curiosity since boyhood, but who has nevertheless been much more enlightened by practice, and what he was taught at home, than by what he has read."[27]

---

*Scipio was another famously cultivated militarist, who had fulfilled Cato's constantly repeated slogan DELENDA EST KARTHAGO 'Carthage must be destroyed'. The deed was done in 146, shortly after Cato's death, and by convenient coincidence shortly after Carthage had paid off the fifty-year indemnity from the Second Punic War.
†C. Lucilius (180–102). Verse satire was the one great literary form for which the Romans could claim originality.

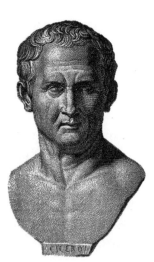

Marcus Tullius Cicero, the eternal doyen of classical prose, who, after a brilliant oratorical career, laid the foundation for Latin as a language for philosophy.

The stance is familiar. Even the most intellectual of Roman politicians were determined to keep their thinking in touch with common sense and (since they were Romans after all) the practice of their distinguished forebears. Nonetheless, they could not overlook that the source of so many interesting ideas was Greek.

Cicero,* whose own political career—to his great sadness—had coincided with the final collapse of traditional values in Roman politics, filled the enforced vacuum at the end of his professional career by writing. The task he set himself was to transmute Greek philosophy into a corpus of Latin works that would make sense to Romans. In so doing, he found himself struggling to give Latin some means of expressing abstractions. The word *qualitas*, for example, is one of the technical terms Cicero invented, turning up here for the first time in his *Academic Questions*:

> "... they called it *body* and something like *quality* ('how-ness'). You will certainly allow us in these unusual cases sometimes to use words that are novel, as the Greeks themselves do who have long been discussing them."

"As far as we're concerned," said Atticus, "go ahead and use Greek terms when you want, if your Latin fails you." Varro replied, "You're very kind: but I'll endeavor to speak in Latin, except for words like *philosophy* or *rhetoric* or

---

*M. Tullius Cicero. The cognomen appears to derive from CICER 'chickpea'.

physics or *dialectic*, which along with many others are already customary in place of Latin words. So I have called *qualities* what the Greeks call *poiotētas*, which even among Greeks is not a word for ordinary people but philosophers, as often. In fact, the logicians have no ordinary words: they use their own."[28]

In such works, Cicero ensured that, just like Greek, the Latin literary tradition would progress from classic works in verse (dramatic especially) to classics of artistic prose, in oratory and philosophy. Of course, he was not alone as a writer in the late Republic; but the copyists' tradition has been kind to him, following the collective judgment of ancient schoolmasters on who was worth reading, and his work now largely stands alone in those fields, along with the historian Sallust (86–35), and Julius Caesar himself (100–44), who also wrote a kind of contemporary history, but of his own campaigns. There is also DE RE-RVM NATURA 'On the Nature of Things', an atheistic epic on science and paleontology written by Lucretius (ca 94–ca 52 BC).*

This corpus was supplemented in the next generation by a small number of poets and historians who were likewise to be selected as classic representatives of their art forms. Three of them were protégés of a single rich and exceedingly well-connected man, Augustus' aide C. Maecenas: these were **Virgil** (70–19 BC), the doyen of epic poetry (as well as pastoral and didactic verse—although Virgil was always inclined to weave in political references); **Horace** (65–8 BC), of lyric poetry, as well as witty, topical verse; and **Propertius** (ca 50–ca 5 BC), of love elegies. Besides them there were the historian **Livy** (59 BC–AD 17), author of *Ab Vrbe Condita* 'Since the Foundation of the City', and the poet **Ovid** (43 BC–AD 17), mostly famous for the wide range of his wit, often on erotic themes. These were the masters of the Golden Age. To them—largely, in deference to later taste—three other love poets are usually added: C. Valerius **Catullus** (84–54 BC) who was marginally involved in politics in the era of Cicero and Caesar; Albius **Tibullus** (ca 52–19 BC), who was a friend of Horace's and Ovid's and **Sulpicia**, the only extant woman poet of the classical era, whose poems have been preserved along with those of Tibullus. With these, the roll call of accepted Golden Age writers is essentially complete.[†]

---

*C. Sallustius Crispus, C. Iulius Caesar, T. Lucretius Carus. CRISPVS means 'curly', CAESAR apparently a place-name (from Rome's Etruscan neighbor Caere), and CARVS 'dear'.
†P. Vergilius Maro, Q. Horatius Flaccus, Sex. Propertius, T. Liuius, P. Ouidius Naso. As for their cognomina, MARO is the title of an Etruscan magistrate, FLACCVS means 'flabby'

Publius Vergilius Maro (Virgil), Latin's great epic poet. His apparent prophecy of a new age brought in by a virgin and child assured his later reputation among Christians.

In their separate ways, all but Catullus (who died too soon) needed to come to terms with the new dominance of Rome's first emperor, Augustus. They were then amply rewarded for their optimistic view of the new regime: only Ovid fell foul of the government, but apparently because of a social or personal faux pas, rather than a false move in the political sphere.

More important for the history of Latin, they were all consciously following, imitating, and sometimes even translating Greek originals—inevitably the best they knew of, with greater ambition as their confidence ripened.

So Virgil started with Theocritus, a Syracusan of the third century who had made his name at Alexandria (then the Greek cultural center) with the invention of highly mannered poetry about the lives of country bumpkins, so-called bucolic ("ox-herding") verse. Virgil then moved on to Hesiod, whose archaic *Works and Days* is a guide to farming, but allowed Virgil (in the *Georgics*, Greek for 'land-workings') to express a Roman's traditional joy in growing things in Italy, while never forgetting the contemporary crisis in land ownership there from a century of civil wars and veterans' demands for settlement. At last he attempted the ultimate challenge, to measure himself (and Latin) against Homer himself, the author of the universal founding texts of

---

or 'flap-eared', and NASO 'big-nose'. The spelling 'Virgil,' usual in English and enforced in this book, is a corruption that goes back to the fourth century AD: it may be an allusion to the *virgo* hailed in his Eclogue IV.6, identified throughout the Middle Ages as the Virgin Mary.

Greek culture. In the *Aeneid*, by taking the mythical theme of Aeneas' journey from Troy to Italy (via Carthage), he was able to address a resonantly Roman theme, but still have the freedom given by writing about the mythical past— and since the story contained sea adventures followed by a war, he could neatly draw on, and invite comparison with, both the *Odyssey* and the *Iliad*.

Although Virgil is a universal example of Latin literature being built out of Greek, the other authors recognized as great were no less explicit about their models. Horace drew on Archilochus of Paros (mid-seventh century) and Hipponax of Ephesus (late sixth) for his iambics, Sappho and Alcaeus (Lesbos, late seventh century) for his lyrical odes. Even his *Ars Poetica* is based on the prescriptions of an otherwise obscure Neoptolemus of Parium. Both Catullus and Propertius drew much from the learned Alexandrian poet Callimachus (mid-third century), and Propertius even claimed to be carrying on his inspiration in Roman form. Ovid was less clearly imitating Greeks than trying to outdo some of his illustrious Latin forebears, notably Catullus, Tibullus, and Propertius, while consciously exploring new territory. Nonetheless his *Ars Amatoria* 'Lover's Art' is supposed to be indebted to the explicit prose manual *Aphrodisia* by Philaenis;* his *Fasti* 'Calendar' was influenced by *Phaenomena*, an astronomical and meteorological poem by Aratus (early third century, Asia); and his masterpiece, the mythological *Metamorphoses*, has Callimachus' *Aetia* 'Causes' in the background, a mélange of mythological stories in verse, united only in that they sketch the origins of rites and cities.

In Livy's field, Roman history, the first works, even by Romans, had actually been written in Greek.† And Romans were not the only ones interested to write it: one of Livy's major sources was the Greek Polybius (of the mid-second century BC). On occasion, Livy paid fulsome homage to Greek learning, calling Greeks "the most erudite race of all, who brought many arts to us for the cultivation of mind and body."[29] The ground rules for history had largely been set by Greeks, and these were never challenged by their Roman students and successors. Strikingly for moderns, these included a general practice of inventing long speeches to put in the mouths of the protagonists,

---

*Totally lost, except for its unexciting opening few words, which have shown up on a fragment of papyrus: "Philaenis of Samos, daughter of Okymenes, wrote the following things for those wanting . . ."

†Q. Fabius Pictor and L.Cincius Alimentus, of the late third century. Livy several times quotes Fabius as a source, stressing usually that he was SCRIPTORVM ANTIQVISSIMVS 'most ancient of writers'.

Titus Livius (Livy) dramatized Rome's past, from the city's foundation to the present, firmly establishing Latin as a language for history.

dramatizing and analyzing their motivation. This was very much in the tradition of Greek and Roman education, where schoolwork was largely oral. Pupils were encouraged to develop their understanding not through essays, but by working up speeches to examine the strengths and weaknesses of famous past situations.* And modern analysts of Livy[30] tend to emphasize how incidents in early Rome were recast in the light of episodes from Greek history. So the tale of the rape of Lucretia, which led to the downfall of the Etruscan king Tarquinius, is adapted to mirror the story of the homosexual love affair that was the undoing of the Athenian tyrants Hippias and Hipparchus; and the entry of Gauls into Rome, followed by a massacre of senators, echoes Herodotus' classic account of the Persian sack of Athens and destruction of the diehards who held the Acropolis. History was all about telling a good story, and the old (Greek) ones were the good ones.

So keen were the Romans to be seen as successors to the Greeks (but transcending them, of course) that they had elaborated the origin of Rome as

---

*Livy is in fact so bound up with the Greco-Roman school tradition that he even breaks off his narrative in 319 to give a treatment of the stock speculative theme "Would the Romans have been a match for Alexander if, instead of dying in Babylon, he had turned his attentions to the western Mediterranean?" (Livy's answer: Rome, over eight centuries, kept on throwing up generals who could have been his equal, whereas Greece only produced one Alexander, and he didn't even live for a full career; effectively he had quit while he was ahead—so no contest.)

something close to a Greek city: so they had adopted the story of Aeneas the noble Trojan as their foundation myth. Some Greeks had (for unknown reasons) reciprocated early on: both the fourth-century Academic philosopher Heraclides Ponticus and the third-century Macedonian warlord Demetrius the Besieger characterized Rome as a Greek city (*pólis Hellēnís*) in Italy—strange when we consider how little Rome had in common with real Greek foundations such as Cumae, Syracuse, or Tarentum.[31] Pyrrhus, another Greek warlord (and enemy of Demetrius'), had seen a different significance in the foundation myth: if Rome was the new Troy, it was a fitting target for a Greek crusade.[32] But in the next century, Rome, now with military control of Greece, assimilated itself subjectively to the Greek view of the world as a whole. This was not so much a process of trying to win Greek "hearts and minds"; we have seen that, if there ever was such a process, it did not last beyond the first generation of Roman control. Rather, it was that Romans saw themselves as insiders, in a civilized world, where the Greeks had seen all but Greeks as inferiors and outsiders. Hence the Romans' appropriation of the unappetizing Greek term for 'foreigner', *bárbaros* (about as respectful as calling aliens "bowwows").

The first large-scale user of this word in the Latin tradition was Plautus, at the beginning of the Roman wars in Greece, and for him it referred to what was non-Greek, and quite often Roman. It often has a decidedly negative charge: BARBARVM HOSPITEM MI IN AEDEM NIL MOROR 'I can't abide a *barbar* guest in my house,' says a Greek slave to and of an apparent down-and-out, who is as Greek as he is.[33] Still, Plautus could have been a key influence in changing its meaning from "non-Greek" to "neither Roman nor Greek": when watching a Plautine play, the Roman audience had to identify with Greeks and so see the rest of the world as barbarous.

One hundred and fifty years later, the word had become, for Romans, the standard one to characterize those lacking in that Greco-Roman specialty, civilization: Cicero could routinely contrast HVMANVS, DOCTVS 'humane and cultivated' with IMMANIS, BARBARVS 'savage and barbarous'.[34] The quasi-racial claim that only Greeks and Romans enjoyed full humanity and civilization is clear, since Cicero was also happy to cast as BARBARI Syrians and even learned Egyptian priests, whose title to learning and literacy was well-known to predate the Romans certainly, and probably the Greeks, by many centuries.[35] Julius Caesar, about the same time, naturally calls BARBARI not only all the peoples he challenged outside the Roman Empire, but his non-Roman "native troops" too.[36]

Meanwhile, Greeks gave no sign of returning the compliment: the word *bárbaros* and its derivatives in Greek resolutely went on including the Romans, even among Rome's Greek admirers. In the first century AD the Greek geographer Strabo unembarrassedly used the term *ekbebarbarōsthai* 'barbarized out' to describe the process whereby Greeks had been supplanted by Romans in southern Italy.[37] And putting the best face he could on the facts, the enthusiastic historian of Rome Dionysius of Halicarnassus, who knew both languages, but believed that Rome was of Greek origin, claimed that Latin was a kind of Greek-barbar creole: "The Romans speak a language that is neither highly barbarous nor thoroughly Greek, but somewhat mixed from both, with the greater part Aeolic, with this sole benefit from the minglings that they do not pronounce correctly all the sounds."[38]

⟡

This quest of the Romans to be accepted into civilized—i.e., Greek—society, was explicitly pursued in the realm of grammar. As we have seen, Latin and Greek were learned in parallel (pari passu) in the best Roman schools. Since Greek was a "modern foreign language" at the time, as well as the acknowledged classic, it was not at first taught through the grammar rules and translation drills that are familiar to us from more recent classical studies. (The grammar rules had in fact not yet been worked out.) Rather it was taught though memorization and parallel dialogues; something of the style can be seen in surviving *hermēneumata* 'translations', parallel school texts, apparently dating from the third century AD or earlier, filled with everyday language showing how to say the same things in good Latin and Greek, and (like modern phrase books) sometimes illustrating the right words for a crisis:

Πρῶτον ἀσπάζομαι τὸν διδάσκαλον, ὃς ἐμὲ ἀντησπάσατο. χαῖρε διδάσκαλε. χαίρετε συμμαθηταί. συμμαθηταί, τόπον ἐμοὶ δότε ἐμόν. βάθρον. ὑποπόδιον. δίφρος. σύναγέ σε.	PRIMVM SALVTO MAGISTRVM, QVI ME RESALVTAVIT. AVE MAGISTER. AVETE CONDISCIPVLI. CONDIS- CIPVLI, LOCVM MIHI DATE MEVM. SCAMNVM. SCAMELLVM. SELLA. DENSA TE.	First I greet my schoolmaster, who has greeted me back. "Good morning, sir." "Good morning, classmates. Classmates, give me some room." Bench. Stool. Chair. "Pay attention."

Οὐκ ἔστιν οὗτος Λούκιος ὁ τὸ ἐμὸν ἀργύριον ἔχων; Ὅδε ἐστίν. Προσελθὼν οὖν ἀσπάσομαι αὐτόν. χαῖρε, οἰκοδέσποτα. οὐδέπω δύναμαι λαβεῖν τὸ ἐμὸν ὅ μοι ὀφείλεις τοσούτωι χρόνωι; <Τί> λέγεις; μαίνηι. Ἐδάνεισά σοι ἀργύριον καὶ λέγεις μαίνηι; ἀποστερητά, οὐ γινώσκεις με; Ὕπαγε, ζήτει τίνι ἐδάνεισας. ἐγὼ γὰρ οὐδέν σου ἔχω … Ἄρτι καλῶς, καὶ ἀμφισβήτησιν ποιῆσαι οὐκ ἔστιν καλὸν ἐλευθέρωι ἀνθρώπωι καὶ οἰκοδεσπότηι.	NON EST ISTE LVCIVS QVI MEVM AES HABET? HIC EST. ACCEDENS ERGO SALVTABO EVM. AVE, PATER FAMILIAS. NONDVM POSSVM ACCIPERE MEVM QVOD MIHI DEBES TANTO TEMPORE? QVID DICIS? INSANIS. FENERAVI TIBI AES ET DICIS INSANIS? FRAVDATOR, NON COGNOSCIS ME? DVC TE, QVAERE CVI FENERASTI. EGO ENIM NIL TVVM HABEO … MODO BENE, ET CONTROVERSIAM FACERE NON EST BONVM LIBERO HOMINI ET PATRI FAMILIAS.	Isn't this the Lucius who has my money? It is. I go up to him then and greet him. "Good morning, good sir! Can I still not have back what you have owed me all this time?" "What? You're mad." "I lent you money and you say, 'You're mad'? You cheat, don't you know me?" "Go away, ask the person you lent it to. I don't have anything of yours" … "Okay then, it's not right for a free man and a householder to have an argument."
24. Καὶ λοιδορεῖ ὁ θηριομάχος; ἄφες ἐμὲ καὶ τοὺς ὀδόντας αὐτοῦ ἐκτινάξω. Κἀγώ σε ἐκτυφλῶ. Θεωρῶ τί μοι ποιῆις. Ἐγώ σε ποιήσω εἰς φυλακὴν ἀπελθεῖν, ὅπου ἄξιος <εἶ> γηράσαι. Λοιδορεῖς με, φυλακῖτα. οὐ φροντίζω σε. φίλον ἔχεις καί με εὑρήσεις ἔχοντα …	24. ET MALEDICIT BESTIARIVS? DIMITTE ME ET DENTES EIVS EXCVTIO. EGO TE EXCAECO. VIDEO QVID MIHI FACIES. EGO <TE> FACIAM IN CARCEREM IRE, VBI DIGNVS ES SENESCERE. MALEDICIS ME, CVSTODITE. NON CVRO TE. AMICVM HABES ET ME INVENIES HABENTEM …	Is the beast-fighter giving me abuse? Let me go: I'll knock his teeth out. I'll have your eyes out. I know your little game. I'll have you thrown in jail, for life. You're calling me out, you jailbird. I'm not bothering with you. You've got your friend, and you'll find I've got one too …
10. Κατάγετε σάβανα εἰς τὸ βαλανεῖον, ξύστρον, προσοψίδιον, ποδεκμάγιον, λήκυθον, ἀφρόνιτρον … Ἔνθεν	10. DEFERTE SABANA AD BALNEVM, STRIGILEM, FACIALE, PEDALE, AMPVLLAM, APHRONI- TRVM … HINC VIS PER	Get down the bath towels, scraper, facecloth, footcloth, oil bottle, washing soda … Do you want to go through the

θέλεις διὰ τῆς στοᾶς διὰ τὸν <λαμ>πετον; Μήτι θέλεις ἐλθεῖν 'ς τὸν ἀφεδρῶνα; Καλῶς με ὑπέμνησας, ἡ κοιλία με ἐπείγει . . . τήρει καλῶς, μὴ νύσταζε διὰ τοὺς κλέπτας. ἄρπαξον ἡμῖν σφαῖραν· παίξωμεν ἐν τῶι σφαιριστηρίωι . . . παλαίσωμεν διὰ χρόνου μιᾶι ῥοπῆι. Οὐκ οἶδα, εἰ δύναμαι· τὸ πάλαι γὰρ πέπαυμαι τοῦ παλαίειν. ὅμως πειράζω, εἰ δύναμαι. Ἐλαφρῶς κεκόπωμαι . . . περίζωσε σάβανα. κατάμαξόν μου <τήν> κεφαλὴν καὶ τοὺς πόδας. δὸς σανδάλια, ὑπόδησόν με . . . Καλῶς ἐλούσω, καλῶς σοι ἔσται.	PORTICVM, PROPTER LVMEN? NVMQVID VIS VENIRE AD SECESSVM? BENE ME ADMONVISTI, VENTER ME COGIT . . . SERVA BENE, NE ADDORMIAS PROPTER FVRES. RAPE NOBIS PILAM; LVDAMVS IN SPHAERISTERIO . . . LVCTEMVS POST TEMPVS VNO MOMENTO. NON SCIO, SI POSSVM; OLIM ENIM CESSAVI LVCTARE. TAMEN TEMPTO SI POSSVM. LEVITER FATIGATVS SVM . . . CINGE SABANA. TERGE MIHI CAPVT ET PEDES. <DA> CALIGV- LAS, CALCIA ME . . . BENE LAVASTI, BENE TIBI SIT.	colonnade, for the light? Would you like to go to the toilet? A good suggestion, my stomach calls. Let's go, then . . . Keep a good eye on them, don't snooze off in case of thieves. Get our ball, let's play in the ball court . . . in a while let's do a bit of wrestling. I don't know if I can; I haven't wrestled for quite a time. Still I'll try if I can. I am easily tired . . . Put towels round me. Dry my head and my feet. Give me my boots. Do them up for me . . . You gave me a good bath, thanks very much.[39]

The Greek language had progressively been analyzed since the fifth century BC, first by the sophistic rhetoricians and philosophers of Athens, who tended to look for general principles such as the division of subject and predicate, later by Stoic philosophers and Alexandrian textual critics, who emphasized more the arbitrary and irregular, which is apparent to anyone studying the profusion of inflexions on Greek nouns, adjectives, and especially verbs. The two aspects were characterized by the Greeks as "analogy" and "anomaly," and theorists disputed in vain which of the two was truly fundamental to language. Nevertheless, the traditions culminated in the first comprehensive textbook of Greek grammar, Dionysius the Thracian's *Tekhnē Grammatikē* 'The Scholarly Art', written around 100 BC. (Dionysius taught at Rhodes.) At the time, the aim of these studies was said to be the criticism of literature. Although the analysis of Greek's distinctive sounds (largely implicit in the alphabet), and of its noun and verb inflexions, was highly developed, the theory did not cover sentence structure, and this was only to be added by Apollonius Dyscolus ('the Grouch') in the second century AD, based on his analysis of the functions of the "parts of speech."

But despite the detailed description of the concrete facts of Greek, the general approach to the language remained loftily philosophical and conceptual. As in the "ordinary language" philosophy of the later twentieth century, analysis of the home language was assumed to yield generalizations of universal validity. There was no sense among Greeks that any language other than Greek deserved such analysis, much less that such an analysis might lead to interestingly different results.

This theory of grammatical analysis was no doubt known to many of the Greeks who came to teach in Italy in the first century BC, but Romans were the ones who showed concretely how it could be applied to Latin. Before its development, L. Aelius Stilo,* who was born around 150 BC, had paid attention to Latin etymology and tried to analyze archaic texts, but as a Roman had largely been interested in the theory of oratory. Cicero himself studied under him.[40] The analysis of Latin on Greek principles took off with Aelius' student M. Terentius Varro (116–27 BC), whose DE LINGVA LATINA 'On the Latin Language' included a treatment of Latin inflexion, and who can often be seen thinking like a modern formal linguist.[†]

The analysis continued to be elaborated, and simplified versions came to be included in the grammatical syllabus. Q. Remmius Palaemon, a famous practitioner of the first century AD, incorporated most of Greek terminology into Latin in translated form, including the famous mistranslation of *aitiatikḗ*, the 'caused' case, as ACCVSATIVVS 'accusative'. The most definitive compilations turned out to be the ARS MAIOR ET MINOR 'greater and lesser treatise' of Aelius Donatus[‡] in the fourth century, and the monumental INSTITVTIONES

---

*Cognomen from STILVS 'spike'.

[†] Varro saw that the noun stem is shown more clearly in the plural than in the singular, and that the pattern of declension shows up most distinctly in the ablative singular. Overall, he succeeded in identifying three of the four verb conjugations and five principal noun declensions, familiar to all subsequent foreign students of Latin—in fact, well before a similar overall classification was applied to Greek inflexion. Varro, *De lingua Latina*, x.56, x.62, ix.109.

[‡] The Greek cognomen PALAEMON 'wrestler' shows Remmius to have been a freedman. DONATVS means 'gifted'.

GRAMMATICAE 'grammatical educations' of Priscianus Caesariensis in the fifth and sixth.*

Scholars' adaptations of grammatical theory to Latin gave the language a new source of status, putting it effectively on a par with Greek even at this, most abstract, level. But there was another motivation for developing grammar, one that brings us back to the schoolroom. Foreigners aspiring to learn the language well, especially as it began to change, needed instruction on what was good style; seeing examples of it held up for imitation was no longer enough for learners. Grammatical theory began to be presented, often in simplified form, in the classroom. The word *bárbaros* / BARBARVS came to be at least as commonly used to denigrate failures in grammar and style (in Greek or Latin) as to point something out as truly foreign. A. Gellius, a scholar of the second century AD, naturally described a correct usage as NON BARBARE DICERE, SED LATINE 'saying it not barbarously but in Latin'.[41]

And while such implicit snobbery against the outsiders continued to prevail, a curious fact was missed. Already by the first century AD, Latin scholars had demonstrated that Greek was not the only language reducible to rule, even if those very rules were inspired by looking at Greek. Other languages too could have a grammar.[†42]

Yet it would be another millennium and a half before Europeans would realize the implications of this for languages at large.

---

*Priscian wrote in Byzantium for Greeks who wanted to learn Latin, in a very different age, when the priority was for Greeks to learn a Latin that was rapidly being forgotten, even as they aspired to run the Roman Empire from the east. Although the most comprehensive, Priscian's work was for a long time lost to the western tradition; it was only rediscovered in the twelfth century, but thereafter became the classic treatment of Latin grammar for all of medieval Europe.

† Varro, original as ever, glimpsed this, writing in almost Chomskyan style: "Declination [i.e., inflexion of nouns and verbs] is a feature of all human languages, not just Latin, for a good and necessary reason: without it we should not be able to learn so many words (for the natures in which they are declined are unlimited) nor should we be clear on the facts that we infer from these declinations, namely how the words are related in meaning." But the hint of grammar's universality was not taken at that time.

❖❖❖❖

CHAPTER 6

Felix coniunctio—
A Partnership of Paragons

GRAECA DOCTRIX OMNIVM LINGVARVM,
LATINA IMPERATRIX OMNIVM LINGVARVM

Greek teacher of all languages, Latin commander of all languages

Honorius of Autun,
Gemmae Animae, iii.95 (twelfth century AD)[1]

A T THE VERY END of the Roman Republic, when normal politics had
been made impossible by Julius Caesar's dominance, Cicero withdrew to
his study. He would attempt something radically new, to give Latin its own
corpus of philosophical writings and, in so doing, put it on a par with Greek, a
language that would be adequate to express all aspects of civilization. Amazingly, in the twenty-two months between February 45 and November 44, this
he achieved. His writings, especially those that covered the gamut of philosophy from theory of knowledge through to practical ethics, gave Latin the
vocabulary to tackle any subject, no matter how abstract. As he put it himself,
writing to his good friend Atticus, "You'll say I must be pretty sanguine about
the Latin language, writing such stuff. But they're copies, not too hard to do. I
just bring the words, which come pouring out of me."[2]

Possibly more important, since they were respected and remained available from generation to generation, Cicero's philosophical works allowed the
Roman writers who followed him to share his self-confidence in addressing
serious factual subjects in Latin. As he said himself, "But my sense is (and I
have often discussed this point) that Latin is not only not poor, as they commonly believe, but even richer than Greek. Has there ever been a time, whether

for good orators or poets, at least after they had someone to imitate, when their style was lacking in any fine feature, in quantity or quality?"³

Even if the inspiration in the early days was often Greek, the result of Roman writers' efforts was to be a body of literature that stands alone. Latin literature became "the universal receptacle," a basis for all the western European literatures that were to follow.⁴ For all its derivative roots, it has become an independent treasury of classical models, in every age mostly read and appreciated by people with no knowledge of Greek.

Few contemporary Greeks will have been as generous as Cicero's tutor, Apollonius Molon, who is supposed to have made these prescient remarks to his amazingly accomplished student, when he heard him declaim in Greek as well as Latin: "I praise and admire you, Cicero, but it worries me for the

Mestrius Plutarchus (Plutarch), a moral philosopher and antiquarian who wrote a series of paired biographies of great Greeks and Romans. He never learned Latin well.

fate of Greece when I consider that through you the only advantages which we have left, culture [*paideía*] and language [*lógos*], are also to pass to the Romans."[5]

Until they started to write in the language themselves, Greeks passed over in silence any serious literature in Latin: evidently it never played any part in their education.

A good example is Plutarch, a Greek gentleman of the first century AD, who was interested enough in Rome and its history to write a series of parallel biographies comparing Greek and Roman statesmen. He even volunteered that, in his day, "pretty much everyone used the Roman language."[6] Nevertheless, on his own command of it he is modest:

> . . . having had no leisure, while I was in Rome and other parts of Italy, to exercise myself in the Roman language, on account of public business and of those who came to be instructed by me in philosophy, it was very late, and in the decline of my age, before I applied myself to the reading of Latin authors. Upon which that which happened to me may seem strange, though it be true; for it was not so much by the knowledge of words that I came to the understanding of things, as by my experience of things I was enabled to follow the meaning of words. But to appreciate the graceful and ready pronunciation of the Roman tongue, to understand the various figures and connection of words, and such other ornaments, in which the beauty of speaking consists, is, I doubt not, an admirable and delightful accomplishment; but it requires a degree of practice and study which is not easy, and will better suit those who have more leisure, and time enough yet before them for the occupation.[7]

But the balance was going to shift. Already in the first century AD Greek translations of Virgil's work at least were appearing, and Virgil's popularity beyond the Latin-speaking world was reinforced when his Fourth Eclogue began to be interpreted as a prophecy of the Christ child.[8] By the second century a well-to-do North African such as Apuleius could prepare for a career at home by a Greek education at Athens followed by a Latin one at Rome, then go on to write what he called a 'Greek-style story' (FABVLAM GRAECANICAM) in Latin, although he laughingly dismissed himself as a 'rough speaker of that exotic, courtroom language' (EXOTICI AC FORENSIS SERMONIS RVDIS LOCVTOR).[9] Greek literature went on being written in profusion, but Greeks were becoming increasingly disadvantaged as candidates for imperial service in that they just did not have the Latin for it.[10]

In practice, Apollonius Molon's fears for Greek were coming true. Augustine (354–430) was the first top-rank philosopher brought up in Latin to find (with relief) that he could get by without any Greek at all.

> But what was the reason why I hated Greek literature, when I had been so steeped in it as a child? Not even now have I fully worked it out. I had fallen in love with Latin . . . I think it is the same with Virgil for Greek children, when they are forced to learn him as I was [Homer]. The fact is that the difficulty, the difficulty of learning a foreign language at all, wiped out with its gall all the Greek sweets of fabulous stories.[11]

And now that an education in Latin alone was totally respectable, the value of Greek tutors was plummeting. Libanius, a consummate Greek rhetorician of Antioch (and a friend of the emperor Julian), wrote ruefully in 386 of the poor career prospects awaiting would-be Greek teachers, indeed any who stayed in the east:

> You know how the present age has transferred to others [the Latin teachers] the rewards for our language studies, and reversed the ranking of respect to our disadvantage, presenting them as giving access to all good things, while suggesting that we only offer mumbo jumbo and a formation for hard grind and poverty. That is why there are all those frequent sailings, voyages with only one destination, Rome, and the cheers of young people off to fulfill their dreams: of high office, power, marriage, palace life, conversations with the emperor.[12]

Some Greeks were prepared to make the ultimate sacrifice and write not in their own language but in Latin. One of the most famous in this line is the last great Latin historian of the Empire, Ammianus Marcellinus (ca 330–95), an older contemporary of Augustine's.[13] Although educated in Greek (like Libanius) in Antioch in Syria, he had a varied military career, which took him all round western Europe, but also to Mesopotamia, where he took part in a failed campaign against the Parthians. His service no doubt gave him a thorough exposure to Latin. In the 380s he moved to Rome and started to write. He took the very Roman historian Tacitus as his model, writing an opinionated history that took up where Tacitus left off (AD 96) and continued to his own day (around 391). He frequently cited Cicero with approval, but with a bicultural touch unknown to previous historians, now and then also quoted in

Greek. He appears to have been rewarded with public readings of his works at Rome, a source of reflected glory on his home city of Antioch. Even Libanius was pleased.[14]

In the eyes of the Empire as a whole, then, Latin was in time able to match and just about supersede its master Greek as preeminent language of culture. This new standing of Latin was clear when viewed from Rome, and the Greek cultural centers that had once attracted so many students from abroad, but felt themselves disfavored; it was less so when viewed from the rest of Greece, or the provinces of the east. This was because of the stubborn limit on the progress of Latin there: Latin remained unable to displace Greek in the east, as a language actually spoken in daily life, a fact which stands in vivid contrast with the pervasive tendency of Latin in all other parts of the Empire.

This linguistic deficit of Latin in the east was noted at the time. The famed Bible translator Jerome (Eusebius Hieronymus), a native speaker of Latin from Dalmatia, who lived from 331 to 420 and learned to read and translate Hebrew as well as Latin and Greek, spent the latter half of his life in Palestine. In a letter to Augustine, he wrote, "We suffer a great poverty of the Latin language in this province." In a commentary, he noted by contrast that the Greek language was spoken all over the east.[15] Egeria, a pilgrim from western Europe to Jerusalem around the fifth century, noted that Christian services there were conducted in Greek always, with Syriac interpretation; but in addition, Latin speakers could receive interpreting into Latin "lest they be saddened."[16] Yet it had been some 450 years, perhaps twenty generations, since those lands had been absorbed into Rome's empire.

In all the sixteen centuries that the Roman Empire was to last in the east, Latin never spread as a popular language. Some say the Romans themselves were at fault, in never making a determined effort to require its use. But what cultural inducement were the Romans able to offer to the Greeks? They were not offering any serious political rights comparable to Greek aspirations before the Roman conquest, and both Greeks and Romans agreed that the Greeks already had privileged access to the finer side of private life. A passage of particular pomposity from the first century AD suggests that it was usual for Romans to stand on their linguistic dignity:

How much the magistrates of old valued both their and the Roman people's majesty can be seen from the fact that (among other signs of requiring respect) they persistently maintained the practice of replying only in Latin to the Greeks. And so they forced them to speak through interpreters, losing

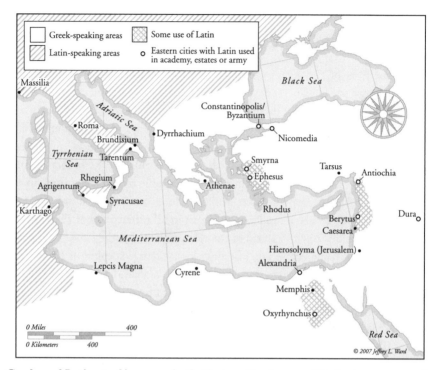

Greek- and Latin-speaking zones in the Eastern Empire, 300 AD. Latin never spread widely in Greece or the Levant, except in army bases and academic centers.

their linguistic fluency, their great strength, not just in our capital city but in Greece and Asia too, evidently to promote the honor of the Latin language throughout the world. They were not lacking in learning, in everything they held that what was Greek should defer to what was Roman, thinking it improper that the weight and authority of the Empire should be sacrificed for the charm and attractions of literature.[17]

But be this as it may, the language never expanded out of the functions (army, law, government, and the administration of imperial estates) and the particular cities (Constantinople, Nicomedia, Smyrna, Antioch, Berytus, Alexandria)* that had attracted larger Roman populations. Roman citizen

---

*Modern Istanbul, Izmit, Izmir, Antakya (Turkey), Beirut (Lebanon), Iskandariyah (Egypt).

colonies in the east had been few (notably Corinth, refounded by Julius Caesar in 44 BC amid the century-old ruins left by L. Mummius) and soon effectively hellenized.

As long as the Empire was united and looked only to Rome as its capital, there was an inducement for the elite, at least, to learn Latin and seek advancement in imperial service. There was even a brief surge in the use of Latin in the east, when the capital was moved to Constantinople in 324. Berytus became a great center of Latin studies, with a practical bias preparing its students for careers in law.* But even so, Latin speakers were increasingly hard to find in the fourth century: Ammianus recorded two high officials appointed to service in the east specifically for their bilingual skills.[18] In the fifth century, from the reign of Theodosius II (408–450) the eastern and western halves of the Empire increasingly went their separate ways. The use of Latin in the east was becoming purely a formality. From 397, governors had been permitted to issue judgments in Greek; from 439, wills too were confirmed to be valid in Greek. The emperor Justinian (527–565), himself a Latin speaker from Illyria, tried to boost Latin again, calling it PATRIA VOX, and (still in Greek) hē pátrios phōné; but he had no choice but to publish most of his famous law code, the CORPVS IVRIS CIVILIS, in Greek as well as Latin, to make sure it was widely understood.[19]

This period is documented among other sources by the memoirs (in Greek) of John the Lydian (490–ca 560), whose high judicial position in Constantinople, *exceptor* in the Praetorian Prefecture, had been achieved partly on the strength of his Latin. He witnessed with foreboding the courts' abandonment of Latin, which happened in his time in office, recalling a prophecy attributed to Romulus, that Fortune would abandon the Romans whenever they should forget their paternal language.[20] Declining use of Latin had become a symbol of the fading importance of traditional learning, especially in the law, where clarity was being sacrificed for ease and accessibility.[21] Still, we know that Latin was hanging

---

*The use of Latin in the law itself had legal backing until a late date. The Digests of Justinian (a codification of existing laws, issued in 533) contains the simple requirement DECRETA A PRAETORIBUS LATINE INTERPONI DEBENT 'Judgments are to be given by the praetors in Latin'. And in civil law too the role of Latin was guaranteed, up to a point: LEGATA GRAECE SCRIPTA NON VALENT; FIDEICOMMISSA VERO VALENT 'Wills written in Greek are not valid; but informal bequests to third parties are' (Gaius, *Institutiones*, ii.281). This shows the Roman ideal; but both these were dead letters by the time these Digests were issued.

on in some of its traditional functions: the emperor Maurikios (who reigned 582–602) wrote in Greek a field manual for the army in which the words of command were listed in Latin.* And a new emperor was in these days formally acclaimed in Greek by the populace, but in Latin by the army.[22]

Then in the early seventh century, after the death of Muhammad in 632, the eastern Empire was buffeted by a series of military disasters that deprived it of all but its solidly Greek-speaking heartland. Egypt, Palestine, and Syria, where Greek had only ever been an elite language, and most spoke Egyptian or Aramaic, would never again be under Roman control. This turned out also to give the quietus to even official uses of Latin: there was no longer a need for it as a distinct, formal unifying language when everyone in the eastern Empire spoke Greek anyway. Looking back from the mid-tenth century, Emperor Constantine VII Porphyrogenitus judged that it had been in this early seventh century that the Romans "had been Hellenized and discarded the language of their fathers, the Roman tongue."[23]

In a confusing footnote to the career of Latin in the east, the Byzantines were soon calling Greek itself *rōmaíika* 'Romanish' (in contrast with *latiniká*), a term for Greek that lasted at least until the nineteenth century. When Emperor Michael III (reigning at Constantinople in the mid-ninth century) was reported to have called Latin a "barbarian and Scythian language," Pope Nicholas I riposted by suggesting that if that was his opinion, he should give up the title *Emperor of the Romans*.[24] Of that there was never any question. The eastern Empire had abandoned Latin, but that did not mean its citizens had given up on their Roman identity. Quite the reverse: the Byzantines were known as *Rūmī* to all their threatening neighbors to the east, Arab, Persian, and Turk, for more than eight hundred years, at least as long as their previous allegiance (as *Graeci*) to Rome in Italy. And when the Seljuk Turks, after 1071, succeeded in dislodging them from most of Anatolia, the Turks called their successor kingdom there the Sultanate of Rum.

In some sense, the Greeks had never "got the point" of being Roman.

---

*E.g., LARGITER AMBVLA 'Open order, march', AD LATVS STRINGE 'By the flank, close', IVNGE 'Close ranks', SILENTIVM 'Silence', MOVE 'March', STA 'Halt', EQVALITER AMBVLA 'In line, march', MANDATA CAPTATE 'Stand by for orders', NON VOS TVRBATIS 'Steady', PERCVTE 'Charge', TRANSFORMA 'About-face'. When about to attack, according to the drill, an officer shouts ADIVTA 'Help', and the soldiers must respond DEVS 'God!' Dennis 2001: 35–39, 145, 146–47.

They had never agitated for the kind of citizen rights (of trade, marriage, the vote) that exercised their fellow peoples subject to Rome in the west—and which meant that the Roman conquest and assimilation of Gaul, Spain, and Africa was like a continuation of the earlier struggle to expand across Italy. The Greeks' loyalty to Rome, such as it was, was shown rather through participation in novel religious cults: first they hastily conjured into existence a new goddess, Roma (honored in Alabanda, Chios, Miletus, Smyrna, Rhodes, as well as Athens); later—bizarrely—they affected to worship the most popular of the proconsuls sent to govern them; and ultimately they offered adoration to the emperor himself. In the first century AD, cities vied for dedicated shrines of worship to the emperor, since they were some kind of badge of status, entitling the city to call iself *neōkóros* 'temple warden'. This was most un-Roman behavior. But religion had always been an important mark of *tò Hellēnikón* 'Greekness'—Herodotus[25] related how the Athenians had appealed to it in seeking alliance with the Spartans against the Persian menace in 480 BC. It would be again, after the Christianization of Greece in the fourth century AD. This would offer scope for almost endless doctrinal dispute: henceforth the Greeks would be able to combine the two traditional Greek propensities, for worship and for argument.

⚛

Ultimately Greek was little affected by its eight hundred years of cohabitation with Latin, but Latin on the other hand derived much of permanence from its cohabitation with Greek. We have seen that Latin drew from Greek the conception it had of its own grammar, and also the tradition that a gentleman's education should be general, based on literary classics and the skills of public speaking. But Latin is an heir to Greek in many other ways.

Most concretely, there are far more loans of Greek words into Latin than the reverse, starting with the philosophical and intellectual vocabulary, which has largely been transmitted through Latin's later career into all the modern European languages at large. But Greek was also the source of many everyday words in the more colorful side of spoken Latin. Although this type of Latin is little known to us directly, outside graffiti, many such words have survived into Latin's daughter languages. They also bear out the general hints we get from classical literature of the particular sociolinguistic role of Greek (and hence Greek borrowings) in the Latin world.

Gastronomy was a particular strength of the Greeks—the very words for olive and its oil (OLIVA, OLEVM) are old borrowings from Greek (*elaiwā, elaiwon*)—but this shows up in many names for sauces (GARVM 'fish sauce', HYDROGARVM 'diluted fish sauce', TISANA 'barley water', EMBAMMA 'ketchup'), vegetables (ASPARAGVS, RAPHANVS 'radish', FASEOLVS 'kidney bean', CRAMBE 'cabbage') and seafood (ECHINVS 'urchin', GLYCYMARIS 'clam', POLYPUS 'polyp', SCOMBER 'mackerel', SEPIA 'cuttlefish'), as well as some foreign delicacies that were to become common (AMYGDALVM 'almond', DACTYLUS 'date', GLYCYRRHIZA 'licorice', ORYZA 'rice', ZINGIBER 'ginger'). The word for liver, which has been absorbed by so many Romance languages (French *foie*, Spanish *higado*, Italian *fegato*, Rumanian *ficat*) is from Latin FICATVM, which originally did not mean 'liver' at all, but 'figged'. This was a loan translation of Greek *sukótón*, since the liver of animals raised on figs was such a popular delicacy. The word MASSA (which just means 'mass') is another borrowing, from Greek *mâza*, generalized from a mass of barley cake. The whole set of equipment for drinking wine, delivered in an AMPHORA, diluted in a CRATER, and ladled out with a CYATHVS into a large CANTHARVS or SCYPHVS, or an individual CARCHESIVM or CYMBIVM, was labeled in Greek. The culture of drinking too was named in Greek: an aperitif was a PROPIN 'foredrink', a toast PROPINATIO, a game of drunken marksmanship with wine lees had the Greek name COTTABVS.

Most musical instruments had Greek names: SYRINX 'panpipes', CYMBALA, TYMPANVM 'drum', LYRA, CHORDA 'string', PLECTRVM as well as MVSICA itself. More sophisticated engineering tended to be named in Greek, such as the construction terms TROCLEA 'pulley', ARTEMON 'block and tackle', ERGATA 'windlass', POLYSPASTON 'hoist', CNODAX 'pivot', COCLEA 'screw mechanism'; and so were the ORGANA of high-tech warfare—CORAX 'crow' (battering ram), HELEPOLIS 'city-taker' (siege tower), CATAPVLTA 'off-swinger', BALLISTA 'shooter', ONAGER 'wild ass' (all forms of catapult). So, of course, were many terms in the world of school and writing: SCHOLA, ABACUS ('checkerboard' as well as 'abacus'), EPISTVLA 'letter, missive', PAPYRVS, CALAMVS 'pen', ENCAVSTVM 'molten wax, ink', GRAMMATICVS 'language teacher', RHETOR 'oratory teacher', BIBLIOTHECA 'library'.

Physical culture too was a Greek speciality. Medical terms taken from Greek have often had a long life (e.g., *plaster* from Latin EMPLASTRVM, Greek *emplastron* 'molded on', *palsy* from PARALYSIS 'detaching', *dose* <

DOSIS 'giving', French *rhume* < RHEVMA 'flow', for the common cold).* The Roman institution of the bath was clearly heavily influenced by its Greek origins too: BALNEVM (from Greek *balaneîon*) 'bath', THERMAE 'hot baths', APODYTERIVM 'dressing room', LACONICVM 'sweat room', HYPOCAVSTVM 'underfloor heating', XYSTVS 'running track', PALAESTRA 'wrestling ground', LECYTHVS 'anointing bottle', ALIPTA 'masseur/trainer' (from Greek *aleiptēs* 'anointer'), were all terms of everyday use at the bathing establishment, all derived from Greek. Perhaps even more interestingly, a number of words for parts of the body in Latin are borrowed from Greek. The usual Romance words for leg (e.g., French *jambe*, Italian and Old Spanish *gamba*) are derived from a Latin word, GAMBA, itself derived from veterinary Greek *kampḗ*, 'bend, joint'. STOMACHVS, originally meaning 'maw', the opening of the digestive tract, was a Greek word for which the Romans had a lot of use, since they thought of it as the seat of anger: STOMACHOSVS meant 'testy' and STOMACHARI meant 'to lose one's temper'. And curiously the Romans too borrowed their (and hence our) word for mustache: Latin MVSTACEVS, never found in Latin literature, is derived from a Doric Greek word for the upper lip, *mustákion* or *mústax*.† Its close relative *mástax* 'jaw' was also borrowed in Latin; MASTICARE, a verb derived from it, has resulted in French *mâcher* 'chew' as well as modern English 'masticate'. What became the favorite word for a punch or blow (seen in French *coup*, Italian *colpo*, Spanish *golpe*) was COLPVS, derived from COLAPHVS, already used in Plautus; in Greek it originally meant 'a peck', the blow from a bird's beak.

---

*Pliny the Elder remarked in the first century AD: "[Medicine] is the only one of the Greek arts not practiced by the serious Roman: few sons of Rome have attainments in this profession, and those few have immediately gone over to being Greeks. Indeed, use of the Greek language here is the key to reputation among those [patients] who don't know it, and people have less faith in a remedy if they understand it" (*Natural History*, xxix.17).

†Classical Latin had no word for mustache (though Greek had two, *mústax* and also *hupḗnè*). Over many centuries a personal statement of north-European identity, they were famously sported in the centuries BC by Gauls (in walrus style, 'wine strainers' according to Diodorus Siculus, v.28); and in the fifth and sixth centuries AD, a clipped mustache was called *barba Gothica* and worn ostentatiously in official portraits by Kings Theoderic and Theodahad. (Ward-Perkins 2005: 72–79, citing coins and the poet Ennodius, who lived 474–521.)

Colloquial Latin was also full of Greek-sounding interjections: BABAE or PAPAE 'wow', PHY 'ugh', VAE 'oh no', ATATAE 'ah', AGE 'be reasonable', APAGE 'get outta here', EIA 'come on', EVGE 'hurrah', all have identical equivalents in Greek. Cicero had been embarrassed to use the seemingly innocuous BINI 'two each', since it sounded the same as the Greek imperative *bínei* 'fuck!'[26] (Spoken Greek had, in any case, always had, for Romans, overtones of the bedroom.)* BASTAT 'enough', though unknown in classical Latin, went on to a lively career as a verb in Spanish and Italian and seems to have come from Greek *bástaze* 'hold it'.

This last example points to one of the persistent differences between Latin and Greek, namely the accentual patterns. The accent on Greek *bástaze* made it sound like a two-syllable word in Latin; hence it might be heard by Romans as BÁSTAT. By contrast, Greek names imported into Latin were given new accentual patterns, based on the Latin rule, which have largely stayed with them in modern western European languages: not, as per the original Greek, *Athená, Aléxandros, Euripídes, Heléne, Menélaos, Periklés,* or *Sokrátes,* but ATHÉNA, ALEXÁNDER, EVRÍPIDES, HÉLENA, MENELÁVS, PÉRICLES, SÓCRATES. Meanwhile, modern Greek has retained the patterns of ancient Greek.[27] Stress patterns, in the languages that have them—French, for example, and Japanese do not—can be remarkably persistent over the millennia, and modern English has turned out in many ways similar to classical Latin; but Greek and Latin are very different and have remained so.[†]

Latin, particularly colloquial Latin and poetic Latin, was peppered with Greek words. But to get this in proportion, let us consider some comparisons. Sampling in a moderate Latin dictionary (of about twenty thousand headwords) shows that, excluding proper nouns, some 7 percent of vocabulary in the classical era (200 BC to AD 200) was derived from Greek.[28] By contrast, in 1450, after an equal four hundred years of Norman and Angevin dominance of written expression, something like half the recorded vocabulary of English was of French origin. Another language with

---

*Lucretius (iv.1160–69), Martial (x.68), and Juvenal (vi.184–96), from the first century BC to the second AD, all show from their different points of view that Romans, especially Roman women, liked to talk dirty in Greek.

[†]Except in the way that British students have traditionally been taught to pronounce ancient Greek. I myself was brought up to stress Greek as if it were Latin, despite the written accent marked on every printed word.

massive borrowing, Turkish, has derived 28 percent of its core vocabulary from Arabic, 8 percent from Persian, mostly in the eleventh to sixteenth centuries; but since the nineteenth it has gained as much as 25 percent from French.[29]

◈

Beside vocabulary, Latin writers and orators absorbed from Greek a particular attitude toward sentence structure, what is called periodic style. Greek language analysis did give rise to what we now recognize as grammar, but no one sways an audience or wins an argument by grammar alone. Greek analysis of how oratory or dialectic becomes effective was every bit as structured as—and considered much more important than—their analysis of declensions, conjugations, or parts of speech. The Greek word *períodos* means 'circuit', literally a 'go-round', as in a race. Aristotle, no doubt following up a doctrine that had been elaborated by the Sophists in the height of fifth-century Greek rhetoric, defined a *períodos* as "an utterance with a beginning and an end in itself, and a length that can be easily taken in," contrasting it with a strung-out utterance, which has no end in itself, stopping only when what it is talking about comes to an end. The idea was that audiences are made restless by this strung-out style, not knowing what is coming up; and as an added bonus for the speaker, a speech made up of periodic sentences, the so-called terminated style, is much easier to memorize, since it consists of balanced parts, called 'limbs' (*kôla*, MEMBRA) each of them neither too long nor too short. It can even have rhythm, like verse, making it easier to remember; but the actual meters of poetry should be avoided.[30]

We can get an idea of what Aristotle was talking about, and what every *rhetor* of Greek or Latin put across to his pupils, by looking at a short period (*períodos*) of Cicero's, indeed the sentence that follows on from the sentence cited above, when he was praising the stylistic resources of the Latin language. For immediate convenience, a parallel translation into English is included, but the meaning is not the main point here. Since the structure is, the English phases more or less correspond to the Latin originals, even if the grammatical relations in the sentence are somewhat changed.

EGO VERO, QVONIAM FORENSIBVS OPERIS, LABORIBVS, PERICVLIS NON DESERVISSE MIHI VIDEOR PRAESIDIVM, IN QVO A POPVLO ROMANO LOCATVS SVM, DEBEO PROFECTO, QVANTVMCVMQVE POSSVM, IN EO QVOQVE ELABO- RARE, VT SINT OPERA, STVDIO, LABORE MEO DOCTIORES CIVES MEI, NEC CVM ISTIS TANTOPERE PVGNARE, QVI GRAECA LEGERE MALINT, MODO LEGANT ILLA IPSA, NE SIMVLENT, ET IIS SERVIRE, QVI VEL VTRISQVE LITTERIS VTI VELINT VEL, SI SVAS HABENT, ILLAS NON MAGNOPERE DESI- DERENT.	But I, since my services, hard work, and risks in the courtroom have not been the better, I think, for the guard under which I have been placed by the Roman people, I have a clear duty, as far as I can, to engage too in the struggle, through my service, effort, and toil, to educate my fellow citizens, and while not fighting so much with those who prefer to read works in Greek, as long as they really read them, without simulation, yet at the same time serving those who wish to benefit from literatures in both languages, or if they hold to their own, do not miss greatly those others.

This is fairly typical of a well-structured period in a Ciceronian speech or essay. Formally it is a balanced structure of measured clauses, with all sorts of measured contrasts and internal echoes, but it is not really an aid to clarity of thought. The whole thing is contrived, and its meaning is disguised rather than revealed by the form preconceived for the sentence. It starts with a sideswipe at the political constraints under which Cicero was laboring and finishes with a statement of his self-imposed duty to give the Romans a literature they could be proud of, linking them only with the observations that his talents are unused and he does not wish to quarrel with people who are happy enough reading Greek. Aristotle's "utterance with a beginning and an end in itself" has largely taken leave of the natural form of whatever it was talking about.

The whole sentence can be analyzed with a kind of Chinese-box structure, with parallel constituents signaled by comparable styles of underlining.

EGO VERO,

But I,

A. QVONIAM FORENSIBVS OPERIS, LABORIBVS, PERICVLIS

NON DESERVISSE

since my services, hard work, and risks in the courtroom have not

been the better,

MIHI VIDEOR PRAESIDIVM, IN QVO A POPVLO ROMANO

LOCATVS SVM,

I think, for the guard under which I have been placed by the Roman people,

---

DEBEO PROFECTO,

I have a clear duty,

B. QVANTVMCVMQVE POSSVM, IN EO QVOQVE ELABORARE,

as far as I can, to engage too in the struggle,

VT SINT OPERA, STVDIO, LABORE MEO DOCTIORES CIVES MEI,

through my service, effort, and toil, to educate my fellow citizens,

---

C. NEC CVM ISTIS TANTOPERE PVGNARE,

and while not fighting so much with those

> QVI GRAECA LEGERE MALINT,
>
> MODO LEGANT ILLA IPSA, NE SIMVLENT,
>
> who prefer to read works in Greek,
>
> as long as they really read them, without simulation,

D. | ET IIS SERVIRE,

yet at the same time serving those

> QVI VEL VTRISQVE LITTERIS VTI VELINT
>
> VEL, SI SVAS HABENT, ILLAS NON MAGNOPERE DESIDERENT.
>
> who wish to benefit from literatures in both languages,
>
> or if they hold to their own, do not miss greatly those others.

This, then, was the basis of the Greek theory of how to structure sentences in a formal speech. (A full exposition of it would be far more elaborate, naturally.) The theory was widely applied in Latin, and not just by orators. For in the ancient world, all reading was reading aloud, and public recitations of poetry and prose works were common. In this context, some writers—notably the perverse genius Tacitus—delighted in disappointing the expectations raised by periodic theory. His *Annales* starts with what is almost a hexameter line (the classic epic meter), precisely what was not supposed to happen in a well-regulated prose stylist.* And here is his one-sentence analysis of the decline of history writing during the early Empire:

TIBERII GAIQVE ET CLAVDII AC NERONIS RES (FLORENTIBVS IPSIS) [OB METVM] FALSAE, (POSTQVAM OCCIDERANT) [RECENTIBVS ODIIS] COMPOSITAE SVNT.

Of Tiberius *and* Gaius *and* Claudius *and* Nero the events (while they themselves still flourished), [out of fear] were misrepresented, (after they had passed away), [in a setting of recent bitterness] were recounted.[31]

The translation gives some sense of the rhythm of the whole, but notice how the "limbs" are deliberately mismatched. Three different words for *and*

---

*ūrbĕm | Rŏm(am) ă | prīncĭpĭ | ō rē | gĕs hăbŭ | ērĕ; lībĕrtāt(em) 'The city of Rome in the beginning kings held; liberty' The only flaws are the long *I* in *lībĕrtāt(em)*, and the absence of a word break (caesura) in the middle of the third foot, *prīncĭpĭ*.

(underlined) link the four emperors' names, and then two fairly simple clauses follow, each begun with two short adverbials. In sense they are parallel (as shown by the parentheses and square backets), but formally they jangle, and the two that ought, by their similar endings (*-entibus*, *-īs*), to be parallel and so in contrast, simply are not. Aristotle and Cicero would not have appreciated this monkeying with hard-won stylistic norms. But it only makes sense if readers knew the rules that Tacitus was breaking.

And to counterweight the periodic balance further, Latin had always had some maxims of its own that emphasized substance over style. They tended to be associated with Cato the Censor (see pp. 70–71). For him, the essence of a fine orator was VIR BONVS DICENDI PERITVS 'a good man skilled in speaking'. Virtue will out, and damn your technique! Instead of spending too much time planning well-balanced periods, he recommended as preparation for a speech the policy REM TENE: VERBA SEQVENTVR 'get a grip on the facts and the words will follow'.[32]

◇

Besides these explicit rules on how to put a text together, both the Greeks and the Romans were extremely selective in whose work they accepted as models for good language. They showed extreme prejudice in favor of particular eras, which were thought to have nourished the best writing.

For Greek, the model was always the language as used by authors writing in the Attic dialect in the fifth and fourth centuries BC. This was the dialect of the city of Athens, and the linguistic mark of quality was naturally discerned in all the writers of this period whose works had survived: they include the tragedians Aeschylus, Sophocles, Euripides; the comedian Aristophanes; the historians Thucydides and Xenophon; the philosophers Plato and Aristotle; and orators such as Demosthenes, Isocrates, and Lysias. "Atticism" has been the ideal that Greeks have striven for in every age over the succeeding twenty-three hundred years until (at long last) the last quarter of the twentieth century. Flexibility and freshness may well have been the virtues that had first made those authors great; they have not been virtues, at least as far as choice of linguistic style is concerned, for any generation of Greek writers until the modern era.

The value of Atticism remains hard to perceive from outside the charmed circle of the Greek-language community. It really had to do with keeping up technical features of the old language, such as the distinction between genitive and dative cases for nouns, the use of optative mood in inflecting verbs in certain subordinate clauses, and in general the conscious maintenance of words and usages that had come naturally in the fourth century BC, but were stilted already in the first AD. Greeks came to think it a superior way to use the language because of its association with the great works of the past—which none felt able, or perhaps even worthy, to match— and because the ability to use it was the unforgeable proof of a good education. But what to an insider are associations with quality are, to an outsider, difficult to distinguish from sheer obscurantism and snobbery. English has a much shorter continuous written tradition than Greek, but it is as if all modern English writing could only be taken seriously if it employed the spelling and phraseology of the Elizabethan Age.

For the Romans too the best language was defined *ad hominem* as the language of the best writers, but they gave themselves somewhat more latitude. Schoolmasters were to define a Golden Age, which covered the century to the death of Augustus in AD 14, and a following Silver Age, which lasted up to AD 150 or 200. The Golden Age included the historians Sallust, Caesar, and Livy, the orator and philosopher Cicero, and the poets Lucretius, Catullus, Virgil, Horace, Propertius, Tibullus, and Ovid. The Silver Age would take in letter writers Seneca the Younger and Pliny the Younger, epic poets Lucan and Statius, epigrammatist Martial, historians Suetonius and Tacitus, satirical poets Persius and Juvenal, novelists Petronius and Apuleius, and the encyclopedists Pliny the Elder and Aulus Gellius. (Curiously, this meant that some of the most widely read authors, the dramatists Plautus and Terence, from the second century BC, were simply timed out.)

The term *classic* itself was invented by M. Cornelius Fronto in the middle of the second century AD, on the analogy of the topmost class of citizens: "Go now then, and when you have the time, ask whether 'QVADRIGAM' or 'HARE-NAS' was said by anyone from that cohort, at least the more ancient one, whether a significant orator or poet, I mean a significant, ranking [CLAS-SICVS], landed [ASSIDVVS] writer, not a common sort [PROLETARIVS]."[33]

The focus on a small subset of extant authors as being the sole proponents of good language—and hence fit as models for imitation—was certainly accepted by the Romans; but it was less an obsession for them than the Greeks, who as the centuries wore on increasingly had only their language, and strict rules for using it well, to fall back on as a prominent symbol of their identity.*

---

*Perhaps because it was invented for Roman literature, the term *classic* was never accepted by the Greeks, although the approach it symbolizes was certainly a Greek heritage in

Stylistic quality, apparently so important for ancient writers and readers, was a deceptive thing. In essence, language was seen as high quality in itself just because it was associated with writers whose work was judged to be elegant and important. Although the Latin-using world imitated the Greek in taking this cultural stance, the content of the preferred styles for the two languages can hardly be equated, beyond the patterns for periodic sentences that have been described. As different languages they had different stylistic hangups, of no more concern universally than the split infinitive is in English. Furthermore, the next great cadre of Latin writers, the Church Fathers, would pride themselves on dispensing with what they saw as artificial classical norms.

Time, though, would bring a full turn of the wheel of fortune. Ironically, the greatest vogue for classicism in Latin did not occur in the second or third century AD, but over a millennium later, in the Renaissance and the centuries afterward. Then, to achieve liberation from the perceived turgidity of Christian and medieval Latin, the fashion would dictate a return to the classic authors and, in writing, a renewed fidelity to their language.

✧

The Greeks were extremely lucky to have the Romans as their cultural successors, though they seldom recognized it. (They would naturally have preferred to continue their own tradition, without the need for any alien—i.e., necessarily barbarian—followers or replacements at all.) Although Rome had disabled them militarily, it was content for a good five centuries to be their cultural disciple, and indeed to use its unprecedented power to project aspects of Greek culture to the farthest parts of northern and western Europe: *paideía* the Greeks had called it, but for the Romans it was nothing less than HVMANITAS. We have already noted how it was taken up, even to the extent of a demand for formal rhetoric as far away as Britannia. When Q. Sertorius was attempting to establish Roman influence in Spain in the 70s BC, "nothing appealed to the Spaniards more strongly than Sertorius' provision for their sons. He brought the noblest of them to the large town of Osca [Huesca]. They may

---

Latin. It has no clear equivalent in what we call "classical" Greek (which Greeks can only call αρχαία ελληνικά 'ancient Greek') and has subsequently only been represented by the borrowed term κλασσικός, a modern word that is now used more for talking about music or ballet than language.

have been hostages but, for all to see, they were given schooling by the teachers of Latin and Greek whom he had appointed.[34]

Latin literature was shot through with references to Greek antecedents; except for satire, the source of every Latin literary form was Greek. And in the Roman Empire, no literature oral or written, nor even folklore, survived beside the works written in Latin and Greek. Moreover, Greek inspirations in drama, athletics, geography, geometry, astronomy, sculpture, painting, architecture, pantomime, medicine, veterinary science, music, cookery, perfumery, viticulture, weapons technology, and religious mysteries went wherever Romans settled—all interpreted through Latin. Under Roman tutelage, the reputation of the Greek oracles, at Delphi, Didyma, and many more, was projected across the continent. Even Roman aqueducts made a contribution to spreading Hellenism: bringing running water to the heart of cities everywhere, they always terminated in a nymphaeum, a shrine to the nymphs of the watercourse. The association of girls with running water is at source a Greek conceit. Modern nymphaea can still be seen in European civic fountains from Cíbeles in Madrid to Moscow's Friendship of Peoples.

The long-term result was to project Greek civilization far beyond its self-created heartland of the eastern Mediterranean, indeed to make it the main founding culture of western Europe. To take a single example, this is why, in the modern state that holds the island of Britannia, Homer and the Greek myths of the far Aegean have remained central, much better known than the Gaelic Táin and all the related Irish stories, although this world of comparable depth, beauty, and diversity was conceived just across the Irish Sea, and the people that conceived it have been in constant touch ever since.

The Cibeles Fountain (left) in Madrid and the Friendship of the People's Fountain in Moscow. The association of nymphs with fountains goes back to Roman aqueducts.

Britain is at an extreme distance, but in this cultural obeisance to Greece it is typical of the whole continent. Through Roman power in the first few centuries AD, and the resulting spread of Rome's people and language, every corner of western Europe became a cultural colony of Greece.

This strange but fertile relationship of Greek with Roman, the disempowered inspirer with the powerful transmitter, has become a common theme of subsequent European thought. German Romantics in the nineteenth century saw Napoleonic France as Rome to their Greece; and in the twentieth century notable figures in Britain and France, looking to the United States, have hoped to interpret their own countries' greater age but lesser power through the same analogy.[35]

In fact, the same kind of relationship can be projected backward as well as forward in history. Might Livy, instead of pondering whether Rome's strength would have been equal to Alexander's had he chosen to attack it, have asked whether in the dramatic struggles with Philip, Perseus, and Antiochus, Rome was herself the new Alexander, defending the Greek cities against the new Persia (even if under Greek management)? Had it been left to Rome to pull together the disorderly but unmatched intellectual strengths of the Greek cities and successor empires and lead them to new glories? This jeu d'esprit was probably not for Livy, since the point of such an analogy is primarily to console the party who has lost the power, but hopes to be respected for wisdom and useful experience. But a Greek might have drawn the analogy, for solace to their self-respect.

But by the third century AD, speakers of Latin no longer felt any need for Greek mentorship, and the respect for ancient Greek learning began to be replaced by a Christian-inspired contempt for Greece's pagan past. When the center of the Empire was moved to Constantinople, the Greeks were recast as Romans themselves and at last were left no option but to see the world as if through Roman eyes.

There were many ironies in this reversal: Greek and Latin were destined to share the European space for many centuries, lending each other their different strengths as often as they competed head-to-head. Yet the most pervasive aspect of Rome's heritage from Greece was as diffuse as it was significant.

Greeks confronted the surrounding world as if they were its natural masters. When the supremely analytic Thucydides started to write his history of a war of Greeks against Greeks in 431 BC, he nevertheless anticipated that "it would be more worth writing about than any of those in the past . . . the greatest commotion in the history of the Greeks, affecting also some part of the barbarians, and indeed, I might almost say, the majority of mankind."[36] When Alexander declared aggressive war on the Persian king in 332, whose domains extended at the time from the Indus to the Nile, he said, "Constituted as leader of the Greeks as I am . . . send to me as king of Asia, not your equal, but as lord of all that is yours."[37] Given this powerful self-image of the Greeks, backed up by their centuries-old impact all across the Mediterranean far away from their homeland, it is unsurprising that the Romans in the first instance took them at their own valuation and counted themselves favored to be invited to join the charmed circle of competitors at Greek games: Rome was proud to count itself "a Greek city" and adopt the Greek term *bárbaros* for any that could not.

By implication, Rome would be among the insiders, no longer a small player attempting to muscle in on the big game. In the following century, as the inability of any Greek city, league, or empire to resist Rome became apparent, the Romans came to think of their city as the unchallenged center of this inside circle. It took another century, and the work of Cicero and his successors, for them to see their language too as the equal of Greek. But when they did, they had already learned from the Greeks that once this was done, there were no more worlds to conquer—or indeed to learn from. Italy had been subdued, Carthage destroyed, Greece ingested. Rome learned from the Greeks to believe that there were no other significant challenges worthy of the name.

VT ENIM SIMONIDES LYRICVS DOCET, BEATE PERFECTA
RATIONE VICTVRO ANTE ALIA PATRIAM
ESSE CONVENIT GLORIOSAM.

For as the lyric poet Simonides teaches us, he who would live blessedly on
the perfect plan should first of all have a homeland that is glorious.

Ammianus Marcellinus, *Histories*, xiv.6.3

PART II

LATIN RECRUITS

CHAPTER 7

◇◦◉◦◇

Urbi et orbi—
Taking Over the Church

Tres sunt autem linguae sacrae: Hebraea, Graeca, Latina,
quae toto orbe maxime excellunt. His enim tribus linguis super
crucem Domini a Pilato fuit causa eius scripta.

There are three sacred languages: Hebrew, Greek, and Latin, which are
supreme all over the world. For in these three languages, above the cross
of our Lord, Pilate wrote the charge against him.

Isidore, *Etymologiae*, ix.1.3 (early sixth century AD)

F IRST OF ALL COMES the story of growing power and numbers.
The Christian contribution to Latin, and to the character of Latin-
based culture, came about only because the Christians were able, over three
centuries, to convert their community from a small, and for most purposes
insignificant, minority within the Roman Empire into its dominant force; ultimately, they became its overwhelming majority. As a result, Christian Latin
is recognized as a new era in the development of the language. By contrast, few
seek to identify Mithraic, Manichaean, or indeed Jewish Latin, although
many Latin speakers were followers of Mithras, Mani, or Moses in these same
centuries AD. These cults were never able to grow to a size, and to a status, at
which they could command the loyalty of an emperor, and through him to
build a congregation in the Empire as a whole.

Christianity achieved a double religious triumph: not only did it supplant Rome's traditional religion (with worship of the emperor at its center),
but it also swept away Rome's traditional tolerance for variety in people's
personal devotions. Christianity was first encouraged, and later—from the
fifth century—enforced. When this process was complete, Latin too stood

transformed. For the rest of its natural life on the lips of the common people, it became nothing more nor less than the single speech of Christian folk in western Europe. The Latin language was retuned, from the ancient and pagan babble of a multiethnic empire, to a much more modern-seeming Christian unison.

How did it come about, this "strange triumph of Christianity"?[1] The population of the whole Roman Empire in the first century AD is estimated at about equal to a single modern major European state, 60 million. Within this, fewer than ten thousand would have been Christians in AD 100, and perhaps two hundred thousand a century later, just 0.3 percent of the Empire. The growth was rapid, but inevitably from a small base. Even if it continued at the same 3 percent annual rate until 312 in the following century, there must still have been no more than 5.5 million Christians in the Empire, then still under 10 percent. Nevertheless, in that year the emperor Constantine stunningly chose to place the Christian Chi-Rho symbol* on his forces' shields and, with that device, went on to win the crucial battle of the Milvian Bridge outside Rome, against an opposing candidate emperor, Maxentius, who was himself apparently claiming to have a prophecy on his side, but one with the more traditional authority of the Sibylline Books.[2] Thereafter, Christianity would hold priority among the religions of the Empire, with the explicit support of the emperor himself; and Constantine, first among emperors to do so, was baptized a Christian in 337, shortly before he died.

The period of Christianity's early growth, the first and second centuries AD, was untypical in the history of Europe: because of the mass mobility brought about by the Empire, newly stabilized by Augustus, there was something of a sectarian melting pot and free-for-all in the populations of large cities. This was particularly so in Rome, but also in other major centers such as Antioch, Athens, and Ephesus in the east, Carthage and Marseille in the west. Christianity, in various doctrinally divided forms, was part of this melee, but so were Mithraism and Judaism; they were joined from the third century by a new entrant from Parthia, Manichaeism, which purported to be an improvement on both Judaism and Christianity, and on Persia's indigenous Zo-

---

*☧, combining the first two letters of ΧΡΙΣΤΟΣ *kʰristos* 'the anointed' in Greek. The sign came to be known as the labarum. It may have had a previous history as a symbol of Khronos, Father Time. The resonant Latin phrase IN HOC SIGNO VINCES 'In this sign you shall conquer' does not appear in any of the contemporary sources.

roastrianism to boot. Into the mix add the cults of Cybele and Sabazios from Phrygia, and various Egyptian cults, of which the most successful export was that of Isis and Osiris (which like Christianity and Manichaeism involved death and resurrection). And in 361–363 the emperor Julian, in his brief attempt to disestablish Christianity, could still see a coherent core worth fostering and reviving in the cults of the traditional pagan gods of Greece and Rome, cults that—until the advent of so many easterners—had never been seen as being in competition with each other, nor with outsiders.

Except for the strictly traditional—and actually quite impersonal—cults associated with Rome, and Etruscan augury, all these religions had an interesting linguistic aspect in common: wherever they came from, their rituals were largely conducted in Greek, the lingua franca of the east. Christianity and even Judaism were no exceptions. The Hebrew Scriptures were consulted in the Greek translation known as the Septuagint, which had been commissioned in Egypt by the Greek pharaoh Ptolemy II (308–246 BC). Christianity, though founded as a reformed Jewish sect among Aramaic speakers, was documented (outside its basis in key prophecies of the Septuagint) first in Church Fathers' letters written in Greek, and then increasingly in Gospel narratives likewise written in that language. Only a small minority of adherents would have been literate; but there was no doubt heavy reliance on bilinguals to interpret the written documents to the rest of the congregation, whatever the faith being interpreted.

The great eighteenth-century chronicler of the decline of the Empire, Edward Gibbon,[3] had listed five causes that favored Christianity's growth, implicitly at the expense of the others:

1. the inflexible and intolerant zeal of the Christians, derived from Judaism, but purified of the narrow and unsocial spirit that had deterred gentiles from accepting the law of Moses;

2. the doctrine of a future life after death;

3. the miraculous powers ascribed to the early Church;

4. the pure and austere morals of the Christians; and

5. the union and discipline of the Christian republic, gradually forming an independent and increasing state in the heart of the Roman Empire.

None of these has been questioned since, but the emphasis is usually placed on the first and the fifth, as offering a clear advantage in a struggle for descendants among different faiths. Strange as it now seems, early Christians were often called atheists (*átheoi*): their difference from other sectaries lay not so much in their having a god of their own to worship, as in their denying that anyone else's gods were there at all, unless perhaps they were really not gods but malevolent demons. Other faiths were happy to accept, perhaps agnostically, the existence of other gods; only the Christians and the Jews militantly refused the existence of any but their own, One, God. This exclusivism, combined in the Christians' case with an active endeavor to preach and recruit new followers, meant that accepting Christ was a one-way street: new believers might check in, but they did not check out. Nor in general did their children. Like modern Catholics, or Muslims, children born to a believer were expected to be baptized and likewise brought up in the faith. Those who for any reason left the faith and withdrew from the Christian community, rejecting the authority of its *epískopoi* 'guardians, overseers' (the origin of the English word *bishop*,)* were reviled as *apostataí* (literally 'deserters, runaways, rebels'). Especially in the early days, before there was any state support, the self-sustained discipline of the Christian communities themselves must have been crucial to the bishops' authority.

And as Tertullian (AD 160–ca 220) pithily put it, the blood of the martyrs was the seed of the Church.† Official persecutions were particularly directed at Christians (whose atheism made them unable to join in loyal worship

---

*And its bewilderingly multiform equivalents across Europe, e.g., Welsh *esgob*, Scots Gaelic *easbuig*, Dutch *bisschop*, German *Bischof*, Norse *biskup*, Catalan *bisbe*, Spanish *obispo*, Portuguese *bispo*, Italian *vescovo*, French *évêque*, Romanian *episcop*, Russian *episkop*, Latvian *bīskaps*. In Albanian (*dhespot*) it appears to have been confused with the word for 'master', Greek *despótēs*.

†Tertullian actually wrote (*Apologeticum*, 50.13): NEC QVICQVAM TAMEN PROFICIT EXQVISITIOR QVAEQVE CRVDELITAS VESTRA; ILLECEBRA EST MAGIS SECTAE. PLVRES EFFICIMVR, QVOTIENS METIMVR A VOBIS: SEMEN EST SANGVIS CHRISTIANORVM 'However exquisite your cruelties they achieve nothing; rather they are an enticement to join us. We are made more whenever we are harvested by you: the blood of Christians is seed.' This, immediately after pointing out (less memorably) that a Christian would far rather face a lion (LEONEM) than a pimp (LENONEM). Augustine then recast this in his *Sermones* (xxii.4.4): SPARSVM EST SEMEN SANGVINIS, SVRREXIT SEGES ECCLESIAE 'the seed of blood has been scattered, the Church's crop has grown up', and this became a favorite metaphor for him. By an irony of fate, Tertullian himself died a heretic, condemned by the Church. (Mohrmann 1951.)

of the emperor), and not only when they were still a tiny minority during the first century AD. They were especially severe in 250, 257, and 303, in the two generations before Constantine's reversal of their fortunes. Although Christian allegiance may have been deterred in some by the Roman persecutions, those who were already committed found their dedication only reinforced by these clear fulfillments of the prophecies that they would be tested. For Christians forced to choose between membership in a severe (but in principle loving) community and a loyalty to the Roman state, which only recognized them as lowly subjects, there was little competition. To come out as a CONFESSOR (freely declaring adherence to the Church) and even as a MARTYR (literally in Greek 'a witness'—like the modern suicide bombers who call themselves in Arabic *shāhid*) was after all to become a hero or heroine of the Church, equal to a bishop in presumed authority to forgive sins, at least while the persecutions lasted.

Whatever the causal mechanism, the Christian community grew until it received supreme blessing from fortune: a Roman emperor who publicly embraced it. After this act of Constantine it was bound inevitably to become influential in the circles of the Roman elite, and hence important for literary Latin. We do not know when it formally became the absolute majority of the Roman Empire's population. (If the 3 percent annual growth was maintained, it would have happened around 370, a generation after Constantine's baptism, with total saturation achieved in the generation following.) But its continuing growth with worldly as well as personal inducements, meant that from the fourth century on, on every level, Latin would essentially be Christian Latin.

⬦

But if the majority of its followers in the west were inevitably soon to be people whose first language was Latin, Christianity still had a liturgy, and a canon of scriptures, that were overwhelmingly provided in Greek. As we have seen, there was nothing unusual in this for a religion of foreign origin seeking converts in Rome and the western provinces: all such spiritual support had always been given in this second language of the Empire, for as long as foreign religions had been on offer. Nevertheless, western Christianity was to change, dropping Greek and asserting Latin as its primary language, for liturgy, for theology, and indeed for all kinds of literature. Three steps were involved. First, Christianity required Latin translations of its sacred texts and pastoral works. These were already becoming available in the second century.

Next Latin began to be used in the official administration of the Church, something that is visible in the record through correspondence, and began in the mid-third century. And finally, in the papacy of Damasus (360–82) Latin became accepted into the liturgy itself, a place it would hold in the Church of Rome for the following sixteen centuries.[4] It was at this last stage that the first was redone, in elegant perfection: Damasus commissioned Jerome to produce a revised Latin translation of the Bible as a whole, and this, Jerome's life's work, was to be accepted as the Vulgate.

This was a big change, at least for the Roman elite. For the first time in five hundred years—and just at the time when their control of the Empire was finally slipping, as a result of foreign pressures—they were to become monolingual in Latin. The question arises why the whole population should have ceased to learn Greek.

For the vast majority of the general public in the west, the motive for a switch to Latin may have been fairly straightforward. Latin was, after all, their vernacular language. Writing in the late fourth century (366–88), one important author* evidently thought that spiritual value was lost if people conducted their religion in a language that they did not understand. Commenting on St. Paul's text, 1 Corinthians xiv.14 (literally: "If I pray with tongue, my spirit prays, but my mind is fruitless"), he wrote:

> It is evident that our heart is ignorant if it speaks in a language it doesn't know, just as Latin people often sing in Greek, enjoying the sound of the words but not knowing what they mean. The spirit given in baptism knows what the heart is praying when it speaks or mouths off in a language unknown to itself; but the mind, which is the heart, is without fruit. What fruit can it have if it does not know what it is saying?[5]

He also felt that the lack of clarity could be interpreted as a lack of sincerity, reminiscent of the delusions he associated with paganism:

> The simple man understands him and is understood, hearing him praise God and hearing Christ worshipped, and sees clearly that the religion is true and to be venerated: in it he can see that nothing is done in obscurity as the pagans do, for their eyes are kept blindfolded in case they should see the things they

---

*He is known as Ambrosiaster 'pseudo-Ambrose' because his works were transmitted under the name of St. Ambrose.

call holy and so realize that they are being cheated by gaudy vanities. For every imposture seeks the darkness and shows falsehoods as if truths: therefore in our case nothing is done slyly, or under wraps, but quite simply the one God is praised.[6]

This way of thinking resonates with the usual modern view: both for inward understanding, and for outward show, the clarity of the vernacular is seen as desirable. And since that vernacular was also at the time the official language for the whole western Empire, a decision to move away from traditional Greek and into plain speech had apparently few disadvantages in diminishing the unity of the Church, at least in the west. In this, the move was easier than the decision taken at the Second Vatican Ecumenical Council (Vatican II) in 1962–65 to drop the use of Latin from the Roman Catholic liturgy.

The nature of the Christian faith itself meant in any case that vernacular languages tended to be preferred when the faith was spread to new places. Christianity, as an egalitarian religion, appealed first of all to common people, who had less to lose and more to gain; and they needed to receive the appeal in direct terms if they were to take up something so new. Egypt gives a good example of this. In the third century AD the newly rising force of Christians there had seen the Egyptian language as best suited to advance the conversion of the people, not Greek, even though Greek was both the language of Christian texts and in almost universal use among Egypt's elite. In another popularizing gesture, the Christians had discontinued the ancient writing in demotic script, derived from hieroglyphs, inventing instead the first (and only) phonetic writing system used for Egyptian, the Greek-based script now known as Coptic. First came translations of the Bible, then original works, such as the lives of the Fathers of the Egyptian desert, led by St. Pachomius. Homilies, letters, and polemics followed, all widely read in Egypt, and laying the basis for the Coptic Church.

Another such example of Christian linguistic populism was the work of Ulfilas (or Wulfila),* bishop of the Visigoths from 341 at the age of thirty, a man who had grown up on the northwestern shores of the Black Sea, trilingual in Greek, Latin, and Gothic. His people were by origin Greco-Roman kidnap victims from Anatolia, taken in a Gothic raid in the preceding century,

---

*'Wolf-ie'.

but his bishopric was given to him by the Roman emperor Constantius. To reach his Gothic parishioners, Ulfilas translated much of the Bible into Gothic (thus creating the only record of that language that has survived).[7] But still Christianity, even preached in Gothic, may have been seen as too Roman a religion for his Gothic overlords: his flock was expelled by them, to be then resettled by Constantius just south of the mouth of the Danube. Despite his concern to reach those without a traditional education, Ulfilas also took a full part in the intellectual disputes of his era, defending right up to the Council of Constantinople in 381 the Arian theology that was to remain an abiding article of the Goths' Christian faith.[8]

A third example of early Christians' readiness to adapt their faith into a new language was the introduction of Christianity into Armenia, which in 301, after two and a half centuries of missionary activity, had become the first state to accept it as its official religion. Evidently, the Scriptures had still to be consulted in a foreign language, probably Greek, for Armenian itself was not at the time a written language. It took another century for the language to be given an alphabet (by St. Meshrop Mashtots in 406); but when it was, the Bible was immediately translated, as the founding text of Armenian literacy, and indeed of Armenian education until the nineteenth century.[9]

However, in the Roman case there were also more political considerations, which would have favored a move out of Greek, as much as a move into Latin—which was of course the vernacular for most in Rome. Unlike its recent peers, all those other foreign religions, Christianity was to assume an official role, and as such it began to be affected by *raison d'état*, or the perceived public interest.

First of all, Constantine was the emperor who, besides accepting Christianity, also set up a competing capital for the Empire in Byzantium, newly refounded in 324 as Constantinople. This immediately put a premium on knowledge of Latin in the Greek-speaking east. But it also created a rift between the two halves of the Empire, which was only to deepen over time, as first the western half fell to Germanic invaders, then was partly reconquered only to be lost again by the irredentist east. There was, for the first time perhaps, a sense of "Rome (and Latin) for the Romans," a need to assert the western identity over an increasingly powerful, independent, and indeed Latin-ignorant Greek east. This was seen in the increasing theological estrangement between Roman and Greek bishops, which was already severe in Constantine's reign; while the ruling dispute was expressed in Greek as to whether Christ was *homooúsios* or merely *homoioúsios* with the Father ('of the same essence' or 'of like essence'), the issue was effaced by the proffered Latin translation CONSVBSTANTIALIS (literally 'of shared substance'). It became important for the bishop of Rome, the pope, to assert his continuing Roman identity, both before 364, when the Empire was often effectively governed from Constantinople, and even more afterward, when the domains of the western and eastern emperors were, as it turned out, finally sundered. And how better than through demonstration of the total competence of the Latin language in matters of true religion?

This self-assertive preference among Italian and other western Christians for use of Latin was also reinforced by the long-standing association of Greek literature, and hence—for outsiders—the Greek language, with the pre-Christian cults of all kinds, but especially the traditional Olympian deities from Zeus to Dionysus. By the fourth century, *Hellene* had come to mean "pagan" as well as "Greek," and the emperor Julian, whose first language seems to have been Greek, took this as a badge of pride when he attempted, during his short reign, 361–63, to turn the clock back and reinstate a kind of paganism as the official religion of the empire.* Christian Greeks, of whom there were a fair few, were highly offended, especially as he seemed to be saying that their language was essentially reserved for paganism. The contemporary Christian Greek intellectual Gregory of Nazianzus wrote to Julian, of "the words and the speaking of Greek": "Nay, if they *be* thine, how canst thou show that *we* have no part in them, according to thy legislation and unreasonableness? Whose property are the words of the Greek language?"[10]

Whatever the merits of Julian's combative claim that Greek was the language for pagans par excellence, Greek was in its use clearly far too promiscuous (and indeed, in the original sense, catholic) to have built up any privileged link with the Christian faith; and for those with a literary education, it had a heavy load of pagan associations. How much better for westerners to leave all this behind and express God's truth in the simple language of daily Roman speech, Latin!

---

*For this, if for no other reason, it is highly unlikely that his last words were, as popularly attributed, a rhetorical apostrophe to Jesus (in Latin): VICISTI GALILAEE 'Thou hast won, Galilean'.

CHAPTER 8

❖❖❖❖

Vox populi vox dei—
Latin as the Bond of Unity

ET SINE FINE DICEMVS VNVM LAVDANTES TE IN VNVM
ET IN TE FACTI ETIAM NOS VNVM.

And without end we shall say, "One," praising you as one,
and ourselves made one in you.

Augustine, *On the Trinity*, xv.28.61

N OT THAT LATIN WAS a language without a pagan past, indeed an all
too glorious one. Jerome, authorized to standardize the Latin text of the
Bible, recounted a nightmare in which he was told at the gates of heaven that
he had been more deeply devoted to Cicero than to Christ (*Ciceronianus es, non
Christianus*).[1] Christians with a literary education always worried that a good
style, as traditionally defined, would distance them from true piety. Nonetheless, they could not avoid rephrasing simple Christian prayers with the elaborate parallelisms that we know had been a prominent feature of Rome's pagan
prayers. In the Mass, for example, *hunc panem sacrum et calicem vitae aeternae*
'this holy bread and cup of eternal life' was reconfigured into the more orotund
panem sanctum vitae aeternae, et calicem salutis perpetuae 'holy bread of eternal
life and cup of perpetual salvation', with a parallel structure and rhyming
parts.

But sometimes it was the pagan, rather, that seemed to be prefiguring
the noble sentiments of the Christian faith itself. This had occurred most
famously in Virgil's Fourth Eclogue: ". . . the Virgin returns . . . a new prog-
eny is sent down from heaven above . . . favor the child being born, through
whom the iron age of men will give place to gold . . ." On the strength of
this, in fact, Virgil, Rome's great imperial epic poet, was accorded the status

of an unofficial pagan prophet throughout late Antiquity and the Middle Ages.

Christians' Latin did have some distinguishing features before it was merged into the standard for the language as a whole. Augustine, for example, who had converted in 387, noted the linguistic consequences of his conversion to Christianity. He had to adopt the *ecclesiastica loquendi consuetudo* 'the Church style', even when he would have preferred to establish his own style. There was a vocabulary that Christians used, and this went beyond the details of their own rituals and theology. 'Kill' in Christian Latin, he said, is not *occidere* (the usual Latin word, which has survived in Italian as *uccidere*) but *occurrere* (literally 'run into'), or else *compendiare* (literally 'abridge').* Augustine said he would have liked to call the Christian martyrs *heroes*, but the Greek, i.e., pagan, overtones (and association with the goddess Hera) were just too strong.[2]

A general feature of Latin as used by Christians was its aggressively vulgar, plebeian, tone, quite happy to commit what traditionalists would call solecisms or barbarisms. This is unsurprising, since it was the converse of their worries about excessive eloquence. As Arnobius had put it, writing in 303, "When the point is something serious, beyond showing off, we need to consider *what* is being said, not how elegantly; not what soothes the ears, but what brings benefits to the hearers."[3] But the fact that it seemed easier to write ungrammatically also shows that maintaining the full traditional grammar of Latin was becoming a burden even to native speakers, within the fourth century AD. Augustine observed:

> For what is called a solecism is nothing other than putting words together on a different rule from that followed by our authoritative predecessors. Whether we say *inter homines* ['among men'—accusative case] or *inter hominibus* [ditto—ablative case] does not concern a man who only wishes to know the facts. And likewise, what is a barbarism but pronouncing a word differently from those who spoke Latin before us? For whether the word *ignoscere* ['pardon'] should be pronounced with the third syllable long or short is indifferent to the man who is praying to God, with whatever words he can, to pardon his sins. What is correctness of diction beyond sustaining usages that happen to be hallowed by the authority of former speakers?[4]

---

*He compared the Roman soldiers' equivalent *allevare*, which is literally 'lighten', an idiom perhaps like English 'neutralize'.

He even explicitly enjoined breaking the grammatical rules on occasion:

Feneratur [a deponent verb, with passive form but active sense] is the Latin for giving a loan, and receiving one: but it would be clearer to say *fenerat* [i.e., the corresponding active form]. What do we care what the grammarians prefer? Better you understand through our barbarism, than get left behind [*deserti*] through our elevated finesse [*disertitudine*].[5]

Besides these almost routine abuses of the language's norms, Christianity also had its own rituals and concepts that needed to be couched in Latin. In many cases, Greek words were simply borrowed (*anathema, angelus, apostolus, baptizo, charisma, diabolus, diaconus, ecclesia, episcopus, presbyter, propheta*, etc.), and the familiarity of these words shows that they were to stick. There were neologisms such as *Trinitas* for the threefold Godhead; and indeed *salvare* 'save', *salvator* 'savior': the obvious Latin words *conservator* or *salutaris* had been besmirched since they had been used by pagans to refer to Jupiter. But Christianity also began to reinterpret Latin vocabulary, playing especially strongly on the ruling metaphor that the faithful were the soldiers in the army of *Imperator Christus*: the loyalty oath of a Roman soldier, the *sacramentum*, was adapted to "we are called to the militia of the living God precisely when we answer to the words of the sacrament."[6] Faithful Christians could expect at the end of their service, like Roman veteran soldiers, a *donativus* 'grant'; however, in their case it would not be a land settlement, but eternal life. Those who were not in the army were termed dismissively by Roman soldiers *pagani* 'villagers'; what better term for those outside the Church? *Pax*, as we have seen, was a favorite word for the main achievement of the Roman emperors, even if they had mostly aimed at this outcome through waging almost perpetual wars; but it too was now reinterpreted, not only to mean absence of war or persecution, but the state of mind and being that Christ offered. Christians after death would sleep *in pace*, but far more they were part of the *pax*, the Church itself, in this world, and they greeted each other with the *osculum pacis* 'the kiss of peace'. A memory of this has been preserved through Irish Christianity, for in Gaelic *póg* still means a kiss.[7]

Christian Latin overall, then, was the Latin of the street, and perhaps especially the Latin of recent-generation speakers, who had never gained perfect command of the language.* Lactantius, a mid-third-century Christian

---

*It is notable, though, that wherever we find nonliterary Latin recorded, e.g., for the first century AD in the preserved graffiti of Pompeii or the wooden cards from the Vindolanda

writer who did strive to follow the classical rules, noted that his recent prede-
cessor Cyprianus, bishop of Carthage, who had happily embraced the vulgar-
isms, had attracted among pagans the nickname Coprianus 'Mr. Merde': the
Greek for dung is *kópros*.[8]

◈

Self-consciously rough at the outset (since even early Christian Latin was far
removed from Latin's classical era), this common language was going to give a
whole new character to Latin literature. Changes transformed a vast range of
the old ways—affecting the substance of the Latin language, its literary forms,
its publishing technologies, its approach to personal literacy, and ultimately of
the very nature of poetry itself. Christianity brought *res novas* 'new things',
which in Latin signifies revolution.

Christian Latin was happy to identify itself with common speech
patterns—what indeed is commonly called Vulgar Latin—and to set them
down in writing, or, to fix them just as permanently, in the endlessly repeated
phrases of the liturgy, sung or spoken.* Augustine noted explicitly how the
popular hymn had the phrase FLORIET SANCTIFICATIO MEA 'My sanctification will flourish', although there was no reason but habit for not singing the
grammatically approved FLOREBIT SANCTIFICATIO MEA.[9] In this period, the
fourth century AD, Latin word-order began to change and become more
rigid, with the verb in particular moving up from the end of the sentence into
second position: sentence structure was becoming more like what is typical in
a modern European language.

Latin became, in a way, more straightforward and explicit. There was a

---

garrison on Hadrian's wall in Scotland, the grammar strikes us as imperfectly classical.
So spoken Latin must always have been more varied than the norms hallowed in the era
of Cicero and Virgil.

*So literary constructions like the "accusative + infinitive" were replaced with simpler
clauses using *quod/quia/quoniam* 'that': no more CREDO ILLVM SALVATOREM MEVM
ESSE 'I believe him to be my savior', but CREDO QVIA ILLE SALVATOR MEVS EST
'I believe that he is my savior'. Irregular verbs became regular (e.g., the indispensable verb
odi odisti odit 'I/you/he hate(s)' was replaced by *odio odis odit*), and there was flux in the
complex system of verb conjugation, with verbs changing from one pattern to another:
instead of *exerceo* 'I exert' *exercēre* 'to exert', we now find *exercio exercēre*, but instead of
fugio fugĕre 'run away' we find *fugio fugīre*. Prepositions *in/de* 'through/with' were used
where classical Latin had used just a special ending (ablative) on the noun.

general process whereby the shorter but less predictable words came to be replaced by more regularly inflected extensions: instead of *os* 'bone' (plural *ossa*), we read *ossuum* (*ossua*); for *rete* 'net' (plural *retia*), the plural was taken as a singular: so *retia* (*retiae*), and even *retiaculum* (*retiacula*). And with similar, more downright effect, words were inelegantly extended, with weighty endings: not *corona* 'wreath' but *coronamentum*, not *gaudium* 'joy' but *gaudimonium*, not *poena* 'pain' but *poenitudo*. But diminutives were also used more, so that although the word became longer, its effect might be lighter, almost childish in tone: for *auris* 'ear', *leo* 'lion', *agnus* 'lamb', we find *auricula, leunculus, agniculus*— 'earsy-wearsies', 'liony', 'lambkin'. These developments in Latin gave a new linguistic sense to Christ's dictum: "Except ye be as little children, ye shall in no wise enter the kingdom of heaven."

While the words and texture of Latin were changing, the Christians also brought new literary forms into popularity. No form was abandoned (though erotic verse was certainly discouraged for a few centuries), but the primary historical texts became gospels and hagiographic lives of the saints and martyrs. Instead of geographies we find accounts by pilgrims of their travels to holy places. Formal speeches were replaced in popularity by homilies or sermons, and also by long letters of advice. Philosophical texts were often formulated as "apologies," not requests for forgiveness, but argued statements of the case for the Christian faith, formulated with ever increasing doctrinal exactitude.

The Christians were also innovators in the distribution and publication of their literature. Relying as they did on written texts, but because only a minority of their congregation was literate and able to read them, they maintained a culture of the public reading of letters. Such "epistles" are well represented in the New Testament, and in fact represent the earliest documents in that compilation. Public readings had always been a feature of the Roman literary scene, but previously these had been opportunities for select writers, especially historians and poets, to declaim finished, and highly elaborated, works. The Christians, by contrast, pioneered this as a means of making devotional literature available to congregations at large. These epistles were effectively recorded homilies, broadcast to whoever was in the audience.

Often the speakers at these gatherings were not reading out others' words, but delivering their own. In such sermons, preachers liked to be able to quote from Scripture. Early on, such scriptures were usually selections from the Jewish prophets (in Greek, or later in Latin translation), which the Christians naturally believed they understood better than the Jews themselves. Later on, they included Christian epistles and gospels. This posed a problem for the preacher, since these scriptures were extensive and indeed not written in the kind of deathless prose or verse that was readily committed to memory verbatim. To solve the problem of random access to texts, the answer seems to have been to invent, or at any rate to popularize, the book as we know it.

An ancient Greek or Roman book was a *volumen*, literally a 'roll', i.e., a scroll that was designed to be read from beginning to end, being simultaneously unrolled on the right and rolled up again on the left. Bookmarking, and ready reference to passages for citation, was cumbersome or impossible. But about the second century AD a new form of book was being pioneered, called the *codex* 'wood block': it was in the form of a hinged set of pages, originally sheets of wood (hence the name) but later of parchment. The codex had long been used for account books, with relatively few pages, but once ordinary writing materials replaced wood, they were able to hold considerable amounts of text. Now the pages could be consulted individually and in random order. The all-round convenience of this device for text storage and retrieval won out, though evidently it was more laborious to make a codex than a scroll. The exigencies of the Christian sermon had given rise to the text-publishing format that is still in use, and indeed dominant, to this day, after almost two millennia, including a major intervening revolution in the form of the printing press.

As if these innovations were not enough, Christianity also seems to have been the catalyst for a new kind of reading, closer to thought itself. Reading in the ancient world had always been a kind of performance, in which the characters written on the page were converted into a stream of spoken language, available to be understood by the reader himself, but of course also for any others present, in the living room or in the classroom, wherever the reading was taking place. Silent reading does not seem to have been considered, despite the inconvenience that must have been encountered when more than one person in a room wished to read different books at the same time.

The first reference in the western tradition to silent reading was Augustine's almost incredulous report in his *Confessions*, of how he first witnessed it being practiced by Bishop Ambrose of Milan, when he knew him in the 380s. He described it as a sort of book communion: "But when he read, his eyes were led over the pages and his heart sought out the understanding, while his voice and his tongue were quiet."[10] Augustine, a highly vocal man, whose career was one of open discussion and oratory, and who indeed wrote his many books by dictating out loud to a secretary, could only conjecture that Ambrose might have been doing it to save his voice, or perhaps to save potential listeners from perplexity, in case they might have overheard him reading something that was just too difficult for them. But in this Ambrose, and not Augustine, was the man of the future.

◈

Perhaps the most fundamental change for literature in this period was the revolution in poetry, unseating the kind of verse that had been written ever since the Greeks had taught the Romans how to write poetry in the third century BC. The new style would encourage stress-based rhythm, and ultimately neat rhymes that would lock lines together in couplets and verses, though it would take more than seven hundred years for the transition to run its full course.

The classical tradition was of "quantitative verse": in this the poet used rhythmical patterns of heavy and light syllables (such as the iamb [ti-tum], the dactyl [tum-ti-ti]) regardless of the stress pattern of individual words. Greek words had originally had light stress (if any at all), but a keen sense of whether vowels were long or short, so this was a natural way of structuring its verse, going back to Homer and presumably before.* Latin's oldest verse, on the other hand, had been based on a sprung stress rhythm (like the earliest Germanic verse): typically there were four stresses in a line, but its length was otherwise not determined. It had been seen as a cultural advance (associated with the transition from Livius Andronicus and Naevius to Ennius) to adopt the Greek verse patterns and was not too alien, since early Latin was evidently also a language with clearly sensed long and short vowels. But by the fourth century AD, the distinction between long and short vowels was breaking down (it has been lost in all the Romance descendant languages), whereas stress was—if anything—becoming more prominent. The result was the revival of stress-based verse, but now (after five hundred years of Greek meters) with the lines much more regularly measured than they had been in the days of Naevius. Essentially, a Christian hymn, with regular patterns of stressed and unstressed syllables, became the prototype for future verse.

The preference for balanced clauses remained in Christian diction, almost against Christians' better judgment—as it had in all literary Latin:

---

*See the brief overview of the hexameter in the note to page 61.

panem sanctum vitae aeternae,
et calicem salutis perpetuae

But Latin is a language where verbs, nouns, and adjectives have suffixes to show their grammatical functions: e.g., subject and object, dependent nouns, and their qualifying adjectives. The result is that the balanced clauses often rhyme, simply because the parallel parts have parallel functions in the sentence, and so the same endings. To gloss the above:

[bread OBJECT] [holy QUALIFYING OBJ] [life DEPENDENT] [eternal QUALIF DEP]
and [cup OBJECT] [salvation DEPENDENT] [perpetual QUALIF DEP]

So rhyme would occur as almost an incidental feature, just because of the patterns of the language, and the structure of Latin itself. But regular stress rhythm came first, required for a text to be sung by a congregation to a simple tune.

An early stage of the new poetry can be seen in the first few lines of a 'psalm' composed by Augustine himself, "against the party of Donatus" at the end of the fourth century. I have marked the long vowels and the stresses, and marked the beat (*ictus* in Latin), with bold type. Some verbs are evidently being pronounced differently from their classical form (e.g., *accipére* as against classical *accípere*). Syllables that are elided before a following vowel (or after a preceding vowel) have been parenthesized.

In this verse, there is a tendency (no more than that) to put the beat on the stresses, rather than the heavy syllables. (A heavy syllable has either a long vowel, a diphthong, or is followed by two consonants. Cf page 336, note 6.) And one can see assonances, the first glimmers of a movement toward rhymes.*

Vōs quī **gaūdétis** dē **pá**ce,	You who rejoice in peace
módo **vé**rum iūdi**cá**te.	right now judge the truth.
Foéda	**est** rēs **caús**(am) au**dí**re	It is foul to hear a case
et per**só**nās acci**pé**re.	and put on masks.
Ómnēs ini**ús**ti nōn **pós**sunt	All the unrighteous cannot
régnum **Dé**i possi**dé**re.	possess the kingdom of heaven.

*Full rhyme in the modern sense would come very much later, not before the twelfth century (pp. 182–83).

Vést(em) aliēnam cōnscíndas	That you should rip another's shirt
nēmō potest toleráre:	no one can abide:
Quánto mágis pácem Chrístī	How much more, the peace of Christ,
quí cōnscíndit dígnu(s e)st mórte.	he who rips it deserves death.
Et quis est ísta quī fécit	And who it is who has done this
quaerámus hoc sin(e) errōre.	let us find out without mistake.

The character of Christianity, then, served in two rather different ways to bring literary Latin away from its old existence. In Christian use, public Latin was less predominantly a medium for rhetorical displays and became a more ambivalent vehicle. Before, the essence of Latin literature had been well-crafted speeches and open debate, seeking plausibility rather than truth, and the only participants were the well educated, leaving everyone else firmly excluded. From the time Christianity took over the language, the democratic emphasis on SERMO HVMILIS, literally 'ground-level speech', meant that substance would be emphasized over style, and artistic productions would remain in close touch with popular culture and indeed, from time to time, popular song.

But besides developing its common touch in the use of Latin among the congregation, Christianity also brought another side to Latin. The close relationship of the preacher with his (written) texts, and the emphasis on personal or introspective thought, also meant that Latin would increasingly become a medium for speculative, confessional writing. The culture of monastic Latin, with its emphasis on private study and conscientious reading while copying, was also being prepared.

◇

Constantine's embrace of Christianity, and its subsequent instatement as the established religion of the Empire, had created a major problem for the Roman state. Since the collapse of the Roman republic in the first century BC, and the constitutional reconstruction then carried through by Augustus, loyalty to the person of the emperor, expressed through the deification and formal worship of his forerunners, had provided the linchpin for the whole body politic. The formal cult of the emperor in dedicated temples was a feature of the eastern provinces, but even in the west, private and public banquets involved a libation, the pouring out of wine, to the emperor, as to a god. Petronius recorded the words used: AVGVSTO, PATRI PATRIAE, FELICITER 'To Augustus, Father of the Fatherland, blessedly'.[11] In principle, this was more than a loyal toast; it

Flavius Valerius Aurelius Constantinus (Constantine the Great) was the first emperor to accept Christianity. This was crucial in its advance to become Rome's official religion.

was an act of worship, explicitly a holy moment in an otherwise secular occasion. Direct worship of the emperor was required of all citizens, at least in the sense of making fealty to him a priority over all other duties.

This the Christians could not accept. The emperor might well thrust himself into theological issues, as Constantine did, and demand a special status, precisely in virtue of being the emperor, summoning bishops to Rome to resolve theological issues that he felt were causing unrest ("I do not intend to tolerate schisms or dissension anywhere," he wrote)[12] and calling and presiding over the first ecumenical council of bishops, in Nicaea in 325. (Although the council's discussions were largely in Greek, he chose to make his opening speech in Latin, with an interpreter.)[13] The status was duly accorded, but nevertheless the Church was never in doubt that its members' first duty was not to the emperor, but to God.* Moreover, one of its fundamental beliefs was that the end of this world was nigh (what they called more poetically "the sunset of our era"—*occasus saeculi*), an event that would inevitably bring with it the annihilation of the Empire.

Christ was indubitably on record[14] as having said: "Render unto Caesar the things that are Caesar's, and God the things that are God's." But three

---

*Later, in 355, Constantius II apparently declared, "What I wish must be regarded as the canon," before exiling two bishops. The testimony, though, comes from one of those two: Athanasius, *Historia Arianorum*, 33. And no such doctrine was ever established.

centuries of demonizing the Roman state in the literature of Martyr Acts—as well as many real memories of oppression—had left a rather weak and ambivalent basis for civic cohesion by Christians in the fourth century AD. Fidelity to God and his Church they knew; loyalty to Rome had always seemed like the mark of a pagan. Since the second century Christians had been used to thinking of themselves as a third kind (*tertium genus*), different both from Jews and the (fully Roman) gentiles.* If the emperor, first among gentiles, wished to clothe himself in the prestige of the Church—divine grace, no less—Christian subjects might well feel he had something to prove first.

Meanwhile, dedication to Christ was not exclusive to the Empire, its citizens and slaves. It became increasingly difficult to distinguish friend from foe as Goths and other tribes outside the Empire first accepted Christianity themselves, then went on to press their demands to enter the Empire's borders, if necessary (as at the battle of Adrianople in 378) by force. Traditional patriotism and cultural chauvinism were now supplemented either by a heightened racism or else with a concern for heresy. Bishop Ambrose of Milan was writing, just after Adrianople, "Have we not heard, from all along the border—from Thrace, and through Dacia by the river, Moesia, and all Valeria of the Pannonian—a mingled tumult of blasphemers preaching and barbarians invading? What profit could neighbors so bloodthirsty bring us, or how could the Roman state be safe with such defenders?" Ambrose explicitly equated Gog, in Ezekiel's biblical prophecy of catastrophe, with the Goth.[15] From the strict doctrinal point of view, in fact, Goths were just as much to be execrated: they were Arians, after all, holding firmly to a doctrine of Christ's difference from God the Father, which was to be formally repudiated at the Council of Constantinople in 381.

In 401, Sulpicius Severus, resident in Gaul, was reading the book of Daniel, chapter 2. He read Nebuchadnezzar's vision, of the idol with feet of iron and clay mixed, which was about to come crashing down, and saw it as applicable to the Roman Empire. According to Sulpicius, the problem lay in the fact that the foreign populations ("barbarous tribes mixed up across the cities and provinces") were not assimilating to Roman ways. Jerome, reading the same text in Palestine around 407 (the year of the successful Germanic invasions of the west), saw the problem in the fact that Rome's army was no longer

---

*There had been a biblical basis for this, of course. Zechariah 13.8: "And it shall come to pass, that in all the land, saith the LORD, two parts therein shall be cut off and die; but the third shall be left therein." See Cracco Ruggini 1987: 199.

of homogenous stock.[16] Either way, it was clear that Christian faith alone could not do what the imperial cult had achieved in previous centuries: to unite the western Empire, in a way that would set it apart from those people that many Romans, including senior bishops and intellectuals, wished to see as "lesser breeds without the law."*

But in the event Latin itself provided what was necessary. In a world where *Pax Romana* aspired to represent itself as *Pax Christiana*, the Latin rite became the linking bond of the *familia Christi*, the Roman Catholic Church, linking its members to Rome as well as to each other. And if that excluded the Roman east, well, so be it. By the fourth century, competence in Latin could be used to mark out outsiders, as when in 358 Athanasius claimed, in dramatizing his dispute with the emperor Constantius II, that Auxentius,† the bishop summoned from Cappadocia to take over the see of Milan, was "an intruder rather than a Christian . . . this person was as yet even ignorant of the Latin language, and unskillful in everything except impiety."[17] Latin was to become the distinguishing mark of a (western) Christian, and hence a Roman, even after the collapse of the Empire and consequent disappearance of any emperor. In 533 the senior official Cassiodorus, in flattering his young master Athalaric, king of the Ostrogoths ruling from Ravenna, thought it best to say that his history of the Goths, compiled in Latin from far-flung sources, had made it into a Roman history.[18] No higher praise could be found.

But if Latin was to provide a visible, or audible, talisman of *Romanitas*, hence unity, for Christians after the collapse of the Empire, Christianity too may have been vital to the survival of Latin.

---

*Augustine did not understand this. In the 420s he was quite prepared to set the bounds of Christian charity at the boundary of the Roman Empire: slavers might rightfully kidnap people beyond the African border, but not within it. (*Letters*, CSEL 88: 8 and 10, discussed by Cracco Ruggini 1987: 198.)

†Auxentius spoke Greek and was of Gothic extraction. But his most famous work, the letter in which he praised his foster father Ulfilas and stated sympathetically what Arians believed, was in Latin. (See chapter 7, note 8 on page 342.)

CHAPTER 9

Dies irae—Staying On

DIES IRAE DIES ILLA | SOLVIT SECLVM IN FAVILLA | TESTE
DAVID CVM SIBYLLA

Day of wrath, that very day, turns the mortal world to ashes,
as David and the Sibyl have witnessed.

Thomas of Celano, ca AD 1250

ECCE OMNIS TERRA AD POTENTISSIMAE GENTIS FREMITVM
CONTREMISCIT, ET TAMEN ROMANO AD TE ANIMO VENIT,
QVI BARBARVS PVTABATVR

Lo, the whole world trembles before the clamor of the most powerful race,
and yet he who was thought a barbarian comes to you with a Roman spirit.

Sermon from southern Gaul, ca AD 477[1]

T HE POLITICAL CONTROL OF western Europe was thoroughly and permanently overturned by the invasions of German speakers in the early
fifth century. Within a single generation Franks and Saxons, Goths and Vandals, surged westward and southward to master France, Britain, Italy, Spain,
and even north Africa. Yet remarkably, Latin was displaced in only one of
these provinces, Britain, and the conquerors largely took up the language of
their subjects.

First the Goths, who had been Rome's neighbors in the eastern Balkans
(modern Rumania) but were under pressure from Huns invading from the east,
applied to enter the Empire, essentially to come under the Roman defensive aegis.
Meeting with Roman resistance, they decided to come anyway and so defeated

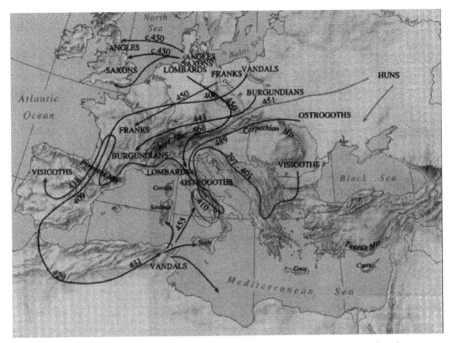

Routes of the Germanic invasions. The Goths' conquest of Italy was immediately followed by their attempts to stem other foreigners' advances into Gaul and Spain.

and killed the Roman emperor Valens near Adrianople in 378; then, after attempting but failing to take the Romans' capital, Constantinople, and a four-year war of attrition, they finally settled as they had originally intended, as sworn allies (*foederati*) of the Romans, on land just south of the Danube, which in southeastern Europe marked the *limes*, the Roman frontier. They had shown, however, almost inadvertently, that the *limes* could no longer offer the firm defense that the Romans had hoped for.

In the next generation, the protagonists were at first German-speaking Vandals and Suevi, resident farther north in Pannonia (modern Hungary), together with the Alans, who spoke an Iranian language and who had not long before been nomads roaming the plains of Ukraine. Again under pressure from marauding Huns in the east, their leaders decided they should migrate westward. They met little resistance as they moved along the northern bank of the Danube, until entering Frankish territory along the Rhine, they found their way blocked. Famously, on New Year's Day 407, the Rhine was frozen over: the Vandals, Suevi, and Alans surged across and went on a rampage across the domestic heartland of southern Gaul. The Franks (and Alemanni and Burgundians) moved in behind them, settling on the western as well as the eastern banks of the Rhine. By October 409 the Vandal alliance had reached the Pyrenees, which they crossed. Once in Iberia they were granted *foederati* status by Rome and settled in various, largely coastal areas.

Within a year, however, they were to find themselves the victims of a hot-pursuit army of Goths.

The Goths had sporadically been moving westward since their settlement in 382: in 396 southward to Greece, and then in 402–3 northward through the Balkan peninsula and into Italy. There they had at first been repulsed by the Romans, led by the great general Stilicho (himself, as it happened, a Vandal). However, the drawing down of Roman troops into northern Italy had fatally weakened the Rhine frontier, soon to be breached by the Vandals and their allies. And when in 408 Stilicho was killed by a Roman emperor fearful of an overmighty subject, there was no effective resistance when the Goths returned, under their leader Alaric. It took the Romans too long to awaken to the weakness of their position: by the time they offered terms, the Eternal City had been taken and sacked. The seat of government had already been moved to Ravenna, but nonetheless this event was memorable: the city of Rome, great conqueror of nations, had not been taken by a hostile power in eight hundred years.

The Goths, however, being—despite everything—the most Romanized (and indeed Christianized) of Germanic tribes, immediately took over the effective government of the Empire and proceeded to act as if they owned the place, entering Gaul to crush an army of Franks and Alemanni that was even proposing a competing emperor, and in 414 entering Spain to defeat the Vandals and Alans. Before they could turn on the Suevi, they were persuaded (by the Romans) to return to Gaul, where they settled in the southwestern region, Aquitania, setting their capital in Tolosa.

In the next generation, the Germanic peoples demonstrated their new power. The remnant of the Vandal-Alan alliance, tiring of Spain, moved south (428–42) across the Strait of Gibraltar and drove into what was then the much richer province of Africa; when St. Augustine died in 430, the Vandals were at the gates of his home city, Hippo. For the ensuing century, Vandal naval control of the western Mediterranean from its base in Carthage became an inescapable fact—a fact that was cruelly underlined by their sea-borne sack of Rome in 455. The Goths of Aquitania expanded south to the

Mediterranean in 469 and then over the next decade reestablished themselves in central and southern Spain. The Burgundians moved south too, to occupy the Midi region of modern France. Meanwhile, their eastern cousins, attempting to salvage Roman imperium in Italy, carved out what was in fact an Ostrogothic kingdom: by 528 its king, Theoderic, controlled the whole of Italy and Sicily, as well as the areas of southern France, Austria, and northern Yugoslavia. And the Franks too expanded at the expense of their neighbors eastward and westward, so that by this same date they controlled most of what had been Gaul, from the Atlantic to the Rhine, and a good swath of what is now the west of Germany.

In 533 the Empire struck back. From the eastern Mediterranean, the emperor Justinian's general Belisarius regained control of northern Africa (from the Vandals), southern Spain (from the Visigoths), and all of Italy, thus ending the kingdom of the Ostrogoths. But only the African gains were to prove solid. The Vandals were finished; but the Visigoths soon rallied in Spain and by 575 had confined the Romans to a coastal strip, finally taken only in 631; and in Italy, east-Roman rule was soon challenged in 568 and then diminished by a new group of invading Germans, the Lombards, who came over the Alps from the area of modern Austria. From bridgeheads in Milan and Pavia, they had come by 600 to control most of north and central Italy, but their power was exercised through a patchwork of duchies that were never to be fully united, nor in possession of Rome itself.

While these convulsions had been shaking the heartlands of the western Roman Empire, one ex-province had been left largely isolated. Characteristically for its future, this was Britain. Its detachment from the Empire is said to have begun in the year of the German crossing of the Rhine, 407. As it happened, Britain was home to a substantial military force, but this was in revolt against Rome and had in that year put up no fewer than three contenders for the imperial throne. The last of these was a general named Constantine. He moved into Gaul with his army, but instead of opposing the invaders, he largely used these troops to substantiate his claim. The claim was not ultimately successful and hence in itself is irrelevant; but it seems that his action had stripped Britain of its principal defense. According to the Byzantine historian Zosimus, writing probably a century later:

> The barbarians above the Rhine, assaulting everything at their pleasure, reduced both the inhabitants of Britain and some of the Celtic peoples to defecting from Roman rule and living their own lives disassociated from the

Roman law. Accordingly the Britons took up arms and, with no consideration of the danger to themselves, freed their own cities from barbarian threat; likewise all of Armorica and other Gallic provinces followed the Britons' lead: they freed themselves, ejected the Roman magistrates, and set up home rule at their own discretion. Now, the defection of Britain and the Celtic peoples took place during Constantinus' tyranny, the barbarians having mounted their attack owing to his carelessness in administration.[2]

This somewhat vague account of the threat to Britain, and the response to it, is all we have; and it is quite possible that Zosimus, writing from the other end of the Empire after a century's interval, may have confused different barbarian intrusions, since no other reason exists to suppose the German invasion of the Rhineland and Gaul was any threat to Britain itself, nor indeed to Armorica (Brittany). Although it is not strange that the British were thought capable of looking to their own defense (since forces raised in Britain had previously been sent to intervene on the Continent,—recently, under Maximinus in 388), it is surprising that they were ultimately so much less successful at ensuring cultural survival than their cousins in Gaul or Spain.

For Latin died out in Britain, as in no other part of the Roman Empire in the west. The language, religion, and way of life that were to survive in the exposed parts of Britain were not Roman, nor even British, but English—i.e., a composite of the ways of the Frisians, Angles, Saxons, and Jutes (northern Germans), who were beginning to establish themselves aggressively westward across the country from Kent to the Firth of Forth, no later than the mid-fifth century.

The narrative of these conquests is the stuff of legend rather than history, but evidently the British were in these years having to fight a war on two fronts. The polemical monk Gildas wrote in the mid-sixth century that the British had petitioned Rome (and specifically Flavius Aetius, the general who was later to defeat Attila the Hun in 451) for help against northern barbarians, the Picts and the Scots, in a plea dated to 446: "To Aetius, now consul for the third time: the groans of the Britons . . . The barbarians drive us to the sea; the sea throws us back on the barbarians: thus two modes of death await us, we are either slain or drowned." The Romans, however, could not assist them. Later, Gildas went on, "Then all the councillors, together with that proud tyrant Gurthrigern, the British king, were so blinded that, as a protection to their country, they sealed its doom by inviting in among them like wolves into the sheepfold, the fierce and impious Saxons, a race hateful both to God and men, to repel the invasions of the northern nations."[3]

The great chronicler Bede wrote in the early eighth century that the Saxon brothers Hengest and Horsa were recruited in 449 by British king Vortigern to fight Picts of the north, but stayed on after a dispute about payment.[4] And Hengest is stated by the Anglo-Saxon Chronicle to have died in 488. Gildas added, "Sometimes our countrymen, sometimes the enemy, won the field, to the end that our Lord might in this land try after his accustomed manner these his Israelites, whether they loved him or not, until the year of the siege of Badon Hill, when took place also the last almost, though not the least, slaughter of our cruel foes, which was (as I am sure) at an interval of forty-four years and one month, and also the time of my own nativity."[5]

Depending on whether this date was being given as forty-four years from the advent of the Saxons, or forty-four years from the time of writing, the battle occurred between 493 and 503. And whatever the respite achieved at Badon Hill, the battle of Deorham (probably Dyrham, close to Bath) in 577 (again attested by the Anglo-Saxon Chronicle) appears to have reversed the outcome and set the seal on the Saxon conquest of England, taking them to the Severn and yielding up the cities of Cirencester, Gloucester, and Bath.

Over the fifth and sixth centuries, then, western Europe had changed from an integral structure of Roman provinces to a mosaic of fairly large kingdoms, less unified in the east than in the west, but each dominated by an established Germanic court and ruling class. Of these erstwhile provinces, however, only Britain had ended up beyond the pale, without even a historic link with Rome.

⟡

In the newly ordered western Europe that gradually emerged from the Germanic *Götterdämmerung*,* one feature that remained constant was language. In practice, when the dust and ash from conquering armies and devastated cities cleared in the early eighth century, Latin was the only language left standing. Western Europe was still *Romania*, the land of Romans.[6]

However, for some time, especially during the fifth and sixth centuries,

---

*This, Wagner's translation of the Scandinavian *ragnarøkkr* 'twilight of the gods', is a fittingly Germanic word for what the Romans had foreseen as *occasus saeculi* 'setting of the age'.

the future had appeared very different. Although the Gothic forces that took control of Italy and Rome in this period were set on defending the Roman world, rather than destroying it ("The glory of the Goth is the maintenance of civilization,"[7] as Cassiodorus, minister of the Gothic king Theoderic, put it), they did represent a new power, which might have attracted acolytes, fellow travelers, and perhaps—in time—fellow speakers. We know of a few examples where this began to happen, among the upper classes, in the later fifth century. Sidonius Apollinaris, a Roman aristocrat with estates in Gaul, who had tried in vain to mobilize effective resistance to the Goths in his area, was writing around 465 to an old friend, Syagrius, evincing amazement, and typical Roman snobbery, at his acquired fluency in German: "I can hardly express my astonishment at your speed in picking up a knowledge of German . . . what a joke: I often hear that in your presence a barbarian is afraid of committing a barbarism in his own language. Bowed old Germans fawn on you to interpret their letters and take you as an arbiter and judge in their dealings . . . I only urge you, as a gentleman, to keep a measure in this: hold on to our language to avoid being a laughingstock, even as you practice theirs, for a laugh."[8] Two generations later, well-born Roman children were being brought up in Gothic: the minister Cassiodorus praised Cyprian for his foresight in bringing up his sons this way: "The boys are of Roman stock, yet speak our language, clearly showing the future loyalty that they will hold toward us, whose speech they are now seen to have adopted."[9]

This might have been expected to lead to a language divide between the rulers and the ruled, at the least. But to first appearances, the outcome could well have been far more extreme. Later in this same era (635–37), when Roman (i.e., Greek-ruled) Palestine and Syria were conquered by the Arabs, both the main languages in use, Greek and Aramaic, were swept away, replaced by Arabic. Much the same thing had, after all, happened, though then to the benefit of Latin, when Rome had conquered western Europe in the previous millennium.

In the event, no such change occurred. The numbers of Germans entering Roman territory were never and nowhere preponderant; nor did they have a tendency to grow their communities faster than the Romans. The most substantial figure we have is for the numbers of the Vandal-Alan force embarked from Spain for Africa in 429—claimed by their commander to number eighty thousand males, based on the fleet's logistics; but this was small by comparison with an estimate of the then population of Roman Africa, 3 million. The Visigoths in Spain and southern Gaul are estimated at one hundred thousand.

The population of the western Roman Empire as a whole is estimated to have
been falling at the time, with higher concentrations in Gaul (5 million), Italy
(5 million), and Spain (4.5 million)—precisely where the Franks and Goths
were heading. One can estimate, then, that in the fifth and sixth centuries,
at most half a million Germanic speakers came to settle among 20 million
speakers of Latin: some forty speakers of Latin remained for every one of a
Germanic language, more if Germanic women and children tended to be left
behind.[10]

Nor did the Germans, as they might well, have an ethic that saw themselves as lords of creation, and the Romans as inferiors who might do well to
look up to them. Instead, once established, they seem to have accepted the
rules of the Roman society. They suffered painful disdain from the Romans
when they were forced to mix with them—as witness a supposedly clever comment from Sidonius Apollinaris to a Roman friend: "You shun barbarians
should they have a bad reputation. I shun them even with a good one."[11] But in
response, the dominant Goths and Franks in particular were not set on destruction, but rather reconstruction, even if they expected for themselves a
position of greater honor and power. In words attributed to Athaulf (Gothic
king, 410–15):

> He had at first ardently striven to obliterate the name of Roman and make the
> whole empire Gothic in fact and in word; to speak plainly, Romania would
> have been turned into Gothia and Caesar Augustus into Athaulf. But when
> through long experience he realized that Goths could never obey laws owing
> to their unbridled barbarity, whilst the laws of a state should never be effaced,
> since without them there is no state worthy of the name, he had chosen at
> least to seek glory for himself by using Gothic strength to restore and pro-
> mote the Roman name, to be considered by posterity the architect of a Rome
> restored, since he could not change it.[12]

It is difficult to know how seriously to take this Roman report of a Germanic king's admission that his race should know its place. But such testimony
is not isolated: on a tombstone in southern Gaul, two Germans abjectly noted
that the stain of their race had been washed away through baptism.[13]

But a large part of the reason for the loss of Germanic *Gemeinschaft* 'community' and hence Germanic languages within *Romania*, the old Roman
domain, must have been the demise of the Germans' own Arian churches.
Christian faith, with its rituals observed and its texts recited in Latin, was to

prove the great survivor through the time of massive tribal upheavals that began in the fifth century. Civil administration, the Roman tax base, and the
easy circulation of mass-produced goods may have been eroded and eventually
swept away, but the rock on which Christ had famously built his Church stood
firm. As the annual sequence of plowing, sowing, reaping, and threshing confirmed the identity of farmers and laborers, so the regular observance of religious services in Latin kept vivid the eternal verities of life and language in
their hearts and on their lips.

When the invaders finally settled down, to rule—as they had previously
pillaged—through military prowess, the rhythm of religious observance was
largely respected. The one major German tribe that had not previously been
Christian, the Franks, from northern Germany, were content (in 496) to accept baptism into the Roman Catholic Church—which meant liturgical use of
Latin. But the Goths, and most other Germans of Arian belief, would initially
set up their own, separate churches, with their own hierarchies, worshipping
in their own languages, perhaps seeing this religious divide as a useful mark
of their separate identity from their subjects. Only the Vandals, who after two
decades of wild progress through Gaul and Spain established their permanent
kingdom in Carthage, were determined to persecute their African Catholic
subjects and did so almost without remission for a century (439–534).

In situations like this, conquerors who are self-consciously a minority are
keen to avoid being assimilated and hence disappearing. They typically appeal
to the law. Consider the Manchus who conquered China starting in 1644, also
no more than 2 percent of the population. They were forbidden by law from
intermarrying with Chinese or adopting Chinese customs and were compulso-
rily educated in Manchu. (Nevertheless, within 150 years all those of Manchu
ancestry were speaking Chinese.)[14] And likewise after two centuries in Dublin,
the Anglo-French Normans in Ireland passed in 1364 the Statutes of Kilkenny,
with the clause:

> Also it is ordained and established that every Englishman do use the English
> language, and be named by an English name, leaving off entirely the manner
> of naming used by the Irish; and that every Englishman use the English cus-
> tom, fashion, mode of riding and apparel, according to his estate . . .

In similar circumstances, in 484 (after two generations of Vandal rule in Africa), King Huneric ordered that no one in Vandal dress should enter a Catholic church—a ruling that was said to have caused special difficulty for the

Roman Catholic servants in Vandal households. But their significant presence reminds us that chatter in Latin would have been the constant background noise in the nurseries of the rising generation of Vandal nobility.[15]

In the end, the disappearance of these distinctively German churches was as often a military event as a religious or a social one. After their century of rule in Africa—and despite the bishops' complaints, it had been a century of economic recovery, probably due to the lower tax burden[16]—the aggressively Arian Vandals had fallen in 534 to an invading army from Constantinople; trade might suffer, but the Latin Mass would no longer be opposed in Carthage, and the Arian rite no longer celebrated. By the end of the seventh century, all the other Arian churches in Europe had either been conquered by Catholic powers or voluntarily dissolved: the Burgundians in south-central Gaul were conquered in 534 by the Franks, the Ostrogoths in northern Italy in 563 after a sustained massive onslaught from the eastern Roman Empire, which for a time reclaimed Italy and southern Spain. More pacifically, the Visigoths in Spain were brought to Catholicism by their own king Reccared in 587; and the Lombards, the new Germanic power in northern Italy from 572, were split from the first between Catholics and Arians, the Roman-leaning Catholics gradually gaining ascendancy in the seventh century. When the Lombards gave themselves a legal code in 643, the *edictum Rothari*, it was written in Latin, replacing their Germanic *cadarfada*, which had been preserved through oral tradition.[17]

The shock of Germanic conquest was a common theme in the literature of the time, as witness these self-pitying words of Orosius:

> [If I may be permitted a personal reference] I saw the barbarians at first as unknowns, I avoided them as hostiles, I flattered them as masters, I begged them even as infidels, I shunned them as tricksters, in the end when they chased me into the sea and attacked me with rocks and darts, and had almost got me in their clutches, I took advantage of a sudden mist and escaped, wishing that all who heard of it should be moved to tears, but grieved silently at those who felt no grief, thinking of the harshness of those who do not believe whatever they have not themselves suffered.[18]

But even though the Germans' all-dominating military forces had been commanded and led in their home languages, and their leaders became landowners out of all proportion to their numbers, nevertheless the literate structures by which civil society was still ordered—tax collection, trade, and business—remained in Latin. As Germanic society settled down, and the armies were dissolved, only their churches remained as centers for a distinctive German identity. When they too were dissolved, German status and the Germanic languages went with them.

Catholic Christianity ultimately proved the most significant institution throughout this period: it sustained the identity, and language, of the Romans' descendants in the centuries after the Empire's defenses collapsed, even when their temporal rulers found it impossible to defend fixed borders or define a clear law of succession. Through their Church, they remained Romans; and their religion reminded them to speak Latin.

❖

But there is a curious exception to this story of massive linguistic continuity, which throws a sidelight on the factors at play: the tribes that invaded Britain did succeed, alone among Germans, in imposing their language in the fifth and sixth centuries. Britain had been a Roman province almost as long as Gaul, and yet it was swiftly reconfigured in the linguistic image of its invaders.

Britain, for all its four centuries as a Roman province, had always been considered marginal. Since before its conquest under the emperor Claudius in AD 43, *Britannia* had been a byword for remoteness. A century later, the satirist Juvenal was still linking it with "farthest Thule." Except as a source of tin to make pewter plate and bronze weaponry—and exotic glory for the then presiding emperor—the Romans' decision to invade the island must long have seemed a poor one. The northern parts were never subdued and, despite massive investment in Hadrian's and Antonine's walls, required serious guarding for centuries. Florus penned a telling little verse at the time of Hadrian's visit in AD 120:

EGO NOLO CAESAR ESSE | AMBVLARE PER BRITANNOS | SCYTHICAS PATI PRVINAS

I'm glad I'm not Caesar | On tour in Britain | Suffering from its Scythian frosts

The reputation of Britain as a hardship posting persisted. In later years, it became notorious as a place to send exiles, a hotbed of disloyalty to Rome, and (in perhaps natural consequence) a nursery of would-be emperors. In the sixth century AD, Gildas was to comment that the Britons had been to the Romans "neither brave in battle nor faithful in peace." The province was de facto independent from 286 to 296 under two rebellious generals, Carausius and Allectus, but then reclaimed for Rome. In 312 Constantine had launched from Britain his successful play for Rome itself; in the second half of the fourth century five more generals were to attempt the same, prompting Jerome's quip that Britain was "a province fertile in tyrants." But it was also fertile in something else: finally, in the latter fourth century, Britain rewarded its conquerors: it became the breadbasket for the western Empire.[19]

Strangely, in the historical record there is no clear sign of what language the British had been speaking before English replaced it. Preconquest Britain, to judge from the names of its leaders, had spoken a language much like continental Gaulish; yet there is little evidence that Latin ever trickled down to become the usual language of the common people in Britain, as it did in Gaul. Evidence of any kind is scarce in Britain, where (again unlike Gaul) there is no trace of any literacy in the pre-Roman language; after the conquest, documents do survive—curiously focused on the cursing of undetected thieves—but all are in Latin.

> Honoratus to the holy god Mercury: I complain to your divinity that I have lost two wheels and four cows and many small belongings from my house. I would ask the genius of your divinity that you do not allow health to the person who has done me wrong, nor allow him to lie or sit or drink or eat, whether he is man or woman, boy or girl, slave or free, unless he bring my property to me and be reconciled with me. With renewed prayers I ask your divinity that my petition may immediately make me vindicated by your majesty.[20]

Politically severed from the Empire in the early fifth century, Britain was left in fact to fend for itself, in a way that no other province was. It is hard to believe, though, that the governing classes of Britain, with four hundred years of Romanization behind them, would have accepted invading Germans as their superiors any more easily than their peers did in Gaul, Italy, and Spain. Nevertheless, cut off as they were from Rome, from its tax collectors, its trade routes, and its bishops, as well as its armies, they may have had less to bargain with than those peers had. When the historical record recommenced after a break of two centuries (around 597, with Pope Gregory's mission to Canterbury), Latin-speaking Christian landowners, living in Roman villas, were no more; pottery was home-produced, and coinage had become treasure rather than a commonly used means of exchange. Above all, the clear, and unique, fact of the use of a new vernacular, English, shows that in this province something very different had happened from the fate of all the others.

Basically, there are three possible explanations for this unique surge in the linguistic fortunes of the Germanic invaders in Britain, an outcome quite unlike their linguistic submergence everywhere else in western Europe. One possibility is that they succeeded in overwhelming the natives and recruiting them into their Germanic settlements. A second is that the native Britons suddenly became thin on the ground in precisely this period, leaving the country essentially empty for Germanic speakers. A third is that the Britons included a large, perhaps even a dominant, population who already spoke a Germanic language.

Against the suggestion that the invasion was more a peaceable social transformation of Celts under Germanic leadership than a storm of rapine and aggression, there are some clear contemporary statements: Gildas after all—who knew them—referred to the invaders as "those ferocious Saxons of unspeakable name hateful to God and men."[21] And a population that considered itself superior (as Romans, even recent ex-Romans, always did) would not have easily accepted cultural or linguistic reeducation from their perceived inferiors. It had also long been assumed that the population was much lower in Britain than other Roman provinces, at most eight hundred thousand, faced with say one hundred thousand Germanic invaders, thus making the task of recuitment, and language replacement, less infeasible. But Britain's late reputation as a granary province—in an era long before capital-intensive farming—also argues that it must have had a substantial workforce. More recent archaeological surveys too have revised these estimates upward, putting late-Roman Britain's population on a par with that quantifiable in the Norman Domesday Book (of 1086), at 2 million or more. British density was still much lower than that south of the Channel; but even so, how could such a large incumbent people be subdued and assimilated by marauders whom they outnumbered twenty to one?[22]

In fact, recent genetic evidence tends to confirm the prima facie view that English speakers do not in the main descend from Celts who were converted or recruited out of their Roman ways. Comparing the pattern of Y-chromosome DNA from samples in a line across from Anglesey to Friesland, a recent study found that Welshmen were to this day clearly distinct from those in central England, but that the English and Frisian samples were so similar that they pointed to a common origin of 50 to 100 percent of the (male) population.[23] Where, then, did the millions of Britons living in southern and eastern Britain go? Genocide on a national scale seems unlikely, and even widespread enslavement would not have bleached out the long-term population record in this way (unless British males were largely denied any chance of having children).

The apparent fact of a population collapse by the Celts is much more suggestive of an epidemic, and this is just what seems to have happened. Bubonic plague, the "Great Plague of Justinian," had started around 532 in Egypt and spread through the Middle East and the Mediterranean basin in the following years, reaching Turkey, Constantinople, and Greece in AD 541–42. (It was described by Procopius in his *Persian War*, written in 550.) Around 547, a generation or two after the great battles of Badon and Dyrham, with central Britain still reeling from the Saxon advance, the plague would have entered Britain, along trade routes from the Mediterranean. Britain (the west and center of the island) would have been hit far harder than England (the southeast), because only Britain maintained trade links with the Empire. Saxons did not consort with Britons and, outside the established Roman towns and cities, may have been more thinly spread.

In this same year a *mortālitās magna* did indeed hit Ireland, according to the Annals of Ulster, devastating the aristocracy. According to the *Annales Cambriae*, Maelgwn, a famous king of Gwynedd in southern Wales, also died in 547 or 549, in a plague that affected both Ireland and Britain. Besides this direct evidence, the Arthurian cycle of heroic stories, conceived in this period, seems to contain an echo of just such a devastating event. The horrors of the disease, and the depopulation it would have caused, make sense as the inspiration for the legend of the Waste Land, in which hunger (from untended farms) and military defeat swept the land, the king suffering from a mysterious sore in the groin—as with bubonic plague. Entering in the aftermath of a devastating plague, the Saxons were effectively granted a walkover.[24]

But in these troublous times of population changeover, another underlying fact about the British population may have been even more crucial. This brings up the third possibility, which is quite compatible with the first and second, but perhaps more significant than either for the origin of English itself.

The traditional assumption that Britain's indigenous population before the Roman and Saxon invasions was purely Celtic (Welsh-speaking) may itself have been wrong. Recent linguistic and genetic studies[25] suggest that when the coastal regions of northwestern Europe—in Friesland, Denmark,

Norway, and Sweden—had received their (Germanic-speaking) population, a fair number of them had settled beyond the North Sea in Britain too. Some literary evidence also bears this out. In their brief comments on the British, both Julius Caesar and Tacitus noted a significant difference in type between coastal and inland British populations. Julius Caesar wrote:

> The interior of Britain is inhabited by those of whom they say the tradition is that they were indigenous to the island; the coastlands by people who had crossed from the Belgae's territory for plunder and war; almost all these tribes kept their original names when they settled down after the war . . .[26]

Of the Belgae, he had also remarked:

> When Caesar asked the Remi what states were under arms, their power and military capabilities, he was told that most of the Belgae were of German origin and, having early crossed the Rhine, had settled there on account of the richness of the land and had expelled the Gaulish inhabitants . . .[27]

Tacitus added:

> Who were the original inhabitants of Britain, whether indigenous or foreign, is as usual among barbarians, little known . . . The red hair and large limbs of Caledonians [in modern Scotland] indicate a German origin. The dark complexion of the Silures, their usually curly hair . . . are evidence that Iberians anciently crossed over to settle here. Those who live nearest to the Gauls are also like them . . . The language differs but little.[28]

Since no ancient author ever recognized the major linguistic divide between Gaulish and Germanic languages, this last could be taken as evidence that the Belgae in the southeast of Britain spoke a Germanic language, like their cousins on the Continent.

Roman Britain has left behind no direct evidence in inscriptions of the languages spoken by the non-Roman population; so in essence this is as far as the evidence goes. But in sum, the invaders could have found already sizable Germanic, proto-English communities settled in the eastern and southern parts of the island. If so, it is less surprising that, with the Roman-connected population in the west hit hard by plague, Germanic-speaking communities expanded to dominate the whole of central Britain, boosted as they were by Frisian, Saxon, and other Germanic invaders speaking closely related languages.

◈

Events in the other provinces where Latin was spoken were complicated and extended by the fact that other invaders became involved, overrunning lands that Goths and Vandals had for some time held—the Arabs and Berbers in Africa and Iberia, the Slavs in the Goths' erstwhile homeland of the Balkans. The outcome of these invasions is difficult to describe in simple terms. Although as a political unit the Greek-speaking eastern Empire was to survive for a millennium longer than the Roman Empire in the west, the Latin language after invasions proved sometimes to a surprising degree more robust than Greek—and this even when confronting the same conquerors.

Despite the collapse of government from Rome, for the duration of the seventh century the southwestern provinces of the Empire remained Latin-speaking. In Iberia, the Visigoths, who had by then confessionally been Catholic for two generations, had finally expelled in 631 their fellow Christians, the Byzantines, from their last redoubts on the southern coasts of the Algarve and Andalusia; while north Africa itself had been under renewed "Roman," i.e., Byzantine, rule since the expulsion of the Vandals in 534.

But this century was to be the last—after 850 years—in which government in Africa was exercised in Latin. The second surge of the Muslim expansion was beginning, carrying the new faith, and with it religious use of Arabic, from one end of the Mediterranean to the other. This onslaught had begun in the conversion of the Berbers to the west of Egypt. But like Muhammad's Arabs, these desert peoples developed into a formidable fighting force, once inspired by the new, righteous, motive of a *jihād* to guarantee their raids and serial conquests on unprecedented scale. In 698 they took Carthage, capital of Roman north Africa, and in 711 they had crossed the Strait of Gibraltar, defeating King Roderik in one decisive battle, and within three years completing the conquest of Iberia (except for the narrrow northern strip of Asturias).

This single decade was enough to determine the utter elimination of Latin from north Africa. Much of the populace had in any case spoken Berber from time immemorial; but it is perhaps surprising that the cardinal Christian center of Carthage and its surrounding cities yielded so smartly to the new elite, accepting the Koran in Arabic and special taxes on non-Muslims, where they had previously known only Catholic Christian scriptures, and Roman administrative documents, expressed in Latin.

In Iberia—which for the next eight hundred years was to be known as el-Andalūs—the outcome must have seemed to contemporaries equally final. Christian claims to the land were ineffectual and ignored, as for several centuries it became the theater of competitive wars between different tribes of Berbers. Culturally, the Muslims established themselves in style, and the city of Cordoba especially became one of their treasures, marked out as one home of poetry in Arabic. At the summit of their influence, in 929, Emir 'Abd el-Rahman III considered himself strong and magnificent enough to declare a claim, as "Commander of the Faithful," to be true caliph of all Islam. Linguistically, the elite naturally spoke Arabic, and the armed forces Berber. Use of Latin among others—known as Mozarabs or *musta'rib* 'arabized'—seems to have survived, but weakened, along with Catholic Christianity—which, as usual in Islamic countries, was never banned, although non-Muslims were subject to a special tax; their rights were restricted (e.g., Christians were not allowed to own Muslim slaves and were in later centuries forbidden from building new churches); and hence there was a continuing tendency for Mozarabs to migrate northward into Christian-held territory. Under the Muslim dispensation, society was segmented by religion, while maintaining the Islamic umma in a distinct position of leadership, a trick that had eluded the Goths and Arianism. There was also the demographic advantage that, of the three major faiths, Islam, Christianity, and Judaism, only Islam permitted mixed marriages (for Muslim husbands), whose issue would themselves become Muslim.[29]

Some conversion spread through all levels of society in the eighth and ninth centuries, but then a wholesale switch to Islam occurred in the tenth.[30] Spain had become overwhelmingly a country of *muladí*, people of mixed Spanish and Arab/Berber origin. It is suggested that Latin, or the Romance language into which it was turning, had almost died out in the Muslim realms by the twelfth century, being replaced not by classical but by *Andalusī* Arabic.[31] (And unlike Arabic in contemporary Iran, which was always said to be "of the best"—thus showing that it never spread beyond elite circles who learned it formally—the dialectal nature of this Spanish Arabic shows that the language had been taken up in earnest by the people.)

As such, the fate of Latin in Spain (as in north Africa) should have been totally on a par with what happened to the languages of the eastern Mediterranean—as a result of the same Muslim onslaught. Something about the Muslim proposition made it highly effective in long-term acculturation. Within two centuries of the conquest, Greek and Aramaic, each a foundation of elite communication and common conversation all over the Near East for a thousand to fifteen hundred years, had been reduced to the speech of small isolated communities, as Arabic took their place in every major function.

Yet, amazingly in Iberia, from their bridgehead in Asturias and the Basque country, Christians from the north were gradually able to reclaim the land for their faith, and for their language. It would take many centuries of campaigning and population growth, unlike the Arab conquest, which had been over in decade. But Christian kingdoms grew stronger in León and Navarre in the west, and later in Castile and Aragon in the center and east. Toledo fell in 1085, bringing half the peninsula to the Christians. A new force of Berbers, the Almoravids, was then called in to redress the balance between Christian and Muslim. But after a long respite, the tide continued to run against Islam: Cordoba fell in 1236 and Seville in 1248. By this time more than 90 percent of Iberia was in Christian hands, and a kind of modus vivendi between Christians and Muslims set in for some two centuries, the *reconquista* not being completed until the capture of Granada in 1492.

Although reciprocal tolerance of Muslims (as of Jews) was at first offered in Christian domains, in practice these rights were steadily eroded. In addition, extreme action was taken to eliminate Arabic speech for at least the next three generations after the fall of Granada, starting (in 1501 and 1511) with the banning of ownership of all books in the language. Even in 1566 Philip II still found it important enough to decree that within three years all Moors must speak Castilian Spanish only, not Arabic.

In Iberia then, Latin did not so much survive as grow back, its fortunes—here as everywhere in medieval Europe—strongly linked to those of the Catholic Church, and the population of Christian Spain, which had been growing faster than the Muslims since the later eleventh century.[32] Islam had shown that it could be the equal of the Church in a peaceable society, and in this it held the key to the undoing of Latin. But in Spain, its armies had not ultimately been able to withstand those of Christendom. In north Africa, by contrast, where no reconquest was ever attempted, religious identities, and with them the availability of future languages, were permanently redefined by those invading Muslims of 698.

Meanwhile, at the eastern end of the Roman world, other Latin speakers were also endangered in the fifth to seventh centuries, by the Slav invasions of the provinces of Dalmatia and Moesia. These territories (which correspond to the areas of the former Yugoslavia, and Bulgaria) were long-term Roman provinces, unchallenged since Trajan had conquered the whole area of the Balkans in AD 106–7. But in the sixth century, the Slavs took possession of the arterial route from Aquileia on the Adriatic to Constantinople, the road that had kept this part of the Empire, alone in the east, strongly linked to Latin-speaking Italy.

In fact, very little can be said of the detailed effect of the Slav migrations in the Balkans, since they were only seriously documented when they made their impact farther south, among the Greeks themselves. It was a time of great turmoil, since the Slavs were only the last in a series of incursions: from Germanic-speaking Goths in 378, Turkic-speaking Huns in 441–47, Germanic Ostrogoths in 479–82, and Turkic-speaking Bulgars in 493. Fifty years later, the Byzantine historian Procopius recounted:

> Illyricum and all of Thrace, i.e., the whole country from the Ionian Gulf [the Adriatic] to the outskirts of Byzantium, including Greece and the Chersonese, was overrun almost every year by Huns, Slavs, and Antae, from the time when Justinian became Roman emperor [viz 527], and they wrought untold damage among the inhabitants of those parts. For I believe that in each invasion more than two hundred thousand Romans were killed or captured.[33]

The Balkans were evidently lightly populated, and indeed ill-defended, areas of the Empire, and had Latin not survived the onslaught of the Slavs, this would have needed little explanation. Yet somehow, some vestige of Latin did survive in this area, even though little other trace of Roman traditions seems to have come through the turmoil. *Bláxoi hodîtai* 'Vlach nomads' prowled the northern marches of the Empire, up until the eleventh century. And there were surviving Romance speakers (known to the Greeks as *Rhōmânoi*) up and down the Dalmatian coast until the beginning of the twentieth century.[34] There are loanwords from Latin in all the languages of the region. Albanian shows distinctive influence in the realm of kinship terms: *prind* from *parentem* 'father', *emtë* from *amita* 'paternal aunt', *fat* from *fatum* 'spouse', originally 'fate', *ndrikullë* from *matricula* 'godmother'. Slavic languages have borrowed building terminology: e.g., Serbo-Croat *kal* from *calx* 'limestone', *komin* from *caminus* 'forge', *kòsao* from *casale* 'hovel'.[35] Above all, modern Rumanian is a remnant of the Latin once spoken in this region, although its current territory is well to the north of the Roman border, the river Danube.

Perhaps, once again, some of the nomadic invaders had abandoned their language in an area where they faced a more organized culture, and specifically the Roman Catholic Church. But more likely, when the turmoil of repeated invasions had ensued (and it would continue sporadically until the final inroad of the Mongols in 1242), few groups succeeded in any settled life at all. Rather, small groups had survived as best they could, either in villages or nomadically, and among them, against all the odds, there remained some communities of Latin speakers.

⟡

So Latin too, in this period of tumult after the collapse of the Empire in the west, can be recognized as a beneficiary of that same "Shield of Faith" that has protected so many languages in troubled times: a religious tradition has sustained a language that would otherwise have been lost, along with the culture of which it is the vehicle.

Evidently, a minimum precondition for any survival is the maintenance of an adequate population of speakers. As the case of Roman Britain showed, when that fails, a community under pressure may be shattered, and its religious and linguistic traditions annihilated. When absolute numbers fail, a community cannot defend itself, nor, importantly in the longer term, renew itself. A disease like the plague also tends to have a particularly severe effect in cities and high-density settlements, thus tending to wipe out political and social leaders, who might have been able to organize their communities in these times of stress, rather than let the weak die, and the survivors merge with stronger surrounding social groups.*

But if the population holds up, a religious link can be crucial in maintaining a community in the presence of a more powerful, and even a more numerous,

---

*This is what seems to have also happened in the next great epidemic stress on Britain, the Black Death, which struck repeatedly eight centuries later. It told particularly against the elite populations in courts, cities, and monasteries, and so discriminated de facto against any distinctive language that they spoke: curiously, by the fourteenth century, this was once again Latin (along with Norman and Angevin French). In this case, though, there was no competing society of invaders like the Saxons who could step in to take over as the holders of past power tottered and fell. When the Black Death receded, people from the countryside—typically less educated speakers of English only—found their labor much more in demand and took the vacant jobs. Use of Latin and French at court, in the law, and in the Church never recovered. For the second time, bubonic plague had asserted the role of English in the island of Britain.

ambient society; and such a community may well also sustain a distinctive language. The history of the Old World and the New is rife with examples.

The most famous example of community survival is the Jewish diaspora. This has not only preserved Hebrew as its sacred language, but also a number of other languages that the Jewish community has carried from one part of the world to another, such as Judezmo (Judeo-Spanish) in the Balkans and around the Mediterranean, and Yiddish (Jewish German) in eastern Europe. Furthermore, the Khazar empire, a Turkic state of nomadic origin that converted en masse to Judaism around AD 800 has preserved to this day its faith, and its Turkic language, in the Karaim community of Lithuania.

Many Christian sects too have preserved languages. Nestorian Christians spread Aramaic-speaking communities along the Silk Route for well over a millennium, from Urfa and Nusaybin in the Near East to Karakorum in Mongolia and Chang-an (Xian) in China. The Coptic Church in Egypt retained, in the midst of Arab Muslim rule, the use of its ancient language as a vernacular for almost a thousand years, before seeing it regress to the status of a purely liturgical language in the latter half of the second millennium. An Armenian merchant community preserved its language in Poland from the eleventh to the seventeenth century, until the union of the Armenian Church with the Roman Catholic Church; Armenian then died out in the eighteenth century. And in the United States, the nineteenth- and twentieth-century Amish have continued the use of German (also known as Pennsylvania Dutch) in small, isolated communities totally surrounded by English-speaking areas.[36]

In fact, when any language community is set under the domination of an elite who speak a different tongue, the attitude of religious authorities to the language's role in worship may be critical to the long-term survival of the language. After the Welsh language was barred from an official use in court and government in 1536 and 1542, only the translation of the Bible into Welsh in 1588 saved it as a literate medium. Later, arguably, the very different linguistic attitudes and practices of the predominant churches in Wales and in Ireland during the eighteenth and nineteenth centuries laid the foundation for the fundamental difference in speaker strength between those two languages that exists today: Welsh Nonconformist chapels would function fully in Welsh, while the Roman Catholic bishops were content to staff Irish parishes with priests quite ignorant of Irish.[37]

And so it was well for Latin that Christianity had adopted it in the second and third centuries and ultimately came, in the fourth, to identify its congregation with the Roman world (a world that was mistaken—as ever—for the world as a whole). Latin had sustained the ideal of *Romanitas* when the Church had fatally supplanted loyalty to the emperor. But when the borders of *Romanitas* were overrun, it was the Roman Church that sustained Latin. First Latin, then the Church itself, had become the *vinculum unitatis*, the bond that would unite all the Romans.

> BAPTISMVS IGITVR VINCVLVM VNITATIS SACRAMENTALE
> CONSTITVIT VIGENS INTER OMNES QVI PER ILLVM
> REGENERATI SVNT.
>
> Baptism then forms the sacramental bond of unity, which thrives
> among all who are reborn through it.
>
> Catechism of the Catholic Church, 1271

CHAPTER 10

Ultra vires—
Beyond the Limits of Empire

*[lingua] Latinorum, quae meditatione scripturarum ceteris
omnibus est facta communis*

[the tongue] of the Latins, which through the study of the Scriptures has
become common to all

Bede (writing of Britain in the early eighth century)
Historia Ecclesiastica Gentis Anglorum, i.1

U SE OF LATIN CAME to be extended far beyond the limits of the erstwhile Roman Empire. This expansion began through the individual
missionary activities of some heroic churchmen. But it continued because of
the politicial and military ambitions of German kingdoms to expand their
domains to the east. And there was a tendency for the faith, especially as planted
in the British Isles, to spread as through a contagion, as converts turned to
missionaries in their own right. Roman Christianity always entailed the sacred
use of the language, and Latin thereby became the language of learning among
peoples whose natural languages included Irish, English, German, Polish,
Hungarian, Norse, Latvian, and Estonian. The only effective limits to this
expansion were reached when German conquerors came into contact with
lands of eastern Orthodox Christianity, simultaneously being spread (usually
by international diplomacy) northward from Constantinople.

The first known missionary to Ireland was Palladius, sent from Rome in
the early fifth century.[1] More significant was Patricius (better known as St. Pat-
rick), who, later in that century, was kidnapped as a child from the Scots borders
and sold into slavery in Ireland; he escaped, but later returned there on his own
initiative to spread the Gospel. A few generations later, the monastery of Iona in

the Hebrides was founded by the Donegal Irishman Colmcille (glossed as *Co-lumba* 'dove') around 563, and from there Christianity was gradually reintroduced into Britain, with an early base at Lindisfarne (643) on the coast of Northumbria. (The Saxon invasions, and perhaps the British revolt, of the fifth century had largely swept aside the Church as planted during the Empire.)

Columba's Latin, like much of the "Hiberno-Latin" of the time, was obscure and gratuitously overwrought, often peppered with Latinized Greek and Hebrew, suggesting not only that it was still a struggle for writers to compose in it, but also that native canons of *filidecht* 'bardship' were enriching the tradition. It seems that for them the difficulty of classical learning was part of its point. They seem never to have read, or at least accepted, the famous maxim of Horace: ARS EST CELARE ARTEM 'the art lies in hiding the art'. Here are the first few lines of a long hymn attributed to Columba, which in twenty-two verses, each beginning with a successive letter of the alphabet, contrives a summary of the Christian faith, with heavy emphasis on the punishment of sinners in hell. Its Latin is just as stilted as my translation.

Altus prosator, vetustus	High fore-sower, aged
dierum et ingenitus	of days and unbegotten,
erat absque origine	was outwith origin
primordii et crepidine,	of beginning and the abyss,
est et erit in saecula	is and will be in ages
saeculorum infinita . . .	of ages unending . . .

And here the second coming of Christ is laboriously prefigured in the skies:

. . . girans certis ambagibus	. . . gyring with certain vagaries
redit priscis reditibus,	he returns with former returns
oriens post biennium,	rising after two years,
Vesperugo in vesperum;	the Evening Star in evening,
sumpta in problematibus	[these are] taken as puzzles
tropicis intellectibus	with figurative meanings.

Simultaneously, there was missionary activity into the south of the country sponsored by Rome, beginning with the arrival of the pope's emissary Augustine in 597. The contending influences of Roman and Irish missionaries in southern England are marked in styles of handwriting, and it was the Irish script which prevailed.[2] Soon a student like Aldhelm (ca 640–710) could receive an education in the West Country at Malmesbury from the Irishman Maeldubh, then move to Canterbury for higher studies (law, meter, astronomy, and *computus**) under the Roman Gratianus. The competition that developed between the two traditions was settled—in favor of Rome—at the Synod of Whitby in 664.[†]

One effect of vernacular English on Anglo-Latin culture is clear in the prevalence of riddles, an Anglo-Saxon speciality that it would be nice to think still echoes in the modern crossword. Here is one of Aldhelm's, written in hexameter verse. (The answer is *arca libraria*, a book box.)

> *Nunc mea diuinis complentur uiscera uerbis*
> *totaque sacratos gestant praecordia biblos;*
> *at tamen ex isdem nequeo cognoscere quicquam:*
> *infelix fato fraudabor munere tali,*
> *dum tollunt dirae librorum lumina Parcae.*

> Now my bowels are filled with divine words
> and my whole breast carries hallowed tomes;
> but still from the same I cannot learn anything:
> unhappily I am cheated of such a gift by fate,
> while the dread Fates take the lights of the books.

In the next generation the English grammarian Wynfrith (around 675–754), renamed in Latin by Pope Gregory II as Boniface (*Bonifatius* 'well-fated'), took the faith eastward, preaching to the Germans beyond the Rhine, and famously felling the holy oak sacred to Thor at Fritzlar in Hessen in 727, to build a chapel out of its timbers.[3] By the time he died, martyred on a mission to Frisia in the north, there were bishoprics all over Germany, under the authority of his

---

*Arithmetical studies, culminating in techniques for calculating the date of Easter.
†Missions planted abroad could also have offshoots closer to home. Those in Ireland came to benefit continental Christianity itself, since from the end of the sixth century until the mid-ninth there continued a tradition of *peregrinatio pro Christo*, whereby missionary "White Martyrs" made their way from Ireland to the Continent. Irish Christianity had by then had 150 years to develop, while education had become scarce in the realms of Franks and Burgundians, and northern Italy was disrupted by the campaigns of the Lombards. The White Martyrs founded monasteries all over eastern France, western Germany, Switzerland, and down the length of Italy. The one who went farthest was Cathal, elected bishop of Taranto in the heel of Italy ca 666, now better known as San Cataldo.

Tenth-century drawing of Charlemagne (left) with his son Pippin the Hunchback. Charlemagne was the first Frankish king with an empire large enough to recall Rome's domain.

archbishopric at Mainz (Roman *Moguntiacum*). Only the northerly Saxon kingdoms were still holding out for paganism, to be crushed by Charlemagne and his Catholic Franks in the last decades of the century. (But in the way of the world, it would be from Saxony that a successor German empire would arise a century later—militantly Catholic, and nostalgically Roman in aspiration.)

Farther north, in Scandinavia, there had been scattered missions since 700. Another Englishman, the Northumbrian Willebrord, had withdrawn to Denmark after being expelled (like so many other missionaries) from Frisia. But no lasting Christian presence was established there. In the next century, Charlemagne had got no closer than setting up a church in Hamburg, but his son Ludwig the Pious strongly supported Ansgar (801–65), bishop of Hamburg-Bremen, who led missions to Denmark and Sweden throughout his life, laying the foundations for permanent Christianization. It took another two centuries, however, for the faith to spread widely, not least because it was bloodily resisted by many of the kings there. Christianity, after all, represented foreign influence from Rome—cultural, and by implication possibly political. Denmark was in fact only finally converted when its king Sweyn Forkbeard, previously a determined heathen, conquered the serenely Christian realm of England in 1013 and came himself to accept baptism; his son Cnut (reigning 1019–35) completed the conversion of Denmark with the help of English priests and monks. Southern Sweden too was largely secured in the same era by the exertions of Sigfrid, another missionary from England, who converted its King Olof around 1018.

In the continental domains abutting Germany, power politics was to prove ultimately at least as significant for Christianization as conscientious preaching. In the tenth century, after five generations of Christianity, most of Germany stood united politically. Its Saxon emperors Otto I–III (reigning 936–1002) not only conceived themselves as successors of Charlemagne, but intended to excel him: Otto III's conscious aim would be nothing less than the *renovatio imperii Romanorum*. This was the origin of the Holy Roman Empire. To judge from the Saxon monk Widukind's account of Otto I's coronation at Aachen (Charlemagne's old capital), the Christian part of his duties was impressed upon him from the first:

> *Accipe hunc gladium, quo eicias omnes Christi adversarios, barbaros et malos Christianos, auctoritate divina tibi tradita omni potestate totius imperii Francorum, ad firmissimam pacem omnium Christianorum.*

> Take this sword, with which to cast out all enemies of Christ, the barbarians and the bad Christians, by the divine authority given to you [and] every power of the whole empire of the Franks, to the strongest peace of all Christians.[4]

Besides annexing northern Italy as the key part of the plan, the empire became a powerful force for the spreading of the Roman faith—and hence by implication, the use of Latin—eastward into central Europe. In its administration too, far more than in the feudal west, bishops played the key roles. The German empire's political aspiration to be the new Rome would fail, undermined and discredited by its long-running dispute with the papacy in the twelfth century over which had the right of "investiture" (the appointment of bishops). But its Christianization (and Latinization) of the east was to prove lasting.

The western Slavs, in Austria, Bohemia, Moravia, and Croatia, had briefly been a part of Charlemagne's Frankish empire from 796 to 846, and German priests had begun the (Roman) Christianization of the region. But in 863 the Kingdom of Great Moravia chose to assert its newfound independence by inviting (Greek) Orthodox missionaries from Constantinople. It received the famous brothers St. Cyril and St. Methodius, who diplomatically instituted a vernacular service (and the first Slavic literacy, using their new invention, the Glagolitic script), but arranged a concordat with Rome.* In 880, Pope John VIII wrote to

---

*It was in just this period (865) that the Byzantine emperor Michael III was calling Latin a "barbarian and Scythian language" to Pope Nicholas I. (See page 90.)

Svątopluk, king of the Moravians, "In all the churches of your land the Gospel must be read in Latin because of its greater dignity, and afterward it should be announced to those who do not understand Latin words in the Slav language, as seems to be done in some churches . . . If you and your judges wish . . . we recommend that you celebrate the rites of the Mass in Latin." By 885, Pope Stephen V was attempting to restrict use of the Slavic liturgy.[5]

However, in the last decade of the ninth century, central Europe was disrupted by a massive warlike invasion of Magyars, nomads from the east. They hit the Moravian kingdom hard and it collapsed, taking with it the vernacular (Slavic) Church. In the aftermath, German influence was reasserted, and so was the Latin liturgy.

Moravia had already made the first missionary attempts to reach into Bohemia (to its west) and Poland (to its north), but had encountered stiff opposition, even though preaching was supplemented by some key dynastic marriages of Christian brides, and then by large-scale immigration of the Moravian elite after the collapse. Now in the tenth century, sustained military and political pressure from Otto I's Holy Roman Empire established the Latin rite not only in these lands, but even among the recently nomadic Magyars themselves. Otto III was able to set the crown on three generations' work. In 983 an archbishopric was established in Prague, in 1000 at Griezno (Gnesen) in northern Poland, and in 1001 at Gran (Esztergom) on the Danube in western Hungary. In 1027 King Mieszko II of Poland was told that the Poles could use their own language "as well as Latin" in a missive that even contains some enthusiasm for linguistic diversity: "Who has gathered so many languages for the praise of God?" But in 1080, Pope Gregory VII would by contrast refuse permission for Bohemia to celebrate its Masses in Slavic. It is clear that the Church pressed strongly for the widespread use of Latin in these new dioceses.[6]

The language became firmly established in worship and for learning, as in lands to the west. Soon native chroniclers were writing in it, notably Cosmas (Bohemia, end of eleventh century), and Gallus anonymus (Poland, twelfth century). By the fourteenth century, these lands would be among the foremost intellectual centers of central Europe, with universities founded at Prague (1345) and Kraków (1364), well ahead of most of Germany.[7]

Norway too was not reached until the tenth century, but Christianity came there exclusively via usurping kings, as a cultural attainment picked up in England. First Haakon, who had been brought up at the English court, attempted to introduce it, but was killed in battle in 961. Then Olaf

Tryggvason, a no-nonsense Christian who had accepted the faith while raiding England as a Viking, entered the country in 995 and spread Christianity quite literally at the point of his sword. (Once at Moere, he gave the assembled throng a blunt option: Christian baptism, or the immediate sacrifice of twelve of their notables to Thor.) The faith stuck, although Olaf himself fell in battle against the Danes and Swedes in 1000—Sweyn Forkbeard in alliance with King Olof, no less, though neither had yet accepted Christianity. There followed a short interregnum under Danish control; but on the death of Sweyn, Olaf II (who ruled 1014–30 and was later canonized) was able to step in and take up where Tryggvason had left off, proceeding with the ecclesiastical organization of the country until he was himself deposed by the Danish king Cnut, who was evidently not going to reverse the conversion. Meanwhile, Iceland, at the time a Norwegian dependency, officially accepted the Christian faith without conquest or heroics, but by democratic vote at its parliament, the Althing, in 1000.*

As the bells rang in the new millennium in January 1001, Latin was the language of Church services across Europe from Poland to Portugal, and from Sicily to Iceland; from the Arctic to the Mediterranean, and from the Atlantic to the Baltic.†

---

*In Iceland, the missionary who had given concrete meaning to the new faith was actually not English, but a Saxon, named Frederic. Christianity brought with it the Roman alphabet, and a consciousness (derived from two hundred years of German literacy) that Latin was not the only language for writing. The result was a feast of literary creativity, as the ancient Norse myths, and the sagas of the Icelanders' recent adventurous and turbulent history, were all set down.

†The conversion (and Latinate education) of eastern Europe was nearly completed in 1226–42, when (German) Teutonic knights conquered and settled the eastern Baltic regions from East Prussia to Estonia, having received a papal license to campaign to convert the heathen. Only Lithuania eluded them; even after 1385, when their Grand Duke Jogaila (Jagiello) was baptized in order to marry Jadwiga (Hedwig), king of Poland in her own right, Lithuania remained an Orthodox (and hence non-Latin) country; and this continued during its long and close alliance with Catholic Poland. Lithuania's Latinization would wait until the sixteenth century, when Augustin Rotundus, burgomaster of Vilnius (Wilno) wrote a Latin chronicle (1576) and translated the laws into Latin. He claimed that Latin was by then an attractive alternative to the Polish of the rulers. (Burke 2006: 53.)

PART III

WORLDS BUILT ON LATIN

CHAPTER II

❖⊙❖

Lapsus linguae—
Incurable Romantics: Fractured Latin

*Latinas autem linguas quattuor esse quidam dixerunt, id est
priscam, latinam, romanam, mixtam . . . mixta, quae post
imperium latius promotum simul cum moribus et
hominibus in romanam civitatem inrupit, integritatem
verbi per soloecismos et barbarismos corrumpens.*

Some have said there are four Latin languages, the Ancient, the Latin,
the Roman, and the Mixed . . . The Mixed is the one that burst into the
Roman state after the Empire was more widely advanced, together with
its culture and its people, corrupting the wholeness of the word
through solecisms and barbarisms.

Isidore of Seville (AD 560–636), *Etymologies*, ix.6–7

AFTER THE COLLAPSE OF the Empire in the west, Latin began to split
into what we now see not as a language but a language family, the vernacular languages of western Europe, collectively known as Romance. It
turned out that this, not the spread of alien languages, was the ultimate linguistic effect of the Germanic invasion from the northeast and the Afro-
Asiatic (of Arabs and Berbers) from the southwest. The middle and latter
part of the first millennium AD was a period of social "hamletization," when
horizons became narrower for many people, and the chances of wide-scale
activity, e.g., travel, correspondence, or trade, were highly restricted outside
the topmost elites. Without an overarching government, movement beyond
the local market town became too costly and too dangerous to be undertaken
without an exceptional reason. The resulting fragmentation of Latin, hitherto
a highly unitary language across its wide range, is the best example we have of

how a former imperial language can split when the political conditions of unity and mutual contact are no longer maintained.*

Latin was transformed on the lips of its speakers into a profusion of different dialects that were one day to become recognized as languages in their own right. The intrinsic changeability of language, the code passed on not quite perfectly from generation to generation, began to assert itself, and the speech of the different communities went off in separate directions. The story of how this happened is fascinating in itself, although the changes took place largely unconsciously. To tell it or understand it requires a certain tough-minded determination to see Latin not (as contemporaries did) as rule-governed text on the page, but as a vast set of spoken words, each taking its part in a system, the mental grammar, that made the language make sense. As local accents changed the pronunciation of certain sounds, various words' grammatical relations to other words became less obvious, or even quite impenetrable. New generations of language learners made sense of how the language worked in slightly new ways. The changes rippled thoughout the system, causing new systems to form, which became the grammars of the new, Romance languages. First and foremost, then, Romance is the name for any more or less distorted form of Latin, as the language gradually evolved and split apart in the latter first millennium.†

Over the long centuries in which the new kingdoms established themselves, the stories of Rome's continentwide imperium and single invincible army came to seem like legends. Societies became more strictly hierarchical, with most people bound into the feudal network of personal relationships, each man (and woman) recognizing his superior lord, but few outside the Church active in that wider world that had once been ruled through Latin. Within three hundred years from those fateful crossings of the Rhine, the people of France, Italy, and Iberia began to find it difficult to understand one another when they did meet. Ordinary speech, wherever it was spoken, was more and more called *romanica* rather than *latina lingua*. Latin, as a single

---

*As such, there may even be an analogy here for a possible future for English, if someday global communications break down or somehow become less important.
†The word goes back to the Latin adverb *romanice*, which (like all such adverbs applied to language names, *latine, graece, hebraice, punice, gallice, anglice* . . .) could mean 'in (the language)'. It meant 'in the language of *Romania*'. Recall that *Romania* meant the whole of Rome's old dominion, and this is how it is used in this chapter. (The eastern European country, Romania or Rumania, was indeed named for its Romance language; but this name has only been used since the union of Moldavia and Wallachia in 1861.)

written language, was still taught in classes of *grammatica* and increasingly took its name from that. Meanwhile the inhabitants of Rome's old domains increasingly spoke a multitude of dialects, each called an *idioma*: this, when it could be recognized, arbitarily marked out the origin of speakers. But the differences between them seemed to have no meaning. Nevertheless, there remained the constraint of the need to communicate with the neighbors; in practice the result was not so much a set of distinct *idiomata* as a dialect continuum, which varied gradually across the whole field of Romance speech. Picking out particular local varieties within this continuum as "national languages" came much later.

Looking at the resulting languages—rather than at contemporary documents, which, since they are written in their authors' best Latin, largely disguise any changes that might have been taking place*—we can see that a number of common changes were affecting Romance wherever it was spoken.[1] Modulated differently in the various regions, it gave rise to the grammars and vocabularies of many modern languages, among them Italian, French, Spanish, Portuguese, Catalan, and Rumanian.†

In overall pronunciation of all the languages both the vowels and the consonants were being modified. Consonants were getting slacker, tending to be lost at the end of words (e.g., *bonus cantat canticum* 'a good one sings a psalm' became Italian *buono canta cantico*), or pronounced rather more laxly.[2] The most common inherited diphthongs *ae* and *au* everywhere had a tendency to turn to simple *e* and *o* respectively (e.g., Latin *causae* became Italian *cose*). The vowels were losing the contrast between short and long, which had not only distinguished many words (*mălum mālum* 'bad, apple', *lĕuis lēuis* 'light, smooth') but also often marked the contrast between singular and plural (*exercĭtŭs exercĭtūs* 'army, armies') or present and past tenses (*fŏdit fōdit* 'digs, dug'). The contrast had also been crucial to the meter of Latin verse, as well as determining the

---

*But there is some evidence of the changes in progress: many examples are specifically noted in the so-called *Appendix Probi*, a grammarian's list of common errors needing correction, in a document that has survived from the Africa of the third century AD. When a grammarian notes that something is wrong, it means that many people are already doing it.
†There is little point in wondering where these changes came from. Some of them may be due to the accents and natural word order of Germanic, Gothic, Berber, or Slavic speakers, trying and failing to master Romance. This is called "substrate" influence, as if the language of foreign learner is lurking underneath. But many changes seem more like effects of random drift, even if the drift is applying a pressure for change all across the language. Historical linguistics can sometimes answer how, but seldom why.

stress pattern of every word. Nevertheless, even though the long-short distinction was lost, these stress patterns on words largely remained unchanged. Stress became a law unto itself; yet by the same token it became an intrinsic, often arbitrary feature of every word, and for that reason much more important in word recognition.*

A difference developed between hard and soft *C* and *G*, something quite foreign to classical Latin, where all *C* and *G* had been hard. But before the vowels [e, i], many consonants (and particularly [k] and [g]) tend to acquire a following [y] sound, which combines with the consonant to produce the "soft" *C* and *G*, whose actual quality differs across the Romance languages—e.g., Italian, Rhaeto-Romance, and Rumanian [č, ǰ] (*ch*urch, *j*udge), Spanish [θ, x] (*th*in, lo*ch*), French [s, ž] (*c*ertain, mira*g*e). This change came to be accepted in people's pronunciation of Latin itself, giving what is called the Florentine pronunciation, popular with the Catholic Church to this day. But there was never any change in the spelling. Hence arose the need for a rule to tell when *C* and *G* are pronounced soft, and when hard.†

A largely common set of changes applied in different ways, and in different periods, where Romance was spoken. Almost everywhere the loss of the long-short distinction in vowels was not simple, but first resulted in changes to the color of the vowels: except in the case of *a*, long vowels became tense, and short ones lax. The differences (tense:lax) were much as those between the vowels in *mate*:*met* [e:ɛ], *meet*:*mitt* [i:ɪ], *moat*:*motte* [o:ɔ], and *pool*:*pull* [u:ʊ] in modern English, which are often said to differ as between long and short, but really differ as between tense and lax tongue position. The resulting system of nine vowels [a:e:ɛ:i:ɪ:o:ɔ:u:ʊ] was then widely resimplified by dropping some: in brief, e replaced ɪ, and o ʊ, reducing the nine vowels to seven [a: e:ɛ:i:o:ɔ:u], as in modern standard Italian. The net effect is that, from the outcome in most modern Romance languages, you cannot tell that *pĭrum* 'pear' and *uērum* 'true' once had different vowels, nor that *nŭx* 'nut' and *uōx* 'voice' did not rhyme in Latin.‡

---

*The effects on verse we have already seen (p. 123).

†French has applied palatalization before the vowel [a] too, giving the distinctive [š, ž] in *cheval*, *joie* (from Latin *caballum*, *gaudia*). But this is explicit in the spelling, replacing *c* with *ch* and *g* with *j*.

‡It seems that the origin of this change was in southern Italy: early confusions of *E* and *I* are seen in first-century AD graffiti from the walls of Pompeii, perhaps a remnant of Oscan accents, which found it hard to distinguish them; e.g., PVTIIOLANIS FILICITIIR OMNIBVS NVCHIIRINIS FIILICIA ET VNCV POMPIIJANIS PETECVSANIS representing

One effect of the greater importance of stress was to efface unstressed vowels toward the end of the word: *másculus* 'male' evidently became *másclus* (Italian *maschio*, French *mâle*)—as indeed *románice* 'in Romanish' became *románce*. But this tendency was stronger in some parts of *Romania* than others: *duódecim* 'twelve' must have been *duó(d)cim* in the west (giving Spanish *doce*, French *douze*) while its latter vowels survived in the east (Italian *dódici*).

These changes taken as a whole set had catastrophic effects on Latin's old system of case endings in nouns and person endings in verbs.* In this circumstance, Romance grammar changed radically from Latin. A system of six cases (nominative/vocative/accusative/genitive/dative/ablative) and three genders (masculine/feminine/neuter) was reduced to one or two cases and two genders. Among nouns and adjectives, the distinction between nominative and accusative was abandoned everywhere (except for the Romance of Gaul), and word order came to be the principal marker of subject and object in a sentence. All the languages lost the genitive, dative, and ablative cases, except for Rumanian, which alone maintained the genitive. (It may be significant that Rumanian's neighbor Greek, which was to change in many ways analogously to Latin, also retains its genitive.) The functions of these cases were expressed by use of prepositions such as *de* 'from', *ad* 'to', and *per* 'through'. All the languages lost the neuter gender, a class of nouns that Latin had preserved from the Indo-European system. It was just not different enough from the masculines in the singular, and as for the confusions of the neuter plural with the feminine singular (*ova* 'eggs' versus *vita* 'life'), the results bedevil the grammars of Italian and Rumanian to this day, where some masculine singular nouns have feminine plurals.

Latin, a free word-order language that tended to place verbs at the end of a sentence, changed, in all its Romance descendants, into a relatively fixed subject-verb-object language. (It may be significant that those Germanic languages that for a few centuries had permeated western Europe usually have a firm principle that the verb will come second in a main clause.)

The verb system too was radically simplified. Nevertheless, verbs in all the Romance languages are still highly inflected (far more so, for example, than in any of the Germanic or Slavonic languages, let alone Iranian or Indo-Aryan).

---

classical *pŭtĕōlānĭs fēlīcĭtĕr ōmnibŭs nūcĕrīnĭs fēlīciă ĕt uncum pompēiānĭs pĭthēcūsānĭs* 'Bliss to the Puteolians, blessings to all the Nucerians, and a hook for the Pompeians and Pithecusans'.

*The tables in Appendix III show how the changes combined to make the inflexional system of Latin less clear and, ultimately, quite dysfunctional.

Why is this? On the one hand, the profusion of different forms that survived in classical Latin had been exceptionally rich, so that even pruned, it remains luxuriant; and on the other, Romance reconstructed, using auxiliary verbs, almost everything that it discarded from the Latin inflectional system and even added a few categories of its own, so it can even be maintained that the new system was richer and more flexible than the old one.* Romance languages can make the distinction of present perfect as against simple past, "he has gone" vs. "he went," whereas Latin has only the perfect.

In all its different local varieties, spoken Romance used other means than Latin did, expressing the functions of its nouns through word order and a wide range of prepositions, and employing auxiliary verbs, equivalent to *have* and *be*, to mark the explicit sense of its verbs. The new means must have seemed less than elegant to schoolmasters across Europe, who throughout this period continued to teach the elite the full rigors of Latin *grammatica*; but the new ways of speaking grew fully adequate for precise and detailed expression, quite equal to that of Latin in their descriptive power, if not in their concision.

While these restructurings were going on in the architecture of the language, Romance vocabulary was also receiving new local colors in the different parts of Europe from the various aliens who, usually by main force, had entered *Romania* and settled among its inhabitants. Although the invaders were not overwhelming in numbers, they were highly influential, especially in the ruling levels of society. The sustained contact of Goths and Germans across wide swathes of the west has left its mark in a common set of words in all the Romance languages that has nothing to do with their shared roots in Latin.†

---

*In practice, every category of inflection that was dropped was replaced by a work-around. So, the inflected passive *amatur* 'she is loved' was restated as *amata est*, using the participle and the verb 'to be'; the inflected future *amabit* 'she will love' was replaced, throughout western Europe, by *amare habet*, literally 'she has (the prospect) to love', with the infinitive and the verb 'to have'. The perfect system, three tenses formed with a special (often irregularly formed) stem, was largely replaced by the past participle and various tenses of the verb 'to have': *amavit, amaverat, amaverit* 'he has loved, had loved, will have loved' were now expressed by *amatam habet, amatam habebat, amatam habere habet*. (The old perfect inflection was in fact retained in all the languages, with its meaning refined as simple past, *amavit* 'he (once) loved'. Four tenses of subjunctive were cut down to two without any great sense of loss, and there was even a gain, since many of their old uses would now be expressed by the new conditional, 'he would love' *amare habebat*, combining the infinitive with the imperfect.

†Examples are found not only in the expected matters of war, peace, law enforcement, and equipment (e.g., *werra* 'war', *treuwa* 'truce', *riki* 'rich', *brando* 'brand', *marka* 'border', *warda, wahta* 'guard, watch', *rauba* 'booty', *wadjo* 'pledge', *warnan, warjan* 'supply, defend,

But others left different marks in the words of regional speech that have remained more localized.*

The grammarians struggled to keep all these new words out of the written language, viz Latin proper. They were fairly successful at least in ecclessiastical and philosophical writing, but much less so in legal documents and historical descriptions, where practical utility and the need to express accurately facts on the ground were paramount. From these sources medieval Latin comes to have a vast new vocabulary, so vast that it has discouraged any attempt at a comprehensive dictionary of it; those that have been compiled are restricted to the areas of what became individual countries, and so—in a sense—foist on Latin the regional limitations of spoken Romance in this period.†

Yet despite these local effects due to the influence of particular invaders or particular neighbors, the direction taken by the spoken Romance dialects was broadly similar across its whole geographic range. The only explanation for these shared trends is that some system of "tensions" within the language—the pattern of what was hard to learn, and what was easy, from generation to generation—was pushing toward certain changes and reconfigurations in the language's grammar. The changes occurred without any educational sanction. Such schools as there were taught Latin grammar only, as traditionally as they could manage it; and they conceived their duty as the reversal of any change in language, with extreme prejudice, not its conscious shaping.

The scarcity of communication with people in distant areas would have

---

care for, cure', *spehôn* 'spy out', *skiuhan* 'escape', *bastjan* 'build', *helm* 'helmet', *hosa* 'trousers', *sporo* 'spur', *want* 'glove'), but also emotions (*haunitha* 'shame', *urgolî* 'pride'), colors (*blank* 'white', *brûn* 'brown', *gris* 'gray', *gelb* 'yellow'), parts of the body (*hanka* 'haunch', *kruppa* 'crupper'), and other quite mundane matters (*krattón* 'scratch', *furbjan* 'polish', *frisk* 'fresh', *thwalja* 'towel', *laubja* 'lodge').

There are some semantic curiosities here: a "robe" turns out to be originally just a piece of booty; a living "wage" is by origin just a pledge, and the best "warning" was originally a delivery of supplies to a garrison (Fr. *garnison*), not the garnish on a dish.

*So Italian has received from Goths and Lombards *stecca* 'stick', *bandire* 'ban', *smaltire* 'digest', *romire* 'make a row', *scherzare* 'joke', *spaccare* 'split', *mondualdo* 'guardian'. French has from Franks and Burgundians *hache* 'ax', *bacon* 'salt pork', *gonfanon* 'war banner'; *écurie* 'stable'. Arabs and Berbers have given to Spanish *mezquino* 'poor, mean', *achacar* 'accuse', *halagar* 'flatter', *aceite* 'olive oil', *algodón* 'cotton'; and Slavs in the Balkans have worked particularly thoroughly on Romanian with *iubi* 'love', *dărui* 'give', *gol* 'naked', *zid* 'wall', *plug* 'plow'.

†For the vernacular languages, in fact, the true successors of Romance, it was only in the fifteenth to eighteenth centuries, when descriptive grammars, and later dictionaries, were compiled, that a full account was attempted of the outcome of this era of innovations.

allowed each community, in principle, almost total freedom for variation in its vernacular speech. Yet the internal logic of Latin as a spoken language, underlying all the dialects, must have been at least as important as any tendency to drift at random in each separate community. Despite its political fragmentation across a dozen kingdoms and hundreds of lordly domains, the language of the Roman world—in its sound system, in its systems of noun cases and verb tenses, in its word order and its receptivity to foreign loans—in some sense moved as a unit.

At the same time, the fact that written Latin, doggedly unchanging, became separated from its spoken version, the hodgepodge of Romance vernaculars, was not in the least surprising. Exactly the same happened in China between the fifth century BC and the fifteenth AD, as classical Chinese monopolized written expression and the "dialects" remained unwritten; and the same phenomenon can been seen in the lands where Arabic has flourished since the eighth century AD to the present, classical Arabic remaining the unique expression of the literate while the Arab vernaculars have gone their own ways.* This seems, in fact, to be the standard outcome in a literate society that lasts for many centuries, if only a minority ever become literate. What does call for an explanation is why western Europe was to break out of this norm toward the end of the first millennium and bring its popular Romance vernaculars onto the page in their own right.

◇

Why did *Romania*—the cultural domain of the old Roman Empire in the west—need to make its vernacular languages into written ones? Why was Latin not enough as a means of written expression for western Europe in the Middle Ages when other classical languages—Arabic for West Asia and north Africa, or Chinese for East Asia, indeed Greek for Europe's southeast—evidently were? By the standards of the wider world, what happened in Europe at the end of the first millennium AD looks decidedly odd.

First of all, it is clear that some exceptional development would have been needed to change the status quo. In the four hundred years after the German invasions, Latin, and at first Gothic, were the only written languages current in continental western Europe. With the suppression or sidelining of the Arian

---

*The survival, indeed the reclamation, of Sanskrit in medieval India falls within the same pattern, although here we have the paradox that the elite language was sustained almost as importantly by an oral tradition of education.

churches over the first two of these centuries, the tradition of written Gothic had disappeared. But Latin lived on, taught as *grammatica*, and a language increasingly seen as inseparable from the very fact of writing itself. Above all, it was the written language of the Catholic Church, cultivated in monasteries and churches, and the language of literature. It also persisted as the language of government and the law, and (where necessary) of commercial transactions, for there had never been any other used for these purposes in western Europe. In such traditions based on a classical language, writing was the business of specialists, above all clerks (*clerici*—a word that had, revealingly, originally meant members of the Christian clergy, but was applied to all those with written work).

Between the tenth and the twelfth centuries, all over the west, this ceased to be true. From then on the skills of reading and writing would widely be found outside the clergy; more significant, those skills were going to be applicable not just to Latin, in its traditional form and grammar, but to spoken languages too. Writing became clearly an art applicable, in principle, to any language, even if for many centuries more—essentially until the advent of printed books in the fifteenth and sixteenth centuries—it would be seen as rather rough and ready when used to represent living languages. Unlike *grammatica*, whose rules were clear, set down by Donatus and Priscian, a spoken language seemed constantly to be in flux. As Dante put it, around 1303:

> Therefore if over one people the language changes, as has been said, successively over time, and can in no way stand still, it is necessary that it should vary in various ways quite separately from what remains constant, just as customs and dress vary in various ways, which are confirmed neither by nature or society, but arise at human pleasure and to local taste. This was the motive of the inventors of the faculty of *grammatica*: for *grammatica* is nothing but a kind of sameness of speech unalterable for diverse times and places.[3]

This new, vernacular literacy came about in a western Europe that had begun to resemble a little the world of the Roman Empire. At the end of the eighth century, the Frankish kingdom that ruled northern France had become mightier than any other. Under Charlemagne (768–814) it united all of France, western Germany, and northern Italy, with an enclave south of the Pyrenees, and began to act in concert with the papacy in Rome in a way that recalled the glorious old alliance of Church and Empire in the century after Constantine. This political revival had an immediate cultural manifestation, what is today called the Carolingian Renaissance, when Charlemagne called scholars to receive his patronage at his court in Aachen. They came, first from Italy, but later and more notably from monasteries in England and Germany, and in 781 Alcuin, head of the cathedral school at York, was appointed the director of Charlemagne's Palace School.

Alcuin was above all a teacher and a regimenter. He presided over the establishment of new standards for the spelling and pronunciation of Latin, an attempt to return it to its classical roots, seen as the source of its fundamental value in education, thought, and culture. Alcuin enjoined a new, universal style of pronunciation for Latin, deliberately reconstructed to be close to its original sound. Rather than allow each local community to pronounce its Latin as came naturally, he proposed that all should follow a single norm. In his own words:

> *Me legat antiquas vult qui proferre loquelas;*
> *Me qui non sequitur vult sine lege loqui.*

> Let him read me who wishes to carry on the ancient modes of speech;
> He who does not follow me wishes to speak without law.[4]

This would perhaps give scholars closer access to the true sound of Latin poetry and rhetoric; importantly, it would certainly make it easier for them to communicate orally in Latin, wherever in Europe they might hail from. As a reform, it did not in itself tend toward vernacular literacy: indeed, quite the reverse, for the immediate effect of the new pronunciation was to make priests reading out their sermons or their church offices more or less incomprehensible to their illiterate parishioners. In the favorite—somewhat extreme—example, the word *viridiarium* 'orchard' could no longer be pronounced in northern France as vair-jair, by then its natural rendering in the local variety of Romance.[5] With each priest following his home pronunciation, it was possible—at least in Romance-speaking countries—for the Latin text to have been read pretty much in line with the local language, hence understood by those who could not read. The newly antiquated, universal Latin, by contrast, was a foreign language everywhere, accessible only to those who had studied it. So quite soon after Alcuin's reforms, rulings were needed to guarantee that Church services would still make sense. At the Council of Tours in central France in 813, as at the Council of Mainz in Germany in 847, an explicit exception was made, to guarantee the continued understanding of the countryfolk: ". . . and that each should work to transfer the same homilies into rustic Romance or German language [*rusticam romanam linguam aut thiotiscam*], so that all can more easily understand what is said."[6]

Alcuin of York, from a ninth-century Bamberg Bible. Called to preside over Charlemagne's Palace School, he set new standards for Latin education across Europe.

One effect of Alcuin's reforms must ultimately have been to impress on everyone that Latin, as written and spoken, was actually now a foreign language, not just the written, quasi-eternal form of Romance speech. This message would have been reinforced by the wider knowledge, given by academic and political contacts within Charlemagne's Frankish empire, that Latin was not the only written language of western Christendom: Irish, Anglo-Saxon, German, and even Welsh were all appearing in manuscripts in this period, and it would have been clear to those who read them—all clerics who would also have known their *grammatica*—that they were much closer to contemporary speech than Latin was to any form of Romance, especially in northern Europe.

But now Alcuin had shown that Latin too could be interpreted phonetically. He had invented a system of pronunciation that correlated directly and simply with the language on the page. The thought must have arisen, why not try the same trick, in reverse, for the spoken language?—that is to say, provide a version on the page that correlated directly with a Romance dialect, just as it was spoken?

A couple of centuries were needed for these written versions to become a widespread reality in the realms of Romance speech. But even before this happened, Latin had already consciously been used as a common written language in lands beyond *Romania*. Inspired by this, a successful experiment had been conducted, in many of them (e.g. in Ireland, England, Saxony, and Germany), to represent the home language directly in Roman script, and as a result it had become clear that the value of the letters went far beyond their use for Latin alone. As a result, the Latin-writing world as a whole would have gained an awareness of the possibility of a different, vernacular literacy—in parallel with the writing of their classical language (Latin)—in a way that was certainly never available in China. This may provide the answer to why Europe's Romance vernaculars became written languages, independent of Latin, whereas the vernaculars of China largely did not.*

Meanwhile, starting in the mid-seventh century western Europe's population had steadily begun to increase. The unsettling turbulence from two centuries of invasions and dynastic feuding had subsided, and a new social regime, more locally based than the Roman system, but again stable, was now becoming established.† There was, of course, no Roman army left to support, nor Roman imperial infrastructure of cities, roads, and officers to keep up, and consequently the tax take—or its equivalent in services rendered to one's lord—had become considerably lighter. New agricultural practices were taking root across Europe: a new asymmetric iron plow, and a three-year crop-rotation system, allowing less fallow time and more production, were boosting yields, and allowing more animals to be kept. In the late ninth century there was even an improvement in the climate: we know that beeches advanced up into the Alps, birches retreated in northern climes, and coastal marshes receded.[7]

With greater prosperity came a growth in disposable income at least at the top end of society, and a new beginning for Europe's towns and cities,

---

*The clearly nonphonetic nature of Chinese characters, when used to represent Chinese, acted as a barrier to any widespread application to non-Chinese languages, although there are some early examples of the experiment being tried, ultimately successfully in the case of Japanese, Vietnamese, and Korean. But the only sustained success, namely Japanese kana, entailed a radical simplification of the characters, which was not reexported anywhere in the Chinese-speaking world.

In the case of Arabic in the Islamic world, the use of its script to represent Mozarabic (Spanish), Persian, and later Turki does seem comparable to the early writing of Irish, Anglo-Saxon, and German. The absence of any feedback to represent more directly the Arabic vernaculars needs to be explained in parallel with the absence of independent states, which would have given status to those vernaculars, if they had become written languages.

The Aryan languages of India, on the other hand, like the Romance, did largely achieve status as written vernaculars in competition with their classic, Sanskrit, and at much the same time; Pollock 2006, chapter 12, considers this parallel from various points of view.
† But the new system may have taken some time in the building: the first surviving document with the word *feodum*, meaning tenancy by military service (a borrowing from the Frankish *fehu* 'cattle, property, fee', dates to 898 from southern France (Fossier 1999: 27).

which began to expand, filling up with those who lived by trade. Shopkeepers, specialized tradesmen, innkeepers, merchants, began to multiply. For those with a secure income, possibilities of travel began to beckon, whether for gain (to markets and fairs), for worship (on pilgrimages), or for a heady mixture of motives (on Crusade). There was also increasingly a demand for secular education, as reading and writing and accounting—evidently in Latin, since there was as yet no alternative—were becoming skills important for business. And in the households of the very rich, and the very powerful, there was a greater prospect for artists to find patronage. Some of those artists were *troubadours*, 'inventors' in Provençal, who would found Europe's vernacular literature; but the term in English, *minstrels*, emphasizes how much these supposedly traveling entertainers depended on a patron: it derives from *ministerial* 'on the staff', ministering to a lord or lady.

The first occasions when Roman script was used to represent the phonetic reality of Romance languages were fairly lackluster, without any sort of literary aspirations. They may be classed together as "teleprompter" uses, in that they were all occasions when a written document was needed to support an oral performance with an illiterate audience. The earliest, and most famous, was the Strasburg Oaths of 842, taken by two brother princes, Charles the Bald and Ludwig the German, in the hearing of respective troops of followers who actually spoke different languages: the Romance of France, and German. Then, in the proceedings of some monasteries between Rome and Naples (Monte Cassino, San Salvatore di Sessa, Santa Maria di Cengla, 960–63), there are some *verbatim* statements in the Romance of Italy, recorded as sworn, to validate ownership for lands.*

These deliberate attempts at phonetic accuracy, particularly as used in legal statements, were to give rise to a new tradition, namely to use Romance by default when one's proper Latin gave out. This we could call the "stopgap" use of Romance, represented by the sporadic "glosses" in the margins of literary manuscripts,

---

*But touchingly, the first surviving example of imperfect written Latin—if not yet conscious Italian—is an elegant riddle apparently used when trying out a new pen:

se pareba boues | alba pratalia araba | & albo uersorio teneba | & negro semen seminaba

'he yoked his oxen | white fields he plowed | & white plow he held | & black seed he sowed.' The manuscript (Biblioteca Capitolare di Verona, codex lxxxix [84]) dates to the turn of the eighth-ninth centuries and is a riddle on the act of writing itself, with black ink on a white page.

such as, the *Glosas Emilianenses, Glosas Silenses* in monastery copies of religious texts from the tenth century. In fact, informal aide-mémoire must often have been written in the vernacular, like one cheese-larder list from a Spanish monastery also datable to the late tenth century, preserved because it had been scribbled on the back of a document of donation.[8]

But more important, stopgap uses began to occur in legal documents. In Iberia, fragments of Leonese in legal depositions occurred from the mid-tenth century, in Castilian from the early eleventh, and in Aragonese and Catalan from the mid-eleventh, as if a contagion of imperfect Latin education was spreading across the peninsula.* Likewise, in the south of France (from Foix around 1034 and Narbonne around 1053), legal deeds were written with short sections in Occitan. The scribes must have felt that in such a text it was most important to get the details correctly understood, whether or not anyone knew how to express them correctly in Latin.

From this, it was a small leap, but nonetheless a leap to a different intellectual world, to draft an entire legal document not in formal Latin, but in Romance, as it would naturally be spoken. This happened for Occitan about 1100 (in the south of the Massif Central, as it happened, in the monasteries from Toulouse to Millau); for Catalan (from Pallars, high in the Pyrenees) the first known text is from this same period; for Castile it was a little earlier; and for Portuguese, there is no example until 1192, in the monastery of Villão. French itself seems to have brought up the rear, since the first attested document is from Arras in 1230, four generations after the appearance of written epic poetry (*chanson de geste*) in the mid-twelfth century, and indeed well after the translation of the rule for Knights Templars into French, for the less well-educated aspirant (1160–70).[9]

Nevertheless, the writing down of artistic literature in Romance languages then seems to have followed everywhere. In Occitan, Guilhelm, ninth duke of Aquitaine (1071–1127), led off a two-hundred-year tradition of lyrical poetry in that language. (It is often known as Provençal, although it was used much more widely than in Provence, and Guilhelm himself hailed from the other end of its range, in Poitou.) Around 1140 in northern Castile, the *Cantar de mio Cid*, a romance that culminates in the war to retake Valencia from the Moors, shows

---

*Charitably, one should remember that comprehensive reference books such as dictionaries were nonexistent in this age—indeed incompatible with the medieval educational spirit of achieving an active oral command of knowledge through constant *repetitio*—although partial glossaries of difficult words had been available since the seventh century. Bilingual glossaries, though, were never available in Romance areas.

Castilian epic poetry making the transition from oral performance to the manuscript page. Later, Castilian was established as a language for prose at the court of Alfonso X (who lived 1221–84). Alfonso also lent his weight to Portuguese, but as a language for lyrics, composing his own *Cantigas de Santa Maria*.

E assi Santa Maria	Thus Saint Mary
ajudou a seus amigos,	helped her friends,
pero que d'outra lei eran,	although they were of another law,
a britar seus eemigos	to shatter their enemies,
que, macar que eran muitos,	for although they were many,
nonos preçaron dous figos,	they did not give two figs for them,
e assi foi ssa mercee	and thus was her mercy
de todos mui connoçuda.[10]	made well known to all.

This specialization of language by genre was also seen at the other edge of Iberia: Catalan literature began in the thirteenth century, but exclusively in prose, verse having been preempted by Occitan. Some of the earliest works in Catalan were chronicles, including the royal *Llibre dels Feyts del rei En Jacme* on the reign of Jaime I "the Conqueror" (1213–76); but Ramon Llull (around 1233–1315) was famous for highly theoretical and speculative works, of a kind that had previously been exclusive to Latin. Among them was a treatise on chivalry itself (*Libre de l'Orde de Cavalleria*).

Perversely enough, the beginnings of any literary Italian language were delayed by the popularity of what was already available in French and Occitan. No dialect of Italian, in fact, had a preeminence in Italy comparable with Francian (from the Paris region) or literary Provençal, north and west of the Alps. Moreover, the largest state in twelfth-century Italy was in fact the Norman kingdom in Sicily, where (as in Norman England) French was the language of the court. The delay lasted perhaps a century, but after 1200, a "Sicilian School" of Italian poets came into being, basing its style on the Provençal troubadours. They were followed by poets in Tuscany, and others such as St. Francis of Assisi, who saw the evident potential of the vernacular for expressing not just courtly love among the upper classes, but popular religious devotion.

Laudato si' mi Signore, per sora nostra	Praised be, my Lord, for sister our
Morte corporale,	bodily Death,
da la quale nullu homo vivente	from whom no living man can
pò skappare:	escape.

guai a quelli ke morrano ne le peccata   Woe to those who will die in
    mortali;   mortal sins;
beati quelli ke trovarà ne le Tue   blessed those whom she will find in
    sanctissime voluntati,   your most holy designs,
ka la morte secunda no 'l farrà male.   where a kindly death will do them
                  no harm.[11]

Meanwhile all prose writing, including merchants' account books and business letters, remained conservatively in Latin alone, even though some cities of northern Italy were already pulsating centers of international commerce. In fact, not until the thirteenth century did the merchants too break down, and all types of literature and documents came to be written in Italian, with the dialect of Florence taking the lead.

The salience of chronicles and histories, and indeed royal authors, in these early Romance literatures points to another reason why vernacular literacy became a distinctive development of western Europe, although Latin was still preeminent as the language of the elite. The link of language and people, an early form of nationalism, could be asserted precisely in those areas where the writ of the Frankish king no longer ran. Charlemagne's unified state, while it lasted, may have created the stimulus for written vernaculars, through indirect effects of the Carolingian Renaissance; but later, the breakdown of its power in the south, together with the growing power of Christian kingdoms in Iberia, made possible the flourishing of the newly recognized languages as media for court, government, and patriotic literature.

It is fascinating to trace the transition of vernacular literacy from "teleprompter" experiments in phonetic transcription, through "stopgap" supplements for imperfect Latin, to fully functional legal documents. Western Europeans were gradually realizing that the convenience of reading and writing useful texts could be disconnected from the vast educational overhead of learning the grammar and lexicon of the traditional written language, Latin. Following this was the leap to full-blooded literary uses, as people realized that literacy was not just for the serious things in life.

But a problem arose, similar to what inhibited the origin of vernacular literacy in Italian. A writer's own vernacular might have been the simplest language to write down, and indeed the most direct way to express his or her thought, but it was essentially a local thing, easy for neighbors and close colleagues to understand, but perhaps difficult for those far away, whether they were business associates or readers of literature. By being straight from the heart—and from the tongue—it lacked the regularity of a standard. How then could vernacular texts be made more widely accessible?

In practice, two answers were possible. The one adopted by the lyric poets of Provençal was to identify strongly with the idiosyncrasies of the first writers and so create a new literary language in its own right. For more than two hundred years, some 450 troubadours, of a wide range of social classes and from all over southern France, maintained a single language, abstaining from the various dialectal words and forms with which they must have grown up. This meant that the vernacular language needed to be learned, though clearly with much less effort than Latin would have required. Effectively, a single standard was accepted, though we know little of how it was arrived at.

The alternative answer was to look at the problem analytically, compare the various dialects, and attempt to formulate a rational compromise standard, by selection and elimination. It could be claimed that this was just a painful way of reconstructing an alternative to Latin—which already existed. Nevertheless, it was precisely this task that the Florentine master poet Dante took on in his work on the theory of language and literature, *De Vulgari Eloquentia*.

Dante was writing around 1303, after the first ill-disciplined surge of Italian vernacular poetry, and just before the prose writers were about to take up Italian. After the fun of pricking the pretensions of every dialect he could quote, he enumerated the necessary properties of this desirable new standard, the *vulgare illustre* as he called it: it must be *illustre* (of shining celebrity), *cardinale* (a leader that is followed), *aulicum* (associated with a royal court), and *curiale* (balanced). Dante claimed that he found this paragon in the *vulgare latium*, which—perversely—was neither vulgar Latin, nor the dialect of Latium, but *istud, quod totius Ytalie est* 'that which belongs to the whole of Italy'.* Apparently, the illustrious doctors who had written vernacular poetry in Italy, from Sicily to Le Marche, had been using it all along—a sadly classic example of petitio principii, assuming what was to be proved.[12]

Dante's declaration that the search was over, doubtless ingratiating to contemporary readers, is doubly infuriating for modern linguists since Dante had shown in his introduction that he was capable of quite penetrating definitions of dialect areas within Romance and had also made some suggestions on the nature of language change. In his later poetry and prose works, which went on to stun Italy by their comprehensiveness and manifold literary virtues,

---

*The interpretation is complicated by the fact that Dante used *latius* as a synonym for 'Italian', as when discussing the Sardinians (p. 176).

Dante Alighieri by Andrea Del Castagno. A pioneer in his awareness of language change, Dante sought a new style for Italian poetry among the various dialects.

Dante in practice chose basically to use the Tuscan dialect of Florence, his home city, while accepting features of other dialects as and when they were convenient.

Despite his linguistic insights and panoramic view of languages in Europe,[13] suggestions that Dante is the father of Romance philology should probably be restrained: he did see the various Romance languages and dialects as similar in greater or lesser degree to the *inalterabilis locutionis identitas* that is Latin, but he never explicitly stated that Latin was their origin nor apparently conceived that Latin might once itself have been a *vulgare*.* Nor was he above ethnic prejudice, hardly a fitting stance for a descriptive linguist. Sardinian, which he correctly noted was closest to Latin, received no credit for this: "The Sardinians too, who are not Italians but apparently to be associated with Italian, let us cast aside, since they alone appear to have no *vulgare* of their own, but imitate *grammatica* as apes do men: for they say *domus nova* and *dominus meus*."[14] Grammatically faultless, then, it would seem, but evidently, Sardinians—no-account islanders—could not be considered serious competitors in the Italian *vulgare* game.

---

*The question of what language the ancient Romans had actually spoken was still a live issue among the Italian scholarly elite over a century after Dante. (See footnote on p. 237.)

❖❖❖❖❖

CHAPTER 12

Amor vincit omnia—Latin Lovers

Et ieu prèc en Jesú del tron,	And I pray to Jesus enthroned,
Et en romans et en latí.	Both in Romance and in Latin.

Guilhelm, ninth duke of Aquitaine,
seventh count of Poitiers; composed in 1117

Quando appar l'aulente fiore,	When fragrant blossom appears,
Lo tempo dolze e sereno,	The weather sweet and serene,
Gli ausciulletti infra gli albore	The little birdies under the trees
*Ciascun canta in suo latino;**	Each sings in his Latin;
Per lo dolze canto e fino	By the sweet, fine song
Si confortan gli amadore,	Lovers are reassured,
Quegli ch'aman lealmente . . .	Those who love truly . . .

Bonagiunta Urbiciani (ca 1220–ca 1300),
Tuscan poet of the "Sicilian School"

T HE TONE OF THIS new literature trilling out across western Europe was very different from the continuing Latin tradition. Rather than staid prose chronicles, it resounded with heroic verse, imbued with the new values of chivalry and manly prowess; rather than hymns of sacred devotion to the Virgin, it sang of courtly love for an idealized mistress, a real woman but

---

*This conceit, of birds in spring each with his own Latin, seems taken from a poem of Guilhelm of Aquitaine, written a century earlier. It begins, *Ab la dolçor del temps nòvel | folhon li bosc, e li aucèl | chanton chascús in lor latí,| segon lo vèrs del nòvel chan* 'From the sweetness of the new season, the woods are in leaf, and the birds sing each in their Latin, according to the verse of the new song'.

one set high on a pedestal of admiration; rather than philosophy and theology, it developed flights of fantasy, its heroes pursuing incredible adventures in unknown lands.* These were the preoccupations of literature in Romance language, in the eleventh to thirteenth centuries: Europe was to come to know them as the stuff of "romance."

To understand how this hinterland of the heart became associated with a particular language, it helps to remember how, within a literature that is known across a widespread language area, particular genres tend to become associated with particular dialects. This had famously happened at least once before in European history: in the Greek of the eighth to fifth centuries BC, Homer's mixture of Ionic and Aeolic was the language for epic poetry, Alcman's Doric for lyric poetry, Herodotus' Ionic for history, Aeschylus' and Sophocles' Attic for tragedy. As noted, this phenomenon took over almost at once within the new Romance writing. Within Spain, Castilian was for heroic verse, but also for prose, so Galician or Portuguese was available, indeed obligatory, for the lyricism of love poetry. And sure enough, its accent was perceived—perhaps only by outsiders—to breathe haunting melancholy. In the Midi, Occitan was already the home language of courtly love lyrics, but that meant that neighboring Catalan to the west had to be for prose narratives. (French in the north and the *vulgare illustre* of Italian in the south were never so specialized.) In sum, many Romance languages came to seem the right way to tell of matters of the heart, innocent of the convoluted thought processes of those who could express themselves through grammar.[†]

This is the root of the strange fact that the word *romance* left behind its original meaning ('popular language derived from Latin') and began to pick up romantic overtones. The word *romanice* had achieved some currency after the Carolingian reforms, when those in western Europe had needed to say what

---

*In *Blanquerna* (written in Catalan ca 1283), Ramon Llull pursued fantasy in a linguistic direction, with "Tartars" and Christian friars learning one another's languages, then decamping to "Turkey" where they convert the khan (lxxx.9, lxxxviii.5). The potential of foreign languages, as well-defined, learnable, and useful skills, was beginning to become clear in Europe.

[†]In the Romance languages, *grammatica* (or grammar) too has given its name to a hinterland, but perhaps not what the schoolmen would have expected. The word was rather mangled as it was converted to French, its *-atica* ending becoming *-aire*. (Similar things happened to other such words: *medicum* 'doctor' is *mire* in Old French, and *artem magicam* or *mathematicam* collapsed to *artimaire*.) Once in French, the dialectal *grimoire* came to mean an arcane text, while as borrowed north of the Channel, *gramarye*, or in Scotland *glamour*, achieved a vivid association with enchantment and witchcraft.

language they understood if it wasn't Latin. The phrase *rustica romana lingua* had been used at first, and subsequently just *romana lingua*: adding *–ice* to the root must have begun the process of according it the dignity of a proper language, rather than a mere slipshod lingo. In these languages, the *c* would have been softened before the *e*.* But French had another trick up its sleeve: *–nce*, shortened to *–nz* (with *z* pronounced as 'ts'), looked like a nominative case, suggesting an accusative in *–nt* (cf *piez ~ piet* 'foot'). *Romanz* was therefore assumed to have another form *romant* or *romaunt*, and this became the origin of the common continental form *roman*, now meaning a novel. (The great medieval classic was originally known as *Romaunt de la Rose*.) This must be the basis for Italian *romanzo* and also the adjective *romantic*, which now exists, borrowed from French, in some form independently of the noun *romance* in all the languages.

The words have gone on resounding down the centuries in European languages. For the first few hundred years, they focused on tales of adventure and affecting action. In fourteenth-century Spain, *romances* were episodes taken from heroic popular epics of knights in armour and derring-do, the (mostly French) *chansons de geste*. But in the nineteenth century the words were applied to a new literary tendency, "Romanticism." Paradoxically, this was strongest not among the Romance languages (derived from Latin) but in German literature, which accentuated emotional response, and novelly contrasted it with the supposedly calm characteristic of "Classicism." In the twentieth century, "romance" was remade once again, focusing on stylish and emotive relations between the sexes, particularly in courtship and wooing.

In a way, this progression from armor to amour is all grounded in the cultural complex of courtly manners expressed in Romance literature. In the tenth and eleventh centuries, the armored, mounted knight (*chevalier, cavaliere*) became the warrior par excellence in western Europe, the backbone of its military forces, and the charge with lance fixed horizontally was established as his principal mode of operation. The chevalier's code required that he never be caught in a situation that could be made to look like cowardice, and so he had to fight when given the chance. Of a knight who counseled discretion, as Olivier does in the *Chanson de Roland*, the best that could be said is *Olivier est sage* 'Olivier is wise'. This contrasted with the headstrong

---

*This of course varied regionally: Rhaeto-Romance (Rumansch!) and Rumanian to *č*, north-Castilian to θ, French and Andalusian to *s*. Loss of the *-i-* in this context is general (cf French *manche* 'sleeve' from Latin *manicam; comte* 'count' from *comitem; bonté, santé* 'goodness, health' from *bonitatem, sanitatem;* Occitan *domna* 'lady' from *domina*).

and fatal, but necessary, prowess of his friend and commander, Roland: *Rollant est proz* 'Roland is proud'.[1]

This was the world of the *chanson de geste* 'song of deeds', where amid the contesting demands of knights' honor there was no serious role for their ladies. To this military ethic, the Occitan poets—led off by the extremely aristocratic ninth duke of Aquitaine—added the manners of *cortesía*. Knights might not all have been noble, but they alone were deemed worthy of love for or from a lady: classically, she would have been the wife of their feudal lord, with a superior status that made her at the same time both desirable and (almost) unattainable: a medieval "Mrs. Robinson," tempting the (graduate) *bachelier*, the entry-grade knight. Some have seen this as a kind of subtle power play by which the older lord might guarantee the attachment to the household of his young knights; if so, it would of course have required the active collusion of his lady wife. This situation, with the noble lover striving to win the favor of his lady, amid the suspicions of the *gilós* (jealous husband) and the malice of the carping *lauzengiers* in the background, is the ground of *fin'amor*, what might well now be translated as 'romance'. Both military and courtly sides are brought together in the romances of Chrétien de Troyes (fl. 1160–85), articulating the drama within the context of Arthur's legendary court of Camelot, with Sir Lancelot the adulterous lover of the queen, but somehow simultaneously faithful to her, his king, and the people whom he must protect.

From the standpoint of Latin, the question arises where all this comes from. The prominence given to erotic love, and the emotions to which it gave rise in both sexes, is what most needs explaining. This culture might, after all, be seen as a completely new strand in what it means to be Roman. While the heroic themes of the *chanson de geste* were common to most epic literature, they arose most naturally in entertainments for military camps based on individual lordships rather than a civic, conscripted army. Erotic love had explicitly been condemned as intrinsically sinful in the western Roman tradition since the time of Augustine at least, so that to dwell lovingly on the contradictions and sufferings arising from it was quite alien to what had gone before.

In this context, south of the Pyrenees something unprecedented seems to have occurred in the eleventh century. Arabic literature, which like Latin had been a product of higher education not open to the general public, started to include vernacular poetry, dedicated to love affairs. Some of this poetry occurred as the coda (in Arabic *kharja* 'exit') to songs in the *muwaššaḥa* 'crossover' form. These songs were highly elaborate in classical Arabic or Hebrew, and the coda was written in Arabic or Hebrew script like the rest of the document, but its language was different: usually it was written in colloquial Andalūsī Arabic, but sometimes in Romance, in the Mozarabic dialect of Muslim Spain. Here is a typical coda in full, transcribed as well into Roman script, with interspersed Arabic words and their translations in bold. Comparison of the Latin source words and a Castilian version give some idea of the distinct flavor of the Mozarabic Romance.

MOZARABIC	ENGLISH	LATIN SOURCE	CASTILIAN
mio sîdî ïbrâhîm	my **lord Ibrahim**	MEVM . . .	*mi señor Ibrahim*
yâ tú uemme dolge	**oh,** you sweet man	. . . TV HOMINEM DVLCEM	*oh tú hombre dulce*
fente mib	come to me	VENI TE MIHI	*vente a mí*
de nohte	by night	DE NOCTE	*de noche*
in *non si non keris*	**if** not, if you don't want to	. . . NON SI NON QVAERIS	*si no, si no quieres*
irey-me tib	I'll go to you	IRE HABEO ME TIBI	*ireme a tí,*
gari*-me a ob*	**tell** me where	. . . ME AD VBI	*dime a dónde*

The *kharja*, always brief, was definitely there to add a little vernacular spice to a formal poem in Arabic or Hebrew, rather than as an independent composition. But another kind of composition of the same twelfth century, the *zajal* 'utterance', while similar to the *muwaššaḥa* in that it had verses and refrains, was in vernacular Andalūsī throughout. Here is a translation of some verses of a *zajal* by the genre's supposed originator, Ibn Quzmān.*

> O joy and spirit of the lover
> Cause of his death and his very life
> As soon as he saw your eyes, they slew him;
> Murder through the eyes takes no prisoners for ransom.
>
> You tear my heart, little one. If you only knew what I endure . . .

---

*But his dates (1095–1159) make him too late to have influenced personally Guilhelm of Aquitaine, the apparent originator of Occitan love lyrics. It is tantalizing that Guilhelm would have grown up with the presence of Arab female slaves captured by his father at Barbastro in 1064. And Guilhelm could have maintained his Moorish links, since he later went to Syria on a Crusade in 1101 and enlisted with the king of Aragon against the Moors of Spain in 1120.

The lover is told, "Just look at her, and have patience."
"What is it like," he replies, "this patience?
Drawn out or round? And what color is it, friend?
Green? Yellow? Then is my lute its reflection?"

You tear my heart, little one. If you only knew what I endure . . .

God has given no one gifts to equal yours.
Among women there is none so fine.
You are heiress to three virtues:
a fair complexion, purity, and faithful love.

You tear my heart, little one. If you only knew what I endure . . . [2]

The *zajal* seems to have influenced the composition of verse in Portuguese at least, including the *cantigas* of King Alfonso. From there the style spread to the Occitan *dansa*, Italian *ballata*, and Old French *virelai*, all popular song forms accompanied by dancing. In fact, since this kind of composition was new in both Iberia and France, it is still disputed whether the Romans got the idea from the Arabs or vice versa. This Andalusian poetry, putting vulgar language into classical form, was unique in its era. Although the *zajal* was to go around the Arabic literary world, it would later die out there, along with vernacular verse in general. Only in western Europe did this verse in popular spoken language begin the tradition of love lyrics that has continued to the present.

In another aspect too Arabic verse probably had a crucial influence on western European verse—in the matter of rhyme. Only in this same period of the eleventh to twelfth centuries did Latin—and other western—verses begin to be fully and systematically rhymed at the end of lines, in couplets or quatrains, so that the poetry with rhythmical stress that had begun in Augustine's time came into its final state. In Arabic, by contrast, rhyming verse with a stress meter had been known since the sixth century at least, and this cultural tradition had coexisted with Romance in Spain since the eighth. The dominant form throughout had been a single (feminine) rhyme persisting throughout a poem.* Although early Latin rhyming poetry had often

---

*Another poetic tradition on the periphery of the Roman world that had had rhyme since the early Middle Ages was Irish. However, this was interpreted by a very different set of rules: stressed syllables could deliberately be rhymed with unstressed, and the rhymes were not exact in requiring matching consonants. It is unlikely, therefore, that Latin verse ever imitated Irish rhyme.

been similar to this, it was not so rigorous, with rhyming endings being a tendency rather than a rule. Yet when the rigor began to be applied, in the eleventh and twelfth centuries, far more complex patterns were soon normal, with a different rhyme in each stanza perhaps, or internal rhymes within a line contrasting with those that mark the end of a line, as in Bernard of Cluny's deathless lines:

Hora novissima, tempora pessima   Hour is the latest, times are the foulest,
 sunt, vigilemus.   let us be wary.
Ecce minaciter imminet arbiter ille Lo ever threatening, cometh upon us
 supremus.   the highest of judges.*

A rhymed hexameter couplet, found on countless tombstones, reads:

Quisquis eris qui transieris, sta, Whoever you will be who has crossed,
 perlege, plora: stand, read, weep.
Sum quod eris, fueram quod es. Pro I am what you will be, I had been what
 me, precor ora.   you are. I beg you, pray for me.[3]

In Leonine hexameters, the old versification combined with the new, the first two and a half feet up to the caesura rhyming with the end of the line.

Vos, qui sub Chri_sto_ ‖ mundo You who under Christ fight in this
 *certatis in i_sto_*   world
discite virtut_um_ ‖ conflictus learn of virtues the conflicts and
 et vicior_um_.   of vices.

Erotic poetry in this era was found in Latin too. Wandering scholars outside the monastery were evidently singing away in Latin, with some of the same themes that came to be associated with Romance, and even with a little psychological realism.

Iam nix glaciesque liquescit, Now snow and ice are melting,
folium et herba virescit,   the leaf and grass is greening,
philomela iam cantat in alto, the nightingale sings high above,

---

*Bernard of Cluny, *De contemptu mundi*—a poem on the last judgment and paradise. The pattern of this couplet is maintained for some three thousand lines.

ardet amor cordis in antro.	love blazes in the heart's cave.
Karissima, noli tardare;	Dearest girl, do not delay;
studeamus nos nunc amare,	let us be zealous now to love,
sine te non potero vivere:	without you I can never live;
iam decet amorem perficere.	now we should perfect our love.
"Non me iuvat tantum convivium	"I don't enjoy festivity
quantum predulce colloquium,	as much as I love colloquy,
nec rerum tantarum ubertas	nor joys of such extremity
ut clara familiaritas."	as much as charming company."
Quid iuvat differre, electa,	Why put off, O my chosen darling,
que sunt tamen post facienda!	what anyway must happen after!
Fac cito, quod eris factura,	Do quickly what you are about to,
in me non est aliqua mora.	for patience I cannot hold out to.[4]

But in the Latin tradition, love was not courtly. The lover did not dwell on the unattainability of his mistress, nor yet that everything depended on her will. And often, a degree of restraint was still required in the telling, not to say self-censorship. Here, for example, is a snatch of a song about birds each singing in its own language, evidently leading into thoughts of maidenly love—the birds and the bees, no less:

Velox impellit rugitus hirundo,	The swift swallow throbs its twitter,
Clangit coturnix, graculus fringultit;	The quail pips, the jackdaw squeals;
Aves sic cuncte celebrant estivum	So all the birds cry forth everywhere
Undique carmen.	Their summer song.
Nulla inter aves similis est api,	None among birds is like the bee,
Que talem tipum gerit castitatis	Bearing such an image of chastity
Nisi que Christum baiulavit alvo	Only she who bore Christ in her belly,
Inviolata.	Inviolate.[5]

In the eleventh century, shaking free of his avian simile, the Latin poet must lead us back to the sanctified, noncarnal love of the Holy Virgin.

❖

There now comes a strange transformation of reputations. Whereas the Romans of southern Europe had once been reputed for their seriousness, and flightiness was deemed the province of the Celts in the north, after the Middle

Ages it would be the "Latins" of the south who would be seen as unstable romantics, while their neighbors speaking Germanic languages became known
for their humorless gravity.

Gravitas 'heaviness' had been a traditional aspiration for Romans of quality. It went together with other ponderous signs of character, such as *maiestas,
constantia, integritas, severitas.* Cicero would often try to see it in those he was
praising, even when it was leavened by less severe virtues: he talked of *comitate
condita gravitas* 'gravity founded in courtesy', *gravitate mixtus lepos* 'wit mixed
with gravity'. Its opposite, *levitas*, was seen as culpable weakness. *Quid est
inconstantia, mobilitate, levitate turpius?* 'What is fouler than inconstancy,
changeability, levity?' *Contemnamus igitur omnis ineptias—quod enim lenius
huic levitati nomen imponam* 'Let us despise all such follies—to which I may
give the gentler name of levity'. And as a byword for depravity he could think
of nothing worse than "dancing in the Forum."[6]

For the Romans and their ideologists, the Greeks, the Gauls' levity was
a crucial flaw. Polybius, in the second century BC, describing the first encoun-
ters of Roman with Gaul in northern Italy in the third, referred to the Gauls'
undisciplined habits of drinking and gorging themselves after a successful
raid. Strabo, a geographer writing over a century later later in the age of Augustus (and quoting the eyewitness report of Poseidonius, a Greek philosopher
who had traveled among the Gauls) wrote: "In addition to being frank and
emotional, they are also childishly boastful, as well as vain about their appearance: they wear gold, with torques round their necks and bracelets on
their arms, and their high-ups are dressed in dyed and gold-spangled clothing. This levity makes them unbearable in victory, but totally panic-stricken
in defeat."

Diodorus Siculus, in the same era, perhaps quoting the same source, was
shocked by their (male, homosexual) promiscuity: "The strangest of all, without a regard for their personal dignity they lightly offer the flower of their
bodies to others. They do not think this obscene, but rather take offense
when somebody so approached does not accept the favor they are offering."

And we can see in some of the few Gaulish artifacts that have survived
a certain twinkle of the "romantic temperament": female nudity, lovingly de-
picted, placed gratuitously on a potter's stamp; affectionate obscenities from
boy to girl, inscribed on the spindle whorls—weights for wool—that were common as lovers' gifts.[7]

But this reputation died away as the Gauls were integrated into the
Roman Empire, forgetting their language and the culture that had gone with

An early potter's stamp from Rouen in Gaul. This gratuitous use of a sexy image, essentially for advertising, shows one characteristic feature of Gaulish culture.

it. They adapted themselves as model Romans, and it is notable that, outside Italy—and with due exception made for the British Isles—the lands which had been full of Celtic speakers became precisely those that made up *Romania*, the western domain of the Romance languages.

Christianity was a true heir to Roman virtue in its respect for *gravitas*: the faith as characterized by Augustine and Ambrose was no laughing matter, and in this Christians once again distinguished themselves not only from frivolous pagans but also from the other eastern religions. There are no comic works with a Christian intent: perish the thought! Paul had decried wit, along with foul language and whimsy, as disallowed by Christ.[8] Latin as used in literature might continue to have its lighter side, sometimes in the most surprising places,* and popular songs still liked their fun. But the Church was above all a place for contemplation of one's soul's eternal prospects, and hence for long faces. This was made quite explicit for the monastic life: in the rule of St. Benedict, the "Instruments of Good Works" include the injunctions "not to speak words vain or apt for laughter" and "not to love great laughter or bursts of it"; under "Taciturnity" "scurrilities and unnecessary words and those that provoke laughter are to be condemned everywhere with eternal exclusion." Indeed, the tenth degree of humility was when a monk "is not easily moved

---

*Ausonius, the premier Latin poet of the fourth century AD, who ultimately rose to the rank of consul, hailed from Burdigala (Bordeaux). In the midst of a variety of work that includes a Christian celebration of Easter, his *Cento Nuptialis* 'wedding quilt' is a patchwork of fragments taken from Virgil cleverly reconstructed into a hexameter poem that gives a blow-by-blow account of a defloration. In the preface, he claims he was put up to it by a challenge from the emperor Valentinian himself.

and quick for laughter, for it is written: *The fool exalteth his voice in laughter (Sirach 21:23)."*⁹*

It was from *gravitas* like this that Romance literature gave some worldly relief. The celebration of righteous warriors was in any case, by the eleventh century, sanctified by the Church's new zeal for the Crusade. The celebration of lovers was more difficult, and many may have paid the price rued in this anonymous verse:

Abbatissae debent mori	Abbesses deserve death
quae subjectas nos amori	who us sufferers for love
claudi jubent culpa gravi,	order to be confined and shamed,
quod tormentum jam temptavi.	a torment that I have now tasted.
Loco clausa sub obscuro,	Shut up down in a dark place,
diu vixi pane duro.	long I lived on stale bread.
Hujus poenae fuit causa	For this penalty what the reason?
quod amare dicor ausa.	Because they say I dared to love.¹⁰

But such feelings could forcibly be rechanneled, if necessary, into contemplation of the Holy Virgin, or of the love of Christ for his Church. As witness this ardent twelfth-century interpretation of the Hebrew love poem that the Council of Trent in its wisdom had included in the Bible, the Song of Solomon—*Canticum canticorum*:

> It is not heard by the ears, it does not echo in the streets: only they who sing it can hear it, and He for whom it is sung, the bride and the bridegroom. It is a nuptial song. It describes the chaste and ecstatic embrace of the senses, the harmony of customs, emotions in unison, and mutual love.¹¹

Christianity never thought—as Islam by contrast did, and quite explicitly, in its three major literatures in Arabic, Persian, and Turki—to reinterpret the whole genre of love poetry as a lyrical quest for the spiritual union of the soul with God, thus according it the full blessing and support of the religious establishment.

---

*This appears only in the Bible's Apocrypha, actually at Ecclesiasticus 21.20: FATVVS IN RISV EXALTAT VOCEM SVAM. But St. Benedict was clearly scraping the barrel for an adequate text: the verse goes, on, VIR AVTEM SAPIENS VIX TACITE RIDEBIT 'but a wise man will scarcely smile in quiet'.

Curiously, as the Latins' enthusiasm for Romance secular literature took hold in the south and west, the Germanic northeast of Europe responded by rejecting frivolous vernacular verse. German *Minnesang* 'love song' had grown and flourished in precise analogy and parallel with the Romance *fin'amor*. Now the new self-appointed heirs to the Roman Empire, the "Holy Roman Empire" of the Germans, would in the thirteenth century seek a new seriousness, a new source of *gravitas*.

Uns sint unsenfte brieve her von
    Rôme komen:
 uns ist erloubet trûren und fröide
    gar benomen.
 Daz müet mich inneclîchen (wir lebten
    ie vil wol),
 daz ich nû für min lachen weinen
    kiesen sol.
	Hard tidings have arrived from
	    Rome:
	 mourning is allowed, and joy is utterly
	    banned.
	 It troubles me deeply (we always lived
	    so well)
	 that now I must choose tears instead
	    of laughter.

Walther von der Vogelweide (ca 1220)[12]

They would ultimately find it in vernacular culture, turning away from the inherited collective certainties of the Church, and focusing on the struggle of each individual to achieve a personal understanding of, and relationship with, his or her God. This would give a new, but quite different, role to the written vernacular, not to express the martial nostalgia and romantic love longings of the less-educated aristocrat, but the word of God, in language that everyone could understand, schooled or not. Martin Luther would find a use for written German that Walther von der Vogelweide had overlooked. The Reformation, then, largely dividing the Germanic north of western Europe from its Romance, Catholic, south, would definitively—if rather caricaturishly—contrast the grave Teutons, who used their literacy for Bible study, with the lighthearted Latins, who used theirs for stories of chivalry and romance.

The vicissitudes of *gravitas* and *levitas* during those fifteen hundred years from the first century BC are strangely repetitive. In each stage, a group that valued heaviness opposed lighter-hearted opponents. Whether the lighter-hearted party was worsted and eliminated or simply expelled to start a new tradition, the confrontation of heavy and light always returned. In the first century BC, the well-disciplined and systematically exploitative Romans conquered the less organized Gauls. In the fourth century AD, within a victorious Roman Empire, the seriously driven Christians subverted and suppressed the traditional power of the (less ardent) pagans. In the tenth century, the innovation came from the less serious side: within a Christian but no longer purely Roman west, the pious (and grammar-observing) Church witnessed the rise of a new literature and new kingdoms, buttressed by straight writing in the vernacular. Part, at least, of this new movement was suppressed: the crusade against the Albigensian heresy of the south of France in the early thirteenth century destroyed the independent Occitan courts, homes of *fin'amor*. But in the fifteenth century, the Church's own tradition came to be seen as not sufficiently grave: this time, the serious, Protestant faction was unable to take control of the organization and so itself seceded.

In each new revolution, vernacular literature was stressed: authentic language, taken straight from the lips of the people, was made to serve the cause of the new ideas, whether they were on the side of levity or gravity. Ultimately, this recurring vernacularization would break the hold of Latin itself, but not before the sixteenth and seventeenth centuries. Until then the force of the vernacular was only to redefine, and nuance, the persistent role of Latin.

So much for grave analysis of *la longue durée*. On a lighter note, we might comment that it had taken a thousand years for tendrils of the Gauls' intuitive, generous spirit finally to find their way through the concrete of rational stolidity set in place by Julius Caesar's legions. Spring had at last returned, and the birds were singing again. In the influential triumph of *fin'amor* across the courts of western Europe, could the Celts be having a last laugh?

❖❖❖

CHAPTER 13

Litterae humaniores—
The Fruits of a Latin Education

Dicebat Bernardus Carnotensis nos esse quasi nanos, gigantium
humeris incidentes, ut possimus plura eis et remotiora videre, non
utique proprii visus acumine, aut eminentia corporis, sed quia in
altum subvehimur et extollimur magnitudine gigantea.

Bernard of Chartres used to say that we are like dwarfs dropping onto the
shoulders of giants to see more than they and farther, not as by the sharpness of
our own sight or the tallness of our body, but because we are carried on high and
lifted by the giants' stature.

John of Salisbury, *Metalogicon*, iii.4

A S THE CONTINUOUS SEQUENCE of manuscripts shows, for most of the
millennium that started in AD 500, Latin remained the language of organized life in western Europe. And this Latin, although its vocabulary was
massively expanded to keep track of the new feudal and ecclesiastical society in
which it was used, was palpably the same language that the grammarian Donatus had described in the fourth century AD to preserve the usage of the first
century BC. Church fathers such as Augustine at the beginning of the fifth
century had already been skeptical about the value of the schoolmasters' rules.
But those rules were to prove much more durable than any attempts at populist
innovation.

Latin, after all, was what was presented in school *grammatica*. As popular speech changed and began to lose touch with it, Latin came first to seem
stilted, then emerged as a language artificially maintained. But as such, there
was less and less point for writers to try to assert their ordinary usage over the
strictures of the schoolroom. The Frankish chronicler Gregory of Tours, his

Latin famously ropy, might well remark (around 575), "The rhetorician philosophizing is understood by few, but the plain man speaking by many."[1] But those plain men would have less and less call to use actual Latin when they spoke, whereas the words of the rhetoricians were increasingly only to be found on the written page. Ultimately, it helped communication—as well as one's posthumous reputation—if writers could at least get their Latin right, rather than each stay true to his or her own dialect. Uniformity meant that all Latin users would understand one another, not only in the present but also across the centuries. Levels of education might of course lapse, as they did in the unruly *Romania* of the sixth, seventh, and eighth centuries, before Alcuin and the Carolingian Renaissance restored a clear sense of the standard in the ninth. But the standard itself was not lost beyond recall, as long as the great writers of the past were still being read and copied out.

The Latin that survived in these conditions was in many ways more circumscribed than the natural lingua franca that had emerged from Rome and been spread by its empire. Above all, it became a 'clerical' language, the province exclusively of *clerici* who had learned it at school, and used mostly for institutional purposes, in Catholic churches, temples, and monasteries, in the chanceries and courtrooms of civil government, and—to a limited extent—in the countinghouses of commerce. The word *clerici* itself had originally meant clergymen, those in holy orders who had received the *clerus* (an early loan from ecclesiastical Greek, *klêros*, the 'lot' or title to officiate in the temple, defined for the Levites in Deuteronomy xviii.2, and extended to Christ in Acts of the Apostles i.17). From the fifth century on, however, the *clerici* were largely the only people who were literate, and so the word came to mean people whose duties involved reading and writing, the class previously known as *notarii* 'notaries'. There came to be *clerici regis*, 'clerks of the king', signing their names on documents of state; *clerici cauponarii* 'innkeeping clerks', who kept the books in hostelries; *clerici camerae computorum* 'clerks of the counting chamber', i.e., petty clerks. It also included those still in education, as in the words of Robert of Sorbonne: "He who is a more frequent attender at class and listens more intently to his master should be thought a better clerk."[2] But it was still used to single out the members of a congregation who could officiate at services and, as such, usually covered those who had taken monastic vows, as well as those in holy orders proper. To this extent at least, it could include women; so *clerica* is one word for a nun.

Some few women continued to get the chance to learn Latin throughout the Middle Ages, and there are female authors of literature, as well as writers of letters, whose works have survived. This small company of exceptional people includes the English nun Hygeburg (late eighth century), who wrote lives of saints; a Frankish noblewoman, Dhuoda (early ninth), who wrote an extended letter of advice for her elder son; and the Saxon nun Hrotsvitha of Gandersheim (late tenth), who in the midst of a wide-ranging oeuvre wrote Latin comedies in the style of Terence to celebrate the deeds of holy virgins. Here is a characteristic scene of hers, where female observers get the better of a deluded and lustful male.

c. What's all this crashing of pots, cauldrons, and frying pans?

H. I'll look. Oh, come here, do, take a peek through the cracks!

A. What?

H. Look, this idiot has taken leave of his senses. He thinks he's got us in his arms.

A. What is he doing?

H. Now he's caressing the pots against his groin, now he's cuddling the pans and cauldrons, showering them with tender kisses.

c. What a joke.

H. And his face, hands, and clothes have got so dirty, so filthy that you'd take him for the blackest Ethiopian.

A. Serves him right to have a body like that, when the devil's taken over his mind.[3]

Hildegard of Bingen (1098–1179) was another unique figure. While a major presence as the head of her convent, she was a writer of visions and a composer of music, ready too at the age of eighty to accept excommunication rather than obey orders and desecrate an excommunicate's grave.

Visiones vero quas vidi, non eas in somnis, nec dormiens, nec in phrenesi, nec corporeis oculis aut auribus exterioris hominis, nec in abditis locis percepi, sed eas vigilans et circumspecta in pura mente, oculis et auribus interioris hominis, in apertis locis, secundum voluntatem Dei accepi. Quod quomodo sit, carnali homini perquirere difficile est.

But the visions that I saw, not in dreams, nor sleeping, nor in a frenzy, nor with bodily eyes or ears of an outward person, nor in hidden places did I see them, but awake and alert with a clear mind, with eyes and ears of an inward person, in open places, according to the will of God I received them. As to how it may be, it is hard for a fleshly person to investigate.

Nevertheless, female voices in Latin were a distinct minority: Latin became over these centuries a language predominantly for men. By the same token, curiously, it acquired the profile of a language for male initiates. Such languages, as they are known worldwide,* are not naturally acquired by young males, but consciously transmitted to them through an inherited but quite artificial procedure. For Latin too competence was largely the preserve of a class of high-status males, and this competence was not likely to be achieved before the age of puberty. The artificial procedure of transmitting Latin (namely school learning) turned out to be an extremely effective substitute for natural language acquisition by word of mouth, preserving the language essentially unchanged over many centuries; it worked in countries where the native language was unrelated to Latin just as well as—perhaps even more easily than—where it was Romance. And by 1000, as we have seen, these countries where Latin came as a book language, to be learned ab initio, had become exceedingly numerous.

◈

Latin, generally known in these centuries as *grammatica*, achieved a kind of timeless status. Characterized by Dante as "a certain immutable identity of language at diverse times and places"[4] it was generally seen as an unchanging link with the past. The list of *auctores*, the celebrated authors, came in an unbroken succession since Terence, Cicero, and Virgil, including the Bible and the Church Fathers, but—with the exception of Holy Scripture—all of comparable *auctoritas*, and to be interpreted where necessary allegorically or metaphorically, to accord with divine revelation, all equally witnesses to truth about the world. This was an era when the ancient, discriminating concept of "classic" had been lost to sight, as had the late Empire's troubling dilemma about the evident literary merits of pagan, as against Christian, authors. Everything that had survived was an *auctor*, to be read and respected, and somehow to be understood as part of the literary heritage of Christendom. Only when "humanistic" thinking began to spread, late in the fifteenth century, was an attempt begun to appreciate each author in the temper of his own time. As we shall see, the medieval syllabus had no space for history as a subject; and the

---

*Two well-known examples from the anthropological literature are Demin, acquired by Lardil aboriginal men in Mornington Island in Australia, and the Isikhwetha initiation-language of the Xhosa in South Africa. Ong 1959 develops the idea of acquiring Latin as a rite of puberty.

idea of the past as a foreign country, where they do and think things differently, was quite alien to it.[5]

Where scholars did see a conflict of values was not between ancients and moderns, but in an ongoing debate on what was the practical value of the skill in Latin once acquired. This was dramatized most vividly in their attitudes to the science of rhetoric, which had always been developed as the science of language in use, and hence an eminently practical discipline. We now trace the development of understanding this in the first and early second millennia AD.

In Greece and Rome, where politics and leadership had been understood as the highest priority in life, this had been conceived as the art of effective speaking. To support this, formal principles had been discerned and laid down. Following those principles rigorously, however, tended to lead to a rather labored, not to say artificial, style of speaking. Nevertheless, rhetorical handbooks from ancient Rome, the *Rhetorica ad Herennium* and Cicero's *De Inventione*, remained primary sources on techniques of composition throughout the Middle Ages.

Early Christianity could make good use of this approach: who stood more in need of effective oratory, after all, than the preacher? But Augustine, who had himself been a student of rhetoric, was skeptical: look at the Holy Scriptures, he says in book 4 of his *De doctrina Christiana*, and you will see that they owe their power to the intrinsic force of their content, not to any oratorical tricks or, as they were known, *colores*. He illustrated this with examples of plain, measured, and majestic styles in the Bible and the works of the Fathers of the Church, always in his view well fitted to the tone of their subject.* In this, he claimed, they were quite naturally in line with Cicero: "To be eloquent, then, is to say what is slight unassumingly, what is reasonable temperately, what is great grandly."[6]

Six generations later, Cassiodorus (who died around 580) had retired from distinguished service in Italy's by then Gothic administration to write on

---

*Augustine, *De doctrina Christiana*, iv.20.39–44. There is a problem, however, in analyzing what he meant, one characteristic of much literary criticism ever since. The *colores* of rhetorical language had explicitly been labeled and defined and could hence be recognized unequivocally. But the stylistic traits that, according to Augustine, inhered in content by its very nature could not be stated: they had simply to be displayed and (with luck) recognized by the reader. (In fact, Augustine's "temperate" style seems to have involved heavy use of parallel phrases, and his "majestic" style constant rhetorical questions and direct address to the audience.) A skeptic could see this as having no conscious style at all. Rhetoric, while still respected in name, was left empty, with an unhelpful injunction to "Do the right thing."

culture, rather as Cicero himself had done in his latter years. Cassiodorus started his *Institutiones* 'General education' by deploring the current vogue for secular authors and urged his readers to begin with sacred learning. Wrapping up his account of rhetoric, he noted that its techniques of memorization, delivery, and voice training, although they were developed for men of affairs, could also be useful to the monk, in reading Scripture, declaiming holy law, and singing psalms. "Thus instructed, one returns to holy work, even if one deals for some time with secular books."[7]

This was indicative of the future trend of western culture. The best minds of the latter first millennium were going to retire to the cloister, where there would be precious little call for skills of persuading large audiences or other attainments of public life. One of those minds belonged to Bede, who spent his life (672–735) in monasteries, but nevertheless thought it worth writing a rhetorical treatise, *De schematibus et tropis* 'On figures of speech and tropes'. He found all his examples in the Latin Bible. As the German diplomat Wibald of Corvey was to point out much later, in mid-twelfth century when horizons were beginning to broaden out again, it was impossible to acquire the art of speaking in the monasteries: there was no opportunity to use it. No more did medieval legal practice, whether ecclesiastical or secular, give any scope for pleading, hence oratory.[8]

But by the founding text of those monasteries, the rule of St. Benedict (who had lived a generation earlier than Cassiodorus, dying in 547), time was set aside every day for private reading, and a new book was to be dispensed from the library every year at Lent.[9] Cassiodorus, who had himself founded the monastery of Vivarium, had a vision of valiant scribes striking a blow against the devil with every word they wrote: "What happy concentration, praiseworthy pains, to preach to men with one's hand, to loose tongues with one's fingers, to bring salvation to mortals in silence, and fight against the wrongful wiles of the devil with pen and ink. Truly, Satan receives a wound for every word of the Lord that a scholar writes down."[10]

There is no reason to believe Benedict had quite shared this vision; his rule is in any case a rather more pedestrian document. Nevertheless, written culture had a privileged status in the monastic life: reading in practice entailed producing a copy of the book being read, and the monastery would have to ensure that all its monks were literate and hence provide instruction in reading, writing, and indeed Latin. With the breakdown of city life after the Germanic invasions, monasteries were to take over almost all education, until the reforms associated with Charlemagne in the ninth century required cathedrals too to provide schools. Naturally, the works read would be predominantly sacred, or chronicles and devotions by ecclesiastical authors, but the system did allow space for secular works too. One of the few records that shows what monks might take out of the library, a roll of books lent for the year 1040 at the premier monastery Cluny shows, besides a wealth of Scripture and commentary, the borrowing of a solitary copy of Livy.[11]

In the monastic world, oral culture had given way to scribal transmission: rhetoric, which remained current as the science of language in use, would have to adapt. After a long hiatus—as long as five centuries—during which rhetoric was preserved rather than developed, it did so by focusing on the details of poetic composition. Alberic (1040–1109), a monk of Monte Cassino, was one of the first to make the jump. He seems to have needed to sublimate earthier thoughts when he elaborated on the need to avoid extraneous material, even if apparently splendid, since he saw such composition as whoring after false cosmetics: "Let the meaning run on content with her own limbs, not damaged by the foulness of copulation with another: her own inner beauty will be enough to make her shine . . . So do not give up on simplicity!"[12]

In similar vein, he had also been exercised about the intrinsic value of metaphor in composition: "But it is characteristic of metaphor, as it were, to twist the mode of the expression away from its own nature, and by that twisting to renew it, and in renewing to cover it as with a wedding dress, and having covered it, as it were, to sell it honorably."[13]

This talk of metaphorically selling an idea, however, despite its modern ring, was true to the new, more mercantile attitudes that were going to come in. Alberic was living in an Italy where business was about to boom. His main detractor, Adalbertus Samaritanus, writing a century later as a professor in a Bologna city school, was in fact concerned to get away from literary appreciation: his priority was to give his students a solid grounding in how to draft expository prose for use in their business careers. The title of Alberic's most substantial treatise was *Breviarium de dictamine*, and Adalbertus called his work *Praecepta dictaminum*. Both show that the content of rhetoric was being reconceived as a new subject: the *ars dictaminis* 'art of dictation', which now meant not 'speaking for another to transcribe' (as it had before and would again), but rather just writing. In principle, whatever people needed to write, this art would teach them how to do it. A stream of *Artes Dictandi*, as the manuals were entitled, were written from the twelfth century until the fifteenth, first centered on Bologna and its school of law, with a highly pragmatic tone, later centered on Paris, where a more literary approach was cultivated. Letter-writing alone was the formal subject of these works, but wills, edicts, and legal charters were all seen as subspecies of the letter, so the full range of business Latin was supported.

Unlike traditional rhetoric, which had been organized notionally around the anatomy of a courtroom speech, the study that replaced it, medieval *dictamen*, was rather subclassified by its possible styles of language: principally, these were prose, quantitative meter (in the style of classical poetry), and rhythmical verse (based on stress and rhyme). These types of written language had in fact all tended to flow into each other and cross-fertilize in medieval literary compositions, to the extent that there was, from the sixth century until the thirteenth, no simple way of saying—nor perhaps need to say—that a writer was a poet.[14] A writer was either an *auctor* on the hallowed list, inherited from the past, or else he was a modern *dictator*.

With this loss of historical perspective, the European world seems for a time to have forgotten its concept of the structure and interrelation of different genres, or what different points they might have had. For five hundred years at least, all the literature that would survive had had to pass the test of being read, and so copied, by monks; and outside the limited discussion pursued in classes of *grammatica*, there had simply been no place for discussions of literary theory. The result, both in the Church and outside, was a kind of genial contempt for the arts as a necessary part of education but lacking in serious value. Bishop Walter of Speyer in 984 recalled how after eight years at the cathedral school studying *grammatica* and the liberal arts he could not wait to leave such childish courses behind and hurry on to the dishes of the sacred feast—the study of the Scriptures—their taste presumed sweeter than any honey: all this recounted in elegant hexameters that were the clear fruit of that education.[15] And this cheerful disrespect for what Alberic had called "the flowers of rhetoric" would be succeeded by different forms of unsympathetic tough-mindedness, whether the logic of the schoolmen, or the calculating pragmatism of the merchants, before the rise of humanism, and a new interest in the original meaning of what the Latin tradition had preserved.

⟡

But the Middle Ages had its own ways of understanding its meaning. Positivsm or minimalism was alien to this era.* Left to itself, medieval semantics developed

---

*Though this too had its precursors, especially in the incurably pragmatic Anglo-Saxon tradition. Witness William of Ockham (1295–1349) and his famous "razor" principle:

into a luxuriant growth. Any text, but par excellence the Holy Scriptures, could signify with meaning on different levels. Beyond the literal interpretation, *historia*, there was a figurative meaning, *allegoria*, if only one could understand it; and beyond that a mystical meaning, *anagogia*, and some moral guidance too, *tropologia*.[16] Coming to appreciate these was the true value of an education.

As one rather profound instance of this, the nature of the world and its workings was, for the medieval intellectual, revealed by the form of the education that gave understanding of it. As John of Salisbury, who had had the best education that the twelfth century could provide, opined:

> *est autem ars ratio quae compendio sui naturaliter possibilium expedit facultatem . . . Natura enim quamvis vivida nisi erudiatur ad artis facultatem non pervenit. Artium tamen omnium parens est, eisque quo proficiant et perficiantur dat nutriculam rationem.*

> An art is a plan [*ratio*] that in its own compass [*compendium*] opens a means of access [*facultas*] to what is naturally possible . . . For Nature herself, however lively, without refinement will not attain to being the means of access that an art is. Nevertheless, she is the parent of all the arts and gives them a form [*ratio*] that nourishes them so that they may benefit and reach perfection.[17]

These arts were a heritage in concept from ancient Greece, where together they had constituted what was known as *enkúklios paideía* ('a rounded education' or 'an education through 360 degrees'). For the Romans, incorporating them wholesale with so much else from Greece in the second century BC, they became the *Artes Liberales*, the arts worthy of a free man (with the leisure to pursue them).

They were seven in number: *grammatica, dialectica, rhetorica, geometria, arithmetica, astronomia, harmonia*. Their names have been somewhat reinterpreted in the modern era, so to give a more specific idea of their content as school subjects, they were: Latin (grammar and authors), logic, and composition/literary criticism, making up the foundation course or *trivium* 'three

---

entia non sunt multiplicanda praeter necessitatem, or more authentically, *numquam ponenda est pluralitas sine necessitate* 'posit no more entities than you need'. (Kneale and Kneale 1962: 243.)

ways'; then a combination of geography with geometry, followed by arithmetic, astronomy, and music, together known as the *quadrivium* 'four ways', or as mathematics.[18] The later medieval mnemonic verse, which preserves the schoolboy slang abbreviations for them, runs:

> *Gram. loquitur; Dia. vera docet; Rhe. verba ministrat;*
> *Mus. canit; Ar. numerat; Geo. ponderat; As. colit astra.*
>
> *Gram* speaks; *Dia* teaches truths; *Rhe* supplies words;
> *Mus* sings; *Ar* counts; *Geo* weighs; *As* studies heavenly bodies.[19]

These subjects would have formed the basis of any structure given to lessons in the monastery schools. But in the ninth century they would have become general across Europe in Charlemagne's empire, in the cathedral schools whose model was Alcuin's academy in Aachen. (Walter of Speyer's Latin poem on his late-tenth-century schooldays at the school in Speyer was naturally organized around them.) They were to remain the basis of the curriculum in Latin classrooms throughout the Middle Ages.

Naturally, since this era loved nothing more than an allegory, they were often equated with the Seven Pillars, which according to Proverbs ix.1—though apparently with no reference to learning—supported the house of Wisdom. But the classic presentation was *De Nuptiis Philologiae et Mercurii* 'On the Marriage of Philology and Mercury', by Martianus Capella (writing AD 410–39), a North African contemporary of Augustine's. This allegory of the liberal arts enjoyed more than twelve hundred years of success as a child-friendly textbook. Translated into German around 1000, it was published eight times in the sixteenth century and even found favor with the young Leibniz around 1670. In it Mercury, the god of trade and business, resolves to get married, and at Apollo's suggestion receives in matrimony the maiden *Philologia* 'Scholarship', who is borne up to heaven by her Latin footmen *Amor* and *Labor*, and Greek handmaidens *Epimelia* 'Application' and *Agrypnia* 'Sleeplessness'. One might have expected the seven liberal arts to appear as the resulting children, but in fact they present themselves as parts of a wedding gift, addressing Philologia one by one in the last seven books of the work, with fairly unrelieved accounts of their specific learning. Still, in the descriptions that introduce them there is some revealing wit.

Grammatica is an old lady with highly polished manners, and various surgical appliances, such as a scalpel to excise the vices in children's tongues,

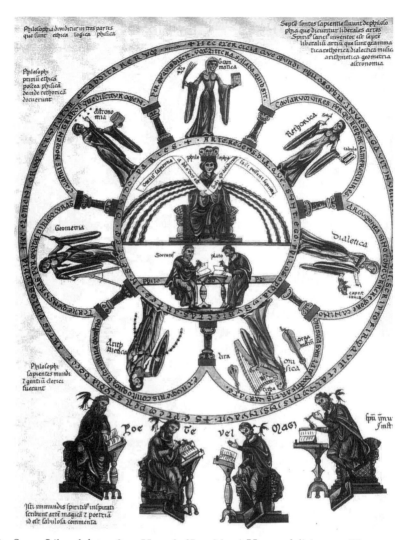

The Seven Liberal Arts, *from Herrad of Landsberg's* Hortus deliciarum. *The arts were the unique basis of Latin education from the second century BC to the twelfth century AD.*

an inky powder that could heal the same, and an extremely sharp medicine, compounded of flower of fennel (used as a cane) and stripped back of goat-skin, to be applied to the throat in case of fetid burps brought on by un-schooled boorishness. *Dialectica* is pale, with a sharp look and constantly ranging gaze, and an exceedingly elaborate hairdo of plaits and curls interwo-ven, but without a hair out of place. Her left arm is entwined in the coils of a serpent, but this is hidden under her cloak, while her right carries a string of wax tablets inscribed with formulas, carefully affixed to a concealed hook. *Rhetorica* strides in with a proud bearing and pout to match her sublime looks in body and face, a helmet on her head and thunderbolts in her hands, for show as well as real damage. Serried ranks of the great orators of the past are in her train.

Geometria appears with a ray of light in her right hand and the earth itself in her left, in a gown decorated with the courses and magnitudes of the heavenly bodies. (*Astronomia* is in fact her sister.) She no sooner enters the Olympian court than she falls to calculating its precise dimensions. *Arithmetica* arrives next, a single beam of light shining from her forehead, which diffuses one by one into a multitude of beams that then come back to a point to focus. She wears an elaborate dress that covers the workings of the whole world, and her fingers are constantly gesticulating. She salutes Jupiter with figures for the number 717, which (according to Pallas) is his real name. *Astronomia* flies in on wings of glass, her body covered in eyes and jewels, a measure in one hand and in the other a book of the courses of stars and planets, illuminated in metallic colors. And a hush falls among the gods as *Harmonia* 'Music' enters, surrounded by celestial music but with no instruments, her clothing a tinkling ensemble of metal chimes. She, of course, begins her address to the throng not in prose like the others, but in verse. Yet her verse form (a string of pentameters only, without the expected hexameters to precede them) is otherwise unknown as a meter.

These then were the personalities whimsically given to the several arts by Martianus Capella, whoever he may have been, personalities that were to stick with them firmly over the next millennium. They became tutelary deities of the Latin language in the sense that nobody would acquire it except through school, and nobody would go to school without making their acquaintance, necessarily in painstaking detail.

It will be noted that they were a totally secular set of characters. They were dreamed up at the end of the pagan era, very possibly by a Christian with a good stock of classical learning, and set in a divine context—a Homeric Olympus—which is evidently taken as a pure literary conceit. Yet they were never going to become the victims of humorless bigotry or rewritten to replace the source of their literary references with Holy Scripture. The long centuries of medieval Latin, militantly Christian though their culture remained, were linguistically and educationally tolerant, at least by the standards of puritan movements that Europe and the world have known since the Reformation.

Pagan learning was to remain valued within the Latin syllabus throughout the Middle Ages.

Crucially, this broad-mindedness can be attributed to the precedent set by Augustine, who was in fact a contemporary, perhaps even a neighbor, of Martianus Capella. Augustine struggled with the question of what attitude Christianity should take to the vast realms of pre-Christian culture, which among much else were the foundation of the educational syllabus of trivium and quadrivium. He found his solution in Exodus xii.36: "And the Lord gave the people favor in the sight of the Egyptians, so that they lent unto them such things as they required. And they looted the Egyptians."

Interpreting allegorically, as ever, Augustine held that Israel stood for the Christians, the Egyptians for pre-Christian pagans, and the things—precious raiment, gold, and silver—were the cultural wealth that the faithful could in fact make better use of than the originators, since they possessed the higher truth with which to interpret its true meaning. "The teachings of the pagan writers not only contain products of their imagination and superstitious misconceptions, a heavy ballast of wasted effort, which each and every one of us must hate and avoid when we leave pagan society, but also the liberal sciences, which are very suitable for the new life in freedom."[20]

This doctrine effectively gave the Church full license to pick and choose from within its vast Latin (and Greek) heritage. With the overarching view that God had managed everything in history, He too must be the source of any truths that classical civilization had discovered. It was not necessary, indeed it was wrong, to be intellectually puritan and condemn anything at all on the grounds of its source. Had not Virgil himself foreseen the birth of Christ? (See pp. 116–17.) And warming to their theme, some controversialists noted with delight that not only was there value to be found in pagan literature, as long as it was approached with proper discernment, but Scripture itself was full of borrowings from pagan authors. As Conrad of Hirsau was to point out much later:

> Where do you think Paul got "evil communications corrupt good manners" from, if not from Menander, the classical poet? Where did the proverb he quotes in the letter to his disciple Titus "the Cretans are always liars, evil beasts, and slow bellies" come from, if not Epimenides the pagan poet? . . . If I went into everything in order to untangle you from the web you have got yourself into, we would range too far and wide, especially as in your own [Benedictine] rule there is a proverb from Terence: "Everything in reason!"[21]

The seven liberal arts had originally been seen as making up an introductory course, to be mastered before moving on to philosophy. This function they lost after the collapse of the western Empire, and of secular Latin education. In the Christian centuries—as the attitudes of Cassiodorus in the sixth century (pp. 194–95) and Walter of Speyer in the tenth (p. 197) have shown—other texts, Walter's "sacred feast" of the Scriptures, would be seen as the summit of human learning. In any case, few philosophical texts in Latin remained available anywhere.* This meant, of course, the exclusion of what we would recognize as philosophy but also natural philosophy as a whole, including such things as the study of physics and biology, in which Aristotle had actually taken rather a keen interest. Alchemy too was excluded. Sacred texts were of course read, and read assiduously, throughout the Middle Ages, but they were never assembled into a syllabus until, with the advent of the universities, starting in the thirteenth century, theology began to be put on an academic basis. Robert of Courçon included it in the first statutes of the Univerity of Paris in 1215.

Other major absences from the liberal arts syllabus, over the millennium from 500 to 1500, are worth noting. It contained no history as such, despite the occasional presence among the authors read in *grammatica* class of such revered figures as Sallust, Livy, and Caesar, and Orosius' *Historiae adversus Paganos* 'Histories against the Pagans'. This last was a tendentious chronicle of all known events to date, written in the fifth century AD at Augustine's behest by a younger friend of his: it continued to be read as the best universal history available throughout the Middle Ages. Neither did the curriculum contain any account of law. This is a strange omission given the Romans' past expertise in this field and its potential for practical utility. By contrast, Jewish education had always centered on the *Tôrāh*, which means nothing else than 'the Law', and indeed focuses on a part of the same Scripture that Christians revered.

---

*Boethius (ca 480–524), a contemporary of Cassiodorus' at the Gothic court of Theoderic, and one of the last westerners to be able to read Greek, had in fact set himself to translate all of Plato and Aristotle into Latin, but was sadly cut off from his books (and ultimately his life) through suspicion of a plot against Theoderic. All Boethius' works that did survive became central to Latin learning, including his translations of some basic works of Aristotle and Porphyry on logic, and above all his masterly "prison diary," the *Consolation of Philosophy*. His *Arithmetica* was to remain western Europe's basic text in the subject during the first millennium AD—an irony of history, since he was not seriously a mathematician. But his major program was left undone, and philosophy remained mostly a closed book until the rediscovery of Aristotle in the later thirteenth century.

It is striking—at least from a modern European standpoint—that there was no place for *artes mechanicae*. These had been esteemed, as early as the seventh century, as "the knowledge or theory in which, in a subtle manner, the *fabrica rerum omnium* 'fabric of all things' comes together."[22] Later Hugh of St. Victor (1096–1141) had noted, "mechanics is the science by which man imitates nature in order to assist him in the satisfaction of his bodily needs." His list of seven such arts, revised by Robert Kilwardby in 1250, comprised textiles, apparatus (which includes ceramics, carpentry, metallurgy, building science, engineering, mining, and architecture), nautics (including commerce as well as navigation), agriculture, and nutrition (including cooking and hunting), medicine, and theater.[23] One gets the sense that, if the transmission of ideas had been just a little different, these might have been included in general education. Varro, in fact, in his *Disciplinae* of the first century BC, had proposed not seven but nine liberal arts, adding medicine and architecture to the canon.

However, the artisan-like nature of many of these, together with the fact that nautics and architecture in particular were dominated by closed guild organizations, meant that they remained excluded from the company of the liberal arts. Neither were they incorporated as higher studies, even after the invention of university faculties in the thirteenth century, which would give a special dignity to law, medicine, and theology alongside the arts. In fact, these latter three had already been singled out in the seventh-century Latin encyclopedia of Isidore of Seville, in which they constitute the next three chapters after the three openers devoted to grammar, rhetoric-dialectic, and mathematics.*

Above all, education in this millennium was language-oriented. The trivium of grammar, dialectic, and rhetoric was central, and that was first and foremost about the Latin language, and that language only. All instruction took place in it. But since there was no teaching of foreign languages, and indeed hardly any recognition of Europe's vernacular languages—the languages that pupils spoke at home—as real languages at all, there was no sense of Latin as a distinct language in its own right: rather, it was, even for the sophisticated Dante, himself capable of comparing dialects, "nothing but a kind of sameness of speech unalterable for diverse times and places." Medieval western attitudes to Latin are

---

*This work is known as *Etymologiae* since Bishop Isidore (who died in 636) delighted to give speculative word origins for his technical terms. It was a standard volume in medieval libraries: at least a thousand manuscripts survive to show how important it was.

reminiscent of those of contemporary Arab Muslims to classical Arabic, as expressed by Ibn Khaldūn (1332–1406): "In every nation, the formation of language takes place according to their own terminology. The linguistic habit that the Arabs obtained in this way is the best there is . . . Cultured people . . . derived certain laws for the Arab linguistic habit from their way of speaking. These norms are of general applicability, like universals and basic principles." Likewise even in the 1960s, Anglo-Saxon philosophers used to like to pontificate for "language" in general, presuming that their concepts would transcend any parochial limits of their own language (usually English). In this context John Searle observed, "Different human languages, to the extent that they are intertranslatable, can be regarded as different conventional realizations of the same underlying rules."[24]

What did they know of Latin who only Latin knew? They certainly learned it more effectively than we do today, in that the courses gave the ability not just to read and write, but also converse in it, listen to lectures, and argue in it, whether passionately or dispassionately; after Alcuin's reforms in the Carolingian Renaissance, it seems that varying regional styles of pronunciation did not affect the overall ability of Latin scholars to communicate orally, whatever their origins. Furthermore, all the textbooks were written in Latin from the outset, and books—as bound manuscript copies—were inevitably scarce. Although introductory lessons may have been bilingual for a time, explaining the vagaries of Latin grammar in a more familiar mother tongue, effective progress would only come when the pupils, having mastered the grammar *memoriter*, by heart, could use their language skills to gain yet more, Latin, knowledge.

As the vernacular languages changed, unheeded by the schools, Latin in its unchanging form, highly disciplined and policed, was becoming a language like none they spoke at home. If that was true in Italy, Spain, or France, where the home language was a form of Romance, how much more so in Ireland, Germany, or Hungary, where it bore no evident relation to their mother tongue at all. For normal children, the acquisition of this language inevitably went quite against the grain. And classroom methods were not soft: it is unsurprising that few references to medieval schooldays are without jokey mention of the *ferula*, the fennel wand used as an instrument of correction.

By the end of the first millennium AD, this was the Latin education current across almost the whole of Europe. The culture that it propagated was a curious complex, in which Roman Christianity, an oriental religion rearticulated in a language not its own, was set alongside traditional knowledge from an ancient pagan empire, which had been developed in total ignorance of it. Both referred exclusively to a world order that had perished more than five hundred years before. Latin, or *grammatica*, the artificially preserved language in which it was all taught, was the single unifying element, its literature defining the bounds of contemporary knowledge. Until the era of translations began, the limits of the Latin language were quite literally the limits of the western intellectual world.

❖❖❖

CHAPTER 14

Ex oriente lux—
Sources of Higher Learning

Quod enim Gallica studia nesciunt, Transalpina reserabunt;
quod apud Latinos non addisces, Grecia facunda docebit.

For what French studies do not know, those beyond the Alps will unlock; what
you will not learn among the Latins, eloquent Greece will teach you.

Adelard of Bath (ca 1080–ca 1160), *De eodem et diverso*, 69

S INCE THE MOORISH INVASION of Spain in the seventh century, Europe's civilization had been self-contained. The inherited wisdom of the
Church Fathers, supplemented by some ancient *auctores*, was somehow preserved through the Dark Ages, to be polished and revitalized in the age that
followed, when Germanic empires of the north aspired to relaunch the spirit
of Rome's old imperium, as best they could. By the eleventh century, this civilization, expressing itself in Latin, had largely mastered and integrated its
source material. It could not yet conceive of anything greater than its heritage
from Rome and the Christians. As so often in the history of Latin, knowledge
of the universe as conceived in this language was resolutely self-sufficient,
and—as far as possible—believed to be perfect and beyond reform. John of
Salisbury had had this dispiriting feeling about the Paris logicians with whom
he had studied:

> So about twelve years passed, with me occupied in various studies. So I
> thought it would be pleasant to see at the Mount the old colleagues I had left,
> who were still pursuing dialectic, to confer with them on old issues in the hope
> of mutual benefit. They were to be found, unchanged in identity or location.

But they had not reached their goal. To analysis of the old questions they had added not a footnote. The same problems still nagged. They had advanced in one point only: they had unlearned modesty or any sense of their limits. So much so that I despair of them ever regaining them. I realized the plain meaning of it: for all the aid dialectic gives to other disciplines, left to itself it is bloodless and barren and does not impregnate the soul with any fruit of philosophy that has not been conceived from elsewhere.[1]

To make the step of transforming itself into something new, Latin learning would need the stimulus of discovery. The store of knowledge from the pagan world was in fact far richer than it had known; and others, notably those despised heretical Saracens,* had developed from this store a corpus of learning that in many ways went beyond their own. Bilingual scholars could see the lack: Alfanus, a monk at Monte Cassino and then archbishop of Salerno, when translating a Greek treatise on the nature of man, stated in his preface that he wrote *Latinorum cogente penuria* 'pressed by the poverty of the Latins'.[†] Despite some kicking and screaming, the masters of Latin would in time come to accept this guidance and make it part of their own tradition. It would then become fundamental to the syllabus when Europe created its new institutions of higher learning, the universities.

The first inkling of another world out there had come from Europe's deep south. Here, in the later eleventh century, a bizarrely new force was at work, emanating from the coasts of the North Sea, the Normans. Duke William had his heart set on an English throne, but others were seeking new worlds to conquer. They ventured southward, perhaps officially on pilgrimage, or as knights-errant, but stayed in some numbers to offer their military services, and then to impose them. From around 1060 two Norman brothers, Robert (*Guiscard* 'the Wily') and Roger, the sixth and seventh sons of Tancred of Hauteville, led their armies in aggressive wars in southern Italy and Sicily, which were amaz-

---

*This, the contemporary European word for Muslims, seems to be a borrowing from Arabic *šarqiyīn* 'easterners'. It was etymologized as a mixture of Hebrew and Greek: *Sarakenoi* 'Sarah-empty', adverting to the belief that they descended from Hagar, Jacob's concubine, not his lawful wife, Sarah. Hence they were also often called *Hagareni*.
†Alfanus seems not to have known the original author of his work, Nemesius of Emesa; but he had great hopes for its intellectual effects: he called his translation *Premnon physicon*, "i.e., the Trunk of Physics: because just as many twigs sprout from one trunk, so from its source a host of streams of natural science will well up." (Per Latin quoted in d'Alverny 1982: 426.)

ingly successful: by the early twelfth century they had annihilated the long-standing rule not only of Lombards and Byzantines but also (and most significantly for Latin) of Saracens. Sicily, after six generations of Muslim rule, was returned to Christendom. There were now Muslims living in Christian lands, and the immediate result was a spread of Muslim knowledge.

Newly Norman Salerno (conquered 1077), just down the coast from Naples and long a noted medical center, became the site for the first of a flood of new publications. Constantine the African (a monk at the nearby monastery of Monte Cassino, who lived until 1087) produced in Latin a text that he called the *Theorica Pantegni*, a book that was by origin an Arabic medical encyclopedia, from the tenth century.* He or his associates followed this up with further medical translations, of Hippocrates, Galen, and Isaac Judaeus ('Isḥāq al-Isrā'ili, a famous doctor from Qayrawān in Tunis, who had lived around 830–930). Southern Italy became for a time the most cosmopolitan part of the Roman world: it had its strong academic links—besides Salerno, Reggio too boasted a *studium generale* active from 1188 to the end of the thirteenth century. Here, for some generations, knowledge of Greek and Arabic remained widespread.† (Hebrew too was strong in Sicily with its communities of Jews who had lived unpersecuted under Muslim rule.) Other major scientific texts would soon be translated. Ptolemy's 'Great Treatise' (*Megálē Sýntaxis*) on astronomy was translated around 1160 in Sicily.‡ This island briefly became central to European affairs in the early thirteenth century, since it was where the heir to the Holy Roman Empire, Frederick II, grew up—his mother being the Norman heiress Constance—and in fact kept his major court for most of his reign (1215–50). As well as giving Salerno its charter as a university, he drew cultural luminaries to his court in Palermo, notably Michael the Scot (educated in Durham, Oxford, and Paris), who had learned Arabic in Toledo, and acquired something of a

---

*Constantine proffered it as his own work. A sequel, the *Practica Pantegni*, was added in 1114–15. The whole book was in fact the *al-Kunnaš al-Malakī* of 'Ali ibn Abbas al-Majūsi, who had died in 994. A new translation, as the *Liber Regalis*, was supplied by Stephen of Antioch ca 1127, saying the previous one had been "corrupted by the shrewd fraud of the translator."

†Stephen of Antioch remarks in the preface to his *Breviarium medicaminum*, 'For in Sicily and in Salerno where most students of these matters are to be found, there are Greeks and experts on Arabic available for consultation' *Nam in Sicilia et Salerni ubi horum maxime studiosi sunt et Greci habentur et lingue gnari arabice quos qui voluerit consulere poterit* (d'Alverny 1982: 438 n. 71).

‡The Arabs had been impressed enough to replace *Megálē* with the superlative *Megístē* 'greatest'. Hence its well-known Arabized title, the *Almagest*.

reputation as a magician, writing on astrology, alchemy, and the occult. In the 1220s and 1230s, Michael translated works of Aristotle (including *Historia animalium* 'Zoology', *De anima* 'On the Soul', *De caelo* 'On the Sky') with commentaries by Averroës (ibn Rushd). But these were only the most famous works in a flood of Greek and Arabic works now newly available in Latin.

And another source of Muslim-preserved knowledge became active only a little later and, perhaps because of its greater proximity to northern Europe, was to have even greater impact. This was central Spain, whose capital, Toledo, had been taken from the Moors in 1085, and which for two centuries thereafter became the focus of Arabic (and increasingly Greek) expertise in western Europe.

Although Toledo was central, cultural contacts were spread through the peninsula. Sporadic contact between Christian and Muslim was not new. Famously, as early as the mid-tenth century, Gerbert of Aurillac (later to be Emperor Otto III's friend and Pope Sylvester II) had visited Vich in Catalunya, home to many Mozarabic exiles, and had come away with knowledge of Arabic numerals, the abacus, and the structure of astronomical instruments. Already at the turn of the eleventh-twelfth centuries, Ibn 'Abdūn was warning as far away as Seville of the dangers of selling books to Jews and Christians: "for they translate these scientific books and attribute them to their own people and to their bishops, when they are really Muslim works."[2] In the early days of the surge of translation, Plato of Tivoli worked in Barcelona during his career, 1134–45, translating medical and astronomical texts.[*] In 1142 Peter the Venerable, abbot of Cluny, commissioned a translation of the whole Koran from the two seasoned translators Hermann the Slav (of Carinthia) and Robert of Ketton (from Chester); this had happened in the valley of the Ebro, in the northeast, where the two were searching for a copy of Ptolemy's *Almagest* to translate. Robert was then in Segovia, north of Toledo, when in 1145 he translated Al-Khwarizmi's *Algebra*, the work that founded higher mathematics in Europe.

---

[*]Another translator who was much impressed by western intellectual poverty, Plato had written in his preface to al-Battāni, 'Blindness to Latin ignorance is all the sadder, and lack of concern for our weakness all the clearer, in that Rome has ended up . . . far worse not only than Egypt or Greece, but even than Arabia . . . Our people have not a single author; instead of books, we have just ravings, dreams, old wives' tales' *Quo magis latinitatis ignorantie cecitas deploranda magisque desidie negligentia redarguenda est . . . Roma . . . non tantum Egipto vel Grecia sed etiam Arabia longe inferior extitit . . . Nostri auctorem quidem nullum, pro libris deliramenta, sompnia, fabulas aniles.* (Quoted by d'Alverny 1982: 451 n. 131 from *Mahometis Albetenii de scientia stellarum liber* (Bologna, 1645), f. b.)

But Toledo does seem to have become focal for translation work, even if the story of an actual school for language and translation, established on the initiative of Archbishop Raimundus (in office 1125–52), is exaggerated.³ The most prolific of the Toledans were two Italians, both known as Gerard of Cremona. The first (who worked ca 1144–87) translated much astronomy (Ptolemy's *Almagest*—independently of Sicily, in this case from Arabic— az-Zarqāli's astronomical tables, al-Farābi on the philosophy of science [*De Scientiis*] and al-Farghāni's *Elements of Astronomy*) and Euclid's *Geometry*, as well as beginning a program on Aristotle's works on natural science. The second (working in the next century, and also known as Gerard de Sabloneta) focused on medicine, notably the *Canon* of Avicenna (ibn Sinā) and *Liber Al-mansoris* of Rhazes (ar-Rāzi).

Some translations were organized cooperatively among scholars working at great distances. Especially, this applied to the translation of the voluminous works of Aristotle. The series that Gerard projected, of Aristotle's scientific works from the Arabic, was completed by a collaboration of Michael the Scot in Palermo and the Englishman Alfred of Sareshel. Meanwhile, in 1136 three young scholars, Burgundio of Pisa, James of Venice, and Henricus Aristippus, had met in Constantinople and planned a joint attack on Aristotle as a whole, in the Greek original.⁴ They went on to pursue it independently in Pisa, Constantinople, and Palermo, in the course of other careers. Burgundio was a judge; Henricus Aristippus became archdeacon of Catania and for a time head of chancery at the royal court, but he was also busy reintroducing Plato to the west, with translations of the dialogues *Phaedo* and *Meno*.*

Other scholars, such as another Englishman, Adelard of Bath (ca 1080–ca 1160), conducted their studies more in isolation. He traveled far to acquire linguistic expertise and important manuscripts, in southern Italy and the eastern Mediterranean, and possibly Toledo too, but then came home to produce finished translations. After 1116 Adelard translated Euclid's *Elements of Geometry*† and al-Khwarizmi's *Zij* 'Astronomical Tables'. Like many of the Latinists, he had probably worked with colleagues with more perfect Arabic, including the Jewish scholar Peter Alfonsi, who was in England at the time.⁵ In 1152 Dominicus

---

*Curiously, he translated just those works of Plato that include a character called Aristippus (Berschin 1988, § 7).

†It is clear, from the duplication of titles translated, that the "bush telegraph" of letters and traveling scholars was an imperfect network in spreading the knowledge of the latest work. Of course, even today it is difficult to find out what works are being prepared before they are published.

Gundisalvi (Gundassalinus), another famous translator, recounted in his prologue to a version of Avicenna's *de Anima* 'On the Soul' his pattern of work with
his collaborator, a Jewish linguist he calls Avendauth (presumed to be Ibn
Daūd):[6] Avendauth *singula verba vulgariter proferente* 'uttering each word in the
vernacular' and Gundisalvi *singula in Latinum convertente* 'converting each word
into Latin'.[7] Gerard of Cremona too had translated the *Almagest*, with a Mo-
zarab named Ghālib: *Galippo mixtarabe interpretante, Almagesti latinavit*, Daniel of Morley reports. Around 1170, this Englishman had tired of the jurisprudence
on offer to students in Paris, and, as he wrote, "since Arabic learning, which is
mostly about the quadrivium [i.e., mathematics and science], is highly celebrated
in Toledo these days, I quickly hurried there, to hear the wiser philosophers of
the world. But being called and invited back from Spain by friends, I came to
England with a precious hoard of books."[8]

Another traveling English scholar, John of Salisbury, would have liked to
taste the springs of new knowledge at their sources. In 1155–56, in his early forties, he had gone on a trip to Beneventum (his companion the then pope, an
Englishman, Hadrian IV) for three months, and there taken lessons in Greek,
but apparently without profit: "While staying in Apulia, I studied with a
Greek interpreter who also knew Latin passably. I should like to thank him, if
not so much for the practical value [of what I learned], at least for his good
graces toward his audience."[9]

Yet even for an old brain like his there was some hope of contributing to
the feast of new learning: he later commissioned a translation of some long-
revered mystical theological works by Dionysius the Areopagite from John Sarracenus, a scholar who was working at Poitiers, and who despite his name
specialized in Greek. Few had been able to make much sense of John Scotus
Eriugena's Hiberno-Latin version from the ninth century. John Sarracenus
noted, "The previous translator, who in my opinion was not as well educated as
he should have been, has added not a few obscurities."[10]

But a theological work was very much the exception. The disciplines
that were directly enriched by the new works were above all medicine, mathematics, and natural science (classified at the time as part of the quadrivium),
and of course philosophy. Medicine was organized according to Avicenna's
Canon, with due deference to the *Aphorisms* of the Greek Hippocrates and the
Ars parva of Roman Galen, but surgery was studied through Albucasis
(Abū'l-Qasim az-Zahrawi). Astronomy was now based on Ptolemy, though
usually through simplified *Elementa* of Alfraganus; arithmetic was still perversely dependent on Boethius, but now supplemented with parts of Euclid,

and John of Sacrobosco's *Algorismus*, his digest of al-Khwarizmi's *Algebra*. Geometry was now based on Euclid (*Optica* and *Catoptrica* as well as the *Elements*), but also Aristotle's *Meteorologica*, al-Kindi's *de Aspectibus*, and the *Optica* of Alhazen (Ibn al-Haitham). Music or harmony remained resolutely based on Boethius' *De institutione musica*. It alone seems to have been unaffected by the new culture available through translation.

Philosophy was revived as a European discipline through a massive infusion of Aristotle. (Plato was a familiar name too, but the translation of his works was going to lag some generations behind Aristotle's: as a fundamentally practical thinker, Aristotle had had a much greater impact on the Arab tradition than Plato.) Aristotle became known as *Philosophus*, the philosopher par excellence. To the simple logical texts transmitted by Boethius were now added, besides his works on natural sciences, the *Analytica Priora* and *Analytica Posteriora*, on logical theory; the *De Anima* 'On the Soul', on philosophy of mind; and the *Metaphysica* 'After Physics', which conceived and developed a whole new concept of reality, based on considerations of being as such, with transcendental attributes (oneness, truth, goodness, beauty) and causal support (material, formal, efficient, and final). There would, ultimately, also be Aristotle's *Politica*, *Ethica*, and *Poetica*.* Together with these new works came commentaries by learned Arabs, by Avicenna (980–1037), but above all the very recent Averroës (1126–98), whose works were all available in Latin by 1230. He became known, by analogy to Aristotle, as *Commentator*.

The implications of all this for theology were incalculable, and profoundly disturbing to the Church. The first reaction was a holding action, to forbid public and private lectures on Aristotle's natural philosophy. (This did not affect the "New Logic" of the *Analytics*, nor yet the moral and literary works on politics, ethics, and poetics. But these were in fact still unknown.) The ban was first promulgated at the Council of Sens in 1210 and reiterated in 1228 and in 1231 by Pope Gregory IX. It first had concrete effect in 1215, in the instructions of the papal legate Robert of Courçon to the arts faculty of the University of Paris. However, as the works of Aristotle became better known, it emerged that they were opening up completely new ground where no previous theology had trodden, and that the heretical doctrines of pantheism and materialism

---

*The (*Nicomachean*) *Ethics* was translated by Roger Grosseteste of Oxford in 1246–47; the *Politics* by the Fleming William of Moerbeke in 1260; and the *Poetics* in 1278. William also revised the whole corpus of Aristotle in Latin with regard to the Greek original in the middle of the thirteenth century.

proposed by some early soi-disant "Aristotelici" (such as David of Dinant, whose works were condemned by a synod in 1210) had been an exaggeration of Aristotle's own theories. In 1255 all the crucial works were not only accepted but made required reading for the Paris master of arts degree.*

The discovery of the new literature had in fact come very much in the same period as the origin of the universities. This development meant the conversion of the old *studium generale*, a school in a city, into a duly chartered *universitas magistrorum et scholarium*, which was a new way of looking at an academic institution, namely as a trade guild or general body (the literal meaning of *universitas*), formed to protect and enhance the rights of masters and scholars over those of their surrounding townsmen. The first universities, which emerged in the last decades of the twelfth century and the first of the thirteenth, were not, with the exception of Paris, in cities that were major political capitals. But the importance of the city of Paris as the seat of France's Capetian monarchy, unmatched across western Europe at the time, combined with the new university—which was partly a development of the royal palace school—meant that Paris achieved an intellectual ascendancy during the twelfth and thirteenth centuries that far exceeded even Rome's. It attracted eminent scholars from all over *Romania* and made many of them famous. Among those who taught there were the Frenchman Peter Abelard (1079–1142), the Italian Peter Lombard (1100–1160), the Englishman William of Shyreswood (1190–1249), the German Albertus Magnus (1193–1280), the Italian Thomas Aquinas (1225–74), the Scot Duns Scotus (1266–1308), and the Frenchmen Jean de Buridan (1300–1358) and Jean de Gerson (1363–1429). Here, above all, in the churches, alleys, and lecture halls of the Left Bank, Latin developed on the lips and the parchments of the schoolmen.

Surprisingly, no clear cause is evident or accepted for the origin of the universities at the turn of the twelfth to thirteenth centuries, or for their spread in the following three centuries.[11] Presumably, they are at root a phenomenon of critical mass: when an academic community reaches a certain minimum size, it becomes impossible to ignore as a political entity in its own right. But except in the earliest cases (Salerno, Montpellier, Bologna, Paris,

---

*By and large, this had all been a peculiarly Parisian brouhaha, since Paris was the only continental university where the Church permitted a faculty of theology, and where as a result there was theological influence on the syllabus in the faculty of arts. Other universities had continued to go their own way throughout the controversy, and these included Oxford and Cambridge, despite their faculties of theology.

Oxford, Cambridge—all with dates of foundation, or rather emergence, that are rather vague), their existence was dependent on formal sanction, the grant of a charter, by some temporal authority: this would be either the pope or the local prince. (All but Oxford and Cambridge finally accepted the same, but sometimes after as much as a century of functioning existence.)

To receive such a charter it was always necessary for a university to have a number of named faculties. In practice in the early period there was a choice of four, of which one, *artes* (covering the familiar liberal arts), was obligatory, and another, *theologia*, being close to the source of Christian authority, was only permitted by the pope in special cases—originally only at Paris, and the papacy's own Curial University in Rome. (Oxford and Cambridge established their theological faculties independently and were never challenged.) The other two faculties were *ius* 'law' and *medicina*. However, all universities had at least two faculties, and many were specialized for excellence in one of these latter two. *Artes* tended to be seen as a kind of foundation course. As in the school system, no provision was ever made for *artes mechanicae*, *historia*, or *philosophia* as such. Where they were taught, they were squeezed into another faculty, typically *artes*.

It is clear that the university as it emerged would have been impossible without the new translated learning of the eleventh, twelfth, and thirteenth centuries. That in effect provided the full curriculum of texts for medicine, revolutionized the content of the arts quadrivium, and even (ultimately) provided the Aristotelian basis that would come to be accepted as the foundation for theology.* The only parts of the syllabus that were not reconstituted were the basic language studies of the arts trivium, and law. Law had had its own radical reworkings since the imperial era, starting from Justinian's collations of laws, defining principles for resolving the conflict of laws (*concordantia discordantium canonum*), and adding a wholly new *ius canonicum*, which defined legitimacy within the Church institutions. But this had not led to any radical change in Latin itself.

◈

Faced with the task of translating technical and often highly abstract texts in Arabic and Greek, the scholars who tried to convert them into Latin were

---

*Full acceptance of this would take some time, however. Thomas Aquinas's thirteenth-century synthesis of Aristotle with Christian theology, although already endorsed by the Dominican order four years after his death in 1274, was only officially accepted as the Roman Catholic Church's standard doctrine in 1879.

conscious of an uphill struggle. One exceptionally explicit statement of these difficulties was made by John Sarracenus to his patron John of Salisbury (in 1167):

> I confess I have been unable to convey in Latin the elegant qualities of the
> style of this most learned and eloquent man [Dionysius the Areopagite]. In
> Greek one finds certain compounds by which things are designated elegantly
> and to the point; Latin must inelegantly, ineptly, and occasionally quite inad-
> equately paraphrase the one word with two or more expressions. To commend
> a person or something fine, they repeat the articles in the proper positions,
> and by means of the same articles many sentences are smoothly linked. And
> then there is the excellent construction of the participle, and the infinitive
> marked with an article: linguistic elegance of this order has no equivalent in
> Latin.[12]

But in a way, their task was similar to that of previous great philosophical
translators, Cicero in the first century BC, Boethius in the sixth century AD:
they were trying to make Greek thought at the highest level comprehensible to
a Latin readership. In some ways, their task was the easier: Cicero had, after
all, had to invent Latin philosophical language from scratch. But the translators of the eleventh to thirteenth centuries could not rely, as Cicero and to some
extent Boethius could, on a public who were totally at ease as native speakers
with Latin. They were secondhand learners of Latin themselves and had been
educated in the skills of writing not through classical rhetoric but its more
businesslike medieval successor, the *Ars Dictaminis*. Furthermore, unlike Cicero and Boethius, they were usually less than fluent in the source languages,
perhaps having only a reading knowledge of them and little cultural background, and hence were vulnerable to unexpected idioms. The work they produced would be more static and pedestrian, and in the first editions less
reliable, than that of the old literary stylists.

Their aim was to translate as directly and literally as possible, with concern only for sense and not at all for style. But this too was difficult. They were
confronted with languages where words often had a significant internal structure more complex than any in Latin, and which seemed to use that complex-
ity far more universally and flexibly than Latin could equal. With such words,
the word-for-word (*ad verbum*) ideal for translation, which largely prevailed
for scientific works until the Renaissance, was almost impossible to fulfill.[13]

Arabic verbs transform regularly and effortlessly into related agent nouns
(*fātiḥ, fattāḥ* 'opener'), patient nouns (*maftūḥ* 'opened'), instrument nouns

(*miftāḥ* 'key'), and abstract nouns of action (*fatḥ* 'opening, commencement', *mufātaḥ* 'opening a conversation', *iftitāḥ* 'inauguration'), state (*futḥ* 'opening, breach'), and potentiality (*mufattiḥ* 'appetizing, aperitif'), as well as adjectives (*iftitāḥī* 'introductory') that show vaguer relationships. Greek readily forms new compound nouns and derives verbs and adjectives from any nouns, though less regularly and clearly than Arabic does (*anoigeus, anoiktēs* 'opener', *anoigma* 'opening, door', *anoiktos, anoiktikos* 'openable', *anoixis* 'opening up'). Greek style also takes full advantage of its great wealth of participles (a maximum of twelve for a transitive verb: present, aorist, future, and perfect, in active, middle, and passive voice) not only to string large numbers of propositions into complex sentences, but also to clarify cross-references among the entities referred to. Both Arabic and Greek have a definite article (*al-, ho*), which makes it possible to distinguish simply definite from indefinite reference in a sentence; in the case of Greek, the article is also highly inflected, just like an adjective (*ho, hē, tó; hoi, hai, tá*; etc.), so that it can be used to clarify the reference of phrases in a long sentence; the neuter article (*tó*) can also turn whole phrases from verbal expressions into nominal phrases or quotations. Arabic can also show indefiniteness explicitly on a noun phrase (with the ending *-n*).

By modern standards, Latin too seems a highly inflected language, but it could not quite match classical Arabic or Greek, the source languages it now had to translate. It had a modest set of derived nouns and adjectives (*apertor* 'opener', *apertura* 'opening', *aperibilis* 'capable of opening'). It only had three participles, with the present (*aperient-*) and future (*aperturo-*) being invariably active, and the perfect (*aperto-*) invariably passive, although the gerundive (*aperiendo-*) could at a pinch step in as a future passive participle.[14] A desperate problem was that the verb *to be*, essential for Greek philosophy, had no present or past participle at all in Latin. Latin's practice in forming compounds and derived forms had hitherto been rather limited, constrained not least by a sense of *modus*, restrained elegance. (Caesar had maintained that a writer should avoid an unusual word as a sailor would a hidden reef.) It had no definite article, but its sense would at least have been clear to most Latin speakers: their native languages, at least the Romance, Germanic, and Celtic ones, did after all have them (e.g., French *le/la/les*; English *the*; Irish *an*). Although literary Latin had once been a match for Greek in fondness for long, complex sentences, at least after it had absorbed the lessons of rhetorical style (pp. 95–99), the second-language learners of Latin in the late first millennium AD would find those increasingly hard to follow.

The answer was found above all in relaxing the constraints on Latin word formation, one part of that *modus* and *decorum* that had once been the hallmark of Latin academic or literary style. We have seen (pp. 164–65) that medieval Latin had always, for practical purposes, admitted vast numbers of borrowed words from the vernaculars, facilitating practical administration and documentation. Scholastic Latin (as the new intellectual instrument is usually called, after the academic "schoolmen" who wielded it) did likewise yield to an extent to the temptation to borrow words from Arabic and Greek. There were after all plenty of new technical terms, and if they were defined in the new documents, with uses far enough removed from the past Latin experience, they could be accommodated. Hence the origin of **algebra** (*al-jibr* 'putting back together'), **algorismus** (a new word for 'arithmetic', name of Al-Khwarizmi 'The Choresmian'), **alchimia**, and **chimia** (*al-kimiyya*, itself a borrowing from Greek *khymeia* 'infusion') from Arabic.* More distinctively, when inventing theological terminology, Thomas Aquinas is also happy to transliterate from Greek **epiceia** (*epieikeia* 'equity'), **eubolia** (*euboulia* 'prudence'), **synderesis** (*syntērēsis* 'observance'), **theandrica** (*theandrika* 'god-man-ly'); and the divergences from Greek spelling suggest that he was receiving these terms not just by reading, but from consultations with Greek speakers.

There are also calques, which only make sense in Latin as translations of technical usages in Arabic and Greek. Hence **sinus**, the trigonometric function 'sine', which literally means 'fold in a garment, bend, curve'. This was adopted to render *jaib* 'bundle, bosom, fold in a garment', which had become the technical term in Arabic, (originally borrowed from the more obviously relevant Sanskrit *jyā* 'bowstring'). **Complexio** 'weaving together' was adopted, after some havering, as the best equivalent for the important medical concept of the balance of elements in the body, Arabic *mizāj* and Greek *krâsis*, literally 'mixture'.[15]† The loan translations from Greek tend to be more philosophical:

---

*Also borax (*būraq*), **camphora** (*kafur*—ultimately [through Sanskrit] from Malay *kapur* 'camphor tree'), **cifra** and **zephirum** *(sifr* 'empty, zero'), **elixir** (*al-iksīr*, itself a borrowing from Greek *xērion* 'drying ointment'), **musa** (*mūza* 'banana'—also known as **pomum paradisi** 'fruit of paradise'), **nadir** (*nāzir* 'looking [toward the zenith]'), **safranum** (*za'farān* 'saffron'), **soda** (*suwwad* 'saltwort'), **talcum** (*talq* 'talc'), **zenith** (*zenit*, a mistranscription of *zemt*, to represent *samt* [*ar-ras*] 'way overhead').

†The phrase for 'pulse' is usually **pondus pulsus**, literally 'weight of driving', translating Arabic *wazn an-nabd*. But *wazn* is ambiguous between weight and (metrical) rhythm, so the translators seem to have picked the wrong sense. The phrase **dura mater (cerebri)** was adopted to represent *umm ad-dimāghi 'j-jāfiyah*, literally 'mother of the brain, the thick one', which meant the tough outer membrane surrounding the brain, and was an example

accidens (*symbebēkós* 'what has happened'), *habitus* (*héxis* 'having'), *materia* (*hýlē* 'wood'). *Surdus* in the mathematical sense of an irrational number is a mistranslated calque from *álogos* 'without *lógos*', i.e., 'without accounting', hence 'irrational', taken as 'without word', i.e. 'deaf'.

But these items were just a new set of borrowings. The really new aspect of scholastic Latin is its festival of neologisms, new words generated from the inherited resources of Latin, but with a freedom that had never before been acceptable.

There had always been abstract nouns in *-tas*, but now they were coined thick and fast, even on adjectives that were comparatives (*prioritas, superioritas, majoritas* . . .) or themselves derivative (*actualitas, animalitas, causalitas, designabilitas, formalitas, immaterialitas, individualitas, intelligibilitas, potentialitas, praedicabilitas, realitas, universalitas* . . . ; *activitas, productivitas, sensitivitas* . . . ; *lapideitas* 'stoniness', *homogeneitas* . . . In exceptional cases, they might even be formed on words that are not even adjectives at all, as when Gundassalinus coined *quiditas* 'whatness' to translate Avicenna's *māhiyyu* (itself a new formation on Arabic *mā* 'what'): it went on to have quite a significant philosophical career in the discussions of Thomas Aquinas and after and has even survived as English *quiddity* (whatever that means). John Duns Scotus and his highly reifying school of philosophy were fond of this approach, building on pronouns, *haecceitas, ipseitas, talitas* 'thisness, selfness, suchness'; verbs, *velleitas*; and even multiword phrases and conjunctions, *perseitas* 'in-itself-ness', *anitas* 'whether-ness', from *an sit aliquid* 'whether there is anything'. For making nouns out of verbs, the natural resource was the ending *-ntia*, and so we find neologisms such as *dependentia, differentia, diffidentia, essentia, exigentia, influentia, intelligentia*. Likewise the adjectival endings *-alis* and *-ivus* took off, added to nouns and verbs respectively.*

The Greek verb-making *-izo* suffix, together with others that went with

---

of Arabic fondness for metaphors drawn from family relationships. Its correlative *pia mater* 'pious mother' involved a bit of religious temporizing on the part of the original translator, Stephen of Antioch, embellishing the original Arabic *umm ad-dimāghi 'l-ḥanūn* 'the tender one'.

accidentalis, canonicalis, causalis, communalis, elementalis, essentialis, fundamentalis, integralis, logicalis, materialis, partialis, totalis, traditionalis, universalis, virginalis; activus, commutativus, confederativus, contemplativus, distributivus, extensivus, laborativus, nocivus, positivus, responsivus, speculativus. In fact, *-alis* often seems also to have been almost gratuitously added to adjectives: *festivalis, maternalis, paternalis, perpetualis*.

it (-*ista* for the agent, -*ismus* for the action, -*isma* for the product), were now miraculously productive, with no concern shown for linguistic purism.* Previously, beside the purely Greek *agonizo, baptizo, canonizo*, etc., there had only been *cicatrizo* 'scar', *latinizo* 'translate into Latin', and *mangonizo* 'tart up' formed from Latin roots. Now we have words such as **carbonizo, decanizo** 'be dean', **festizo, forizo** 'frequent the forum', **guarentizo, incarizo** 'sell at auction', **quinternizo** 'play the guitar', **solemnizo, temporizo** as well as **algorista** 'arithmetician', **artista** 'arts student', **auctorista** 'arts student' (in Spain), **camerista** 'lodger', **canonista** 'canon lawyer', **carbonista** 'charcoal burner', **decretista** 'law student', **humanista, jurista, modista** 'speculative grammarian', **occamista**, **platonista, portionista** 'paying guest', **sacrista** 'church treasurer', **thomista**, **scotista**, as followers of Thomas Aquinas and John Duns Scotus were called. But new formations were still being made on Greek roots: **barbarizo** 'turn someone barbarous' as well as 'speak barbarian lingo', **haeretizo** 'believe heretically', **judaizo** 'observe Judaism', **judaismus** 'usury, Judaism', **'monachismus** 'monastic life', **barbarismatice** 'in the barbarous tongue—viz German'.

The absence of explicitness about 'being' in Latin was addressed. First of all the verb *existere*, originally 'to stand out—to appear or emerge', was pressed into service and given a full range of derivative forms: **existentia, existentialis, existentialitas**. (Greek also has a separate verb *hupárkhein*, which means 'be [there]' without actually being the verb *eînai* 'be'; Arabic *wujida* 'be found' as against *kawana* 'be'.) Evidently other forms related to the roots -*sta*- and -*sist*- were also much used: **status, substantia, subsistere, subsistentia**.

But the irregular verb *esse* was also taken in hand. It had never had a present participle 'being' but was now given one. The vestigial -*sens* (stem -*sent*-), surviving in ancient *absens* 'being away', *praesens* 'being in front', *di consentes* 'gods who are with us', was ignored. Instead, the analogy of Greek was followed, where the present participle of *eînai* 'to be' is just *ōn*, where the participle ending is bald, lacking any stem at all. It is as if the participle of *is* in English were *ing*. Latin therefore invented **ens**, with stem **ent**- (hence the **entia** 'beings', which Ockham believed should not be multiplied), and this then became the basis for more: e.g., **entitas** 'beingness'. Besides this there

---

*As a foreign root, -*izo* was always assigned to the first conjugation, with third singular present -*izat*, infinitive -*izare*, etc. Hence a competing set of Latin derivatives is also sometimes seen: e.g., agent **baptizator, dogmatizator**, action **forizatio**, and **baptizatorium** is found alongside **baptisterium**.

was *essentia,* an abstract noun formed from the infinitive *esse* too, with its adjective derivate *essentialis.* The infinitive was also unconventionally declined in its own right: genitive *essendi,* dative-ablative *essendo.* Latin was now fully equipped for the discussion of what German calls *Seinsfragen,* questions of being itself,* and so Thomas Aquinas can remark—as Cicero never could:

> *Forma tamen potest dici quo est, secundum quod est essendi principium; ipsa autem tota substantia est ipsum quod est; et ipsum esse est quo substantia denominatur ens.*

But the form can be said by which it is, according to which is its principle of being; yet by its very substance it is the very thing it is; and its very being is that by which a substance is defined as a be-er.[16]

Scholastic Latin even found a way to mimic the quotative use of the Greek definite article. Perhaps based on the background awareness of French *le,* philosophers such as Thomas Aquinas in the thirteenth century and logicians as Jean de Buridan in the fourteenth use the little word *ly* (or *li*) to indicate that the following word is quoted, or as they would put it, *materialiter suppositum* 'materially supposed'.

> *Melius est quod dicatur semper natus, ut ly semper designet permanentiam aeternitatis et ly natus perfectionem geniti.*

It is better to say "semper natus," with "semper" designating permanence of eternity and "natus" the perfection of the one begotten.[17]

The masters of scholastic Latin were highly ingenious in applying the inherited methods of their linguistic tradition to the new topics that they wished to develop. Logic (*dialectica*) was their speciality, to the extent that it displaced literature (*grammatica*) from its prime role in the arts trivium at Paris. But their mnemonic for the valid forms of the syllogism was written as a four-line hexameter verse:

---

*Curiously, they were never tempted to coin a past participle to go with the present: perhaps *futus* alongside the future participle *futurus*? But Greek *einai* has no past participle, so morphology envy did not extend this far; and in any case the verb stem *futu-* is unfortunately the obscenest one in Latin.

Bárbara célárént ‖ darií ferió baralíp-ton
Célántés dabitís ‖ fápésmó fríseso mórum;
Césare cámpéstrés ‖ féstíno baróco; darápti
Féláptón disamís ‖ datisí bócárdo feríson.

The stresses mark heavy syllables, and the caesura cut in each line is also marked. The hexameter pattern clearly comes through. However, meaning was harder to guarantee than rhythm. Latin words (*barbara, celarent, ferio, celantes, dabitis, Cesare, campestres, festino*) are present and largely correctly scanned; but the whole has about as much sense as the first verse of Lewis Carroll's "Jabberwocky": "Twas brillig and the slithy toves did gyre and gymble in the wabe . . ."*

Syntactically, scholastic Latin is not distinctive. But its discourse structure is. Here it took its cue from the dominant forms of educational method, the *lectura* and the *disputatio*. Although the words *lectura* or *lectio* 'reading' have given rise to modern words such as English *lecture, lesson*, French *leçon*, German *Lektion*, their original reference was to the reading of a text in class, with copious commentary often of an extremely formalized nature. Each word of the text might be scrutinized individually, a process that could be taken to excess, as one scholar noted in the mid-twelfth century: "And what is even more ridiculous, when commenting on the title of a work, they go right through its contents. The first word has hardly been dealt with after three lectures. This is not teaching: it is a demonstration of ostentatious learning."[18]

This method was determined by the text under study. But a freer format was the disputation, which would be based not on a text but a question. The process of answering it might then be summarized by the master and circulated as a *quaestio disputata*. This could be generalized outside strictly academic questions to become a *quaestio de quolibet* 'question on anything you like', with a lay audience, which was the closest medieval approach to a mod-

---

*The logic represented is due to Aristotle, as supplemented (for the section *baralipton . . . friseso morum*) by the medieval Jewish logician Albalagus. The first three vowels in any word stand for the classic forms of proposition: *a* (all X is Y), *e* (no X is Y), *i* (some X is Y), *o* (not all X is Y); the initial *b, c, d*, and *f* in the words correlate the later patterns with the first four, to which they can be reduced; and some instances of *s, p, m*, and *c* also stand for various technical tweaks. **Barbara** therefore stands for the argument that if every M is L and every S is M, then every S is L; *ferison* for the argument that if no M is L and some M is S, then not all S is L, which can be reduced to ***ferio***—if no M is L and some S is M, then not all S is L.

ern talk show. (The fact that the word *quodlibet* gets a nonstandard, in fact quite "barbarous," plural, *quodlibeta*, shows that this 'whatever' format had taken on a life of its own; and anthologies of these discussions were often circulated in written form.) It came to be realized that the quasi-dialogue form of the disputation was not only applicable to anything at all, but was easier to understand and memorize than the traditional *oratio*, which had after all its inspiration in the rhetorical flights of the Roman barrister. In this sense, despite its unrelenting verbosity, the ideal of scholastic Latin is more dialogue than monologue, though a dialogue of a highly regimented kind. It does not seek to charm through naturalistic conversation, as Plato or Cicero did, but to set down systematically the answers to questions that could be raised by the ideal pupil. Even the most evident truths can, and must, be questioned, to reveal their interrelations and logical support—though not, of course, radically doubted.

This structure is often found in scholastic writing, and par excellence in the vast oeuvre of Thomas Aquinas. Here, for example, is part of his discussion of the nature of God, at the outset of his *Summa Theologica*:

Utrum Deum esse sit per se notum	Whether it is known per se that God is
Ad primum sic proceditur. Videtur quod Deum esse sit per se notum.	To the first question, thus the procedure. It appears that it is known per se that God is.
1. Illa enim nobis dicuntur per se nota, quorum cognitio nobis naturaliter inest, sicut patet de primis principiis. Sed, sicut dicit Damascenus in principio libri sui, omnibus cognitio existendi Deum naturaliter est inserta. Ergo Deum esse est per se notum.	1. For those things are said to be known to us per se whose knowledge is naturally in us, as is evident from first principles. But as Damascenus says in the beginning of his book, the knowledge of God existing is naturally grafted in all. Therefore it is known per se that God is.
2. Praeterea, illa dicuntur esse per se nota, quae statim, cognitis terminis, cognoscuntur: quod Philosophus attribuit primis demonstrationis principiis, in I Poster.: . . . Ergo Deum esse est per se notum.	2. Furthermore, those things are said to be known to us per se that are recognized immediately, on known terms: which the Philosopher attributes to first principles of proof, in Posterior Analytics I . . . Therefore it is known per se that God is.

3. Praeterea, veritatem esse est per se notum: quia qui negat veritatem esse, concedit veritatem esse: si enim veritas non est, verum est veritatem non esse. Si autem est aliquid verum, oportet quod veritas sit. Deus autem est ipsa veritas, Io. 14,6: Ego sum via, veritas et vita. Ergo Deum esse est per se notum.	3. Furthermore, it is known per se that there is truth; because he who denies that there is a truth, concedes that there is a truth; for if there is no truth, it is true that there is no truth. But if something is true, there must be a truth. But God is that very truth. John 14:6: I am the way, the truth, and the life. Therefore it is known per se that God is.
Sed contra, nullus potest cogitare oppositum eius quod est per se notum, ut patet per Philosophum, in IV Metaphys. et I Poster., circa prima demonstrationis principia. Cogitari autem potest oppositum eius quod est Deum esse, secundum illud Psalmi 52,1: Dixit insipiens in corde suo, non est Deus. Ergo Deum esse non est per se notum.	But in rebuttal, no one can think the opposite of what is known per se, as is evident according to the Philosopher in Metaphysics IV and Posterior Analytics I, on the first principles of proof. But the opposite of the proposition that God is can be thought according to Psalms 52:1: the fool hath said in his heart, there is no God. Therefore it is not known per se that God is.
Respondeo dicendum quod contingit aliquid esse per se notum dupliciter: uno modo, secundum se et non quoad nos; alio modo, secundum se et quoad nos.	My answer is that something can be known per se in two ways: in one way, according to itself and not as for us; and in the other way, according to itself and not as for us.

The discussion of the most abstract matter proceeds with a kind of cut and thrust, allowing the master to insert whatever evidence he can think of to back either the objections being rehearsed, or the resolution that he will offer, integrating texts from the Old and New Testaments (here the Psalms and the Gospel of John), the subsequent Church Fathers (e.g., Damascenus), and the Aristotelian corpus (*Philosophus*). No point is allowed to become too prolix. The discussion is organized under a hierarchy of numbered headings, and the resolution is clearly planned from the start. Serious contradictions, where both sides are well backed with evidence, are usually resolved by pointing to a distinction that was hitherto tacit: here, God is in principle known per se accord-

Thomas Aquinas. In his Summa contra Gentiles *and* Summa Theologica, *he summed up Catholic theology from an Aristotelian standpoint.*

ing to his very nature (*secundum se*), but not necessarily from the fallible, human perspective (*quoad nos*).*

The new philosophy revealed by translations had led to an expansion in the scope of higher education in the new university faculties, with concurrent transformations in Latin vocabulary and academic discourse. But it had also affected the content of the liberal arts course itself. At Paris, the intellectual center in the twelfth and thirteenth centuries, more time was being given to the new science of formal logic in *dialectica*, at the expense of grounding in *grammatica*. John of Garlande, an Englishman in Paris writing *Morale scolarium*, complained in 1241 of neglect of the literary greats. The French poet Henri d'Andeli even wrote an allegorical *Battle of the Seven Arts*, in which the forces of Grammar weigh in against Aristotle, Plato, and the hosts of Logic.[19]

But traditional *grammatica*, as a redoubt of literary appreciation, was also beset from within. Simply to read and learn from the *auctores*, in the traditional way, was no longer enough; and from around 1270 the new focus was on deepening the understanding of its linguistic terminology on a rational basis. What did it mean that *homo* 'human' was a noun and *ambulat* 'walks' was a verb? Why did nouns inflect for case, but verbs for person and tense? Here the basic idea

---

*This same structure was still the format for all the textbooks and lectures at the Pontifical Gregorian University in Rome in the mid-twentieth century (Kenny 1985: 45).

was that the parts of speech, and all the other categories that articulated Latin grammar, were not just arbitrary terms, but deeply represented the relations between aspects of language and aspects of reality. They were *modi significandi* 'modes of signifying', which corresponded to the *modi essendi* 'modes of being' of the world itself. By the early fourteenth century, the so-called *modistae* had developed this into a whole new subject, *grammatica speculativa*, grammar conceived as a mirror (*speculum*) to the world.[20] This kind of rationalist approach would develop the vast and complex superstructure of scholastic metaphysics that ultimately provoked the Humanist reaction of the Renaissance, which tried to dismiss it all and get back to simple, concrete reality. But for the thirteenth and fourteenth centuries it remained in the ascendant.

☆

The middle of the twelfth century turned out to be the calm before a time of great intellectual turbulence in western Europe. New sources of learning were about to be revealed in the south of the continent, in Spain, Italy, and Constantinople; and the transmission of learning was about to be radically revised in the establishment of independent, self-governing universities: the Church's monopoly on education and learning was about to be ended, after six hundred years. Even Latin itself was about to be cast into a new mold: having previously had a certain simplicity of expression, henceforth it would look like a thoroughly learned and abstruse language, with a luxuriant growth in its vocabulary for abstractions, and a ponderous, almost judicial style of expression.

But just at this moment, before these new changes came in, scholars in every field had been beginning to feel that they were fully on top of their subjects. They showed it by attempting to codify for their students the contents of each field. These volumes were called *summae*, purporting to be the 'sum totals' or 'summaries' of what there was to be learned in each of these disciplines.* They could be seen as statements of the syllabus, or comprehensive revision notes. But they were in fact granted a much higher status, as systematic statements of the core of each discipline.

In grammar, although Donatus and Priscian remained the ultimate authorities, a first *Summa* (in verse) was provided around 1140 by Petrus Helias, a Parisian master. This was to be overtaken by the *Doctrinale* of Alexander de

---

*The word *summa* is itself of some interest, since originally it was short for *summa linea* 'top line': in Roman arithmetic you entered the total at the top of the column.

Villedieu, another verse confection, but written at the very end of the twelfth century. It was still in use four hundred years later. In rhetoric, various works were written in Bologna (more from a business perspective) and various cities in the valley of the Loire (Tours, Orleans, Blois, Meung—more literary), codifying the new priorities of the *ars dictaminis*. Dialectic had its *Summulae Logicales*, written by Petrus Hispanus, and another *Summulae* written by William of Shyreswood (containing the first known sighting of the *Barbara, Celarent* verse), though these were both written a little later, in the early thirteenth century: logic had after all had a fair deal to digest from the new works of Aristotle, especially the *Posterior Analytics*.

The quadrivium does not seem to have inspired a *summa*. Perhaps it was not taken seriously enough, at this stage; but in any case arithmetic, geometry, and astronomy, as well as medicine, were about to be revolutionized by the translations of books by Al-Khwarizmi, Euclid, Ptolemy, and Avicenna respectively; so any mid-twelfth-century *summa* would have been likely to disappear without trace. In fact, these great authors' works, known as the *Algebra*, *Elements*, *Almagest*, and *Canon*, were each sufficiently comprehensive to have been counted as *summae* in their own right, but in practice European education would include other works alongside them. And as an additional major distraction to potential summarizers, Aristotle's *Physica*, another of the great works of Greek science first known in the period (apparently translated by Michael the Scot), would not have fit neatly into any of the Four Ways, even if it clearly belonged somewhere within the quadrivium.

Law was well served with *summae*. Traditionally, students of secular law could find all they wanted in the great compilations of Justinian from the sixth century, although there were four of them: the INSTITVTIONES, CODEX, DIGESTVM, and NOVELLAE. But in the mid-twelfth century, canon law too received its great standby in the monk Gratian's *Concordantia discordantium canonum* 'Reconciliation of Contradictory Canon Laws', commonly known as the *Decretum* 'Decree'. This was not so much a compilation of received wisdom as a piece of original research, in which he brought all the legal sources into one volume for systematic comparison and evaluated them in accord with stated principles of interpretation.

There were *summae* even of theology, which began to be seen as another science, rather than totally sui generis. The Holy Scriptures could not be challenged or revised, and the writings of the Church Fathers too had to be treated with total respect. Anselm of Laon (d. 1117) had integrated them in his *Glossa Ordinaria*, which was in form a running commentary of the Bible.

But his pupil Peter Abelard (1079–ca 1143) had demonstrated—to his own satisfaction—in his debaters' manual *Sic et Non* 'Yes and No' that there were many apparent contradictions between and among these authorities: the resulting complex interpretations that these made necessary he tried to sum up in his *Theologia scholarium* 'Theology for scholars'.*

Another pupil of Anselm's, Gilbert of Poitiers (d. 1154), taught that theology is unlike the other 'faculties' in that in it faith comes before reason. (He was the first to use *facultas* to mean a subject or discipline, in the academic sense.) Another systematic work of the period was Hugo de St. Victor's *De sacramentis christianae fidei.*† But the full *summa* was provided by Peter Lombard (d. 1160), whose work *Sententiae* 'The Statements' is arranged in four volumes around the major themes of Christianity: God, creation, Christ's incarnation, and the sacraments. Despite the apparent finality of such a work, Peter's prologue represented it almost as a work in progress—perhaps as a means of disarming his critics:

> Folding up in a brief volume the statements of the Fathers, together with the testimonies to them, so that the seeker should not need to open numbers of books, this abridged collection offers him what he was seeking without effort. But in this treatise I am hoping not only for the pious reader, but also the free corrector, especially where there is profound question about the truth: if only the truth had as many discoverers as it has contradictors![21]

Thierry of Chartres (d. ca 1148–53) had even aspired to write *totius philosophiae unicum ac singulare instrumentum* 'the unique and singular instrument of all philosophy'. But philosophy turned out to be the least practicable area for the *summa* treatment. Intended to be definitive, Thierry's work became the last glimpse of a superseded world. Its title, 'the Heptateuch', gives away its basis in the seven liberal arts, and after the absorption of so much lost learning, this

---

*The term *theologia* itself (literally 'God study' in Greek) seems to be Peter Abelard's innovation, typical of his detached style. Previously it had been called by the more deferential-sounding *Sacra Pagina* 'Holy Writ' or *Sacra Doctrina* 'Holy Learning'.

†Another Hugo, of Orleans (ca 1093–ca 1160), memorably summarized the Bible in two (almost identical) hexameter lines:

Quos anguis tristi virus mulcedine pavit	Whom serpent's venom fed with baleful charm
hos sanguis Christi mirus dulcedine lavit.	these Christ's astounding blood hath washed in balm.

simply could not stand. As Thomas Aquinas opined, *septem liberales artes non sufficienter dividunt philosophiam theoricam*—they are not adequate to divide up theoretical philosophy.[22]

The universalist aspiration of the *summa*, however, was due for a last blaze of glory before being abandoned for the Renaissance's acceptance that there would always be "more things in heaven and earth than are dreamt of in your philosophy." The German Albertus Magnus (1193–1280) attempted an encyclopedia of all knowledge old and new, which would be integrated into a philosophical and theological framework, but it ran to forty volumes, and the task of integration was never completed. His Italian student Thomas Aquinas (1224–74) himself came far closer to consummation, restricting his attention to theology but making a serious effort to exhaust his subject, with a full exposition of every question from an Aristotelian point of view. His two greatest works—and they are indeed vast—are both called *summae*: *Summa contra Gentiles* (everything a missionary needs to know before working among the Muslims) and *Summa Theologica*. Although somewhat controversial in its day (at the prompting of the pope, the Bishop of Paris Stephanus Tempier proscribed several of his *sententiae* in 1277), this work has become canonical in the Roman Catholic Church.

◈

This aspiration seems to be characteristic of the Latin intellectual world, the desire for a full and definitive statement of the truth, together with the belief that it could actually be delivered, once and for all, in its own language. It is the mental equivalent of the ancient geographical sense of the *orbis terrarum*, the circle of lands that the Romans had unthinkingly identified with their own empire.

The Christians had known that the source of their faith was prophecy in the Hebrew Scriptures, but only Jerome (a native speaker of Latin from the Balkans) had taken the logical step of going to Palestine, learning Hebrew, and discovering what those Scriptures actually said. The Roman Church accepted his interpretations into the Vulgate Bible, but continued to treat the resulting Latin text as authoritative.

Likewise the schoolmen had known that their latest additions to learning came ultimately from Greek thinkers, courtesy of the Arabic transmission, which had also added much to it. But they did not respond by generalizing the fact that such learning might be continuous, and so leaving open the option that there might be yet more fresh enlightenment on its way, probably from an unexpected quarter. Instead they argued about it among themselves, but ultimately integrated the new point of view into a new *summa* and attempted to make that the last word.

The medieval world viewed through Latin remained a closed world, but not because it rejected the world beyond its limits. Indeed, it was highly successful in converting and absorbing its neighbors in northern and eastern Europe, and ultimately those (in Muslim Spain) to its south. Rather, it remained a closed world because it looked resolutely inward, to Rome, or later—at least intellectually—to Paris. The four Crusades, fought from 1096 to 1204, can be seen as a series of desperate attempts to bring into the Latin-speaking world the main focus of Christianity that lay beyond, namely Jerusalem. They failed, because Jerusalem remained part of a different world, beyond Latin's inward-looking ken. Ultimately, the west did not have the military strength to force Jerusalem into its own image, to see Rome as the center of things.

Strangely, the vast tracts of the world that lay beyond the competing domains of Latin and Arabic were going to prove far more amenable than Jerusalem or the Near East to acceptance of the Roman view. But before this unexpected new career in the New World, Rome would itself change its view of Latin.

PART IV

LATIN IN A
VERNACULAR WORLD

CHAPTER 15

❖⊙❖

Alter ego—
Humanism and the Return of the Classics

*Italice loquentem soli Itali intelligent; qui tantum Hispanice loquatur
inter Germanos pro muto habebitur; Germanus inter Italos nutu ac
manibus pro lingua uti cogetur; qui Gallico
sermone peritissime ac scientissime utatur, ubi e Gallia
exierit, saepe ultro irridebitur; qui Graece Latineque
sciat, is, quocunque terrarum venerit, apud
plerosque admirationi erit.*

He who speaks Italian will be understood only by Italians; he who speaks
only Spanish will have the status of a mute among Germans; a German
among Italians will be forced to use nodding and his hands in place of
his tongue; he who uses the French language with high skill and
knowledge will often be mocked gratuitously when he leaves France;
but as for the man who knows Greek and Latin, he will be admired by
the majority wherever in the world he arrives.

Marc-Antoine Muret (1526–85), a French professor in Rome
(from *Oratio*, xviii, 1583)

IN THE LATTER FOURTEENTH and fifteenth centuries, the focus of innovation in the Latin world passed back from Paris and the universities to
the courts of northern Italy and Rome.

Despite its spread as Europe's universal language, and its currency as a
language of learning, Italians had always felt that Latin in some special way
belonged to them. For them, in fact, the term *Latin* had become a synonym for
Italian. In Dante's *De Vulgari Eloquentia*, at the outset of the fourteeenth century, *Latius*, *Latinus*, and *Ytalus* are used indifferently; 'the Italian vernacular',

which he is seeking to define, is called *vulgare latium*, and *Latium* is even used to refer to Italy in general. Half a century later, in 1368, Francesco Petrarca (known in English as Petrarch) sought to disprove in scholastic style a Frenchman's claim that Latin should be distinguished from Italian, appealing to a text from Augustine: "they traced the succession through Greeks and Latins, then to the Romans, who are themselves Latins." He proceeds, "And furthermore, learned men, in all speech and writing, call Roman eloquence Latin and vice versa, as there are two names but one thing," adding, "We are not Greeks, not barbarians, but Italians and Latins."[1]

There was an ambivalence or equivocation here. Italians still felt that Latin was "a kind of sameness of speech unalterable for diverse times and places," as Dante had still expressed it. Latin had the status of a universal, but it was nonetheless consciously a universal that had been distinctively created and developed in Italy. With the growing wealth, independence, and self-confidence of the cities of northern Italy, and above all in Dante's and Petrarch's hometown of Florence, their citizens saw Latin as 'ours', *nostra lingua Latina*. Even in 1281 the Florentine historian Ricordano Malespini had noted that Emperor Frederick II of the Holy Roman Empire *seppe la lingua nostra latina e il nostro volgare* 'knew our Latin tongue and our vernacular'.[2] Latin was conceived as not only an ideal language, but as one characteristic of the Italian past, an ancient language.[3]

Concurrently, a new sense of history was arising: the past should be understood in its own terms, not simply as a treasury of wise sayings from the *auctores*, and exemplary deeds of the *illustrissimi viri*. Gone was the divinely ordained triumph of the Roman Empire, and its transfiguration in the establishment of the Church, a narrative familiar since Orosius in the fifth century. Instead, the archetypal Florentine historian Leonardo Bruni (1370–1444)— who still chose to write his *History of the Florentine People* in Latin—focused on Rome as a republic, arising as just one amid the city-states of Tuscany, and on the internal rivalry among its great men that made possible the founding of the Empire as such. He still saw history as an inspiration, *vulgaribus fabulosisque opinionibus reiectis* 'when commonly held but mythical beliefs have been discarded',[4] but as an inspiration to those who would be free, as he saw his own city and its neighbors as free.

The ideal was transmuted into a new style of education. Hitherto, education for aristocrats had emphasized chivalric pursuits, and literature read in the vernacular, while for merchants and the professional classes, it had always been more practical.* After the turn of the fourteenth-fifteenth centuries, the rising generation of aristocratic and professional youth in Florence, Venice, and their peers were trained in *humanitas*: to the seven arts were added history and moral philosophy. Within this new system, grammar was based on attention to the actual practice of the ancient Roman writers, rather than the rules abstracted by Donatus and Priscian, let alone the writing of the Church Fathers and their successors; and rhetoric came back to its roots as the discipline of speaking to an audience, not the drafting of documents and business letters. The flash and splendor of classical learning, *bonae litterae*, became part of the array of beauty and elegance that graced any self-respecting Renaissance Italian nobleman or plutocrat. Latin was supposed to be spectacular.

This new self-confidence of the Tuscans might seem not so crucial to the history of Latin, the world language of the day: for after all, who were these jumped-up city-states other than a rump of the Holy Roman Empire, a rebellious region that had asserted independence from Germany only now to be claimed by France? True, the city-states were growing in wealth, but small cities backed by trading houses could hardly compete in prestige across Europe with the established monarchies in France, England, Germany, Spain, and indeed southern Italy, where the Norman power had been succeeded since 1266 by Angevins from France. Yet this was to reckon without Italy's trump card, the papacy, the one institution that, with its spiritual pretensions, has always punched far above its weight in Europe politically, but even more culturally and linguistically.

In the fourteenth century, the papacy had been through an extremely adverse period. Distressed by turmoil and factionalism in Rome, in 1309 Pope Clement V had accepted King Philip IV's invitation to move his court to the safety of Avignon on the Mediterranean coast of France. This, however, had put the pope under the effective control of the French king, which did not enhance his authority or influence in the long term. In 1377 the papal court had attempted a return to Rome, but its prestige was not immediately restored; in fact quite the reverse happened, since when one pope returned to the Vatican,

---

*Even from this book's brief review of Latin in the Middle Ages, the worldly priorities of Italian education emerge clearly: note the bias toward law in the original Italian university at Bologna from the twelfth century; the commercial direction set for the *ars dictaminis* there in the same period; and the north-Italian merchants' early replacement of Roman with Arabic numerals after Leonardo of Pisa's *Liber Abaci* (1202).

the French party of cardinals elected a competing pope, who took up the vacant throne in Avignon. The resulting Great Schism lasted until 1417, when a General Council (using new powers that had been conceived by the logician Jean de Gerson at the University of Paris) managed to get agreement on deposition of the contending popes—there were by then three of them—and a fresh (single) election; but even then, the pope remained locked in a battle of authority with successive councils until 1439.

From 1420, however, to restore and enhance its image and reputation, the papacy embarked on a sustained campaign of cultural relations. The most famous parts of this program were the commissions to such artists as Botticelli and Michelangelo. Over the next century and a half Rome was rebuilt, tellingly in humanist style, i.e., with close attention to remains from the past. Literary archaeologists flourished: Flavio Biondo (who wrote *Roma instaurata*, 1446; *Italia illustrata*, 1454; *Roma triumphans*, 1459) used his wide reading in classical authors to reconstruct the physical details of ancient Rome. Confronting the sad contrast with his own day, he realized that it had been theft of masonry over the centuries, not natural erosion, that had caused so many ancient landmarks to vanish. Three generations later Marco Fabio Calvo (author of *Antiquae urbis Romae cum regionibus simulachrum*, 1527 'An image of the ancient city of Rome and the regions') translated Vitruvius' *de Architectura* into Italian to help Raphael realize his building designs.[5] But language, specifically of course Latin, played a key role in the new dispensation, and humanists were enlisted in the great cause. Important Roman families such as the Colonna and Orsini were already converts to the humanist educational movement, but the list of scholars actually employed on the papal staff over the century to 1526 is legion: it included such luminaries as Leonardo Bruni, Lorenzo Valla, Pietro Bembo the literary theorist, and Maffeo Vegio, an epic poet who dared to complete Virgil's *Aeneid* with a Book XIII of his own devising, carried off with pure Virgilian panache.

Eventually, apostolic secretaries of the papacy were required in practice to be humanists.* These men were responsible for drafting official letters in the name of the pope, the famous Papal Bulls, named for their monumental seal *bulla* (Latin for 'bubble'). Often the pope's personal (or "domestic") sec-

---

*The policy of the papacy to co-opt the best authors went back long before it had accepted the desirability of humanism. In 1352 Petrarch himself, already recognized as a literary lion, had had to use his high Ciceronian style—then still considered unacceptable for papal correspondence—as a diplomatic way to fail the examination in letter-drafting set for the post of apostolic secretary. (*Epistula*, xiii, 5, in Rossi 1937: vol. 3.)

retaries were humanists too, and the pope's antechamber became a place of debates on details of Latin and its history.* Periodic sentences in the style of Cicero came back into favor as the pope's means of expression. More humbly, but more pervasively, in Catholic liturgy the humanists revised the language of the Mass and some holy offices. They wrote hymns in classical quantitative meters; they put classical oratory into pontifical homilies.[6]

Literary excellence, in the classical style, came to seem a virtue in itself when promotions in the Church were being considered. Pope Pius II had before his elevation (1458–64) actually been, as Aeneas Sylvius Piccolomini, a published author, diplomat and poet laureate of the Holy Roman Empire (crowned at Vienna in 1442, this despite being an Italian from near Siena). Jacopo Sadoleto and Pietro Bembo, two eminent stylists who had been domestic secretaries to Leo X (1513–21), went on to become cardinals.[7] The favored idiom of the Roman Church—now even claiming to be home to *principes assertatoresque linguae Latinae* 'the princes and promotors of the Latin language'[8]—had changed from scholastic to Ciceronian Latin.

This favoring of Cicero above all other classical writers had begun as an honest debate within humanism. How was the best Latin style to be achieved? Evidently, for the humanist, by taking as model the best of the ancient writers. But what did this mean in practice? Should it be left to the judgment of the writer (perhaps taking into account his particular purposes)? Or should there rather be an agreement on who the best writer was, once and for all? If so, that must surely be, at least for prose, M. Tullius Cicero. There was an explicit, published debate during the late fifteenth and early sixteenth centuries on how particular the model for imitation should be. For and against the strict Ciceronian model, Poggio Bracciolini disputed with Lorenzo Valla (before 1447),† Paolo Cortesi with Angelo Poliziano (around 1490), Pietro Bembo with Gianfrancesco Pico della Mirandola (1512). In 1516 Cardinal Adriano

---

*Biondo's *De verbis Romanae locutionis* 'On the words of the Roman language' (1435) recalled his discussion with Leonardo Bruni and four other secretaries: what language had the Romans actually spoken? This was still an issue in fifteenth-century Italy. Bruni had maintained that Cicero would have used a vernacular distinct from Latin proper, which was only used in the revised versions of his speeches; but Biondo argued that Cicero had spoken Latin thoughout, Cicero's *sermo vulgi* just meaning unpolished phrasing. He returned to the point in *Roma triumphans*, citing more evidence.

†This was Valla before he came to Rome and joined the papal staff, still best known as the exposer of papal humbug, and author of *De elegantiis linguae Latinae*, a style guide that came closest to the eclectic stance of the Roman educationalist Quintilian.

Castellesi published a short history of the Latin language *De sermone latino*, which placed Cicero at the *perfectum* summit of Latin style, before the unfortunate *imperfectum* of subsequent eras: he represented a *fundamentum quoddam eloquentiae* "a kind of foundation for eloquence". The Church became more and more associated with the Ciceronian side, while it is notable that, in the matches just listed, representatives of independent cities, notably Florence, are to be found on the side of freedom of choice.

Since the Church, seeing itself as a universal teacher, needed a clear, teachable line, one can see the attractions of Cicero, who was as close to a one-man manifestation of classical Latin as could be found, excelling in oratory as well as expository prose and dialogue. His only limitation (besides having been pre-Christian) was his clear espousal of pro-republican, anti-imperial politics—ironically, a feature that had commended him above all, in the previous century, to the northern Italian city-states. This, however, the Church overlooked. Early in the sixteenth century Fedra Inghirami (writing as T. Phedrus), contemplating the New World just being discovered in the west, said Cicero's language had *magnitudinem quae par quidem romano imperio fuit eloquendi* 'a greatness of utterance equal to the very Roman Empire'—but this new Roman Empire (far greater than the old) was to be the spiritual domain of papal Rome.[9] And in the resonant nostalgia of Valla, *Ibi namque Romanum imperium est, ubicunque Romana lingua dominatur* 'For there is the Roman Empire, wherever the Roman language reigns.'[10]

As would have been expected if the Church's real motive was to have a standard that was teachable, Ciceronianism was defined in practice as writing in sentences with a balanced periodic structure, and strict avoidance of vocabulary that was not attested in the works of the great man. But Cicero had not been a Christian. Applied rigorously in a Christian context, this could give bizarre, even embarrassing, results, as in Paolo Cortesi's commentary (*Liber Sententiarum*) on Peter Lombard's theological summa, the *Sententiae*. This was published in 1504, and in it Christianity was repainted with all trappings of ancient Rome's civil and religious establishment: "The saints were *heroes*, priests were *flamines diales* (priests of Jupiter), St. Thomas Aquinas *Apollo Christianorum*, churches *templa* or *publica delubra* (temples or public shrines), decrees of canon law *senatus consulta*, cardinals *senatores*, indulgences *sortes*,* revelation *divina patefactio*, heresies *perduelliones* (acts of treason), and Hell *Orcus*."[11]

Somehow, this degree of stylistic fealty to authentic classical Latin never

---

*i.e., lottery tickets.

caught on. Recall (p. 117) that even Augustine himself had balked at calling the saints *heroes*. But besides the occasional stylistic excesses, the Church became entranced by what now seems like a dream of mystic unity of the Roman Empire and Catholic Church. In 1506–7 Pope Julius II reconquered the Papal States by force of arms and on Palm Sunday was able to celebrate a triumphant return to Rome, borne in a car shaped like an armillary sphere—for universal empire—and drawn by four white horses like a Roman *triumphator*. The Arch of Constantine was reconstructed, decorated with Julius' own victories, and a special medal was struck in commemoration: Julius Caesar Pontifex II. A few years later, in 1521, Pope Leo X was honored by the humanist Blosio Palladio in an oration that totally elided the differences between the Roman Empire and the Church, citing Livy to support his case that Rome had been the most perfect of terrestrial empires, but had been continued in a spiritual dimension by the Christian Church.[12]

This dream was shattered in 1527 by the military sack of Rome, carried out by an imperial army made up of Spanish and German troops. The papacy's political ambitions never recovered. And to add insult, the humanist pretensions of Ciceronianism were punctured in the next year by the publication of Desiderius Erasmus's satire the *Dialogus Ciceronianus*.

In this work written in the most elegant humanist Latin, Erasmus (who had witnessed Julius II's triumph) imagined a character called Nosoponus 'laboring under a disease' exerting himself to work out which inflected forms of each verb were actually found in Cicero's work, and which (more important)

Desiderius Erasmus by Hans Holbein the Younger. A satirist and a New Testament scholar, Erasmus opposed the Catholic Church's adherence to Ciceronian style.

were not. For such a man, even his dreams were restricted to Cicero (*Nec aliud simulachrum in somnis occurrit praeterquam Ciceronis . . .*); and he is described as looking more like a ghost than a man (*Larvae similior videtur quam homini*). Erasmus twits him with the paradox of how a pure Ciceronian could ever say anything more or other than what Cicero had already said. But in it, Erasmus had other concerns than the stylistic: he was concerned to expose the use of Ciceronian style as a cover for crypto-paganism.

> You will find them all full of monuments to paganism. In the pictures too our eyes are more caught by Jupiter slipping as shower of rain into Danae's bosom than Gabriel announcing the heavenly conception to the holy Virgin; there is more joy in Ganymede caught up by an eagle than Christ ascending into the heavens; our eyes linger more longingly on the expression of Bacchanalia or Terminalia full of disgusting obscenity than Lazarus' recall to life or Christ's baptism by John. These are the mysteries that get veiled under the name *Ciceronian*. Under the pretext of an attractive name, believe me, snares are being set for straightforward, easily tricked young people. We do not dare to profess paganism. Our cover is the word *Ciceronian*. But how much better to be totally speechless than to come to this position![13]

For all these concerns about the spiritual crookedness that might be associated with strict Ciceronianism and an overenthusastic embrace of the points of reference in Cicero's world, Erasmus and his reformist friends in northern Europe were just as concerned as the Catholic Church to move Latin away from its scholastic past. By the sixteenth century, reformers everywhere were humanists, in the north as in the south of Europe.

This revision of the Renaissance humanists, essentially a restoration of Cornelius Fronto's ancient idea that Latin was defined by its "classics," its "top rankers" (p. 100), was to be remarkably durable. It has affected classical education, and hence everyone's unthinking idea of what is "the best Latin" to this day. We all see the classical era of the first centuries BC and AD as definitive and have turned our backs on Latin as extended by the schoolmen, even as we have accepted into our own modern languages most of their innovations: as witness the English equivalents of *revisio, humanista, essentialiter, restauratio, antianus, durabilis, definitivus, innovatio*, the words that stocked the last three sentences, all late-Latin or medieval coinages that are now quite standard parts of modern European discourse.

For Latin itself, though, since the fifteenth century it has been considered poor form to use them in writing. And this brings up a long-term charge against the humanists.[14] By insisting on ancient models, the humanists tore Latin away from its old, massive root structure, pruned it, and replanted it in well-weeded display beds, in admirable but alien splendor. Latin remained a privilege of the educated: Renaissance humanism did nothing, for example, to bring Latin closer to the growing multitudes who were learning to read in the vernacular. But even for those who were brought up with it, Latin was now that little bit harder to learn, as its links were cut with modern discourse, however ponderous that discourse might have been. Appreciating Latin neat, in its supposedly purer, pristine form, was an aesthetic achievement; but paradoxically it made the language harder to master, and to use as a living medium of day-to-day expression, let alone as a vehicle for original thought.

Latin, up on its pedestal, began to wilt.

⊹

This wilting was not at first in evidence: quite the reverse. As the Italians of the fourteenth and fifteenth centuries announced the cultural *renovatio* that was happening, they gave proof of it by a surge of vigorous, innovative writing in their new, restored Latin. There was still sufficient force, or accumulated prestige, behind Latin writing for it to rise to the challenge of the humanist filter, rather than to quail at its newly restrictive standards.

Francesco Petrarca (Petrarch), the great pioneer of Renaissance humanism, wrote much in Latin, but also discovered a vast new corpus of Cicero's correspondence.

Petrarch wrote in Virgilian style the epic *Africa*, about the exploits of Scipio Africanus in the third century BC; the heaviness of its verses—far less fluent than what would be achieved as full classical educations became normal over the next century—matched its unpromisingly antiquarian theme. However, on the strength of it Petrarch was elected poet laureate at Rome in 1341, the first since antiquity. Nonetheless, his main contributions to Latin literature were in the variety of his prose: essays, letters, moral biographies, invectives, a guidebook to the Holy Land, and a self-help guide, *De Remedius Utriusque Fortunae* 'Coping with Good Luck and Bad'. In 1345 he in fact achieved the highest conceivable prize in his own terms by discovering in Verona a new corpus of Cicero's works (his voluminous correspondence with Atticus, Brutus, and Cicero's brother Quintus). On that occasion, Petrarch thought fit to write a letter to Cicero himself:

> *Tu quidem, Cicero . . . ut homo vixisti, ut orator dixisti, ut philosophus scripsisti . . . O Romani eloquii summe parens, nec solus ego, sed omnes tibi gratias agimus, quicumque Latinae linguae floribus ornamur; tuis enim prata de fontibus irrigamus, tuo ductu directos, tuis suffragiis adiutos, tuo nos lumine illustratos ingenue confitemur: tuis denique, ut ita dicam, auspiciis ad hanc quantulacumque est, scribendi facultatem ac propositum pervenisse.*

> You, Cicero . . . lived as a man, spoke as an orator, wrote as a philosopher . . . O supreme father of Roman eloquence, receive thanks not from me alone, but from all of us who are decked in the flowers of the Latin tongue; for it is from your springs that we water our meadows; guided by your leadership, aided by your support, illuminated by your light, we honestly confess that it is under your auspices, let me say, we have attained whatever slight skill and purpose there is in our writing.

This, of course, is more a Ciceronian speech than a letter. Petrarch informs Cicero of the sad loss of some of his works, the encouraging success of his great successors Virgil and Seneca, but the lamentable state of Rome itself. (The papacy was at the time in its "Babylonian captivity" in Avignon.) *Crede enim mihi, Cicero, si quo in statu res nostrae sunt audieris, excident tibi lacrimae, quamlibet vel caeli vel erebi partem teneas. Aeternum vale* 'Believe me, Cicero, if you were to hear how our matters stand, your tears would fall, whichever part of heaven or Erebus is yours. Farewell for ever'.[15]

Other great poets in humanist Latin were Maffeo Vegio (1407–58), another admirer of Virgil's, who amid some fifty poems is best known for his short epics on classical themes, Aeneas' final settlement in Italy, the death of the young Astyanax as an atrocity in the fall of Troy, and the tragic success of Jason in winning the Golden Fleece and the dreadly passionate Medea. Later, he wrote an *Antoniad*, on the life of the St. Antony Abbot and his holy adventures in quest of another desert father, St. Paul the Hermit. Curiously, it reads throughout as if Rome's pagan history were more familiar to the reader than the Christian heaven or the lives of saints. This prefigures further Christian epics in the next century, Jacopo Sannazaro's *De Partu Virginis* 'On the Virgin's Birth' (1526) and the *Christiad* of Marco Girolamo Vida (1535).

Angelo Poliziano (1454–1494), two generations after Vegio, had the interesting idea of prefacing his courses at Florence (as professor of *ars poetica et oratoria*) with sustained verse introductions. As a result, he wrote pieces on the *Bucolics* of Virgil, on Hesiod and Virgil's *Georgics*, on Homer, and on the history of Greek and Latin poetry, which were all works of art in their own right, neoclassical Latin poetry inspired by classical Latin poetry. He called them all *Silvae* 'Woods', an allusion to the great work of another Latin poet, Statius, *Silvae* being understood as *indigesta materia* 'untreated timber'. But this is a self-deprecating conceit, in reference to such deftly learned concoctions. Poliziano wrote of poetry (something for which the Middle Ages, remember, had no single word—p. 197) as the driving force toward civilization itself:

> *Donec ab aetherio genitor pertaesus Olympo socordes animos, longo marcentia somno pectora, te nostrae, divina Poetica, menti aurigam dominamque dedit. Tu flectere habenis colla reluctantum, tu lentis addere calcar, tu formare rudes, tu prima extundere duro abstrusam cordi scintillam, prima fovere ausa Prometheae caelestia semina flammae.*

At last the father, wearying in airy Olympus of dense spirits, of senses lolling in long sleep, granted you for our minds, divine Poetry, our charioteer and mistress. You first durst rein the necks of the resistant, spur on slackers, shape the crude, strike a spark hidden in our hard hearts, you first to nourish the heavenly seeds of Prometheus' flame.[16]

This is a very different world from scholastic philosophy. The Italian humanists were attempting to give classical Latin literature the sequel for which it had lost its chance in the ancient period, when the turmoil of barbarians without and Christianity within had put it on the defensive. Now in a world where the Church was a given, not a combative threat, and where there was no external threat to culture as they knew it, they could develop their sensibilities, through the vernacular but also through Latin, from the point where the ancient writers had left off.

Another great original of fifteenth-century Italy was Lorenzo Valla (ca 1406–57), an inveterate controversialist, but also an energetic textual critic. He was a great enthusiast for the Latin language and wrote some substantial works on philosophy. Characteristically in his *Dialecticae disputationes* (1439) he suggested that logic was best seen as subordinate to rhetoric, in fact as an inflated extension of the rules of classical Latin (not even Greek!).[17] But his most influential work was *Elegantiarum linguae Latinae Libri VI* 'six books on the styles of the Latin language', though a modern author has suggested it should be translated as 'Advanced idiomatic Latin'.[18] It was written about 1440, but Valla continued to revise it for the next decade and a half. The work is a style guide for Latin, based on a fresh reading of classical authors, but examining them critically so as to infer general, but often highly specific, rules of good writing. Valla notes for example that *et* is never used in Cicero to mean *etiam* 'even': this usage begins in Virgil.[19]

Besides its detailed content, its prefaces became almost as well-known and much quoted as the text itself, since they developed the idea of Latin—conceived as the language inherited from the Roman Empire—as a thing of awe in its own right:

> Our ancestors excelled the rest of mankind in war and other achievements, but in spreading their own language they outdid themselves . . . Will it be counted less [than all the other gods' gifts of staple crops] to have shared the Latin language among the nations, the best of fruits, a divine one truly, which feeds not the body but the mind? . . . For they realized that their own languages were not diminished by Latin but somehow seasoned by it; just as the use of water was not shaken by the later discovery of wine, nor wool and linen by silk, nor the other metals dispossessed by gold . . . Therefore it is the great sacrament of the Latin language, and its great inspiration, that it has been maintained throughout the centuries sacredly and devoutly among foreigners, barbarians, and enemies . . . by this more splendid dominion we still reign in much of the world. Ours is France, Spain, Germany, Hungary, Dalmatia, Illyricum, and many other nations.[20]

The *Elegantiae* soon became the new standard for higher studies of *grammatica*, or (to speak more modernly) for *latinitas*, and in the next generation it was to become a success in France and the north as well as in Italy. After a first Paris edition of 1471 (one of the first publications of the Sorbonne press), it was reprinted in 1476, 1495, and 1497. In fact, it was to go through fifty-nine editions in sixty-five years.[21] Valla was hailed as *linguae latinae restaurator* by the French grammarian Guillaume Tardif (in 1475), who found in him the inspiration for his own new coinage, the concept of "humanism" itself.[22] Erasmus too in the Netherlands was just as appreciative: "With such industry, such zeal, such efforts, he refuted the stupidities of barbarians, saved from death works that were almost buried, and restored to Italy the splendor of its ancient eloquence."[23]

Of course, it did no harm with such northern audiences that Valla had also achieved notoriety in his early career as a thorn in the side of the papacy, applying his critical method to a number of works associated with traditional Catholicism. First, and most famously, he had written in 1439 the *De falso credita et ementita Constantino donatione declamatio* 'Declamation on the falsely believed and lying Donation of Constantine'. The Donation was in form a transfer of power over the western provinces from the emperor Constantine to Pope Sylvester I; it had been used for at least five centuries to justify the pope's temporal power (and would be for at least one more).[24] But Valla's *declamatio*, despite its reputation, was a rhetorical polemic, and only very slightly a work of linguistic criticism. It did point out that the Donation's author had anachronistic ideas about what a diadem was made of (gold and jewels, instead of cloth); and that he did not understand that *patrician* was a kind of family, *consul* a (highly restricted) office—hence neither appropriate as new titles for the clergy. It noted that, in talking about building cities, the author had confused *civitates* with *urbes*: in classical Latin, only the latter, as physical structures, could be built. And he curiously placed Constantinople in a province named Bizantia. Valla also took issue with a few words that he finds bizarre (e.g., *phrygium* as an imperial headdress, *banna* probably for 'banners', *udones* 'socks', and *concubitores* 'bedfellows'—an unfortunately suggestive malapropism, he jests, for *contubernales* 'attendants'). But Valla was in fact largely frustrated by the very unchanging nature of Latin in giving clear examples of the *stultiloquium* 'idiot speak' that he claimed to see throughout.* After all, clumsy diction in an official document hardly gives an argument against its authenticity.

But besides this case, Valla pursued his historical criticism—seeking to expose fraud or mistakes—in other less political works: he denounced a

---

*Coleman 1922: 92 n. 1, 109 n. 1, points out that Valla actually missed a trick in not noting that *seu*, classical meaning 'or', is used in the Donation anachronistically to mean 'and'.

supposed letter of Christ to Abgarus and questioned Jerome's Latin text of the New Testament itself, suggesting that it should be reexamined in comparison with the Greek, a challenge that would be taken up in earnest by Erasmus, and the new translators of the Reformation, working in northern Europe during the next century.

Despite such a provocative career—which had unsurprisingly attracted for a time the attentions of the Inquisition—Valla actually ended up as an apostolic secretary of the pope. It must have helped that he had always promoted Rome as the true source of the best Latin. He had made his peace with the enthusiastic humanist Nicholas V (the founder of the Vatican library) and died while applying his humanistic style in the service of the Church, having written a sermon, *De mysterio Eucharistiae*, and an *Encomium Sancti Thomas Aquinatis*. Thomism, therefore—unlike the other, denser works of scholastic philosophy—rather strangely received the blessing of humanism, one that would serve it well in the coming century.[25]

Valla was a great precursor, if not exactly the originator, of historical scholarship. (In fact he had been a student of Leonardo Bruni himself, at Rome in 1426.) He applied a historical sensibility systematically to texts and so created what was to be the new foundation for Latin studies, namely classical philology. Clearly, for this to be possible, the idea had to take root that Latin was primarily a language of the past, so that a detailed knowledge of the past would be needed to understand it truly and apply it authentically. Valla had been the required proponent of this view: that Latin was only genuine, only the real thing, if it was used as it had been in the classical era of its history.

Yet, for Latin studies to become historically authentic in this way, scholars of Latin would need an extra skill: they would have to learn to see it in its historical collaboration with Greek. This, after all, was how Latin literature had been born and raised, until the fifth century, when western Christianity, with its enthusiasm for the speech of the common man, and even (if necessary) for broken Latin, had discarded the Greek connection.

For a thousand years, only isolated savants had known Greek in the academic centers of the west. The Greek learning that, in the twelfth century, had been deployed to reintroduce Aristotle and the classics of Greek science and philosophy had remained a technical skill for specialists, concentrated in southern Italy and Spain, and never really entered western European culture, despite attempts to establish it at some universities, notably Oxford. It was, in any case, exclusively applied to serious factual and speculative works: there was no hint of Greek poetry, history, or oratory. Ramon Llull, through the decree of the Council of Vienne in 1312, had called for the founding of ten professorships in Greek across western Europe. In fact, he called for forty such chairs in languages deemed useful for biblical scholars and missionaries, but nothing was done. Greek, associated with the deviant Orthodox Church, seemed sinister. In the fourteenth century, the best library for Greek in the west, at the Papal Curia in Rome, held fewer than a hundred Greek books.[26]

Knowledge of Greek began to come back into western European education through Italy in the fifteenth century. It helped that the Greeks, then fighting for their continued existence against the advancing Ottoman Turks, had become suppliants rather than rivals in the greater world of Christendom; under duress, the Orthodox Church had briefly even accepted the primacy of the pope in 1438–39, and *Latinophrōn* 'Latin-minded' Greeks were more and more common in elite Italian circles. One of them, Manuel Chrysoloras, had taught Leonardo Bruni his language in the last years of the fourteenth century. After the fall of Constantinople in 1453, the flood of Greek refugees coming westward included many learned men, *dotti bizantini*, who converted to Catholicism. The indefatigable humanist Pope Pius II had seriously feared that the fall of Constantinople heralded the end of Greek culture: "Now that the Turks have won and possess all that Greek power once held, Greek letters, I believe, are finished . . . It will all be very different under the rule of the Turks, the most savage of men, the enemies of good customs and good letters."*

Greeks were, in short, now attracting sympathy and solidarity, rather than suspicion.

The new availability of teachers was met by a new readiness to learn in the Italian humanists. Petrarch, their pioneer, regretted that death had robbed him of his Greek teacher Barlaam before he could make much progress,[27] but the humanists of the fifteenth and sixteenth centuries had far better luck.

---

*Pertusi 1976: 2:53. Pius II did not however despair. He had first used his eloquence to write a long (open) letter to the Ottoman sultan Mehmet II, urging him to convert—a difficult brief, and one that might have tried Cicero himself. The pope began by urging Mehmet to give him a fair hearing, in a long, balanced, Ciceronian period: *Pro tua salute et gloria, proque multarum gentium consolatione et pace hortamur ut benigne audias verba nostra, nec prius damnes quam iudices, nec prius iudices quam singula diligenter intelligas* . . . Finally, he pleaded, a few drops of baptismal water would suffice to gain Mehmet the pope's recognition as Emperor of the East. There was no response. Later, moving on to sterner stuff, he tried to mobilize a fleet and an army to reconquer Constantinople, which he would himself lead; but he died in 1464 before he could leave Italy. His latter-day crusade died with him.

Most of the great names of humanist Latin, among them Leonardo Bruni (ca 1370–1444), Leon Battista Alberti (1404–72), Lorenzo Valla (ca 1406–59), Marsilio Ficino (1433–99), Angelo Poliziano (1454–94), and Giovanni Pico della Mirandola (1463–94), learned Greek in their youth. Francesco Filelfo (1398–1481), having married his Greek professor's daughter, made a long career out of Italian-Greek relations and the translation of Greek classics. By 1459, the educationist Battista Guarino could assert:

> I am aware that most say that knowledge of Greek is unnecessary, because, un-learned themselves, they wish others to match their ignorance, so that if they cannot be judged superior then at least not inferior. But for my part, I shall defend until my dying day the error (if error it be) that it is not only beneficial but even essential to our literary education . . . We have the precedents of the most learned ancients, none of whom lacked Greek; and the authority of Quintilian, who says that our literature has its source in the Greek.[28]

Note the consciousness of elitism here, something that has always characterized the learning of Greek in the west, from that day to this; it is even more salient when one realizes that when this was written, Greek was only just beginning to get firmly established in schools and universities as a higher part of classical studies in Italy. Nonetheless it did; Greek libraries too began to be founded, and the advent of printing in the 1470s cemented its presence, since many of those early printed books were in fact Greek texts. By the death of Aldus Manutius in 1515, his Aldine Press in Venice had published most of the Greek classics, as well as school textbooks and dictionaries.

North of the Alps, the new humanist approach to Latin began to spread in the last two decades of the fifteenth century. But by contrast with Italy, here an education in Latin was still mostly the privilege of those intending to be clerics. The first notable northern European humanist, Desiderius Erasmus (1466–1536) fit within this pattern; but his main interest, the reform of Christian doctrine, turned out to be no bar to the new enthusiasm for the Greek roots of Latin culture. Greek, it seemed, had something for everyone. Erasmus was in Italy from 1506 to 1509 (partly at the Aldine Press) and was soon as deeply engaged with Greek as any Italian, but concentrating above all on the Greek original of the New Testament. To this could be added the study of the Greek Fathers of the Church, which fed into the disputes of the Reformation after 1517.

Erasmus published five editions of his *Annotationes in Novum Testamentum* between 1516 and 1535. He was also influential in his travels, in Paris,

Leuven, Oxford, and Basel. While he was at the court of Prince Charles in Brussels, in 1517, a *collegium trilingue* (Latin, Greek, and Hebrew) was set up in Leuven and at the Universidad Complutense in Spain (both academic centers of Charles's empire). One by one, serious scholars arose in the principal academic centers of northern Europe to establish local traditions of Greek studies: notably, Guillaume Budé (1467–1540) in France, John Colet (ca 1475–1519) in England, Johann Reuchlin (1455–1522) and Philipp Melanchthon—sporting a Greek translation of his German name Schwarzerd—(1497–1560) in Germany. The languages were studied with a more sober, not to say dour, attitude north of the Alps, although in Paris particularly this focus changed as the century wore on, with the New Testament yielding to classical Athens.

By the end of the sixteenth century, Greek was being studied in parallel with Latin all over western Europe. It is worth pausing to note how strange these studies had become, by comparison with the language studies of earlier centuries.

Both Greek and Latin were now valued for their associations with a glorious distant past, by teachers and students resolutely oblivious of their actual recent histories. The sad contemporary fate of real Greeks under Ottoman rule was no more of interest to Hellenists than the histories of Charlemagne or Peter Abelard were to Latinists.

Contrast this with the linguistic concerns of Ramon Llull in the thirteenth century. For him, Latin had been a medium for widespread communication with his intellectual peers, in a continuous tradition that went back for over a millennium, and foreign languages were valued as means of contact with the pagan world beyond.

So although this knowledge of Greek, as of pre-Christian Latin, was opening up fascinating new worlds for western Europeans, they were worlds that now only existed in their own reconstructions. In this sense, Europe's new love affair with the classics—dead classics—was profoundly inward-looking.

⟨◇⟩⟨◉⟩⟨◇⟩

CHAPTER 16

Deus ex machina—
Printing and the Profusion of Grammars

Quae enim disciplina . . . tam ornata atque . . . tam aurea ut ius civile?
An . . . ius pontificium, quod canonicum vocant, quod ex maxima parte
gothicum est? An philosophorum libri, qui ne a Gothis quidem aut
Vandalis intelligerentur? . . . An grammaticorum, quorum propositum
videtur fuisse ut linguam latinam dedocerent? An denique
rhetoricorum, qui ad hanc usque aetatem plurimi circumferebantur,
nihil aliud docentes nisi gothice dicere?

What discipline can match the civil law for its expression and sheer quality?
The pontifical, so-called canon law, which is mostly Gothic?
Books on philosophy, incomprehensible even to Goths or Vandals?
Books on grammar, whose aim seems to be to unteach the Latin language?
Or indeed books on rhetoric, very much in vogue nowadays, which
teach nothing but how to speak in Gothic?

Lorenzo Valla, *Styles of the Latin Language*
(best-selling guide to Latin in the sixteenth century)[1]

I TALIANS LIKE LORENZO VALLA might—and did—disdain Germans for
their barbarous "Gothic" Latin, but they had to respect their technology.
Johannes Santritter, a German resident in Venice, noted in 1492 that this competence of his countrymen seemed to cause resentment among Italians.[2] It had
indeed been a German who first combined a usable system of movable type
with the use of paper and so opened up the mass production of books. Some
details of who first did what are disputed, but all the contenders are German,
and most probably the originator was Johann Gänsfleisch Gutenberg, working
around 1450 in the city of Mainz.

Latin was never far from the invention. Some of the first documents printed by Gutenberg had been sections of Donatus' grammar. The Bible he printed was of course the Vulgate. The first book that bore a date of publication (1460) was the *Catholicon* (*Summa grammaticalis quae vocatur Catholicon*), a Latin grammar and dictionary intended for those in holy orders that had been compiled in 1286 by Johannes Januensis de Balbis. And as it happens, eyewitness testimony for the Gutenberg Bible comes from none other than Aeneas Sylvius Piccolomini, Latin author and future pope Pius II, who saw it in production in 1454.

Knowledge had suddenly become cheap, and the growth in the market was explosive. By 1471 the technique—again, usually brought by Germans setting up abroad—had reached many important centers of the book trade, including Paris, Rome, Venice, and Seville; by the turn of the century there were over two hundred printing houses across Europe, from Cádiz to Budapest, and from Oxford to Cosenza in the toe of southern Italy. These first printed books were mostly in Latin, and by 1475 most of the classics were already available in print. By 1500 there had been nearly two hundred editions of Virgil, and over three hundred of Cicero. The concurrent vogue for Greek studies benefited from the boom, especially at the Aldine Press in Venice, so that by 1515 Greek classic literature too was largely all in print.[3]

Printing had, in its first application, a particularly beneficial influence on languages such as Greek and Latin, which existed (by now, in western Europe) primarily as heritages of texts.

Mass production meant that rare books, which had always been in danger of disappearing if the few known copies should be lost or destroyed, could now find safety once and for all in the sheer numbers, and potential widespread distribution, of a print run. (These were usually of the order of five hundred copies.) This was an advantage in terms of brute survival.

But another aspect of printing allowed for actual improvement in the quality of texts. Textual criticism could now make real gains, through collation of manuscripts and selection of the best variants when versions of the same text disagreed, since a new edition could at last be reproduced without the danger of introducing new errors with each new copy. Critical improvements might even be cumulative. The late fifteenth and the sixteenth centuries were a golden age for textual critics. Angelo Poliziano (1454–94), the poetical professor of the *Silvae*, worked out in his *Miscellanea* the basic logic of how to assess the value of written manuscripts as evidence (the idea being to identify independent traditions of copying, select the oldest in each tradition, and discard the rest).

Cultured princes such as the Medici in Florence, and the humanist popes, sent out agents to comb the monastic libraries of northern Europe, paying high prices for classical manuscripts; and a series of enthusiasts in northern Italy, and northern Europe, principally France, actively debated the textual issues, called *cruces* 'crosses', as they emerged from comparisons of the literature.[4]

Evidently, there were dangers in printed editions too, since any single one could as easily multiply corrupt texts as good ones. Printing was an industry and so necessarily was in the hands of businessmen, not scholars. For example, the numerous first editions of Giovanni Andrea Bussi were notorious for their low standard. In the early days especially, there might well be no critically respectable text to hand when a printer wanted to bring out an edition. Even if there were, laziness, and the capital-intensive economics of early printing—Gutenberg himself had gone bankrupt while trying to print his Bible—tended to reinforce reuse of printed text that was already out there as the master for new editions. (It was crucial to estimate the paper costs of a new volume, and the length of a book already printed was clear, while a manuscript's length remained only approximate until it was set up in type.) Yet in general, and in the long run, the consensus of the scholarly world turned out to be well able to police the product of the printing marketplace.*

The new availability of printed texts, and specifically of textbooks, also transformed the Latin classroom. As book prices fell, individual printed copies of textbooks came within the reach not only of teachers but of their students too. Not all the textbooks were new, of course. In the conservative environment of school, notorious old favorites such as the Frenchman Alexander de Villedieu's *Doctrinale*, which recast Donatus' grammar into mnemonic hexameter verse, lived on. Written in 1199, it was reprinted 279 times, all over Europe and well into the sixteenth century. Often parents insisted on it, with a familiar "If it was good enough for me . . ." attitude. "What is the use of it all if parents insist that their children are brought up on Alexander?" bemoaned an Italian grammar-writer around 1475. "Our corrupt values are the misfortune of our children."[5]

But the new trend, as it gradually percolated from the centers of innovation in Italy, was for concision (not a virtue of Alexander's), avoidance of "rules for rules' sake," and giving the boys direct access as soon as possible to real writers. Particularly distasteful was any hint of grammatical theory that

---

*The logic of the situation is emerging again in our own era, with the new, even wider freedom of Internet publishing.

went beyond what was needed for understanding (and composing) good Latin: speculative grammar, often associated in this period with the name Martinus Dacus, was taboo. Erasmus, considering the best textbook in 1511, wrote, "There is not much difference to detect among contemporary Latin grammarians. Niccolò Perotti [*Rudimenta grammatices*, 1468] seems the most accurate, yet not pedantic. But while I grant that rules of this sort are necessary, I want them to be as few as possible, provided they are good."[6]

Aldus Manutius, the prolific Venetian publisher, in the preface to his own *Institutiones grammaticae* (1493), advised teachers, "Do not force children to memorize anything except the best authors . . . not your own composition in prose or verse, or those in the grammar book. They will unlearn in a few days what it took great effort to learn." John Colet, in his teachers' preface to Lily's grammar (1511), which was to become the English standard primer for two hundred years, wrote, "In the beginning men spake not Latin because such rules were made, but, contrariwise, because men spake such Latin the rules were made. That is to say, Latin speech was before the rules, and not the rules before the Latin speech."[7]

In 1540 another grammar writer, Francesco Priscianese, was still inclined to say that the reason Latin and Greek were considered so much harder to learn than modern languages was that grammarians old and new had always taught grammar rather than language.[8] In 1611 the Irishman William Bathe, proposing his *Janua linguarum* 'door to languages' as a new and highly efficient "third way" of language learning, explicitly distinguished "the regular method, where grammar is employed to illustrate concordance, from the irregular method [i.e., direct exposure] which is widely used by those who learn modern languages by reading and speaking."[9] Nevertheless, although there were many conversation guides to Latin (one written by Erasmus himself—*Colloquia*, 1516) and Latin was widely used as the classroom language all over Europe, in practice textbooks and large quantities of explicit grammar were never banished from the Latin classroom. The use of Latin as a spoken language in school and university long coexisted with them.[10]

The conversational guides that were provided to support students' active powers in the language were not restricted to classes and professors: "all student life was there," at least in the authors' intentions, as revealed by a section from *Latinum ydeoma pro novellis studentibus* 'the Latin idiom for beginning students', published by Paul Schneevogel (Paulus Niavis) in Leipzig in 1482. Bartoldus and Camillus are two students, the constant characters in its dialogues.

C:	*Cerne! Numquid clinodium est et pulcrum et preciosum?*	Look! Isn't it a gem, beautiful and precious?
B:	*Ubinam cepisti?*	Where'd you get it?
C:	*Dono datum est mihi. O, quam tenerrime fuerunt ille manus, e quibus accepi!*	It was given me as a present. Oh, how tender were the hands from whom I had it!
B:	*Video bene quod annulus est.* Etiamsi magni pendis, tres quattuorve valet grossos. Ac huiusmodi manus fuerint? Nisi exposueris scire nequeo.*	I can see it's a ring. Even if you think it's valuable it's worth three or four grossi. Were those hands like this? Unless you take it off, I can't tell.
C:	*Non donum, dantis benevolentia placet!*	It's not the present, but the kindness of the giver that pleases me.
B:	*Unde tamen habes, obsecro?*	Where did you get it from, anyway?
C:	*Nulli autem dicas!*	Don't tell anyone!
B:	*Nulli omnino.*	Not a soul.
C:	*Filia maior natu iudicis.*	The judge's elder daughter.
B:	*. . . Si hoc scires ac plane intelligeres, quod ego sencio, procul a te amoveres.*	. . . If you had a clear idea of what I have heard, you'd give her a wide berth.
C:	*Quid hoc est? Eloquere, oro!*	What's that? Spit it out!
B:	*Dicam sed tecum retineas!*	I'll tell you, but keep it to yourself.
C:	*Neque tam rimax sum, ut facile omnia dilatarem.*	I'm not that leaky, to spread everything about.
B:	*Vide, ne laqueus collum stringat tuum et annulus in cathenam vertetur ferream! . . . Enucleabo. Nam eandem dicant violatam. Alius nucleum ceperit si voles, habebis aut testam aut sportam.*	Be careful that you don't put your neck into a noose and your ring will turn into an iron chain! . . . I'll explain. They say she's been taken advantage of. Someone else has taken the kernel if you like, and you'll get the shell or the husk.
C:	*Quid ais? Profecto honestissima est.*	What are you talking about? She's a perfectly respectable girl.

---

*This clause with *quod* 'that' is not good classical Latin. Nor are the spellings *tenerrime, ille, cathenam, sencio, intencio*—for *tenerrimae, illae, catenam, sentio, intentio*. The full gospel of humanist Latin evidently had still to reach Leipzig in 1482.

B:	*Iam sencio, quia in ipsam ardes ac amore eius es inflammatus. Tu verbis si meis fidem non adhibes, conspice ventrem! Numquid tumescit?*	Now I can see that you are burning for the girl, quite inflamed with passion. If you don't believe my words, look at her belly! Isn't it swollen?
C:	*Optime Bartolde, quo ex fonte illa hausisti?*	My dear Bartoldus, what source have you been getting this from?
B:	*Rumor undique in oppido est. Atque iam scito: si poterit, genitor eius ipsam tibi in uxorem copulabit.*	The story's all over town. And be sure of one thing: if he gets a chance, her father will stuff her into marriage to you.
C:	*Et ea mihi intencio hucusque fuit, ipsam ut ducam . . .*	That is precisely my intention, to make her my wife . . .

The new means of book production gave rise to a mushroom growth of printed literature in the vernacular languages, as the less Latinate part of Europe's educated population began to find uses for their literacy. The rise of this new market was revolutionary in itself.[11] But the use made of the print media by the Reformation movement, led by Martin Luther from Wittenberg in 1517, was also telling: Luther's works alone (including his Bible translation) made up 33 percent of all German-language titles published between 1517 and 1525.[12] In time, this momentum would have an adverse impact on Latin as a language of publication, though in the sixteenth century this was still some way off. But, despite this general "rise of the vernaculars" in the sixteenth century, there was no concurrent tendency at all for Latin to be displaced in the classrooms of European schools.

While use of vernacular languages spread in chapel, church, and cathedral within Germany, Switzerland, the Netherlands, and England, Latin remained overwhelmingly the language of their schoolrooms, as it did in all the countries that stayed Catholic. In France, Germany, and Switzerland, children did not even learn to read in the vernacular, but started from day one in Latin.[13] Luther's friend and lieutenant the theologian Philipp Melanchthon himself wrote a Latin (and a Greek) grammar, widely used in Lutheran countries; and as "the preceptor of Germany" he played a key role in the reform of German schools and universities, infusing them with a deeply Protestant, but still highly Latinized, form of humanism. He was determined to counteract the decline in school attendance across Germany, which had partly been due to some early, rather brutish, rejection of education along with all things popish. (Luther's explicit advice to his margrave George

*Philipp Melanchthon by Lukas Cranach the
Younger. An ally of Martin Luther, he was
influential in Latin education for Protestants.*

the Pious was to reinforce Latin schools, but allow the Catholic monasteries
simply to atrophy.)[14]

One of the most successful writers of a Latin grammar in the fifteenth
century was Elio Antonio de Nebrija (1441–1522), a Spaniard from the Seville
region who had been a foreign student of humanities in Bologna from 1460 to
1470. Taking up a post at Salamanca on his return to Spain, to teach grammar
and rhetoric, he published *Introductiones latinae* in 1481, a book that was taken
up with a passion by Spanish schools.* But quite soon, around 1486, and at the
behest of Queen Isabel of Castile herself (the future sponsor of Columbus), he
produced a translation of it into Castilian—which shows that Spanish classrooms, unlike many others across Europe, were not working exclusively in
Latin. To serve this need, he later compiled bilingual dictionaries (Latin-
Castilian and Castilian-Spanish).† Nebrija's grammar was subsequently to go

---

*More specifically: *Aelii Antonii Nebrissensi Introductiones in latinam grammaticem* [sic] *per
eundem recognitae atque exactissime correctae glossematis* [sic] *cum antiquo Exemplari collatis.*
Much later (by the Council of Castile in 1601), it was granted a monopoly in Spain as a
textbook of Latin.
†The best-known previous example of a Latin grammar (and glossary) in the vernacular
goes back to Aelfric, in England at the end of the tenth century. Like Nebrija, he had
been concerned to produce scholars biliterate in Latin and the vernacular, as he states in
his preface: "I have taken the trouble to translate for you into your own language [sections
of Priscian and Donatus] so that your young minds may receive the two languages,
English and Latin, until you attain the fullness of learning."

around the Americas, in the baggage of the first heroic missionaries to Mexico and Peru, and soon reached all the Spanish colonies of the New World.

Besides his success in becoming Spain's doyen of Latin grammar in the new era of printed books, Nebrija developed his grammatical ideas in an original, and ultimately much more significant, direction. In 1492 he published *Gramática de la lengua castellana*, the very first grammar of a vernacular language, and made a splash with it by dedicating it to Queen Isabel. Henceforth, the dialect of her kingdom, Castile, would preempt the title of "Spanish" language, as she and her husband, Ferdinand of Aragon, were constituting Spain as a single state. Nebrija had an eye for history, since the opening words of his preface are some of the most famous in linguistics:

> When I consider well, most illustrious Queen, and set before my eyes the antiquity of all the things that remain written down for our record and memory, one thing I find and draw as a most certain conclusion, that always language was the companion of empire and followed it in such a way that jointly they began, grew, flourished; and afterward joint was the fall of both.

This was written in the first flush of the fall of Granada, the last Moorish kingdom in Spain, but before anyone even knew of the existence of the New World. Even if he spoke more momentously than he knew, Nebrija was deliberately putting Castilian on a par with Latin: it was the new language of the new rising empire, which would need its own monumental grammar, as Latin had had Donatus and Priscian.

The boastful trappings of imperial splendor were perhaps gratuitous, but Nebrija was here doing something highly significant and original. The Romans of the first century BC had been the first to demonstrate that the science of grammar, developed for Greek alone, was in fact applicable to another language. But the Roman aspiration had only been to achieve parity of cultural esteem with the Greeks, not to demonstrate that Greek ideas were more widely applicable. The general point—that every language can have a grammar—had totally been overlooked.

Now, seventeen centuries later—and because another empire, distinct from Rome, wanted top-level cultural recognition—the technique came at last to be applied to a third language. And this time, the general moral was drawn. However preeminent Spain might consider itself to be, for foreigners the kingdom was nothing special: it was clearly on a par with its neighbors, and if Castilian Spanish merited a grammar of its own, then they demanded equal dignity for their languages. In short order after Nebrija's grammar for Spanish, each of the major vernacular languages of western European states would be analyzed and defined with a formal grammar. The word *grammatica* at last became of general application, no longer reserved for basic accounts of the Latin and Greek languages. The sixteenth century was the era of Europe's *grammatisation*.[15]

Perhaps it was only possible because the new profusion of printed books in vernacular languages was showing the world that languages besides Latin and Greek could be set down in black and white, standardized permanently on the page. In any case, the prime motive for the new grammars was not to make the languages easier for foreigners to learn, but to identify each language as something known in its own right: as Nebrija himself put it, "to rehearse in artifice and reason the tongue that by long use they have acquired since childhood."* As it turned out, the main practical effect was to satisfy the new need made urgent by the age of printing: to fix the language in a form that all its users could accept, hopefully once and for all, as a national standard.

But in the light of so many grammars, the link was finally sundered between the status of an empire and the dignity of *grammatisation* for its language. The penny dropped among Europeans that every language could have a grammar, regardless. And the new works came to be valued—as in fact the familiar grammars of Latin had always been—for their utility in teaching or learning someone else's language.† Political status was irrelevant, unless perhaps it decided which language you wanted to learn. Soon, the languages treated were exotic (non-European) languages, such as Arabic and Turkish, and the countless languages of the Americas, just then being revealed. Among the pathbreakers were Pedro de Alcalá, publishing on Arabic in 1505 (*Arte para ligera mente saber la lengua araviga*), and in the Americas, Andres de Olmos on

---

redezir en artificio & razón la lengua que por luengo uso desde niños deprendieron. Nevertheless, Nebrija's grammar did have a final (fifth) book, in which he set out aspects of Castilian that foreign learners would need to master, including all the complex forms of nouns, adjectives, pronouns, and, above all, verbs. He also hoped that Spaniards who read his Castilian grammar would later find it easier to learn Latin, since the sense of the terminology would already be clear to them. (*Prólogo*, fol. 3 r-v, *Libro Quinto, prólogo,* fol. 54 r.)

†Christian missionaries in the east had, in a small way, pioneered this generalized concept of a grammar. The *Codex Cumanicus*, written in Latin and Persian, and compiling works of the thirteenth and fourteenth centuries, includes a partial grammar and dictionary of Qypchaq, a Turkic language spoken in the Crimea, together with some Christian texts and riddles in the language (Golden 1992).

Nahuatl (*Arte de la lengua mexicana*, 1547), and Domingo de Santo Tomás on Quechua (*Grammatica, o arte de la lengua general de los Indios de los Reynos del Peru*, 1560).

In fact, this new concept of a vernacular language, formulated in a description that could be printed in a small volume, would be essential to Spain's understanding of the New World and its varied lands and peoples, as its conquistadores, settlers, and missionaries took possession of them. Experience of Latin grammar had lain at the root of this concept, and classically educated priests and friars would apply it. And Latin itself would have its own important place in the culture that would grow up in the conquered New World.

❖❖❖

CHAPTER 17

Novus orbis—Latin America

Addidit et Deus nostris temporibus foelicitatem siquidem novus terrarum orbis nostris majoribus ignotus ad occidentem Hispanis, ad orientem Lusitanis classibus adapertus, Romanas leges accepit, Romanoque Pontifici, et Christianis legibus paret.

And God has added a blessing in our own day: a new world unknown to our ancestors, opening up to Spanish fleets in the west, to Portuguese in the east, has received Roman laws and obeys the Roman pontiff and Christian laws.*

Blosio Palladio to Pope Leo X
Oratio totam fere romanam historiam complectans, ca 1518[1]

A S THE FIFTEENTH CENTURY turned into the sixteenth, veils fell back from the boundaries of the European world, and a new, vaster world stood disclosed. The gratuitous prophecy of the Roman philosopher and statesman Seneca, uttered by the chorus in his play *Medea* (around 50 AD) was strangely fulfilled:

---

*The phrase *Latin America* itself is of surprisingly recent origin, with little specific reference to Latin, except implicitly as the origin of Spanish and Portuguese. It was coined in 1856 by the Colombian writer José Caicedo and soon popularized by the French, who were then interested in the area as a business prospect. It was taken up by Latin Americans themselves for patriotic solidarity at the end of that century, particularly as against Anglo-Saxon gringos to the north. But *ladino*, first applied to Moors in Spain, had been used from the earliest days of the Spanish colonies to designate non-Spaniards who knew Spanish.

venient annis saecula seris,	Eras will come in later years
quibus Oceanus vincula rerum	in which Ocean releases his bonds on things
laxet et ingens pateat tellus	and a vast universe will spread out
Tethysque novos detegat orbes	and Tethys the sea will disclose new worlds
nec sit terris ultima Thule.[2]	nor will Thule be the farthest of lands.

It was, as López de Gómara remarked in 1552, "the biggest thing since the creation of the world, excepting the incarnation and death of its creator."[3] It was as if the petulant prayer attributed to Alexander, supposedly weeping for lack of new worlds to conquer,[4] had at last been heard and answered by an imperialist deity. Certainly the discoveries were treated as Alexander or the generals who had built the Roman Empire would have wished, subdued with fire and sword—with divine help through the indiscriminate spread of European diseases—to the greater glory, and profit, of their conquerors. In a strange coincidence, almost all the powers that claimed parts of the New World for their own domains—Spain, Portugal, France, the Netherlands, England—had once been Roman provinces.[5] And for the first two at least, their right to take possession of independent countries was assured by Rome itself, in the person of the pope.

But the pope imposed certain conditions: the Papal Bull of 1493 issued by Alexander VI, *Inter Caetera*, and forming the legal title of Spain to its colonies, required the conversion of the natives to be the supreme goal of any Spanish empire in the New World. Likewise the Portuguese in the Indies, intent though they were on a different kind of expansion based on trade rather than direct extraction and exploitation, brought missionaries with them and set up Catholic dioceses in their port towns from Mozambique to Macao. There was an explicit compact in the expansion of these Catholic powers: in return for power, glory, and wealth, it was incumbent on them to spread the word of God and win souls for His salvation. Christianity, which had inherited the Roman enterprise in the fourth century AD, was still seen as the sole justification for any global involvement. The expansion of Europe's interests worldwide was recast by the papacy as a kind of ultimate Crusade.

But if souls, not gold, were the true objective, there was an immediate premium on communication. No one could be brought to the faith without having been made to understand it, and this required a common language between the preacher and the potential convert. When Columbus first made contact in 1492, there was no such language. Direct contact between the native populations of Eurasia and America had lapsed for over two thousand generations, and in any case—by whatever routes America had originally been populated—the parting of the ways had occurred on the opposite side of the planet from the Atlantic Ocean: contrast the age of Christianity, only sixty generations old in the time of Columbus, a period in which there had been plenty of time for the origin of completely new languages such as English, French, and Castilian, none of which had had a single speaker in the time of Christ or for many centuries thereafter.

This was not the first time in the history of the world that a proselytizing, revealed religion needed to be transmitted to peoples who spoke a language hitherto unknown. Buddhism coming from India, Mithraism and Manichaeism from Persia, Islam from Arabia, and indeed Christianity from Palestine in the centuries of the Roman Empire had surmounted this problem in previous ages. The crucial step was always the discovery or creation of bilinguals, people who were competent in the language of the target population, but also knew that of the missionaries. Once they existed and had been recruited to the faith, they could be taught to read and write if they did not know already, and the scriptures of the religion could be translated into the new language. A new generation of preachers, monks, and priests could then be raised, who might even be quite ignorant of the new faith's original language.*

Waiting for bilinguals to arise, as they always do in a situation of sustained cross-cultural contacts, takes time. Columbus, and many of his successors, attempted to accelerate the process by taking—usually kidnapping—young people from the tribes he visited and bringing them to Spain; but this was not a success, because the victims usually took ill and died in the unfamiliar conditions and, even if they did not, were likely to escape once returned to access to their own people. Cortés and Pizarro, a generation or two later, were more successful since there had been time for the first few natural bilinguals to develop. Cortés communicated successfully with the Aztecs through a chain of two of them, one a Spanish priest, Fray Gerónimo de Aguilar, who had been marooned in a Mayan village, and the other the lady Malintzin, a Nahuatl

---

*As examples of this succession process, Islamic missions had been distinctive in requiring their scriptures to be mastered in the Arabic original; by contrast, Christian missions had shown almost total indifference to the original languages—with the perplexing result that for the millennium from 400 to 1400 virtually no one in western Christendom could consult the original texts in Hebrew and Greek.

speaker traded to a Mayan community in childhood. Pizarro, in browbeating the Incas, relied on the linguistic help of Felipillo, a Peruvian boy from the town of Tumbes, on the northern periphery of the Inca empire but visited by the occasional Spanish adventurer. Felipillo had "learnt the [Spanish] language without anyone teaching him."[6] As a juvenile illiterate, he was far less successful in supporting the negotiations between Pizarro and Atahuallpa, and on at least one crucial occasion in Cajamarca hostilities seem to have broken out through impatience with his halting interpretation; but the outcome—in terms of death of kings, slaughter of their people, and triumph of the Spanish invaders—was not much different.

However, in a development that was to have vast significance both for linguistics and for international missionary work, the friars who followed Cortés to Mexico perceived that there might be another, faster, and more systematic way to achieve communication with the indigenous people. Every one of the friars had spent his schooldays learning a language out of a book, usually Nebrija's *Introductiones latinae*. More recently, in the first generation of the colony of Hispaniola, Nebrija's other great work, *Gramática de la lengua castellana*, had been used to spread knowledge of Spanish there. Twenty copies had been delivered to Hispaniola in 1513, sent from the governmental Casa de Contratación de Indias. And the process was effective in the Caribbean. The small, independent village communities there, with their vast numbers of mutually incomprehensible languages, had been the despair of Columbus.[7] Yet in the next generation there are many reports of native chiefs who were literate in Spanish, although the long-term effects were diminished by the tendency of all the Caribbean native populations to sicken and die off in the adverse conditions imposed on them by their new masters.[8]

In Mexico, a new approach would be attempted. Rather than teach the whole population Spanish, which seemed an impossible task amid the teeming multitudes of the Aztec cities, the missionaries would learn the people's languages. The new linguistic insight would be applied that every language could have a grammar—something that, as we have seen, despite more than a millennium of Latin grammar, had until recently been unthinkable. The missionaries themselves would become the necessary bilinguals, using methods that are now the familiar stock-in-trade of field linguists. A contemporary describes what happened:

> And the Lord put them in mind to turn themselves into children like the children who were their pupils to take part in their language, and with it to

bring about the conversion of those tiny people, adopting the sincerity and simplicity of children. And so, laying aside for a time the gravity of their demeanor, they would take to playing with straws and pebbles in the break times they allowed, to get rid of their inhibitions in communication. And they always had paper and ink in hand, and when they heard a word from an Indian, they would write it down, and the circumstance in which he said it. And in the afternoon the clerics would gather and share their scripts with one another and, as best they could, assign to those words the Spanish term that seemed most suitable. And it would happen that what on one day they thought they had heard on the next they thought not.[9]

And as the new linguistic knowledge solidified, they would write it down in the form of grammatical analysis, phrase books, and bilingual dictionaries. Later generations would be trained through the same book-learning skills that they had had from grammar school, given as their models the newly written native grammars, which once printed were seldom if ever revised. So the printing presses—first set up in Mexico City in 1535 and in Lima in 1583—acted as a kind of substitute for the natural increase of a population of bilingual monks and priests. Language acquisition had effectively been mechanized into a process of education, which substituted for the natural transmission from parent to child, something that would evidently have been impracticable in the celibate Spanish missions.

This was a viable approach for effective and rapid language-learning in the remains of the Aztec empire subdued by Cortés. As against the irreducible Babel of the Caribbean islanders, the Aztecs had already made their language, Nahuatl, familiar across most of the territory of Central America. (This language, in its previous history, had in fact conveniently borne out Nebrija's famous claim that "always language was the companion of empire.") The Spaniards dignified it as *la lengua general de los indios*, and from 1558 it was actively taught as a common language in schools for indigenous children of various tongues, by Franciscan and Augustinian monks.[10] Where Nahuatl gave out, other major languages, such as Totonac, Otomí, Mixtec, and the Mayan languages Huastec, Quiché, and Yucatec, were widely spoken and hence efficient means to reach large numbers of Mesoamerican souls in need of the word of God.

Down south in the other great empire, of Peru, the Incas had spread Quechua; and farther south and inland, Aymara and Guarani turned out to be usable lingua francas. To the north of Peru, in what is now Colombia, a kind of empire had been established in the altiplano of Cundinamarca, with the Chibcha language as its medium. These also were all dubbed *lenguas generales* and promoted as common means of contact with the natives, not always successfully. Missionaries endeavored to learn these languages and make them available in the formal descriptions of grammars and dictionaries. As the centuries wore on, they were able to give this attention not only to the *lenguas generales*, but to a vast number of other languages—369 in all by the assessment of the Count of Viñaza in 1892. In these four centuries 667 separate authors had produced 1,188 works, distinguishing 493 languages in all.[11]

One fortunate (double) coincidence that speeded the Spanish missionary efforts was that the repertoires of sounds used in Nahuatl and Quechua, the two principal *lenguas generales*, were not highly distinct from that of Castilian—or indeed Latin. They were not tone languages, and they largely lacked any exotic vowels, consonants, or prosodies (such as nasalization or distinctive intonation). Nahuatl was particularly unexceptional, with no phonemes (except for *tl*) that were unknown to Latin. Quechua too was fairly tractable for the Latin-Spanish alphabet: it did require *ch*, which was distinctive to Spanish. But the glottalized stops of Quechua (represented *p'*, *t'*, *ch'*, and *k'*), and its uvular stop (represented with *q*), were all that went beyond the Spanish system. It was thus possible for missionaries to write the languages immediately and intuitively without any serious difficulty, or indeed any need for lengthy debate on the best innovations in spelling to adopt. In this degree of phonetic similarity to Spanish, Nahuatl and Quechua were rather untypical of the languages of the Americas.

The new grammars, usually called *artes*,* would in time open up an entirely new world of unknown languages. But the grammatical concepts that they used to explore them were mostly drawn from Nebrija's works, with which all the Spanish missionary linguists were familiar. Nahuatl, Quechua, and hundreds of other languages would be analyzed using the eight parts of speech as Nebrija had laid them out, concepts that in themselves had been familiar since Dionysius the Thracian. It would naturally

---

*The term *ars* (*arte* in Spanish and Portuguese) had started as Remmius Palaemon's translation of *tekhnē*, the word used by Dionysius the Thracian for his grammar of Greek. It had then been taken up, memorably, by Donatus. Now it became the usual word for a grammatical treatise of any language.

take time for linguists to realize the true potential generality of human languages, and to devise the best terminology to describe it: arguably indeed, linguists are still struggling to get an adequate grip on this. But in any case, it made pedagogical sense to teach people new languages using, as far as possible, the concepts they had learned at school. Through Nebrija, the content of Latin grammar became the framework for understanding the languages of the New World.

Not only the concepts and categories, but the familiar Latin framework of mnemonic verses to press home the unfamiliar grammar of a learned language was reinvented for American languages. The opening dactylic hexameter lines, with which the inflexion of verbs was being introduced in a grammar of the Chibcha language of the seventeenth century, is a good example.

Eloquio quisquis chibcho cupis esse disertus,	Any who wish to be eloquent in Chibcha speech,
En tibi queis possint formari tempora norma.	Here are your tenses that can be formed by rule.
De praeteritis.	<u>On the past tense</u>.
Praeteritum formas <u>squa</u> et <u>suca</u> facile demptis	You form the past easily taking off *squa* and *suca*.
Addideris vero nonnullis id <u>guy</u> prioris	But to some you must add *guy* first
In quibus A <u>suca</u> praeit, uti <u>zemnypguasuca</u>;	Where *A* precedes *suca*, as in *zemnypguasuca*.
Tum dare pro <u>suca</u> o, tum tollere saepe videbis	You'll see that the Indians replace *suca* with *O*, or
Indos; tumque alias o sumunt, a que relinquunt:	often delete *A*, else take the *O* and leave the *A*:
<u>Zemnypqua</u>, <u>Zemnypquo</u>, <u>zemnypquao</u> que dicunt.	saying *zemnypqua*, *zemnypquo*, and *zemnypquao*.

Gramática Chibcha, Bogotá

first lines of *De las formaciones de los tiempos en verso*[12]

By these means, Spanish clerics were able to gain enough of the native languages to converse, and also to preach in them directly. Fray Andrés de Olmos, the author of no less than four of the first grammars (Nahuatl, Totanac, Tepehuá, and Huastec), was said to have preached in ten languages. Pedro de Quiroga in Peru defended stoutly the practice of preaching in

Quechua, citing St. Paul in his defense against the archbishop of Lima, although in practice many in Peru preached with the help of bilingual interpreters.[13]*

But besides their direct assaults on knowledge of the languages, missionaries also set up schools for the indigenous people; and by teaching them the liberal arts, based as was conventional on Latin grammar, they also contributed to the formation of bilinguals from this new, natural source. Nahuatl-medium schools for the sons of Aztec lords had been established from 1523 (just four years after Cortés had first set foot in Mexico, and two after the fall of the Aztec empire); but before setting up any schools for Spaniards, the Franciscans founded in 1536—with the viceroy to open it—the Colegio de Santa Cruz de Tlatelolco, where a strictly classical education was offered to the same clientele: Latin grammar, followed by rhetoric, poetics, logic, philosophy, and even medicine, all taught through the medium of Latin.† This college, however, became the focus of a political struggle between the Franciscans and their detractors, so that it went into a decline after 1550 and was disestablished in 1576.

But in 1574 had come the founding in Mexico City of the prestige Colegio Máximo de San Pedro y San Pablo, which remained as a stable focus for classical studies in the country.[14] A continent away in Peru, on the very day after its conquest in 1533, the Colegio de San Francisco de Borja had been set up in the old Inca capital Cuzco, again for the children of the nobility. Soon, their teacher, Dr. Juan de Cuéllar, canon of the cathedral, would be exclaiming to his pupils, "Oh, my sons, how I should love to see a dozen of you at the University of Salamanca!"[15]

In fact, as Salvador de Madariaga has observed, all Spanish education of the period tended to emphasize classical themes and Christianity over purely Spanish content, so the American elites were receiving something similar to a general European education. Latin at least had the advantage—over both

---

*Not that these clerical pioneers were linguistically infallible, working as they did in a language not their own. Guaman Poma, a native speaker of Quechua, in his *Nueva Corónica y Buen Gobierno* (pp. 610–12) heartily ridicules the typical mistakes made in these sermons.

† Fray Arnaldo de Basaccio had already been teaching Latin to Aztecs before its foundation. The first headmaster was Fray Bernardino de Sahagún, who was later to win fame as the compiler (in Nahuatl) of a vast encyclopedia of Mexican civilization, *Historia general de las cosas de Nueva España*, especially important since much of the culture was about to be eradicated in a zero-tolerance application of the policy of "extirpation of idols."

Castilian and any translations made into local languages—that the texts in it were solidly canonical, and so free of any suspicion of heresy, something that was always an active concern within the Spanish Church, with the Inquisition on its doorstep. But the Franciscan missionaries also had an ulterior motive in wanting to spread competence in Latin among the Mexicans: how else could they secure their ultimate goal of founding an indigenous priesthood?[16] As against use of the vernaculars, the archbishop of Lima ordered in 1545 that the faith should be preached in Latin or Spanish rather than Quechua, because he could not vouch for the correctness of indigenous texts. He may have had a point. The point of Spanish plays tended to come out quite differently—and much more seditiously—when adapted into Nahuatl for a Mexican audience; and the satirical tone of ancient Nahuatl *huehuentzin* plays meant that even morality plays, the stock offerings of Spanish popular theater, came across with an ironical tone. This different level of intent of formal speech in the two languages may even have played a role in the early misunderstandings between Cortés and Montezuma, which proved fatal to the Aztec defense.[17]

Despite the early demise of the school in Tlatelolco, many of its pupils became distinguished Latinists. Probably the most distinguished was Antonio Valeriano, noted poet in Nahuatl, but also governor of Mexico City for thirty years, who for his Latin correspondence "seemed a new Cicero or Quintilian." Spanish readiness to approach Latin through the vernacular, which we have already noted in Spain (p. 256), was seen in Mexico too. According to Don Santiago Ramírez de Fuenreal in 1533, a friar was teaching with excellent results Latin through the medium of Nahuatl, a process he described as *gramática romanzada en lengua mexicana* 'grammar vernacularized in Mexican'.* In Cuzco, the bishop, Don Sebastián de Lartanín, had written a Latin primer to teach his parishioners the Creed. Latin was taught widely in the Spanish empire, wherever indeed there were settled places of worship, and not only for its role in Church services: in Cali, New Granada, Bishop del Valle's Latin school was putting on comedies in the language.[18]

When the pupils did well, they were, naturally, compared with Cicero:

---

*This contradiction in terms can be seen as a sort of terminological converse of the common phrase *indio muy ladino*, which meant an Indian well-versed in Spanish. *Ladino* indeed is none other than the Castilian development of the word *Latinus*. It was a term often used of non-Spaniards who knew Spanish, first applied to Moors in Spain, then to natives of America, but later also to African slaves.

this was the heyday of ardent Ciceronianism in the Roman Catholic Church, after all. *Hablan tan elegante el latín como Túlio* 'They speak a Latin as elegant as Tully', remarked the viceroy's counselor Jerónimo López of the Tlatelolco pupils, though himself an unyielding anti-Franciscan. But it seems that teaching the Aztecs Latin was at first an uphill struggle. Fray Toribio de Benavente (better known by his Nahuatl cognomen *Motolinia* 'humble'), one of the heroic twelve Franciscans who started the Mexican mission in 1524, stated that progress in the first two or three years had been rather discouraging, but that afterward many of his Aztec pupils became "good grammarians, composing long, well-authorized [i.e. Ciceronian] orations (in prose), and hexameter and pentameter verses"; in fact, he opined, such students kept the school in good order and almost taught themselves. He also handed down this anecdote of punctured pomposity in the sixteenth-century schoolroom:

> A very fine thing happened to a priest recently arrived from Castile, who could not believe that the Indians knew Christian doctrine, nor the Lord's Prayer, nor the Creed; and when other Spaniards told him they did, he remained skeptical; just then two students had come out of class, and the priest thinking they were from the rest of the Indians, asked one of them if he knew the Lord's Prayer and he said he did, and he made him say it, and then he made him say the Creed, and the student said it perfectly well; and the priest challenged one word that the Indian had got right, and since the Indian asserted that he was right, and the priest denied it, the student had to ask what was the correct way, and asked him in Latin, *Reverende Pater, cujus casus est?* ("Reverend Father, what case is it in?") Then since the priest did not know grammar, he was left quite at a loss, covered with confusion.[19]

⊘

In their declared celibacy, the missionaries were very much unlike the secular Spanish immigrants and adventurers to America: the general enthusiasm for union with local women and production of mestizo children almost suggests an intention to create their own bilingual community (which they certainly did). Nearly every famous conquistador is known to have had such children, and their less celebrated troopers undoubtedly did as well. The first generations of mestizos, together with pure-blooded Indians who had grown up just after the conquests, created a particularly fertile period in the literature of the Americas.

This phenomenon seems to have something to do with the level of political and urban development of the conquered society.* The degree of political concentration of a group with a widespread language, what one might call its previous degree of imperial grandeur, is clearly correlated with the development of a literature after Spanish contact. Hence, taking advantage of the transmission of a romanized writing system, Nahuatl and Quechua created substantial literatures in the period after the Conquest, often authored by immediate descendants of the old imperial elites. Mayan, largely outside the Aztec domains but with its own imperial past, and an indigenous hieroglyphic literacy not yet forgotten, did so too, though more as an underground resistance to the Spaniards than as a vindication of the new culture. Aymara, Chibcha, and Guarani, on the other hand, did not develop any indigenous writing, even though they too had each been given written standards by missionary linguists:[20] as far as can be seen, any literature in these languages was written by Spaniards in the cause of Christian indoctrination.

This literary production was not purely in the indigenous languages. One headmaster of the Colegio de Tlatelolco, Pablo Nazáreo, himself an Aztec of noble blood ("chief of Xaltocan"), distinguished himself in 1566 with an eloquent Latin letter to the king of Spain, attempting to assert his family's rights. He was described by Alonso de Zorita, who heard this speech, as "a very good Latin scholar, rhetorician, logician, and philosopher, and no mean poet in every kind of verse, who when he graduated taught the Indians grammar and Christian doctrine."[21] Juan Badiano, a native of Xochimilco and also a professor at the Colegio, translated into Latin the text written in 1552 of a Mexican doctor known as Martín de la Cruz, calling it *Libellus de medicinalibus indorum herbis* 'Booklet on the medicinal herbs of the Indians'. (The work is still extant and was translated into Spanish in 1964.)[22] This was in the context of a regular Renaissance-era college, where all intellectual activities— reading, note-taking, examinations, dramatic performances, and above all public speaking—went on in Latin. *Echar el quamquam* 'pitching the *quamquam*' was the phrase used for working something up in Latin, possibly because *quamquam* 'although' was such a usual word to find at the head of a flowery Latin period, especially in Ciceronian style.[23]

In the reverse direction, Nazáreo also translated the Gospels and New Testament epistles from Latin into Nahuatl. This was an interesting choice in

---

*One can compare the literary flowering in Iceland after the Christian conversion, unparalleled by anything in the rest of the Norse world at the time. See pages 155–56.

a Catholic country of the period, where Christian literature for general consumption was a few short prayers, the Creed, the catechism, and a form of confession.* It is more evidence that the Franciscans were serious in their intent to bring up an indigenous clergy, for clerics would be the main readers of the Bible. But in the sixteenth century too, someone unknown translated the perennial children's text Aesop's fables into Nahuatl, as *In sasanilli in Esopo*. These secular stories allowed for much greater freedom in the style adopted: its Mediterranean beasts were replaced with Mexican animals, notably jaguars, coyotes, turkeys, parrots, and quetzals in place of lions, foxes, cocks, jackdaws, and peacocks, and the whole production was made more status-conscious, more conversational, and generally more florid than the laconic originals. Sometimes the whole point of the fable gets changed, as Nahuatl empathy with the protagonists takes over from a terse Greco-Latin moral.[24]

Latin (in translation):

Nahuatl (in translation):

A lion once heard a frog croaking;
    he turned toward the noise
    thinking it was some great
    beast; when he saw the frog,
    he went up and squashed it.
It is imprudent to be frightened by
    what cannot be seen.

To quieten his heart the jaguar
    looked about him in all directions.
    He prepared himself to encounter
    the one who croaked in such
    manner.
But when the frog saw him at the
    waterside, he quickly fled.
Arriving at the water's edge, the jaguar
    was cross and ashamed for he
    thought of the one by whom he had
    been so frightened. He squashed him
    and killed him.

But the effects of a Latin education could also show up in the style adopted for the new indigenous literature. In Mexico, there were three major indigenous historians: Fernando Alvarado Tezozómoc, grandson of Montezuma and author of the *Crónica Mexicana*; Domingo de San Antón Muñón Chimalpahin Quauhtlehuanitzin, author of some *Relaciones*; but it was Fernando de Alva Ixtilxóchitl, from the line of the kings of Texcoco, who had

---

*The surviving literature in Chibcha, for example, consists of such material and nothing else, except for two panegyrical sonnets to the grammarian Bernardo de Lugo, introducing his own grammar.

helped Cortés to unseat the Aztecs, who became known as the *Tito Livio de Anáhuac*, Anáhuac being the Nahuatl name for the land of Mexico, then known as New Spain. He wrote in Spanish the *Historia de los señores tultecas* and the *Historia de la nación chichimeca*, which together covered the full history from the origin of the quasi-mythical Toltecs up to the appointment of Cuauhtémoc to succeed Montezuma in the final war with the Spanish, and were like Livy both in trying for a universal narrative of his people, and in that they tried to give a credible account derived from legends that were no longer believable—in Fernando's case because of the new, unquestionable truth of Christianity.*

In Peru too, early Inca or mestizo literature is socially significant, with such princely luminaries as the Inca Titu Cusi Yupanqui (baptized plain Diego de Castro) and Juan de Santa Cruz Pachacuti Yamqui Salcamayhua having taken up their pens. But it was also bound up with political controversy, namely the conflict between some culturally involved and sympathetic Jesuit missionaries, in the group known as Nombre de Jesus de Cuzco, and an alliance of hard-liners that included a rather strong combination of Viceroy Francisco de Toledo, the Inquisition itself, and the hard-line wing of the Jesuits. One famous literary mestizo, Father Blas Valera (ca 1550–1619), stood at the center of this.

Blas Valera has long been reputed as the author of a history of Peru (together with a Quechua grammar) in Latin, the *Historia et Rudimenta Linguae Piruanorum*, but it now appears that this work was by two Italian Jesuits, Antonio Cumis and Anello Oliva, though both were sympathizers and allies of Blas Valera. He is also represented as the author of an apologia document in Latin, *Exul Immeritus Blas Valera Populo Suo* 'Undeservedly an exile, B.V. to his own people', written in his last year, which presents a scarcely credible tale of a "juridical death"—effectively a gag order enforcible with a suspended death sentence—imposed on him in Rome in 1597 for his teaching approach judged heretical, and his secret return to Peru via Cádiz. Even more sensationally, it claimed that he afterward inspired and largely wrote, under cover of others' names, two of the principal works of early colonial Peruvian literature, the *Royal Commentaries of the Incas* (hitherto attributed to Garcilaso de la Vega) and the *Nueva Corónica y Buen Gobierno* 'New Chronicle and Good Government' (credited to the pure-blooded Indian Felipe Guaman Poma).

---

*His son Bartolomé attended rather to the modern side of the Spanish inheritance, adapting into Nahuatl two contemporary Spanish plays by Lope de Vega, and another, *El gran teatro del mundo*, by Calderón.

Novelistic as this all seems, four independent scientific tests on aspects of these documents (the apologia and the history-cum-grammar) have vindicated their age: if they are forgeries, they go back to the seventeenth century. There is a further motive for secrecy, in that the documents allege that Pizarro used poisoned wine on Inca Atahuallpa's commanding officer, the *estado mayor*, before the decisive battle of Cajamarca. In addition, Muzio Vitelleschi, then head of the Society of Jesus, who had been involved in the Blas Valera case, burned a number of documents in 1617, without witnesses, "for the good of the Company." Finally, but perhaps most interestingly from the viewpoint of Latin influence, a detailed study in terms of *inventio, dispositio*, and *elocutio* of the rhetorical figures in the *Nueva Corónica y Buen Gobierno*—a book written in a mixture of Quechua and Spanish supposedly by a relatively uneducated Indian—concluded that the author must have studied rhetoric, a subject only taught at the time in Peru in Dominican or Jesuit colleges.[25] The intrigues make it hard to know who wrote these documents or how they were written, but Latin culture was fundamental in setting the terms of the controversies: Blas Valera believed that, on grammatical grounds as well as its past unifying role in the Inca empire, Quechua for the Indians was as important and perfect a language as Latin in Europe.[26]

Regardless of his involvement in the Blas Valera affair, Inca Garcilaso de la Vega (1539–1616) is another highly articulate advertisement for the value of Spanish colonial education. He was born in Cuzco, the Inca capital—or as he himself put it, "another Rome in that empire."[27] He was nothing if not classically conscious, the son of a Spanish nobleman (Captain Sebastián Garcilaso de la Vega y Vargas) and an Inca princess (Palla Chimpu Ocllo, second cousin of both the last ruling Incas, Huayna Capac and Atahuallpa), born just six years after the fall of the Incas. He emigrated to Spain in his early twenties, an accomplished linguist who knew Quechua, Spanish, Latin, and Italian. His first historical work was highly original, not least in its choice of title: *The Florida of the Inca* told the story of de Soto's campaign through Florida, "the Inca" being a tacit reference to the author, not the conquistador. He also published a two-part history of his own country called *Royal Commentaries of the Incas* and *General History of Peru*, though the authorship appears to have at least been shared with Blas Valera, who is explicitly quoted at length at many points.

Garcilaso and Blas Valera held that Spanish power in Peru, with the civil wars and social disruption that it caused, had disrupted the important linguistic unity imposed by the Incas, which should have been used to spread the

Christian faith. And the spread of this faith, on the view then held universally, provided the true justification for the tragic fall of the Inca empire. They certainly believed that a shared language makes for common understanding and good mutual relations "because the likeness and conformity of words almost always tend to reconcile people and bring them to true union and friendship."[28] But after the upheavals, neither Spanish nor Latin were in a position to do what Quechua could so easily have done.

From its height in the generations after the conquest, the use of Latin in the New World traced much the same path of decline as it would in the Old, if with some delay. Spain itself tended to be conservative within Europe, and new fashions and ideas spread comparatively slowly across the Atlantic in those days of sail. There was an early profusion of universities, starting with the inauguration of Mexico's Real Universidad in 1553 (a real achievement—Brazil had none until the nineteenth century); but the Spanish colonies, like Spain itself, did not distinguish themselves as centers of innovation in the seventeenth and eighteenth centuries. Possibly because Spain was a great cultural power in its own right, diffusing its own intellectual priorities through the empire, Latin never played the role it did in Scandinavia and eastern Europe, as a neutral channel by which minor players could contribute to overall European learning and debate. The colonies absorbed the rationalist and secularizing tendencies of the Enlightenment when they came; but the main event in the Spanish colonies was Carlos III's aggressively secular *Real Cédula* of 1767, expelling the Jesuits from the Spanish colonies. Since the Church had, predictably, been the great stronghold of Latin in the Americas, and the Jesuits the great upholders of intellectual interests with the Church, this was a death blow to widespread use of Latin in "Latin" America. It was, in any case, disappearing from Europe; and there was nothing to hold it in the alien territory of the New World but an association with the Church, an institution that was itself fading in importance at the time.

The literary career of Latin in Mexico had, however, rather a bright finish. Three Jesuit theologians who fell foul of the *Cédula* of 1767 were Diego José Abad (1727–79), Francisco Javier Alegre (1729–88), and Rafael Landívar (1731–93). In exile, they all composed long poems in Latin.[29] Abad stuck closest to his profession, writing the *De Deo Deoque Homine Carmina Heroica* 'Heroics on God and the God-Man'. It is in two parts, a theological treatise, followed by a retelling of the New Testament, but the content is extremely wide-ranging, going into aspects of art, science history, and literature. Alegre was more inspired by the Latin tradition, writing first a translation of the *Iliad*

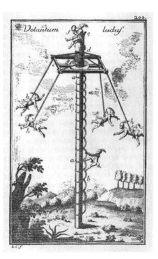

The Volantes *display. This illustration to Rafael Landívar's* Rusticatio Mexicana *shows that an early modern Latin verse narrative could also contain annotated diagrams.*

and then his own account of Alexander's siege of Tyre, called *Alexandrias*. Despite Alegre's membership in the Society of Jesus, this last is a classic piece of epic mythologizing, not above allowing the gods to intervene in the final naval battle.

Most impressive as an original piece of literature, though, is probably Landívar's *Rusticatio Mexicana, seu rariora quaedam de agris Mexicanis decerpta* 'Mexican Pastoral, or some novelties plucked from the Mexican countryside', on the strength of which he has been called the national poet of Guatemala. (He was born there, and the poem includes scenes from Guatemala as well as Mexico.) The poem, with fifteen books and an appendix, has considerable range, since his theme allowed him to describe virtually anything that had happened in these countries, as well as the lakes, volcanoes, and wildlife. In the final book, on games, he achieved some pathos in his description of ancient gladiatorial combats, but part of his illustrated account of an amazing performance may be seen to this day at the Museo Etnográfico in Mexico, the celebrated *volantes*.

Ardua truncatur sudanti cortice pinus,	A tall pine with sweating bark is cut,
Quae impexa feriat lucentia	Which might strike stars with its
sydera fronte.	uncombed top.
Umbrosis deinceps tonsis de more capillis	Then, its shady locks shorn in the
	fashion,

Arbor (a) Olympiaco medio
    Cybeleia circo
Erigitur, circumque obsepta
    ex fune (b) catena
Exhibet illa gradus fastigia summa
    petenti.
Inde coronatur porrecto ex Ilice
    (c) Quadro
Innumeros apto sinuare
    per aethera gyros;

. . .

Tum quatuor lecti vernanti e flore
    juventae
Omnes larvati, fulgentes vestibus
    omnes
Conscendunt Quadrum planta veloce
    supernum
Considuntque aliis alii e regione remoti,
Nectantur donec sinuatis ilia loris.

Restibus ut vero novit se quisque
    revinctum,
Praecipites saltu terram volvuntur
    in imam
Ilia suspensi (h) juvenes: mox
    machina gyro
Flectitur, & bifido evolvens revoluta
    cylindro
Lora, urget subito producto fune
    volantes
Ducere lunatos circum per inania
    flexus,
Nectereque immensis immensos
    orbibus orbes.[30]

The Cybeleian tree (a) in the Olympic
    circle
Is raised, and looped round it a chain
    of rope (b)
Displays steps to one who would reach
    its heights.
Then it is crowned with a square
    produced of oak
Fit to wend countless turns through
    the air;

. . .

Then four chosen ones, all enchanted
    with the
Fresh flower of youth, dazzling in
    raiment,
Scale the upper square with swift foot

And sit down on opposite sides,
While they tie their midriffs with
    sinuous thongs.

But when each knows that he is bound
    with cords,
Headlong they roll with a jump to the
    earth below
Hanging by their waists (h): soon the
    mechanism
Is pulled into a circle, and turning in
    double tube
The thongs, makes those flying on a
    lengthening
Rope, lead crescent loops round
    through space
And interweave immense circles.

Besides its strength as a tour de force, this is interesting as a survival of the old style of didactic verse, when literally anything could be put into hexameters, even a numbered diagram. Ausonius, one feels, would have been pleased with this.

Abad also wrote a *Dissertatio ludicro-seria* (1778), a thirty-page satirical response to the pompous opinion of an Italian Jesuit, Giovanni Batista Roberti, that only Italians could write good Latin. Its subtitle is *Num possit aliquis extra Italiam natus bene Latine scribere, contra quam Robertus pronuntiat?* 'Could anyone born outside Italy write Latin well, as against the thesis of Roberti?' Abad, the Mexican Latinist, may have carried his point, but by the late eighteenth century, he had to go to Italy to get it published.

◇◦◎◦◇

CHAPTER 18

Decus et tutamen—Last Redoubts

Why is the teaching of Latin composition necessary? Without it God cannot
be known. Without it we are mired in damnation. Through Latin
composition we weaken—no, overthrow—the empire of the devil.
It is necessary for the salvation of our souls.

Olaus Theophilus, headmaster, Copenhagen (1573)[1]

*Utinam essem bonus grammaticus. Non aliunde discordiae in religione
pendent quam ab ignoratione grammaticae.*

Oh, to be a good grammarian! Disagreements in religion have
no other source than ignorance of grammar.

Joseph Justus Scaliger, classical scholar, Paris (1540–1609)[2]

T HE GENERAL AURA OF dazzling light, surprising form, and entrancing
color that surrounds our memory of the Renaissance, the life-enhancing
work of Petrarch, Raphael, Brunelleschi, Tintoretto, Dürer, and their peers,
tends to distract us from the lopsided intellectual foundations of the humanist
movement. Who would not listen to the call to sweep away the medieval cob-
webs and pay attention to direct experience of the here and now—even if
curiously allied with enthusiasm for texts over a thousand years old? The Renaissance, and Europe's fifteenth and sixteenth centuries, seem to embody
youth, as the preceding age seems old and set in its ways.

Humanism was an appeal to the heart; and so besides its affirmation of
vivid perceptions and clear thinking, it also rejected the value of large-scale systems and superstructures of theoretical learning. It was the kingdom of the

artista; in medieval terms you could say that the trivium had eclipsed the quadrivium. Even more than in the twelfth century, language studies ruled education. But in its approach to language, humanist effort was devoted first to elucidation, appreciation, and imitation of classical texts, and second to the definition of modern languages. The philosophy of language was nowhere.

In this environment, interest totally ceased in the work of the *modistae*, men such as Thomas of Erfurt and Martinus Dacus, who had tried to look at language structure in its own terms, to make sense of the familiar categories of grammar as clues to something higher, the structure of reality itself. But such systematic, conceptual studies are essential to the development of a science, even if the humanists disdained them. In this sense, humanism was an antiscientific movement. According to its priorities, if they had been observed universally, there would have been no place for the work of Copernicus, Kepler, Galileo, or Newton. As one philosopher put it even in 1492, humanists "took too much delight in verbal cleverness and embellishment; content to know what the words mean, they forget to enquire diligently into the natures and properties which the words express. The result is that they condemn works which lack polish, even though they contain the truth."[3]

As it happened, the sciences benefited from this period when conceptual frameworks were allowed to loosen. New kinds of observation could be admitted, and experiments could be made, not just with the world, but also in rejigging the theories to make sense of them. Despite having lost the centrality to intellectual life that they had achieved in the early medieval universities, philosophy and natural science were still actively pursued through the fifteenth century. And since their critical audience extended across Europe, there was no temptation in their pursuit to drop Latin and slip into the vernacular. Neither did philosophers and scientists accept that their terminology should be limited to the resources of classical Latin, still less to its Ciceronian subset. In the face of snide, humanist mockery, the technical tradition continued.

In fact, for all the humanist hubbub, Europe's scientists were redefining themselves as a community in their own right. Even as use of the different vernaculars spread into new fields, a new kind of linguistic unity—now called *Respublica Litteraria* 'the Republic of Letters'—emerged amid a patchwork of political competition. Although the title itself goes back to 1417—when Francisco Barbaro thanked Poggio Bracciolini in a letter for his signal services to this notional entity in tracking down manuscripts in German libraries—it only becomes generally current in the sixteenth to eighteenth centuries, especially after 1525. It is vague, of course, but it tends to mean not the literary world, but the community of scientists and scholars. Other synonyms included *orbis latinus* (1504, used by the German Conrad von Lowenberg) and "latine Republike" (by the English medic Thomas Browne 1605–82), which referred to this community's common language. Christian Loeber in 1708 submitted to the University of Jena his *Dissertatio politica de forma regiminis Reipublicae litterariae* 'Political dissertation on the constitution of the Republic of Letters'. He concluded that it had no government of any kind, since it was a totally free society. One aspect of this freedom was freedom of religion. Since the Reformation, the principle *cuius regio eius religio* (official religion is determined by the local power) had divided Europe; after Luther, the *Respublica Litteraria* was the only community as comfortingly united as the old *Respublica Christiana*.[4]

For this community, Latin held many evident, and eminent, advantages over the vernacular languages. It was a single language, spoken and written now over most of Christian Europe. Francis Bacon, publishing his *Advancement of Learning* in English in 1605, wanted to have it translated into Latin "to ring a bell to call other wits together . . . and have that bell heard as far as can be." The sixteenth and seventeenth centuries had taken Latin across the Atlantic, and the range of Latin was still growing in the eighteenth century. After the reforms of Peter the Great, the elite of Russia too was educated in Latin: by 1750, twenty-six colleges in the Russian empire were offering a Latin curriculum.[5] The far-flung elite who knew Latin shared not only a language,

Francis Bacon, English statesman and philosopher, was concerned for his works to be translated into Latin, to ensure his reputation in the future.

but knowledge of the classical civilization that had produced it, regardless of their own countries' histories and special conditions. Moreover, Latin—at least when freed from humanist strictures—had built up during two thousand years of continuous development a vocabulary greater than any other European language: it offered technical exactitude when it was needed, for concrete nitty-gritty but also for high abstractions.

Furthermore, from a pragmatic point of view, buttressed as it was by the inveterate conservatism of schools and given its other manifest advantages— as they appeared to those receiving a classical education!—Latin could be expected to be around for a long time, probably forever. In 1623, when his *Advancement of Learning* actually came out in Latin, Francis Bacon commented with relief: "These modern languages will at one time or another play the bank-rowtes [bankrupts] with books; and since I have lost much time with this age, I would be glad as God shall give me leave to recover it with posterity."

◈

Right up to the present, Latin has been seen as a useful basis for timeless (and spaceless) vocabulary. Latin and Greek have remained apparently inexhaustible sources for replenishing scientific vocabulary since the translations of the eleventh century until the research-led intellectual revolutions of the twentieth. Only in the last generation, when physicists at least have begun to draw on native English roots (for such new ideas as *quarks*, *charm*, and *strangeness*), has the enormity of deriving all one's technical vocabulary from a foreign source begun to stand out in relief.

Besides this store of lexical roots, in one scientific discipline at least Latin itself has been enlisted as a language of description. This is the science of botany, and here the terminology was largely established by the efforts of one man from Sweden, Carl Linnaeus (1707–78), though within the framework of a continuous tradition that went back ultimately to the Greeks Aristotle and Theophrastus, preserved in Latin translation by Pliny's *Naturalis Historia* and (as usual) by Isidore's *Etymologiae*. In *Fundamenta botanica* (1736)—all of course written in Latin—Linnaeus outlined his procedure in 365 aphorisms, then selected technical terms from his predecessors, laying out as he did so the basic theory of plant structure. This was then expanded in 1751 into his *Philosophia Botanica*. His contribution was above all in nomenclature. As an example of the procedure, the botanist Stearn, who has written the standard modern text on botanical Latin, looks at floral parts that can be seen with the naked eye. He concludes:

> A few of these terms are Latin words of which the meaning has been re-stricted to one of its classical uses, e.g., *calyx*; some are words of which the present use diverges little from the classical use, e.g., *filamentum*; most of them, e.g., *corolla, petalum, corona, anthera, pollen, pistillum, stylus, stigma*, are classical words given new specialized meanings; the remainder are either new words coined from classical words in a classical manner, e.g., *perian-thium, perigonium, androecium, gynoecium, connectivum, carpellum*, or new words whose connection with classical words is so slender that they are best regarded as quite new inventions rather than adaptations, e.g., *sepalum* and *tepalum*.[6]

Linnaeus was also concerned to constrain the form of the minimal bo-tanical plant description, or *diagnosis*. He held that these descriptions should not exceed twelve words, usually being a "binomial" expression, i.e., made up of two terms defining the genus and the species, followed by a diagnostic phrase in the ablative case, so indicating the distinctive properties of the spe-cies: e.g., *Bauhinia variegata foliis ovatis lobis divaricatis* 'B. v. with ovate leaves and spreading lobes'. Official botanical descriptions remain to this day in Latin of this type, supplemented with a statement of geographical distribu-

Carl Linnaeus. The Swedish biologist used Latin terms and descriptions as the basis for his systems to build taxonomies of all creation.

tion, a phrase in the nominative case describing the species, often followed by an observation in Latin stating more explicitly how the species differs from its allies.

These elaborate developments of botanical descriptions, which may use the full grammatical resources of Latin as well as Linnaeus's restricted terminology, are part of Linnaeus's much greater achievement, which was to establish the system of binomial nomenclature, by which all biological species can uniquely be determined in a combination of two Latin names, representing a genus and species. For this, it was necessary to map out the whole of nature in a hierarchical taxonomy, with kingdoms, classes, order, genera, and species. Again, in Linnaeus's *Systema Naturae* (1735), the use of Latin was proposed, but this time purely its vocabulary. (Although the text is in Latin, it is not proposed to formulate all supporting descriptions in the language.) The details of the assignments of species at all levels have been massively revised since, but the principle of the naming system has survived, giving Latin terminology an apparently unassailable position within biological science.

⬦

Besides its role in the description of creation, in politics too Latin was highly influential for the early modern world. With its aura of antiquity—an aura that grew as the language appeared less and less in day-to-day business—the use of Latin gave majesty and authority to any field. This was most useful precisely where the content to be expressed was least traditional and most radical. Political theorists keen to voice unconventional, even dangerous ideas would cloak them in the "decent obscurity of a classical language" to keep them restricted to a learned readership—one less likely to riot, but one that would extend far beyond their own country and its regime. New revolutionary governments found or invented slogans or mottoes in Latin to make a resonant statement of their legitimacy, drawing on shared lines of education to suggest that the new forms of power were a better means to fulfill age-old aspirations.

The Anglo-Saxon colonies in America, although starting a century later than the Hispanic ones, had been no less in thrall to classical studies. The discovery of the New World was a stimulus to new thinking in England, as almost everywhere; Thomas More's *Utopia*, a fantasy of exotic but rational government published in Latin in 1516, and much admired by his friend Erasmus, is arguably inspired by Peter Martyr's first reports of political thinking in the Americas. To give it the necessary anchor in the real world, More recounts that his adventurer, Raphael Hythlodaeus (Greek for 'knowledgeable in non-sense') was a Portuguese companion of Amerigo Vespucci's; so that, as in Spain, America was part of the Latin world in England even before Latin had come to America itself.

Where the Spanish-speaking world revered Nebrija as the gateway to Latin studies, the English used William Lily's *Short Introduction of Grammar.* Lily (ca 1468—1522) had been a friend and associate of Erasmus's and John Colet's, and the first headmaster of St. Paul's School, which Colet had re-founded. Lily's Latin grammar of 1511, which was said to have been the work of all three on the basis of a much longer Latin grammar by Thomas Linacre,[7] had been made the single required text for Latin studies in English schools by decree of King Henry VIII; later it was duly carried to the Americas as the foundation for Latin studies there. It began with *Carmen de Moribus* 'a poem on good behavior', which for centuries was the first Latin poem that young Englishmen would encounter and gave them good advice on their daily routine. The first few lines run:

Qui mihi discipulus puer es, cupis atque doceri,	You who are my disciple and wish to be taught,
Huc ades, haec animo concipe dicta tuo.	Come here, take these sayings to heart.
Mane situs lectum fuge, mollem discute somnum.	Leave your bed early, cast off soft sleep.
Templa petas supplex, & venerare Deum.	Seek the temples in prayer and worship God.
Attamen in primis facies sit lota manusque	But first let your face and hands be washed
Sint nitidae vestes, comptaque caesaries.	Your clothes shining clean, your hair neat.
Desidiam fugiens, cum te schola nostra vocarit,	Leaving sloth behind, when our school calls you
Adsis: nulla pigrae sit tibi causa morae.[8]	Be present: have no cause for lazy delay.

After two hundred years of yeoman service, Lily was replaced in America by Ezekiel Cheever's abridged version, known as Cheever's *Accidence,* first printed in 1709 and last printed (in a twenty-third edition) in 1838. Cheever (1615–1708) had been a master of the Boston Latin Grammar School, and its name is certainly eloquent of its original priorities in preparing boys to enter

Harvard College. Harvard, founded in 1636, had set the following admission standards in 1642:

> When any schollar is able to read Tully [Cicero] or such like classicall Latine Authore *ex tempore*, & make and speake true Latin in verse and prose, *suo (ut aiunt) Marte*, and decline perfectly the paradigmes of Nounes and Verbes in the Greeke tongue, then may hee bee admitted into the Colledge, nor shall any claim admission before such qualifications.

Once admitted, students were forbidden use of English within the college precincts.[9]

The College of William and Mary in Virginia (founded 1693) and Yale (1701) likewise demanded intermediate Latin and elementary Greek for entrance, and the requirements were maintained in the new seats of learning set up during the eighteenth century, notably Princeton (1746) and Columbia (1754). In a letter of January 27, 1800, contemplating the establishment of the University of Virginia, Thomas Jefferson gave his opinions of classical studies in a letter to the English scientist and educator Dr. Joseph Priestley, endorsing them in the halfhearted manner typical of an Anglo-Saxon radical, convinced that only studies that are practically useful deserve to prevail:

> In my last letter of the 18th, I omitted to say anything of the languages as part of our proposed University. It was not that I think, as some do, that they are useless. I am of a very different opinion. I do not think them very essential to the obtaining eminent degrees of science; but I think them very useful towards it. I suppose there is a portion of life during which our faculties are ripe enough for this, and for nothing more useful. I think the Greeks and Romans have left us the present models which exist of fine composition, whether we examine them as works of reason, or of style and fancy; and to them we probably owe these characteristics of modern composition. . . .

Classics was the staple of general learning in the eighteenth century, in the American colonies as everywhere else under the dominion of Europeans. John Adams, later the second U.S. president, mentioned in his *Diary* (August 19, 1770) how, during an inspection tour of a lighthouse at Beacon Island, the inspectors passed the time by trying to recall any Latin verse couplets that they had learned at school: this one happened to be known in full only to Adams:[10]

Gutta cavat lapidem non vi, sed sepe cadendo.	The drop hollows the stone, not by force but by often falling.
Sic homo fit doctus, non vi, sed sepe legendo.	So a person becomes learned, not by will but by often reading.

In a recent collection of some 350 American poems written in Latin in the two centuries to 1825, the editor notes that most of them were elegiac, dealing with death and misfortune, while the second biggest group commemorated or narrated events.[11] These can be dramatic and vivid in expressing the way the New World struck its visitors from the Old. Here are sections of two early poems, describing relations with the Indians. William Morrell returned to England in 1625, after the attempt to found a settlement at Weymouth in Massachusetts had failed, and there wrote a poem entitled *Nova Anglia* 'New England':

Sunt etenim populi minimi sermonis et oris austeri, risusque parum saevique superbi, constricto nodis hirsuto crine sinistro, imparibus formis tondentes ordine villos mollia magnanimae peragentes otia gentes, arte sagittifera pollentes, cursibus, armis astutae, recto robusto corpore et alto pellibus indutae cervinis frigora contra aspera . . .	For there are people of little speech and austere face, little laughter, savage and proud, with their hair on the left bound in knots, shaving their bristles orderly in uneven shapes, great-hearted peoples who lead leisurely lives, strong in the art of arrows, and running, and clever with arms, of strong, upright, tall body, clothed in deerskins against the harsh cold . . .
Litera cuncta licet latet hos, modulamina quaedam fistula disparibus calamis facit; est et agrestis musica vocis iis, minime iucunda, sonoris obtususque sonis, oblectans pectora, sensus, atque suas aures artis sublimis inanes . . .	Though writing is unknown to them, some tunes they make on panpipes of uneven reeds; there is a rustic music in their voices, not very sweet, bruised with sonorous sounds, delighting their hearts, senses, and empty ears, of sublime art . . .[12]

And Philip Vincent, wrote an eyewitness account of the Pequot War of 1637, a tense and sustained encounter that had led to the extinction of the Pequot tribe. His account was headed by a savage celebration in Latin, which concluded:

Tunc laesi justa arma movent	Then injured, they justly take arms, and
hostemque sequuntur, struxerat	pursue the enemy, having built
haud vanis qui munimenta locis.	forts in suitable places.
Invadunt vallum palis sudibusque	They occupy a wall fortified with beams
munitum—	and stakes—
pax erit: hoc uno solvitur ira modo.	there will be peace: only thus will
	anger pass.
Undique concidunt omnes, pars una	From every side they cut them all down,
crematur:	but some of them are burned:
post, caesi aut capti, caetera turba luit.	afterward, killed or taken, the rest of
	the tribe pays dear.
Utraque laetatur Pequetanis Anglia victis,	Both Englands rejoice at the Pequot defeat,
et novus 'aeternum hic figimur'	and the new settler says, "Here we
hospes ait.	stay forever."
Virginia exultat, vicina Novanglia	Virginia exults, nearby New England is
gaudet, signaque securae certa	glad, and have sure signs of a secure
quietis habent.	peace.
Plaudite qui colitis Mavortia sacra nepotes,	Clap, you descendants who practice
et serat incultos tutus arator agros.	rites of war, and may the plowman
	in safety sow his untended fields.
Quae novus orbis erat, spiranti numine,	She who was a new world, with the
Lector,	support of God, O reader,
Anglia nascetur, quae novus orbis erit.	an England will be born, which will be
	a new world.[13]

With its militant sentiment, there is a truly Roman irony in the line *pax erit: hoc uno solvitur ira modo* 'there will be peace: only thus will anger pass' reminiscent of Tacitus' *ubi solitudinem faciunt pacem appellant* 'they make a desert and call it peace', and Augustus' boast, after the Roman civil wars, of having imposed *pax orbis terrarum* 'world peace'. (See page 10.)

When the colonists of the thirteen British colonies succeeded in establishing their own government, recourse was immediately made to Latin to give due solemnity to the instruments of the new state. On July 4, 1776, the Continental Congress named a committee to design a great seal for the country. But only after almost six years was a design agreed. Charles Thomson, the secretary of the Congress, merged previous work and achieved congressional approval in 1782. The obverse and reverse of the seal contain no less than three Latin mottoes, *e pluribus unum*, *annuit coeptis* and *novus ordo seclorum*. None of them is exactly a quotation, but the last is most messianic, recalling the passage in Virgil's Fourth Eclogue, which was widely taken in the Middle Ages to be a prophecy of Christ (see page 116):

Ultima Cumaei venit iam carminis	The last age of the Cumaean Sibyl has
aetas; magnus ab integro **saeclorum**	come; a great order of the ages is born.
nascitur **ordo.** *iam redit et Virgo, redeunt*	Now the Virgin and the age of Saturn
Saturnia regna, iam **nova** *progenies*	return; now a new Child is sent from
caelo demittitur alto.	heaven above.

Annuit coeptis 'He nodded to the undertakings' is taken from a passage in Virgil's *Aeneid* (ix. 625), *Jupiter omnipotens, audacibus annue coeptis* 'Almighty Jupiter, nod to my undertakings', where Ascanius, the son of Aeneas, is asking for Jupiter's support in a (not particularly risky, but perhaps difficult) arrow-shot at Remulus, an enemy soldier who has demeaned his manhood by calling him a Phrygian. Jupiter complies, with thunder on the left from a clear sky, and Remulus duly falls dead, an arrow through his skull. And *e pluribus unum* 'from more, one' has no relevant classical context at all, although the phrase is used in an ancient poem, the *Moretum* (also long attributed to Virgil, though now not thought to be his). It described the making of a certain sort of savory dish:

The Great Seal of the United States of America. The obverse and reverse contain no fewer than three Latin mottoes.

it manus in gyrum: paulatim singula
uires deperdunt proprias, color
est e pluribus unus, nec totus uiridis,
quia lactea frusta repugnant,
nec de lacte nitens, quia tot
uariatur ab herbis.

the hand goes in a circle: little by little
each loses its own force, and the color
stirred into one, not all green, because
the milky slices resist, nor shining from
milk, because varied by so many herbs.*

The mottoes of the United States were evidently chosen more for what they said than where they came from: sense prevailed over resonance. But the U.S. Constitution itself was explicitly designed after a Roman model. The classically educated founders naturally saw themselves in the traditional Roman mold, deposing a king, and setting up a republic that would be proof against the instabilities natural where there would be no predictable, nor sovereign, head of state. Although they did not go to the lengths of balancing the executive power internally, as the Romans had done with their two equal consuls, they did create in their legislature an analogue to the Roman tension between Senate and Council of the Plebs, and they explicitly set the different arms of government as checks and balances on one another, as tribunician power had limited the freedom of action of the other institutions.†

⬦

The American attempt to draw inspiration from Roman constitutional thinking is a leading example of the indirect role that Roman law, mostly formulated in Latin, has come to play in the modern world. It has had a role certainly in the currency of legal maxims, and in the curt and widely understood expression of such concepts as *stare decisis* 'abide by previous decisions' and *mens rea* 'criminal intent'. Even in the declaredly independent tradition of England, with the United States of America and many others of England's former colonies, known as the Common Law, key institutions go back to rather specific Roman ideas, such as those of trust and trustee based in the *fideicommissum* and *tutor*.

---

*Appendix Vergiliana, Moretum, 101–4. In 1956, Congress officially superseded *e pluribus unum* (although it might be thought a good expression of America's melting-pot ideal) by the deliberately religious (and English) "In God We Trust."
†Like the Romans, they also presided over a state that included slaves as well as free citizens, but unlike the Romans, many found this incompatible with their ideals.

Roman imperial law, codified in the emperor Justinian's *Institutiones, Codex, Digestum,* and *Novellae,* and extensively intepreted in the Middle Ages, ultimately created a largely homogeneous legal culture for the European world, often indicated by the Latin phrase *ius commune.* But the body of the laws had been regarded rather differently in different ages.[14] In the early university tradition created by Gratian's *Decretum* in the twelfth century, it had largely been an ideal, theoretical system. When it was applied in the courts, as happened increasingly from the fourteenth century, this was in competition with other systems, the canon law of the Church, local custom, and feudal law relating to land tenure. The historical sentiment of the humanists who followed in the fifteenth and sixteenth centuries viewed the laws not as valid for all time, but as documents of their (classical) era, to be read skeptically in case later interests had inserted extraneous material into them. And in the theories of international law due to Hugo Grotius* (1583–1645) and his successors, Roman law played a role as an exhibit of a specific legal system, conveniently well-defined and well-known, for comparison with a new concept of law that was supposedly natural. By and large, in every age after the fall of the Empire in the west, Roman law has been residual in function, with an authority that has served wherever it was useful to have a supplement for issues left untreated by more modern laws.

Since the formation of the Code Napoléon in France in 1804 and various other European codes of the same era, it has not been acceptable anywhere— even in supposedly "Roman law" legal traditions—to appeal directly to the laws laid down by Justinian. Law is now seen as a positive creation of the legislative branch of (national) governments, and from this point of view the past, with its laws, is a foreign country. Nevertheless, in the creation of new laws, and in judges' interpretation of old ones, maxims derived from the Roman tradition are still cited to give direction, even if they might seem noncontroversial to the point of being common sense; e.g., *volenti non fit iniuria* 'a willing victim does not suffer an injury'; *de minimis non curat lex* 'the law is unconcerned about trivialities'; *cessante ratione legis cessat lex ipsa* 'when the reason for a law ceases, so does the law'; *optimus legum interpres consuetudo* 'the best interpreter of the laws is custom'; *exempla illustrant non restringunt legem* 'examples illustrate, they do not restrict, a law'; *talis interpretatio in ambiguis semper fienda est, ut evitetur inconveniens et absurdum* 'when in doubt always intepet to exclude the inappropriate and the absurd'; *expressio unius est exclusio*

---

*He was a Dutchman, and his name is a Latinization of *Huigh de Groot.*

alterius 'the expression of the one option is the exclusion of the other'. And in fact there is a Latin maxim that modestly prefers (non-Roman) statutes over the *ius commune* of the Roman tradition: *statuta sunt stricte interpretanda* 'statutes are to be interpreted strictly'.

However, Latin has not for many centuries been used productively to create new law in the Roman mold, and at least in the British courts, even citing such maxims in Latin is increasingly discouraged. Legal Latin has become a remnant within a residue, a set of terms and phrases, not a fully functioning language. Nevertheless, this set of coded utterances has long preserved the common core of European legal principle and so is still of interest to some as a basis for future harmonized legislation with the European Union.[15]

CHAPTER 19

Eheu fugaces—Latin's Decline

MVLTA RENASCENTVR QVAE IAM CECIDERE, CADENTQVE QVAE NVNC SVNT IN HONORE VOCABVLA, SI VOLET VSVS, QVEM PENES ARBITRIVM EST ET IVS ET NORMA LOQVENDI.	Many words that have fallen will be reborn, and many that are now in honor will fall, if usage wills it, for that holds the judgment, the law, and the standard of speaking.

Horace, *Ars Poetica*, 70–72

Quod iam fuit, ipsum est; quod futurum est, iam fuit; Deus requirit, quod abiit.

That which has been long ago is now, and that which is to be has been long ago: and God seeks again that which is passed away.[1]

Ecclesiastes iii.15

LATIN WAS UNITARY, YET widely spoken by the most educated and influential members of every European country; it was culturally grounded; it had lots of words available for use; and it was apparently permanent. Yet those who trusted in this permanence were to be disappointed. By 1751, the French encyclopedist d'Alembert, noting wistfully in his *Discours préliminaire* the declining role of Latin, concluded with regret that there was no hope for its return. What had told against it?

A major drawback was the small matter of who knew it. Knowledge of Latin was widespread, certainly, but only in the highest strata of society, and among men. When education was expanded to take in larger segments of

Europe's population, including many more women, Latin was seen as too impractical for local, daily life to be offered much more widely.[2] Its "classical" bias, as we noted, was originally a Roman metaphor drawn from social class, and as time wore on this came to seem less and less of a metaphor. But the constant political theme all over Europe in the centuries after the sixteenth was the declining influence of the elite before the rising aspirations and, ultimately, rising power of the masses. More egalitarian distribution, though it came only fitfully, might have meant a wider provision of Latin; but in practice it tended not to. When the Bolsheviks seized power in Russia, an almost immediate reform (in 1920) was to eliminate Latin in schools.[3]

And besides the social element, there was also a changing assessment of the value of Europe's heritage, from those Latin speakers of the ancient, medieval, or even Renaissance eras. Latin's carefully cultivated associations with the past, even if they were more evident in the schools where Latin was taught than in the chanceries and universities where it was actually used, told against it in an era that more and more expected Progress and believed that it could achieve it through modern methods. Memories of an older world were no longer an inspiration, but rather an irrelevant distraction to increasingly self-confident moderns.

This is to telescope the story of six centuries of gradual, and indeed fitful, change, over a large area, with much regional variation. But the course of Latin's decline was one familiar in outline to students of endangered languages. Latin lost one domain of use after another. Its uses in commerce had already largely died out everywhere by the thirteenth century. Next to go, in a wave spreading eastward and southward from England and France, were its uses in national government, law,* and local administration. After this, the flow of literary creativity in Latin dried up. In the west of Europe, this was a phenomenon of the early seventeenth century.

Latin developments in philosophy were the next to peter out, perhaps because philosophy—tellingly—was tending to split into different national traditions in the various vernacular language areas. But this still left mathematics and the sciences still largely flourishing in Latin. Before these would be affected, the international basis of Latin was undercut by its disappearance as the language of diplomacy, largely to be replaced by French. And then at last Latin was withdrawn from the latest research in mathematics and the natural sciences, physics and chemistry, lingering only in descriptive sciences, such as

---

*Italy was exceptional in sustaining the use of Latin in the law until 1789 (Waquet 2001: 91).

astronomy, geology, paleontology, medicine, zoology, and above all botany—where the value of the Latin lexicon at least, to provide labels for taxonomy, is unchallenged to this day.

This ratchet of decline was fairly constant in form, but the speed with which the various steps followed one another varied across the continent, being fastest in the centers of political and cultural innovation in the west, and slowest in Europe's eastern periphery. In England, the Statute of Pleading of 1362 required that court proceedings would henceforth be in English, though "enrolled in Latin." France abandoned all official government use of Latin in 1539 by the Ordinance of Villers-Cotterêts.[4] In Poland and Hungary, by contrast, administration was still in Latin throughout the eighteenth century. The Prussians, who annexed half of Poland in 1772, stated in 1798 that Latin was "indispensable not only because of the Roman law, but because of the new Polish territories, where nearly all the educated strata speak Latin." In Hungary, Latin was necessary as the neutral lingua franca among speakers of five languages, Hungarian, German, Czech, Rumanian, and Croatian; it was hence used at higher levels of government. Although the government tried, it proved impossible to replace Latin with German even in 1790.[5]

In England, the last era in which creative literature was written in Latin was the Elizabethan and Jacobean Age, around 1530–1640.* Thereafter, although poetry for example continued to be composed, it tended to be either for use in hymns or else very conscious, stylized imitation of classical poetry, often for occasional pieces. It is noticeable that our own memory of this era, and our evaluation of it, have been reconditioned by the subsequent triumph of vernacular English. Latin culture was doomed, and those who failed to see it have paid with their reputations. The Latin writings of Elizabethans and Jacobeans, even if highly valued in their time, are not read and have largely been eclipsed by vernacular writers of the same era: admittedly, Donne, Marvell, Marlowe, and Shakespeare are among those vernacular writers.[†] When a language is lost, a world of knowledge is apt to go with it. It is chastening to see that this truth has applied even to so well-documented a language as Latin.

---

*It can be pursued in Binns 1990. The great names include John Shepery, John Leland, Thomas Chaloner, and John Parkhurst among poets, Nicholas Grimald, William Gager, William Alabaster, and Matthew Gwinne among dramatists.
†Some do not see this as unjust: Spitzer 1959: 923–44 claims that deep expression of emotion is bound to be weak in a language acquired by both poet and audience after early childhood.

Next came the changeover to the vernacular in philosophy. The seventeenth century was in fact a period of great philosophical innovation René Descartes (1596–1650) marked the beginning of French vernacular philosophy with his *Discours de la méthode* (1637). But in his lifetime, this and all his other French works were quickly translated into Latin, and most of his work was in fact originally published in Latin. In the same period, Thomas Hobbes, the English political philosopher, was writing his early works in Latin, notably *Elementica Philosophica De Cive* (1642). Nevertheless he republished them all in his own English translation—*Philosophical Rudiments concerning Government and Society* (1650)—before issuing *Leviathan* (1651) in English. Although this was a work he had written mostly while living in Paris, its main target audience was his own countrymen, reeling from the Civil War. But the practice was henceforth established for Englishmen to write their general works in English.

In the next generation, the great French philosophers Antoine Arnauld (1612–94), Blaise Pascal (1623–62), and Nicolas de Malebranche (1638–1715) all published in French. Even Gottfried Wilhelm Leibniz (1646–1716), though a German from Leipzig, wrote his major works in French, though resident (as he was for most of his life) at the courts of German princes. But he still often used Latin (and actually proposed a simplified form of it as a scholarly interlingua).[6] Dutch scholars, having less faith in the accessibility of their own vernacular—such as the highly private Benedict Spinoza (1632–77), an excommunicated Jew living in Amsterdam, and Christiaan Huygens (1629–95), a much more sociable mathematician and astronomer—still wrote in Latin. From the eighteenth century, European philosophers who spoke major European vernaculars used them in their publications. But in the Scandinavian countries, such linguistic self-confidence was rare: here intellectual works went on being published in Latin until the late nineteenth century.

In diplomacy, the use of Latin prevailed by tacit agreement until the mid-seventeenth century. (We have seen that Pope Pius II used it for his proselytizing letter to Mehmet II after the fall of Constantinople.) In that century, the strongest power, France, began to press for the use of French, finally persuading the Holy Roman Empire to use it in the treaty of Rastatt in 1714. But Latin was still used for some decades thereafter, especially by the peripheral powers of Scandinavia and eastern Europe, and indeed the Ottoman Empire.* It

---

*There were Latin treaties signed between Sweden and England (1720); France and Poland (Versailles, 1735); Sweden and the Ottoman Empire (1737); Denmark and the Ottoman Empire (1756).

dropped out of use in the latter half of the century, leaving the field to French.

Although Galileo's *Dialogo sopra i due massimi sistemi* 'Dialogue concerning the two chief world systems' was originally published in Italian in 1632, it was translated into Latin three years later, and much important mathematics, and natural science in general, went on being published in Latin until the end of the eighteenth century. As expected, it was mainly in France and England where the vernaculars took over early, Newton's *Principia* (1687) being the last major scientific work to appear in Latin in England. The German Carl Friedrich Gauss (1777–1855) sustained Latin into the nineteenth century, but that was pretty much the end among mathematicians. The Italian Leopoldo Caldani, writing works on anatomy up till 1814, represents the tail end of Latin publishing on medicine.[7] But the medics had, in general, provided one of the strongest markets for Latin publishing: as late as 1779, the Geneva bookseller Gosse had noted, "Anything to do with medicine is generally good in Latin. Spain, Portugal, Italy, even France does not reject them."[8]

This overview of language use, as represented by a few big names, can be supplemented by some publishing statistics.[9] In France, Latin titles outnumbered French ones until the 1560s, but fell to under 25 percent in the last decade of the sixteenth century, held steady at 20 percent for the next fifty years, but then resumed their decline, to well under 5 percent by 1764. In Italy, by contrast, a bare majority—but a majority—for Latin continued throughout the seventeenth century, only to be lost in the eighteenth, when Latin declined below 30 percent, although Rome (50 percent—for the Church) and Padua (56 percent—for the university) held up best. Germany is represented by the records of the Frankfurt Book Fair. Here, after Luther's one-man vernacular boom (1517–25), Latin rebounded: in fact most titles were still in Latin until the 1680s, and Latin publishing remained significant (above 15 percent) for most of the eighteenth century. The collapse came early in the nineteenth. In England, Latin publishing was always at a low level by continental standards, with only 10 percent even in 1530–1640, and a sharp decline thereafter, except at the Oxford University Press.

It is evident, then, that the Republic of Letters did not save Latin publishing, nor the role of Latin in the active and innovative part of Europe's intellectual life. The self-regarding lead of France, and indeed Britain, to express their thinking in their own languages, without appearing to care very much whether the rest of Europe could follow them, was sooner or later taken up in every part of Europe, though later in regions that knew they were not at the center of things. Germany, Spain, and Italy might reassure themselves that there was either enough of an audience in their own languages, or enough foreigners who had taken the trouble to learn them, that they could follow France and England in using their own vernaculars. For the rest, it was a matter of resigning themselves to having a small, intimate audience for their own original works, and making a much greater effort to learn the influential modern languages, and to get their works translated into them. When the great powers did not endorse Europe's old, and now fairly neutral, lingua franca, there was little the smaller powers could do to buttress it, even if—especially in Scandinavia and eastern Europe—they used it for their own purposes as long as they could.

The widespread learning of foreign European languages, especially French, English, and German, clearly grew in the eighteenth and nineteenth centuries, in response to the lack of any alternative, or rather to the loss of the old alternative. The new powers—partly through imperial pursuits quite outside Europe—had reached levels of eminence where they could promote their own ease of communication, expressed through use of their own languages, as what we should now call a new de facto standard. A "winner takes all" philosophy had certainly been no stranger to Rome at the height of its powers; indeed it had widely been taught to boys studying Latin for two thousand years, through Aesop's fable of "the lion's share."* The use of Rome's language, originally based on the convenience of the ruling classes 'and the spread of so many retired soldiers around the Empire, had only come to seem disinterested, and indeed rational, as the power of Rome had declined. Christianity too, adopting Latin just as the Roman Empire had adopted it, had played its role in maintaining Latin's special status. But Christianity was now split and at least half-vernacularized. And the new ideas that were changing Europe were not coming anymore from Rome, or the nostalgics of northern Italy. There was now no basis for resistance when new powers began to assert—at least implicitly—the special dignity of their own languages.

Nevertheless, the problems implicit when different languages compete to express scientific—and supposedly universal—ideas has occasionally provoked a reaction. In 1903 the Italian mathematician Giuseppe Peano, having once received with dismay a letter from another mathematician written in

---

*Ironically, it had even been put proverbially in the mouth of the one Gaul who had undoubtedly got the better of the Romans themselves. When Romans had complained at the unfair dealing of Brennus, their conqueror in 390 BC, he was supposed to have thrown his sword into the balance, crying, VAE VICTIS 'Woe to the conquered', or in plain English, 'Tough luck!'

Giuseppe Peano, a mathematician and logician of the early twentieth century, attempted to develop Latino sine flexione *as a universal language for scientific communication.*

Japanese, made a sustained attempt to rehabilitate a form of Latin as a universal language.

In fact, in Peano's discipline of logic a tradition stretched back at least to Leibniz of attempting to develop a *characteristica universalis*, or ideal language, which would make truth and valid inference crystal clear on formal grounds. Rather than seeking to persuade, the user of such a language would simply "do sums," with the truth of the conclusions rigorously implied by the truth of the premises. Latin had never actually offered this—though the medieval development of the forms of syllogism (pp. 221–22) had been a move in this direction. And it seems that Peano, although he did sometimes suggest his linguistic proposals were related to his logic, was actually motivated more by the sheer waste of effort caused by the language barrier.

Peano's article was written in classical Latin, but which successively divested itelf of its inflected endings, to give a language that Peano called *Latino sine flexione*. It was subsequently renamed *Interlingua*, or more recently as *Europeano*. It gives an outcome like this:

> *Interlingua es lingua universale que omne persona in modo facile scribe et intellige sine usu de speciale studio. Libro in Interlingua es diffuso supra plure regione de Europa, America, Africa, Australia, et Asia ubi cultura occidentale es noto.*

Interlingua adopta omne vocabulo que existe simile in Anglo, Germano, Franco, Russo, Latino, et Graeco. Et adopta omne vocabulo anglo-latino cum forma de thema (radice).

As an artificial language, it has the advantage of having its vocabulary predetermined by the contents of any Latin dictionary, but replaces the resources of Latin inflection with the simple but fixed subject-verb-object word order of the western European languages. Peano was at the time a world leader in logic, and he put his full authority behind it, publishing all his subsequent articles in it, and making it an official language at a number of mathematical congresses. But it did not catch on, being largely abandoned soon after his death in 1932.[10]

❖

In the nineteenth century, Latin in the United States came to betoken a retrospective attitude, and learning it—unsurprisingly, in a new country dedicated to its future prospects—less and less popular, even if wars of imperial conquest were no less a feature of eighteenth- and nineteenth-century America than they had been of the Roman Republic. With the possible exception of the Roman Catholic Church itself, there had been no intellectual institution like the Catholic mendicant orders in Latin America, Dominicans, Franciscans, or latterly the Jesuits, to promote the development of new ideas and debate in Latin. The immigrant population was European but ultimately highly multilingual, and so there might have been a case for Latin as a neutral, but European-flavored, lingua franca. But this is a fantasy: in practice there was no alternative to the English that predominated among some 750,000 European immigrants to the United States in the seventeenth and eighteenth centuries, even if it was spoken by only a small minority of the 40 million immigrants who came afterward. America was the country for enterprise, not educated decorum, all the more so after the destruction of the Southern slave-based society in the 1860s. There was not the slightest basis for Latin in the rip-roaring American West, the powerhouses of its developing industries, and scarcely any more in the aspirant universities or drawing rooms of the East Coast cities.

Nevertheless, the experience of Latin in the New World—in the British as in the Spanish foundations—had been almost a startling vindication of one constant aspect that we have discerned in Latin culture: its faith in what we could call the *Ad Infinitum*, the sense that the culture that it represented would prevail and prove universal. The Europeans' beliefs and practices did indeed prevail to achieve political and economic control of the total landmass, and all the peoples, of the Americas, as they were step-by-step revealed.

When not seeking personal wealth, or land for settlement, the main early motive of the Hispanic settlers had been to extend the congregation of the Roman Catholic Church. It was an interesting irony in their policy to achieve this that their principal, and most immediate, tool was the grammatical inheritance from Dionysius Thrax, Donatus, and Priscian, the very basis by which they had all learned their Latin. This approach to grammar can also be seen as a manifestation of the *Ad Infinitum* spirit, since it progressed largely on the assumption that the categories of Greek and Latin grammar would prove universal. Remember Varro's presumptuous but prescient words (p. 82, second footnote): "Declination is a feature of all human languages, not just Latin, for a good and necessary reason . . ."

In the most literal sense, the Europeans who conquered empires in the New World were realizing the oldest dream of the Romans, to whom Virgil's Jupiter had announced, *his ego nec metas rerum nec tempora pono: | imperium sine fine dedi* 'On them I place neither bounds to their possessions nor limits in time: empire without end I have granted'.[11] But in another sense, the open frontier, the essence of New World society, was the antithesis of this dream. The pioneers' familiar philosophy of quest, epitomized in the Spanish search for El Dorado, and the American maxim "Go west, young man," always suggested that a land of undreamed-of wealth was to be found beyond the known boundaries of the empire. It was characteristic of this attitude that California, where the New World gave out, was named for a fantasy island.* But Rome's dream had been steadfastly serious and metropolitan: Rome had spread its power, its veterans, and its language not to find or create something new, but as the expression and vindication of its own presumed greatness, endlessly

---

*It had been dreamed up by the Spaniard García Ordóñez de Montalvo in his popular potboiler *Las Sergas de Esplandián*: "Know that on the right hand of the Indies there is an island called California very close to the side of the Terrestrial Paradise; and it is peopled by black women, without any man among them, for they live in the manner of Amazons." The book came out possibly in 1496 (though the earliest extant printing is 1510). In 1540 Hernando de Alarcón applied it, perhaps with satirical intent, to what is now Baja California, in a report to verify the purported discoveries of Hernán Cortés in the western reaches of New Spain. The name was only later extended to include the whole southwestern coast of North America.

confirmed because presumed to be boundless. *Ad Infinitum* indeed, but with a persistent focus on the homeland, on the eternal center.

Seen from this point of view, it is no surprise that Latin did not ultimately prosper in the New World. Latin and its tradition fundamentally expressed the soul of a self-sufficient, centered, dominant Europe. All the states established in the Americas sprang from this Europe and, indeed, could perhaps not have been established without it. But when at last the medieval lordships fell away, and the states embraced self-determination, the European heritage, based in Rome, and expressed in Latin, was awkward and out of place.

What then had fundamentally changed, in the seventeenth and eighteenth centuries, to end Latin's two millennia of linguistic dominance in Europe? Evidently, there had been unprecedented technical progress, stemming from the advances in mathematics and science in the seventeenth century—just as Latin was losing its monopoly as the language of higher thought—and leading to paths of economic development and massive populations quite inconceivable to the ancients. Now the achievements of Roman civilization seemed no longer fresh and impressive, as they had been for the humanists, but passé and unenlightened. But even more spectacular immediate progress had come through navigation, backed by guns and metal armor, and by greed for gold, land, or foreign dominion. Europe in the seventeenth century had detailed knowledge of two vast worlds beyond its shores, a world to the west, which seemed unresisting to the imposition of European empires, and one to the east, where immense wealth was becoming available to the fearless European merchant.* Latin's old implicit claim of universality, that Rome's world was all the world that mattered, could not be sustained. And without it, it seemed neither could Latin.

---

*The African world, to the south, although it was on the way to both these other worlds, would strangely only be truly discovered in the nineteenth century.

CHAPTER 20

❖❖❖❖

Sub specie aeternitatis—Latin Today

It was his view that Latin was mostly for looks anyway, and he devoted
himself to the mottoes in order to find the one with the best look.
The one he settled on was *Uva uvam vivendo varia fit*, which seemed
to him a beautiful motto, whatever it meant.

(Augustus McCrae chooses a motto for his ranch sign.)
Larry McMurtry, *Lonesome Dove*

Iuven, 2,81: *Uvăque conspectā livorem ducit ab uvā.*
Schol.: *Hoc ex proverbio sumitur: uva uvam videndo varia fit.*
Juvenal, ii.81: And a grape takes its blue color from the grape it sees.

Commentator: This taken from the proverb "A grape goes
mottled from seeing another."

L ATIN HAD COLLAPSED AS an effective language for the international
community in western Europe, but it nevertheless lived on in humane
education. Exposure to Latin—however superficial—was still seen as the hallmark of a civilized gentleman. Edward Gibbon, writing his memoirs in the
1780s, could already talk of cloaking potentially embarrassing realities in the
"decent obscurity of a learned language." An association with artificiality,
hidebound restrictions, and the cult of civilized leisure has beset the reputation of Latin ever since, as if the life-affirming classical Latin of the Renaissance humanists had once again been submerged in the mustiness of medieval
scholasticism. But the reputation was an effect of the social role that Latin was
being made to play: it had little to do with the content of Latin grammar,

Latin literature, or indeed ancient history. Schoolmasters, dons, clergymen—in short the archetypes of pedants—came to be the sole purveyors of Latin and gave a certain overlay to the language.

No longer seen as a path of access to a very different, and highly stimulating, world—as the Renaissance humanists had seen it—it was presented with reverence as the true basis of traditional civilization, a sort of communion for conservatives. It became accepted that it was the vehicle of a closed corpus, a language for citation, not creation, with the implication that new thinking and fresh ideas should be undertaken, if at all, with due deference to the ancients: a strange message for eighteenth-, nineteenth-, and even twentieth-century Europe, where the pace of technical change and social egalitarianism was rising quite beyond anything conceivable when Latin was the language of the intellect. Composition in the language was never now a straightforward act of communication, or aesthetic expression, if to a rather small but international audience: rather, it was billed as "the proof and the flower of that scholarship which loves the old writers with an unselfish love, and delights to clothe modern thoughts and modern expressions in the dress of ancient metre and rhythm."[1] No wonder it attracted ever greater resentment, seen as the pursuit of a cultural clique, excluding those who had not been exposed to it in their early years, but not—unlike the increasingly widely taught mathematical sciences—able to show that its brand of elite knowledge actually produced any achievement that was impossible without it.

Yet, the analytical training in grammar by which Latin was still taught made it possible to maintain that "Latin trains the brain"—unlike a language taught primarily through exposure, the so-called direct method—thus giving its instruction some kind of qualitative similarity to mathematics. And there has been a tradition for more than two thousand years in Europe of including some of this kind of training in the introduction to literacy even in the vernacular; in this way, some level of explicit understanding of language structure was given to all readers and writers.

When this element was abandoned, as it largely was in the European and American curricula of the later twentieth century, it naturally became far harder for new readers and writers to reproduce the more subtle and elaborated features of traditional text. But some such rules are implicit, even if they remain unconscious, when a language is learned by any means at all. Remember John Colet in 1510 (p. 253): "Men spake not Latin because such rules were made, but, contrariwise, because men spake such Latin the rules were made." By analogy, it can be argued, a training in musical notation and harmony is evidently not necessary for musical enjoyment and even a fairly high level of performance, given application and some talent.

Perhaps the cultural overlay of grammar—the complacent, and hence resented, elitism of those who have learned the rules—had ended up getting in the way of its utility. Rules are learned, after all, not primarily to demonstrate the intelligence of the person who knows them, but as a shortcut to sophisticated performance. To be given rules actually makes the learning of a language quicker and more efficient. The problem comes when a learner gets neither the rules nor sufficient exposure to the language being learned. (And without explicit rules, a lot more exposure will be needed than with them.) In practice, since the eighteenth century when Latin ceased to be the language of the classroom anywhere, there has been little chance of hearing enough of it to dispense with the rules.

Despite these culture wars that have inhibited its effective transmission into the twenty-first century, traces of Latin are still widespread today, in all the language communities that have origins in western and central Europe. It exists there not usually as a language as such, but in various auxiliary roles that supplement the vernacular languages: as a way of organizing scientific terminology, as a badge of traditional allegiances, and—now and again, not doing itself any favors—as a means of catching people out in some subtle solecism or barbarism.*

⟡

In its role as the "alien" language that is closest to us, Latin is now sometimes used as a kind of neutral proving-ground for theories of semantics.

One such field is the testing of the statement of kinship relations, a major field for anthropologists in the twentieth century. It aims to classify the different ways that societies (usually betokened by their languages) can make sense of the hierarchical structures arising from the universal fact of parenthood, where each human being arises from one father and one mother, as it interacts with the much more variable patterns of how such father-mother bonds are formed and sustained, and the constraints that a society wants to put on such bonds. European society is no exception, and indeed our best source of detailed information on Latin kinship terminology comes from the canon law-

---

*Remembering the difference between these two has been a *pons asinorum* (a bridge that separates out the asses) since the first century BC. In brief, as Suetonius put it, SOLOE-CISMVS IN SENSV FIT, BARBARISMVS IN VOCE: a solecism is a mistake in sense (i.e., in sentence structure), a barbarism in sound (including choice of words).

yers of the Middle Ages, concerned to specify the degrees of consanguinity, how closely within an extended family potential brides and grooms might be related.[2] (The least allowable number of degrees was traditionally six, but it was reduced to four at Lateran Council IV in 1215.)

Human kinship is divided into six major types, named for some individual cultures that exemplify them: Sudanese, Hawaiian, Eskimo, Iroquois,

Arbor Consanguinitatis. This tree diagram, taken from Isidore's Etymologiae *(seventh century) but common throughout the Middle Ages, displays the relations within which Catholic marriage is forbidden.*

Omaha, and Crow.[3] The types are in effect an index of which sets of relations get lumped together under common terms. Some examples may clarify. In an Eskimo system—like English, and that of most modern European languages—paternal and maternal relatives are not distinguished: your uncle is your uncle whether he is your father's or your mother's brother. In a Hawaiian system, all kin of the same generation get one term if they are male, and another if female: your mother is not distinguished from an aunt, nor a son from a nephew. Iroquois, Omaha, and Crow show various patterns of "bifurcate merging": essentially fathers are not distinct from paternal uncles, nor mothers from maternal aunts, but relationships in whose definition the sexes are mixed (e.g., maternal uncles, paternal aunts) are kept apart. The different systems are supposed to be correlated with different social patterns: the Eskimo system, for example, emphasizes the role of the nuclear family.

Now Latin, as it happens, has a Sudanese system, with maximal differentiation of all the different relations. In this, it is like, for example, Turkish and Old English.* There are few observable social implications of this, except for the observance of a class system, which certainly fits ancient Roman society well. But it means, when it comes to specifying a degree of kinship, that—very likely—"the Romans had a word for it." This can make it useful as a standard in terms of which to state a given relationship; and it also plays a useful role in developing terminology for anthropology, whether one wishes to talk of avunculolocal, amitalocal, virilocal, or uxorilocal residence after marriage (i.e., living in the family of your maternal uncle, paternal aunt, husband, or wife), a levirate custom of a man taking to wife his elder brother's widow, or the distinction of (social) *pater* and *mater* versus (biological) *genitor* and *genitrix*.

But this maximal differentiation has its limits. Curiously, nephews and nieces are not usually distinguished from grandsons and granddaughters: *nepos, neptis*. And correspondingly, the word for maternal uncle (*avunculus*) is the diminutive of that for grandfather (*avus*).[4] In fact, knowledge of the finer

---

*Revealingly, *uncle, aunt, nephew, niece,* and *cousin* are all borrowings into English from Norman French, ultimately from Latin (*avunculus, amita, nepos, neptis,* and *consobrinus*). They are innovations less than nine hundred years old, whereas the naming of *father, mother, brother, sister, son, daughter,* has not been interrupted for at least three thousand years, and probably much longer. (Incidentally, note that these French terms preserve only the cross-uncle and cross-aunt, i.e., mother's brother and father's sister. It was the parallel uncle and aunt (father's brother, mother's sister—*patruus* and *matertera*) that were dropped. And among cousins, the maternal terms have been preserved, paternal (*patruelis, fratruelis*) lost.)

details of distant relationships seemed to be as difficult to standardize in Latin as it typically is in our own modern European systems. *Patruelis* and *consobrinus/a* were theoretically paternal and maternal parallel cousins (father's brother's, and mother's sister's children); for cross-cousins, we have *amitinus/a* and *matruelis* (father's sister's, and mother's brother's child). But in the long run *consobrinus/a* tended to get generalized and has hence resulted in the modern (vague) *cousin* in French and English. And if *patruelis* and *matruelis* were the children of a paternal uncle and maternal uncle respectively, what to make of the analogous *fratruelis*, from *frater* 'brother'? It tended to be taken as a synonym for *patruelis/consobrinus*, i.e., parallel cousin, but there was another school of thought that wanted to interpret it as *nephew*.[5]

Looking further into the Latin system of in-laws, it is well developed on the side that refers to the husband's relations (*socer, socrus, levir, glos*: 'husband's father, mother, brother, sister' respectively; *nurus* 'son's wife'; and even the wives of brothers are termed *ianitrices*), but hardly at all for the wife's side. (The one exception is *gener* 'daughter's husband'.) Since these are all terms with a long parentage, and no Indo-European language has preserved wife-side terms, the asymmetry may be ancient. But that Latin has preserved it is also eloquent of the undoubted fact that after a Roman marriage a bride joined the husband's family, not vice versa. (Contrast English, another Indo-European language, but one where all "in-laws" are on a par.)

⚬

Another such field where the Latin language can be examined as a specimen is the theory of color terms. A vast range of difference is apparent in the ways that languages describe the spectrum revealed by our senses.

Perhaps though there is some order to be detected amid the variety. The classic study of color[6] has suggested that every language has a small determinate set of basic color terms, fully partitioning the whole range of possible hues, but which could then be supplemented by an open-ended class of more subtle terms. Hence modern English has *black, white, red, brown, gray, green, blue, yellow, orange*, and *purple* as basic, while, for example, *crimson, vermilion, scarlet*, and *pink* can be seen as kinds of red. The set of basic terms differs among languages: to take one famous example, Japanese *ao* covers the space shared between *blue* and *green*, and some languages may have as few as two basic terms. Evidently too the set can change over time: *orange* and *purple* were not even color words in Anglo-Saxon or Old French; and the Romance languages gained from Gothic and Germanic a number of basic terms, which were then added to the set they had inherited from Latin. (They are the words that correspond to modern English *black*, *brown*, *gray*, and *yellow*. See note on page 165.)

The original Latin set, however, has provided ammunition for some dispute about the theory. Some prefer a relativist position that sees the status of colors as determined by culture alone; on this view neither Latin nor Greek had as part of their vocabulary any such basic set at all.[7] That does not stop others from offering such a set complete.[8] It is minimal (*niger* 'black', *albus* 'white', *ruber/rubeus* 'red', *viridis* 'green'), but it has given rise to the only color terms to have survived into modern Romance.* And it is consistent with A. Gellius' disquisition on colors (of the second century AD).[9] Aristotle himself had, in fact, only distinguished three colors in the rainbow: red, green, and purple.[10]

Most striking perhaps is the Latin view of the range from our blue to yellow, where the basic term is clearly *viridis*, much wider in sense than its usual translation 'green', with some specialized hues, *caeruleus* for the sea and the sky, *venetus* for water and air (!), *caesius* for eyes, according to Gellius. Bizarrely for us, Isidore actually defines *caeruleus* as a combination of *viridis* 'green' and *niger* 'black'—'like the sea'.[11] Latterly, the sense of *caeruleus* seems only to be 'a marginal case of *viridis*', so that it is occasionally used to mean yellow as well as blue.† Subsequently, all the Romance languages restricted *viridis* to true green in the modern sense, inserting new terms specifically for the yellow and blue ends of the range, which were all borrowed from other languages.[12]

Several other terms seem to have been omitted from this overall pattern, e.g., *rāvus* 'gray, roan', *helvus* 'light bay', *gilvus* 'light yellow', *rutilus* 'ruddy', *badius* 'bay, chestnut', *cānus* 'white', *flōrus* 'blond', but as the translations suggest, these seem to have mainly been applied to fur or hair. And Greek borrowings such as *glaucus* 'owl gray', *prasinus* 'leek green', and *citrinus* 'lemon yellow' were also quite common, at least in literary texts. Black and white seem uniquely to have specified texture as well as hue: *ater* was another word for 'black' (matt, contrasted with shining *niger*), which had once been more common than *niger* as the general word, but seems to have gone into a gradual decline after the second century BC; and *candidus* was originally 'burning', but hence, as against *albus*, it meant

---

Albus, though, has been replaced everywhere except in Rumanian *alb*.

†This usage is attributed to Albertus Magnus, writing in the thirteenth century. This is less strange than it appears: Middle High German *blā* can mean both 'blue' and 'yellow' (as can Slavic *plovy*), and Latin FLAVVS is etymologically identical to Germanic *blavus* (giving *blau*, *blue*).

'shining white' (the color of kindness rather than straightforwardness in Roman thinking, but also of a Roman political candidate's clothing).

This is enough to show that Latin colors were conceived in a different, and rather simpler, system from that of the modern European languages that arose from it. But it is fair to point out that specifying the system in this way has an element of novelty; it is not a traditional feature of Latin grammars, and the vocabulary—outside the basic terms—is not frequently used in Latin literature.

⟡

The European Union, especially since the recent accession of Bulgaria and Rumania, has a high overlap of territory with the Roman Empire at its height, e.g., in the age of Trajan, and even more so with the extent of the Catholic Church up to the Reformation.

Evidently, there are major discrepancies—the crucially important provinces of the Roman Empire in Asia Minor and Africa on the one hand, the expansion of the European Union to cover most of eastern and northern Europe on the other—but in a sense, their hearts are one: Rome was the functioning capital of the Roman Empire until the fourth century and has continuously remained the seat of the Catholic Church (with the small exception of the "Babylonian captivity" in Avignon for most of the fourteenth century). The European Union too looks to Rome, at least nominally, as the site of its foundation as the EEC, in the Treaty of Rome of 1957. Admittedly, the cohesive forces for these three leviathans have all been rather different: for the Roman Empire the might of the army, for the Church a shared faith, and for the European Union a powerful desire for collective security within and without, buttressed by secular democracy and mutual prosperity. So nostalgia for the old forms of unity is clearly out of place. But surely Latin at least, the working language of the Empire and the Church, could be called on to exercise some of its old magic as glue for the Union?

To a limited extent, it can be seen in practice. In 2000, *In varietate concordia* was adopted as the official motto of the European Union, accepted by the president of the European Parliament, and supposed to be a Latin equivalent to 'Unity in Diversity'.* The official names of all the euro notes, monetized on

---

*No one appears to care about the ill-omened similarity to Cicero's great ideal, *concordia ordinum* 'cooperation among the classes', which he hoped in vain would save the Roman Republic from the rise of Julius Caesar and his like.

The extent of the Roman Empire at the death of Trajan, AD 117.

the first day of 2002, are in Latin, giving attentive Europeans a quick refresher on the Latin distributive numerals, and some use at least—if not quite a new lease on life—to the disregarded color terms: *quinarius caesius, denarius rubens, vicenarius caeruleus, quinquagenarius luteus, centenarius viridis, ducenarius aureus,* and *quingenarius purpureus.** There are occasional cries that Europe should attempt to reinstate Latin,[13] but it has no official status to give it constitutional parity, say, to Sanskrit, which is among the eighteen languages recognized by the Indian constitution. Nevertheless, there have recently been some fairly constructive attempts to give it a substantial status. During its presidencies of the European Union (in the second halves of 1999 and 2006), Finland offered a weekly summary of events in Latin, *Conspectus rerum Latinus.* This is provided by the same scholars who have since September 1, 1989, produced *Nuntii*

---

*This is some compensation perhaps for the loss of the ancient Roman system of currency, whose last gasp had come on Britain's "D-Day" (February 15, 1971) when the pound sterling, having preserved since late antiquity in its £.s.d. the proportions of *libra, solidus, denarius,* yielded to pounds and centesimal pence.

The reach of Catholic Christendom ca AD 1500.

Latini, a spoken and written news service of their national broadcaster (YLE).[14] That this initiative comes from Finland, a country where it is likely that no citizen of the Roman Empire ever penetrated, shows the continuing strength there of the ideal of Latin as a universal but neutral language. This is felt particularly by people who know that use of their own national language will not give them a wide audience in the world at large, but see no reason to privilege anyone else's. The Finnish prime minister's office in 2006 was at one with the Swedish chancellor Axel Oxenstierna in 1653:

> Though he could, yet would not speak French, saying he knew no reason why that nation should be so much honoured more than others as to have their language used by strangers; but he thought the Latin more honourable and more copious, and fitter to be used, because the Romans had been masters of so great a part of the world, and yet at present that language was not peculiar to any people.[15]

This motive should not be underrated: something like it underlies the conversion in the 1990s of *La Francophonie*, the international cultural-solidarity league based on French, to endorse language diversity as an ideal. "Anything rather than English," perhaps; and one can conjecture that, if the choice should fall on Latin, then so be it. But there seems little prospect of such political initiatives turning the tide for the use of Latin in Europe unless they come to be backed up by wider use of Latin in other contexts, international and perhaps even national, and unless some motive is found for reinstating it in the curriculum in Europe's schools. Latin is, in fact, quite widespread on the Internet. Since 2004, *Ephemeris*, a wide-ranging illustrated weekly newspaper in Latin, has been published from Warsaw.[16] There are special-interest lists (e.g., LatinClassicEd, promoting homeschooling with Latin); blog and chat sites come and go. As of the end of 2006, there are approximately 2.5 million pages in Latin. In practice, this includes al-

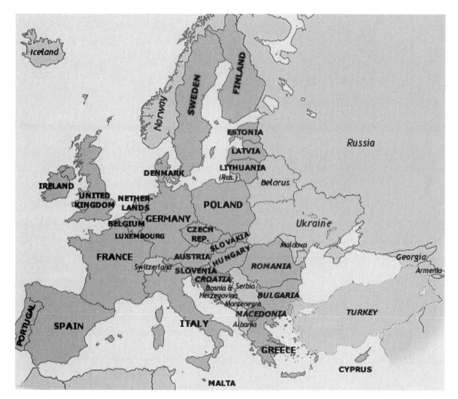

Extent of the European Union, 2007.

most all of the surviving classical literature, but very little of texts dating from after the fourth century. This is small compared with the current 10 billion pages in English, 1 billion each for French and German, and 95 million for Turkish, but not insignificant if compared with 7.5 million for Icelandic, 11 million for Lithuanian, 15 million for Slovenian.[17]

⬦

An important thesis of this book has been that users of Latin have tended to see their world as all the world that counts. A natural extension of this is for them to see Latin not merely as international, but as a heritage and resource for the whole world, a universal and impartial language, in no way specific to Europe where it grew.

The Catholic Church, by its very name, which is the Greek for 'universal', has long tended to make universal claims for Latin. Recall Pope John VIII in 880 (pp. 154–55) lecturing the Moravians that Latin had "greater dignity" than the vernacular that their parishioners could actually understand. The underlying claim, revived down the centuries, was that the mystery of this unfamilar tongue, with its long association with the true religion, was itself an inducement to holy devotion. This argument, if valid anywhere, must evidently be valid throughout the world. It was of course very different from the original motive for introducing Latin into the liturgy in the fourth century AD (p. 112): then Latin had been promoted in the west, to replace the then traditional Greek, because Latin *was* the vernacular. A lot of water had flowed under the bridge since then, of course. But the missionary zeal of the Church was never lost; and from this perspective, it was now clear that Latin the universal language was a decided obstacle in bringing the public as a whole to an understanding of Christianity and its sacraments.

This kind of thinking came to a head in 1962–65, the period of the Vatican II conference. The conference effectively abolished use of the Tridentine Mass, even though it had been universal as the Catholic rite, celebrated in Latin, since the Council of Trent in 1545–63* and contained elements that go back to the time of St. Gregory in the sixth century. Naturally some within the Church resisted this change; but they were proscribed and even, in the extreme case of the French

---

*The decision was actually taken in 1562, after some pleading for a vernacular Mass. The saying of the Mass in the vernacular alone was, however, at that time made anathema. (Feo 1986: 369.)

archbishop Marcel Lefebvre, excommunicated. Since then a multitude of vernacular Masses have been authorized. Despite this, the Tridentine Mass is still regularly said in a few places, by special permission. The matter has remained a live issue in the Church, with rumors that the celebration of the old Mass may soon be permitted anywhere that bishops have not specifically forbidden it. The Catholic Church's links with its ancestral language are not fully sundered, and it seems the pendulum of reaction may yet reinstate some of them.*

⟡

Even as the Catholic Church has endeavored to keep the stock of Latin terminology up-to-date with the modern world,[†] less serious approaches to keeping the language in use are still very much with us. Two volumes in the global children's publishing sensation, J. K. Rowling's Harry Potter series, have been translated into Latin within four years (under the titles *Harrius Potter et Philosophi Lapis*, 2003, and *Harrius Potter et Camera Secretorum*, 2006); so the profile of Latin remains high enough among the rising generation in the Anglo-Saxon world to reflect, at least dimly, the mainstream of commercial culture. Meanwhile the Latin translation of an older pan-European best seller, arguably a classic in its own right, *Astérix le Gaulois*, undertaken by European publishers (twenty-two volumes between 1973 and 2002, all now available in Latin from *Asterix Gallus* to *Asterix et Latraviata*), may well be more useful as a straightforward contribution to school teaching, by putting Latin in a quasi-authentic historical context.[‡]

---

*The Vatican also uses some Latin for administration and teaching and is probably the closest thing there is still to a living Latin community. Nevertheless, here too it seems that the tradition is hard to maintain: Reginald Foster, who has taught Latin at the Pontifical Gregorian University since the 1970s, estimated in 2004 that there are now only about twenty people in the world who speak Latin as well as he does, and only two or three of them are younger than sixty. (*Newsweek*, April 21, 2004.)

†The Church's Gregorian University at Rome was still in the early 1950s attempting to teach wave mechanics through the medium of scholastic Latin (as recalled in Kenny 1985: 48). The Vatican's most recent attempt to keep Latin abreast of the modern world is the *Lexicon Recentis Latinitatis Vaticanense* with Italian translations (Fondazione "Latinitas," 2003), replacing *Antonii Bacci Lexicon Eorum Vocabulorum Quae Difficilius Latine Redduntur* (Studium, 1963).

‡This fact, that *Asterix* is actually about life in the Roman Empire, may explain the otherwise inexplicable fact that his great rival in European children's publishing, Hergé's *Tintin*, has only two volumes available in Latin translation, *Insula Nigra* 'The Black Island' and *De Sigaris Pharaonis* 'The Pharaoh's Cigars'.

Latin continues to play a certain role in the popular imagination of the West. The sense that "Once upon a time the whole world spoke Latin" is still with us, though that world seems increasingly distant and strange. The value systems that came with that world are hard nowadays to take seriously. When it is used productively, rather than simply quoted or misquoted, it is usually in macaronic form, mixing Latin in with the popular language. And when Latin still appears in the mass media, the tone is jokey rather than reverential. In this, Latin is once again being used to reveal the current European attitude to its own past.

◈

Benedict Anderson, the social historian, well characterizes the significance of an enduring language: "Much the most important thing about language is its capacity for generating imagined communities, building in effect *particular solidarities*. After all, imperial languages are still *vernaculars*, and thus particular vernaculars among many."[18] Latin gave its speaker community, evolving over many centuries, a special, and continuing, cohesion.

When it first becomes visible to us, Latin is surviving, perhaps with profit, some centuries of cohabitation with its Etruscan neighbor. It was then spread through the many-faced success of its community. Politically organized as the Republic of Rome, this community achieved a basic political stability, economic and demographic growth, and above all consistent military victories during more than three hundred years of territorial expansion, spreading its speakers as well as its revenue gatherers all round the Mediterranean and western Europe. The expansion largely ceased in the latter first century BC, but when it did—in a highly costly and Mediterranean-wide Roman civil war—a radically new political dispensation, due to the victor Augustus, ensured that despite repeated failures of effective government at the top, and a chronic tendency to wars for the emperor's throne, the western empire, the domain of Latin, remained united as a single functioning state and community for another four hundred years. Latin was therefore firmly established across western Europe by more than seven hundred years as the bond of unity, and the means of communication, for a vast, and stable, single state.

Toward the end of this period, Latin was reinforced by the spread of Christianity throughout this community: this made it a language of liturgy as well as daily life and gave it a stable basis in regular devotions at all levels of society, a basis that proved strong enough to survive the ultimate breakdown of that single state and continental economy. In the four hundred years of social and political confusion that followed the various Germanic, and latterly Arab, conquests of parts of the Empire, the unity of the Church was maintained, and the tradition of Latin learning sustained within the cultural fortresses of the monasteries. Ultimately, when large-scale political order began to be rebuilt by Charlemagne and his successors, the Church still had the means to reconstruct a Latin educational standard built firmly on the old classics. This then became the basis for a new life of Latin as an artificially sustained language of religion and culture, which, despite its dependence on transmission through education alone, would remain the backbone of European learning for a further eight hundred years.

Those eight centuries witnessed the gradual reclamation of full competence in ancient learning, which four hundred years of educational breakdown had largely lost. At the same time, Christianity, and hence Latin, spread to the far north and east of Europe, creating a much wider intellectual community of Latin users than had ever been known before. The styles and the learned vocabulary of the language were revised and extended, but the core lexicon and grammar of the language remained throughout quite unchanged. In this quasi-eternal, artificial form, as a language known only to clerics and scholars, Latin conveyed to all those who used it a sense of European unity that was quite compatible with the concurrent growth of literacy in vernacular languages: Latin provided a basis for European cooperation, conscious of allegiance to a single Catholic Church, while the various vernaculars, more and more conceived as national languages, underpinned a growing competition between nation-states. Europe could have it both ways, for a time.*

Ultimately, though, the independent vernacular traditions outgrew the centrally organized world of Latin. Rather than moving on toward a higher unity, ideas developed in the vernaculars—such as Luther's theology, Hobbes's politics, Galileo's physics—ended up shattering the assured and traditional certainties of the Latin-based canons. Through the Reformation and then the Enlightenment, competition and open speculation beggared the kind of intel-

---

*In western Europe's acceptance that there could be written versions of vernacular languages alongside the unchanging standard for the classical language, Latin assumed a different position from many other idealized languages for elite literacy, such as Greek, Arabic, Persian, Sanskrit, or classical Chinese. The highly conservative standards of these others largely monopolized all written language in their societies, while related spoken languages went on developing independently of them.

lectual consummation willed by the Catholic Church; traditionalists were left scrabbling to catch up with new learning. New ideas were henceforth to be translated into Latin, rather than conceived in it.

Machiavelli was a firm believer in some degree in language as a repository of memory. He wrote:

> ... the Christian sect moved against heathendom, canceling all its orders, ceremonies, and erasing all memory of that old theology. True, they did not succeed in erasing all knowledge of its excellent men; this was because Latin was maintained, under constraint because they needed it to write the new law. If they could have written this in a new language, in view of the other persecutions they carried out, there would have been no record of the past.
>
> Tuscany was powerful, full of religion and prowess; it had its customs and its home language; which was all erased by the power of Rome. And so, as has been said, the memory of its name is all that remains.[19]

Machiavelli had believed that it was the survival of Latin that had preserved large-scale and detailed memory of pre-Christian Rome, in the face of the Church's clear interest that it should be forgotten. The Etruscans, by contrast, for all their ancient glory, were just a name without a history, since the Romans had indeed blotted out their language. Machiavelli's fundamental point still stands. Languages, if they survive, make it easier to foster and preserve traditions of knowledge; loss of languages makes it far easier to dissipate them.

Latin did survive: its twenty-five hundred years of documented history make it unmatched as the language of Europe's memory. But by that same token it is above all a language of the past.

Limes (stem *limit-*) is the word for the boundary of the Roman Empire, and Ludwig Wittgenstein famously wrote, "The limits of my language mean the limits of my world."[20] Admittedly, Latin did establish itself—courtesy of the Catholic Church—well beyond the spatial limits of the Roman Empire, and temporally too it lived on as Europe's central language for a good 1,250 years after the Empire's western collapse. Yet the abiding character of Latin is embedded in the phrase *ad infinitum* 'on and on, without boundary'. The be-all and end-all of the Latin view of the world was European civilization, centered on Rome. The language's fading modern survivals, in the nostalgia of the Catholic Church, as the vehicle of countless aging legal documents and administrative records, in Finnish news roundups, even in the central terminology of the life sciences, all remind us of old aspirations to universality, but in a universe where all roads ultimately lead to Rome.

Latin was always a unifier. It was largely propagated through violence, even if sometimes (as in Norway in the tenth century, or Mexico in the sixteenth) that violence was nominally being deployed on behalf of the Christian God of love, and (just as ironically) knowledge of Latin was until recently passed on to each new generation with ample use of the *ferula*, that painful instrument of educational discipline. Once acquired though, it did provide a powerful means of recruiting European elites and integrating them into a common European tradition. Starting as a unifier of the Roman army, it became the vehicle of Roman law, of literature and the school curriculum, of state administration, of the Christian religion, of monasteries, universities, and chanceries in Europe, and (for a time) even in the New World. In all these fields, it left enduring legacies, which are only now fading, four centuries after its active use came to an end.

But Latin was so assertive of its universal importance and competence that the nature of its actual limits have come to jut out quite starkly. Just as there was always a human world beyond Rome's dominion, beyond Europe and the Mediterranean basin, so there were intellectual domains beyond any ken of Cicero, Augustine, Aquinas, or Erasmus. Influential geniuses of other civilizations, such as Panini in India, Ibn-Khaldun in Arabia, Zhuangzi in China, of course, all achieved their insights outside the Latin worldview; and these have been added to the world knowledge of the twenty-first century. But just as innocent of Latin are the last three hundred years of European thought itself, replete with electromagnetism, economics, psychology, mathematical logic, nuclear and quantum physics, geology, organic chemistry, genetics, informatics, and much else. All of these work with concepts that have no basis in the heritage of the classics, the medieval schools, or indeed the Renaissance humanists. Their technical terms may largely be derived from Greek or Latin—and the Vatican struggles like Sisyphus to keep Latin terminology up-to-date—but a Latin education will leave you quite unprepared for force fields, market equilibrium, archetypes, decidability, radioactivity, plate tectonics, polymers, selective pressure, or transaction processing.

Europe's vernaculars, which were never given universal status nor ever aspired to it, have turned out to be vehicles for the development of sciences that go far beyond the particular concerns of their own communities. The open-ended conception of the world and of the potential for learning, which paradoxically came into its own when the full, finite dimensions of the globe were discovered and explored, is still flourishing; and although a language such as English may find itself as a de facto lingua franca for the world—as Latin was once de jure for Europe—there is now no sense that this is the symbol of an unchanging, let alone a just, world order. The choice of the language that is used worldwide is a result of history; and like any creature of history, it is susceptible to change. Even Latin, with twenty-five hundred years of dominance behind it, found that. *Sic transit gloria mundi* 'so the glory of the world must pass'.[21]

Notes on the Latin Tags
in Chapter Headings

AD INFINITUM To a boundless extent, without end. Mostly used in mathematics.

FONS ET ORIGO Source and origin.

SUB ROSA Under a rose, meaning secret, told in the strictest confidence. Cupid gave Harpocrates, the god of silence, a rose urging him not to betray the amours of Venus. In fact, Harpocrates is a Greek form of the Egyptian god Horus, or Her-pa-khrad, whose symbol was a rose. The word ROSA may be a Latin borrowing from Etruscan.

CUI BONO? To whose (ultimate) benefit? This was a maxim of Roman lawyers, attempting to suggest that he who stood to gain most from a crime was the one most likely responsible for it.

EXCELSIOR Higher. The motto of New York State. Henry Longfellow published in 1841 a poem with this title. It begins, "The shades of night were falling fast, | As through an Alpine village passed | A youth, who bore, 'mid snow and ice, | A banner with the strange device, | Excelsior!"

FELIX CONIUNCTIO Happy union. A quote from the medieval profane lyrics *Carmina Burana*: *Si puer cum puellula moraretur in cellula, felix coniunctio* 'If a boy with a girl should tarry in a little room, happy union!'

URBI ET ORBI To the city (or Rome) and to the world. The focus of the public blessing given by the pope from the balcony of St. Peter's.

VOX POPULI VOX DEI The voice of the people (is) the voice of God. A very old proverb, which Charlemagne's minister Alcuin for one thought was misleading: *Nec audiendi qui solent dicere, Vox populi, vox Dei, quum tumultuositas vulgi semper insaniae proxima sit* 'Do not listen to those who say that the voice of the people is the voice of God, since the riotousness of the common people always is close to insanity' (*Epistles*, 16.9). It is the source of the slang word for consulting popular opinion in a media view, the *vox pop*.

DIES IRAE Day of Wrath. Name of a famous verse meditation on the Day of Judgment by Thomas of Celano, who died around 1255.

ULTRA VIRES Beyond one's powers, or beyond the limit of one's authority. The full legal maxim is *Ultra vires nihil aggrediendum* 'Nothing should be undertaken beyond one's powers'.

LAPSUS LINGUAE Slip of the tongue. Contrasted with *lapsus calami* 'slip of the pen' and *lapsus memoriae* 'slip of memory'.

AMOR VINCIT OMNIA Love conquers all. It is written on a brooch worn by the Prioress in Chaucer's prologue to the *Canterbury Tales*, l. 162. It is in fact a misquotation of a line of Virgil's: *omnia vincit amor: nos et cedamus amori* 'Love conquers all. Let us too yield to love' (*Eclogues* x.69).

LITTERAE HUMANIORES The more humane kind of literature, civilized learning. The phrase came into use in the late Middle Ages to contrast secular literary studies from sacred texts and theology. It is now best known as the title of Oxford University's Classics BA course, also known as "lit hum" or Greats.

EX ORIENTE LUX From the east (comes) light. Evidently a reference to the dawn, but also the origins of Christianity to the east of Europe. The full form of the medieval proverb is *Ex oriente lux, ex occidente lex* 'From the east light, from the west law'.

ALTER EGO Another I, a second self. Usually means a partner in whom one feels complete confidence.

DEUS EX MACHINA God from a contrivance. A reference to ancient stagecraft, whereby a figure representing a god could be lowered from a hoist at the end of a play. Such endings were always felt to be contrived.

NOVUS ORBIS A New World. The first expression used of the Americas, appearing in the title of Peter Martyr's first Latin description of the early explorations: *De Orbe Novo* 'On the New World' (1530).

DECUS ET TUTAMEN Honor and protection. Virgil's description of an ornate breastplate: *viro decus et tutamen in armis* 'a glory to a man, and a protection in war' (*Aeneid*, v.262). It also appears as a legend on pound coins minted for England.

EHEU FUGACES Alas, fleeting. Allusion to a famous lament on age by Horace, which begins *Eheu fugaces, Postume, Postume, labuntur anni* 'Alas, fleeting, O my Postumus, the years slip away' (*Odes*, 2.14).

SUB SPECIE AETERNITATIS From the eternal viewpoint. A phrase derived from Benedict Spinoza, in full *sub quadam specie aeternitatis* 'under some aspect of eternity', to designate what is always true, without reference to the circumstances that change through time.

Etruscan Borrowings in Latin

This is a liberal list, supplementing the list of clearly attested borrowings on the assumption that early words that have no Italic etymology are likely to be Etruscan, especially if they have recognizable Etruscan word endings (*-eus*, *-enna*, *-erna*, *-īna*, *-issa*, *-ō*, *-ulus*, *-urnum*) or are deformed versions of Greek. Such words borrowed through Etruscan from a Greek original are marked in italics. Latin stems, when recognizable, have been underlined and marked with a following 'L'. Hardly any of these words can be identified in Etruscan texts.

ANIMALS
catulus 'puppy'
curc-/gurguliō 'corn
 weevil'
excetra 'water snake'
formica 'ant'
orca 'grampus'
vitulus 'yearling'
voltur 'vulture'

BUILDINGS
ātrium 'forecourt'
cella 'closet'
*cist*erna 'cistern'
columna 'column'
fala 'gantry, mobile
 scaffolding'

favissa 'temple tank'
fenestra 'window'
fornix 'arch'
grunda 'gutter'
taberna 'inn, shop'
turris 'tower'

CLOTHES
balteus 'belt'
burra 'shoddy'
calceus 'shoe'
cappa 'cap'
cimussa 'cloak cord'
lacerna 'light cloak'
laena 'warm cloak'
*pall*a, *pall*ium 'cloak'
 (Greek-style)

tebenna 'toga' (early
 style)
*tun*ica 'tunic'

COMMERCE
aril<u>lāt</u>or L 'huckster'
caupō 'shopkeeper'
cociō 'dealer'
lēna 'madam'
lēnō 'pimp'
mangō 'slaver'
mantissa
 'makeweight'
numerus 'number'
nummus 'coin'
paelex 'whore'
<u>soci</u>ennus L 'partner'

COOKERY AND DINING

amurca 'olive juice'
arvīna 'lard'
botulus 'black pudding'
caepa/-e 'onion'
caseus 'cheese'
cotōneum 'quince'
crāpula 'hangover'
culīna 'kitchen'
lucuns 'sweetmeat'
madulsa 'drunkenness'
mantissa 'makeweight'
mitulus 'mussel'
puls 'porridge'
sagīna 'fattening'

ENTERTAINMENT

ālea, āleō 'dice, gambler'
d<u>oss</u>ennus L 'hunchback'
gānea 'chophouse' harēna 'sand'
histriō 'actor'
lanista 'trainer' (of gladiators)
<u>lūd</u>iō L 'actor'
lustra, lustrō 'low dive, lowlife'
mīriō 'ugly type'
mōriō 'fool'
murmillō 'fish-crested gladiator'
persona 'masked actor, character'
sanniō 'buffoon'
satura 'patter, medley'
subulō 'piper'
tuba 'trumpet'

HOUSEHOLD ITEMS

calpar 'wine jar'
cerussa 'white lead' (for cosmetics)
clarnus 'platter'
cortīna 'cauldron'
crēterra 'mixing bowl'
crumēna 'purse'
fascinum 'phallic charm'
lagēna 'bottle'
lanterna 'lantern'
lepista 'large cup'
<u>luc</u>erna L 'lamp'
orca 'type of vessel'
situlus 'bucket'
sporta 'basket'
tapēte 'rug'
*tīna/tīni*um 'wine jar'
urceus 'pitcher'
urna 'urn'

LITIGATION

aerumna 'trouble'
calumnia 'slander'
damnum 'loss'
rabula 'ranting speaker'
sculna 'arbiter'

MILITARY

cācula 'batman'
lixa 'camp follower'
mīles 'soldier'
satelles 'bodyguard'
tīrō 'raw recruit'
triumphus 'triumph'
vāgīna 'sheath'
vēles 'light infantryman'

NATURE

aevum 'age'
Aprīlis 'April'
autumnus 'autumn'
caelum 'sky'
Idūs 'middle of month'
mundus 'adornment, world, undercroft'
puteus 'well'
tellūs 'world'

PEOPLE

barginna/-ena, bargus, 'dullard'
barō 'blockhead'
buccō 'blockhead'
burrus 'redhead'
carisa 'foxy lady'
catamīta 'catamite'
gāneō 'glutton'
helluō 'splurger'
<u>lev</u>enna L 'wimp'
lurchō 'glutton'
populus 'people'
scurra 'city slicker'
verna 'born slave'

PLANTS

alaternus 'shrub'
fusterna 'knot wood'
genista 'broom'
laburnum 'shrub'
malva 'mallow'
murtus 'myrtle'
rosa 'rose'
viburnum 'shrub'

RELIGION

caerimonia
  'observance'
camillus 'altar boy'
cupencus 'priest of
  Hercules'
lustrum 'lustration rite'
obscēnus 'ominous'
popa 'subpriest'
rite 'duly'
sacēna 'ritual ax'
templum 'temple'
turunda 'sacred cake,
  meal pellet'
tutulus 'priest's cap'

BODY PARTS

caperra 'wrinkle'
cōleus 'testicle'
gemursa 'foot corn'
muttō 'penis'
palātus/-um 'palate'
poples 'knee'
ruma/-is 'teat'
sopiō 'penis'
ulna 'elbow'
verpa 'penis'

SHIPS

ancora 'anchor'
antemna 'yardarm'
aplustra 'stern figure-
  head'
guberna 'steering oars'
guberniō 'helmsman'
prōra/-is 'prow'
saburra 'ballast'
sentīna 'bilge'

TOOLS

bura/-is 'plough
  beam'
catēna 'bracket, chain'
cūpa 'mill handle'
grūma 'surveyor's pole'
lāmina 'blade'
nassiterna
  'sprinkler pot'
santerna 'borax'
tollennō 'swing beam'
tra(n)senna 'bird net'

TRADESMEN

agasō 'ostler'
fullō 'fuller'

laniēna 'butcher's stall'
lanius 'butcher'
nacca 'fuller'
opīliō 'herdsman'
vispillō 'sexton'

WRITING

cēra 'wax'
elementum 'letter'
forma 'shape'
littera 'letter'
titulus 'label'

OTHER ADJECTIVES

āter 'matt black'
celer 'swift'
pulcher 'beautiful'
spurcus 'dirty'
spurius 'bastard'
velox 'swift'

EXCLAMATIONS

hercle (men's oath)
talassiō (wedding)
triumpe (at rustic
  festivals, military
  celebrations)

◇◦◉◦◇

Effects of Sound Changes
on Latin Nouns and Verbs

Some of the more common patterns are set out on the following pages. Taken together with the coalescence of ĭ/ē and ŭ/ō, and the fact that in unstressed syllables there would be little audible difference between e and ε, o and ɔ, one can see that there was not much left of the distinctive markers in the paradigms.

NOUN	OLD (CLASSICAL)				NEW (ROMANCE)			
SINGULAR	'lord'	'life'	'wine'	'dog'	'lord'	'life'	'wine'	'dog'
Nominative	*dominus*	*uitā*	*uinum*	*canis*	dóminɔ(s)	vída	vínɔ	cánɛ(s)
Accusative	*dominum*	*uităm*	*uinum*	*canĕm*	dóminɔ	vída	vínɔ	cánɛ
Genitive	*dominī*	*uitae*	*uinī*	*canis*	dómini	víde	víni	cánɛ
Dative	*dominō*	*uitae*	*uinō*	*canī*	dóminɔ	víde	vínɔ	cáni
Ablative	*dominō*	*uitā*	*uinō*	*canĕ*	dóminɔ	vída	vínɔ	cáne

NOUN	OLD (CLASSICAL)				NEW (ROMANCE)			
PLURAL	'lords'	'lives'	'wines'	'dogs'	'lords'	'lives'	'wines'	'dogs'
Nominative	*dominī*	*uitae*	*uina*	*canēs*	dómini	víde	vína	cáne(s)
Accusative	*dominōs*	*uitas*	*uina*	*canēs*	dóminɔ(s)	vída(s)	vína	cáne(s)
Genitive	*dominōrum*	*uitārum*	*uinōrum*	*canŭm*	dominórɔ	vidárɔ	vinórɔ	cánɔ
Dative	*dominīs*	*uitīs*	*uinīs*	*canĭbūs*	dómini(s)	vídi(s)	víni(s)	cánibɔ(s)
Ablative	*dominīs*	*uitīs*	*uinīs*	*canĭbūs*	dómini(s)	vidi(s)	víni(s)	cánibɔ(s)

VERB	OLD (CLASSICAL)				NEW (ROMANCE)			
	'love'	'send'	'used to love'	'sent'	'love'	'send'	'used to love'	'sent'
I	amō	mittō	amābam	mīsī	ámo	mɛ́to	amáva	mísi
thou	amās	mittis	amābās	misistī	áma(s)	mɛ́tɛ(s)	amáva(s)	misísti
he/she	amat	mittit	amābāt	mīsit	áma	mɛ́tɛ	amáva	mísɛ
we	amāmus	mittimus	amābāmus	mīsimus	amámɔ(s)	mɛ́tɛmɔ(s)	amávamɔ(s)	mísɛmɔ(s)
you	amātis	mittitis	amābātis	mīsistis	amádɛ(s)	mɛ́tedɛ(s)	amávadɛ(s)	misístɛ(s)
they	amant	mittunt	amābant	mīserunt	áman(ə)	mɛ́tɔn(ə)	amávan(ə)	misɛ́rɔn(ə)

Notes

CHAPTER I: *AD INFINITUM*—AN EMPIRE LIVED IN LATIN

1. Virgil, *Aeneid*, vi 851–53.
2. Papyri from Leipzig (P. Lips.) 40 (Hermopolis), recorded in Adams 2003: 385.
3. Tacitus, *Agricola*, xv: SINGVLOS SIBI OLIM REGES FVISSE, NVNC BINOS IMPONI, E QVIBVS LEGATVS IN SANGVINEM, PROCVRATOR IN BONA SAEVIRET. AEQVE DISCORDIAM PRAEPOSITORVM, AEQVE CONCORDIAM SVBIECTIS EXITIOSAM. ALTERIVS MANVS CENTVRIONES, ALTERIVS SERVOS VIM ET CONTVMELIAS MISCERE . . . QVANTVLVM ENIM TRANSISSE MILITVM, SI SESE BRITANNI NVMERENT?
4. Tacitus, *Agricola*, xxxi: AC SICVT IN FAMILIA RECENTISSIMVS QVISQVE SER-VORVM ETIAM CONSERVIS LVDIBRIO EST, SIC IN HOC ORBIS TERRARVM VETERE FAMVLATV NOVI NOS ET VILES IN EXCIDIVM PETIMVR; NEQVE ENIM ARVA NOBIS AVT METALLA AVT PORTVS SVNT, QVIBVS EXERCENDIS RE-SERVEMVR 'Just as among household slaves the newest is pilloried even by his fellow slaves, so among the old slaves of the world we shall be the new boys, in demand as cheap to waste, since we have no farms or mines or ports for which we could be kept to run.' Scotland's people are seen as less valuable because they have no expertise, no civilized institutions that might interest Rome.
5. Tacitus, *Agricola*, xxi: IAM VERO PRINCIPVM FILIOS LIBERALIBVS ARTIBVS ERVDIRE, ET INGENIA BRITANNORVM STVDIIS GALLORVM ANTEFERRE, VT QVI MODO LINGVAM ROMANAM ABNVEBANT, ELOQVENTIAM CONCVPISCERENT. INDE ETIAM HABITVS NOSTRI HONOR ET FREQVENS TOGA; PAVLATIMQVE DISCESSVM AD DELENIMENTA VITIORVM, PORTICVS ET BALINEA ET CONVIV-IORVM ELEGANTIAM. IDQVE APVD IMPERITOS HVMANITAS VOCABATVR, CVM PARS SERVITVTIS ESSET.
6. Juvenal, *Satires*, xv.110–12. Britain was a byword for remoteness to the Romans, and Thule, even farther north, might as well have been the north pole.
7. Ovid (43 BC–AD 17), *Tristia*, v.10.35–42:
   EXERCENT ILLI SOCIAE COMMERCIA LINGVAE: | PER GESTVM RES EST SIGNIFICANDA MIHI.
   BARBARVS HIC EGO SVM, QVI NON INTELLEGOR VLLI, | ET RIDENT STOLIDI VERBA LATINA GETAE;

MEQVE PALAM DE ME TVTO MALA SAEPE LOQVVNTVR, | FORSITAN OBICIVNT EXILIVMQVE MIHI.

VTQVE FIT, IN ME ALIQVID FICTI, DICENTIBVS ILLIS | ABNVERIM QVOTIENS ANNVERIMQVE, PVTANT.

8. Museum of London.

9. 55 RIB 369 (Caerleon): D(IIS) M(ANIBVS) | TADIA VALLAVNIVS VIXIT | ANN. LXV ET TADIVS EXVPER(A)TVS FILIVS VIXIT ANN. XXXVII DEFVN(C) | TVS EXPEDITIONE GERMANICA | TADIA EXVPERATA FILIA | MATRI ET FRATRI PIISS(I)MA | SECVS TVMVLVM | PATRIS POSVIT.

10. RIB 156 (Bath): IVLIVS VITA | LIS FABRICIE(N)S | IS LEG(IONIS) XX V(ALERIAE) V(ICTRICIS) STIPEND(I)OR | VM IX AN(N)OR(VM) XX | IX NATIONE BE | LGA EX COL(L)EG(I)O | FABRICE(NSIVM) ELATV | S H(IC) S(ITVS) E(ST).

11. RIB 163 (Bath): RVSONIA AVENTINAE C MEDIOMATRIC ANNOR(VM) LVIII H(IC) S(ITA) E(ST) L(VCIVS) VLPIVS SESTIVS H(ERES) F(ACIENDVM) C(VRAVIT).

12. RIB 152 (Bath): LOCVM RELI | GIOSVM PER IN | SOLENTIAM DI | RVTVM | VIRTVT(E) ET N(VMINE) | AVGVSTI REPVRGA | TVM REDDIDIT | C. SEVERIVS EMERITVS C(ENTVRIO) | REG(IONARIVS).

13. D(IIS) M(ANIBVS) | AN(N)IA BVTVRRA | VIRIATI FILIA | AN(NORVM) XXX. H(IC) S(ITA).

14. Malone 1924: DIS MANIBVS L . ARTORIVS CASTVS . CENTVRIONI LEGIONIS | III GALLICAE . ITEM CENTVRIONI LEGIONIS VI FERRA | TAE . ITEM & LEG . II ADIVTRICIS . ITEM & LEG V MA | CEDONICAE . ITEM PRIMO PILO EIVSDEM PRAEPOSITO | CLASSIS MISENATIVM PRAEFECTO LEGIONIS VI | VICTRICIS. DVCI LEG COHORTIVM ALARVM BRITANICI | NIARVM ADVERSVS ARMORICANOS. PROCVRATORI CENTE | NARIO PROVINCIAE LIBVRNIAE IVRE GLADI . VI | VVS IPSE SIBI ET SVIS.

15. IMP(ERATORE) CAESARE DIVI F(ILIO) AVG(VSTO) PON(TIFICE) MAX(IMO) TR(IBVNICIA) POT(ESTATE) XXIV CO(N)S(VLE) XIII PATRE PATR(IAE) | ANNOBAL RVFVS ORNATOR PATRIAE AMATOR CONCORDIAE | FLAMEN SVFES PRAEF(ECTVS) SACR(ORVM) HIMILCHONIS TAPAPI F(ILIVS) D(E) S(VA) P(ECVNIA) FAC(IENDVM) COER(AVIT) | IDEMQ(VE) DEDICAVIT.

16. Aelius Aristides, *To Rome*, xxviii–xxix, ci–ciii (my translation of a Greek original). As to the place-names mentioned as making up Rome's "courtyard fence," Aelius literally has *eruthrá . . . thálatta* 'red sea', *Neílou katarráktai* 'Nile cataracts', *límnē Maiôtis* 'lake of Maeotis'. Only the first of these has a reference that is in doubt; but it is unlikely that Aelius' own geography was clear, and the *períplous thalássēs eruthraías* 'voyage round the reddish sea', written about a century before his work, in fact describes the Indian Ocean coasts, not just the Red Sea.

17. Dalby 2002: 46.

18. Pliny the Elder (AD 23–79), *Naturalis Historia*, iii.39: TOT POPVLORVM DISCORDES FERASQVE LINGVAS SERMONIS COMMERCIO CONTRAHERET AD COLLOQVIA ET HVMANITATEM HOMINI DARET, BREVITERQVE VNA CVNCTARVM GENTIVM IN TOTO ORBE PATRIA FIERET.

19. Suetonius, *Tiberius*, lxxvi; *Divus Claudius*, xvi. In both these cases, Suetonius— perhaps representing Roman common sense—sees these actions as eccentric.

20. Cicero, *Brutus*, 37,140: NON ENIM TAM PRAECLARVM EST SCIRE LATINE QVAM TVRPE NESCIRE.

21. Plautus, *Poenulus*, 112–13: ET IS OMNES LINGVAS SCIT, SED DISSIMVLAT SCIENS SE SCIRE: POENVS PLANE EST. QVID VERBIS OPVST?

22. *Tabulae Vindolandenses*, ii.164, recorded in Bowman 2003: 103. BRITTONES NIMIVM MVLTI EQVITES GLADIS NON VTVNTVR EQVITES NEC RESIDVNT BRITTVNCVLI VT IACVLOS MITTANT. Translation mine.

23. Cicero, *Pro M. Fonteio*, xi: REFERTA GALLIA NEGOTIATORVM EST, PLENA CIVIVM ROMANORVM. NEMO GALLORVM SINE CIVE ROMANO QVICQVAM NEGOTI GERIT, NVMMVS IN GALLIA NVLLVS SINE CIVIVM ROMANORVM TABVLIS COMMOVETVR.

24. Cicero, *de Imperio Cn. Pompeii*, 65: DIFFICILE EST DICTV, QVIRITES, QVANTO IN ODIO SIMVS APVD EXTERAS NATIONES PROPTER EORVM, QVOS AD EAS PER HOS ANNOS CVM IMPERIO MISIMVS, LIBIDINES ET INIVRIAS. QVOD ENIM FANVM PVTATIS IN ILLIS TERRIS NOSTRIS MAGISTRATIBVS RELIGIOSVM, QVAM CIVITATEM SANCTAM, QVAM DOMVM SATIS CLAVSAM AC MVNITAM FVISSE? VRBES IAM LOCVPLETES ET COPIOSAE REQVIRVNTVR, QVIBVS CAVSA BELLI PROPTER DIRIPIENDI CVPIDITATEM INFERATVR.

25. Rutilius Namatianus, *de Reditu suo*, I.63–66: FECISTI PATRIAM DIVERSIS GENTIBVS VNAM: PROFVIT INIVSTIS TE DOMINANTE CAPI DVMQVE OFFERS VICTIS PROPRII CONSORTIA IVRIS, VRBEM FECISTI QVOD PRIVS ORBIS ERAT.

26. Juvenal, vii.148–49.

27. Varro, *De Re Rustica*, i.1.6: NEC NON ETIAM PRECOR LYMPHAM AC BONVM EVENTVM, QVONIAM SINE AQVA OMNIS ARIDA AC MISERA AGRI CVLTVRA, SINE SVCCESSV AC BONO EVENTV FRVSTRATIO EST, NON CVLTVRA.

28. Pliny, *Naturalis Historia*, xxix.21.

29. Ovid, *Tristia*, iv.5.2: VNICA FORTVNIS ARA REPERTA MEIS.

CHAPTER 2: *FONS ET ORIGO*—LATIN'S KIN

1. Cato, *De Re Rustica*, I, ll. 3–8.

2. Inscription on drinking bowl found near Cività Castellana. Corpus Inscriptionum Etruscarum, 8179–80.

3. Dionysius of Halicarnassus. At iv.26.4–5 he mentions such a column set up by Servius Tullius (which would be sixth century) still existing in his day (end of the first century BC); and at x.32.4 he mentions another, to record the Lex Icilia, passed in 456 BC.

4. The Forum Romanum cippus, found in 1899. See, for example, Baldi 2002: 202–4. Since the text is fragmentary, preserving only isolated words at the beginnings and ends of alternate lines, it is difficult to say what its purpose was. Since some of the lines were recorded upside down, it might be evidence that the inscriber's work was not actually read very much.

5. Harris 1989, 151–52, elaborates reasons for distrusting the literal truth of this tradition.

6. Polybius, *Histories*, iii.22.

7. I basically follow the interpretation of Pisani 1960. But I have provided what I believe to be a new interpretation of the problematic MITAT, seeing it as a denominative formation from *mītis* 'gentle', comparable formally to *levat* 'lifts' < *levis* 'light', *piscatur* 'fishes' < *piscis* 'fish', *testatur* 'testifies'< *testis* 'witness'. The first ME is then an ablative of the instrument. This seems to fit the aphrodisiac interpretation exactly.

CHAPTER 3: *SUB ROSA*—LATIN'S ETRUSCAN STEPMOTHER

1. *Liber Linteus* (reconstructed from the bandages of the Mummy of Zagreb), v.19–23. The original is written from right to left. I have followed Facchetti 2000: 275 in transcribing the Etruscan sibilants as *s* and *sh*, in accord with our understanding of Northern Etruscan spelling (Facchetti 2000: 20).

2. E.g., in Pindar's ode commemorating Hiero's victory at Cumae (*Pythia*, i.72).

3. Both these inscriptions are illustrated on Cristofani 1984: 46–47.

4. *Tursci* would naturally be simplified to *Tusci* in Latin (cf *Maspiter* < *Mars* + *pater*; *tostu*s < *tors-tus*); but in any case the original form is found in Umbrian as *turskum* (Niedermann 1953: 157). *Etruria* shows the same root before the suffix-ia; it is regular in Latin for *s* to change to *r* between two vowels, e.g., when the word *rūs* 'countryside' adds genitive -is, it becomes *rūris*.

5. This can be equated with Etruscan TRUS because of some extra facts about Etruscan phonology. As it happens, the Etruscan language lacked the sound [o]; in adopting the alphabet from the Euboean Greeks, the letter O was dropped, and this was why a language such as Oscan that derived its alphabet from the Etruscans ended up using *Ú* to denote O. So it is very likely that ancient [o] in Etruscan words had been changed to [u]. For a historical linguist, this etymology is almost impeccable.

6. See Georgiev 1981: 247. The only cautions concern the order of the *u* and the *r*, and the gratuitous *e* that begins the forms where the root begins with tr-. But metathesis of *r* with a high vowel (*u* or *i*) is common in language change; and so is the insertion of a supporting vowel before consonant clusters. E.g., Spanish *estado* from Latin *statum*; Turkish *ıspor* from French *sport*.

7. Herodotus, i.94.

8. Dionysius of Halicarnassus, i.28.

9. Ogilvie 1976: 34.

10. De Simone 1996, Rix 1998, Schumacher 1998; Facchetti 2000: 24–31, 40–43.

11. *Claudii Caesaris Oratio Lugdunensis*, col. i.

12. First, they lack Indo-European etymologies (unlike, for example, the words in Latin's more distant neighbors Oscan and Venetic); second, they tend to have certain characteristic endings: -us(s)a, -is(s)a, -in(n)a, -erna, -erra, -e(n)na, -eus, -ulus, -(i)ō, -es (with stem -it-). Many more are masculine nouns with a one-syllable stem and the ending -a. As borrowed words, they may not have stabilized their ending, alternating say between -is and -a. Recognizing these properties of "Etruscan Latin" has made it possible for modern scholars (notably Ernout 1930) to lengthen the list.

13. Livy, vii.2: LVDI QVOQVE SCENICI, NOVA RES BELLICOSO POPVLO—NAM CIRCI MODO SPECTACVLVM FVERAT—INTER ALIA CAELESTIS IRAE PLACAMINA INSTITVTI DICVNTVR; CETERVM PARVA QVOQVE, VT FERME PRINCIPIA OMNIA, ET EA IPSA PEREGRINA RES FVIT. SINE CARMINE VLLO, SINE IMITANDORVM CARMINVM ACTV LVDIONES EX ETRVRIA ACCITI, AD TIBICINIS MODOS SALTANTES, HAVD INDECOROS MOTVS MORE TVSCO DABANT. IMITARI DEINDE EOS IVVENTVS, SIMVL INCONDITIS INTER SE IOCVLARIA FVNDENTES VERS-IBVS, COEPERE; NEC ABSONI A VOCE MOTVS ERANT. ACCEPTA ITAQVE RES SAEPIVSQVE VSVRPANDO EXCITATA. VERNACVLIS ARTIFICIBVS, QVIA ISTER TVSCO VERBO LVDIO VOCABATVR, NOMEN HISTRIONIBVS INDITVM; QVI NON,

SICVT ANTE, FESCENNINO VERSV SIMILEM INCOMPOSITVM TEMERE AC RVDEM
ALTERNIS IACIEBANT SED IMPLETAS MODIS SATVRAS DESCRIPTO IAM AD
TIBICINEM CANTV MOTVQVE CONGRVENTI PERAGEBANT.

14. We already know enough Etruscan to see *avil* 'year' in Aule, *puple* 'army' in Puplie, and *spur* 'city' in Spurie. To these the Romans added two ordinal numerals (Sextus, Decimus) inspired perhaps by Quintus, which can be understood as 'fifth', Manius for the Di Manes 'the good gods', and Numerius, which did service also as a *gentilicium*. Three more, Salvius, Statius, and Vibius, were added from the Oscan tradition, and this completed the short set of *praenōmina* in use.

A few more male forenames did not get accepted into Latin use, although they often have Latin transcriptions: e.g., *Arnth* 'Aruns', *Vel, Larce/Larth/Laris* 'Lars', *Sethre*. Etruscan also had forenames for females: *Aula/Aulia, Vela/Velia, Sethra, Arnthi, Larthi*, as well as *Thana, Ramtha, Ravntha, Hastia*, and the famous queen's name *Thanchvil*, meaning 'gift of Thana', Latin 'Tanaquil'.

15. Facchetti 2000: 61.
16. Peruzzi 1973.

CHAPTER 4: *CUI BONO?*—ROME'S WINNING WAYS

1. Watmough 1997: ch. iv.
2. Sallust, *Catilina*, 51: MAIORES NOSTRI, PATRES CONSCRIPTI, NEQVE CONSILI NEQVE AVDACIAE VMQVAM EGVERE; NEQVE ILLIS SVPERBIA OBSTAT, QVO MINVS ALIENA INSTITVTA, SI MODO PROBA ERANT, IMITARENTVR. ARMA ATQVE TELA MILITARIA AB SAMNITIBVS, INSIGNIA MAGISTRATVVM AB TVSCIS PLERAQVE SVMPSERVNT. POSTREMO, QVOD VBIQVE APVD SOCIOS AVT HOSTIS IDONEVM VIDEBATVR, CVM SVMMO STVDIO DOMI EXSEQVEBANTVR: IMITARI QVAM INVIDERE BONIS MALEBANT.
3. Greek original in von Arnim 1892: 121–22. Translation mine.
4. The importance of any legal distinction between citizen and Latin colonies has been queried (Sherwin-White 1973: 36, 77); at any rate, linguistically, and in the long term, it has no significance. After 80 BC in any case, all free Italians south of the Po enjoyed full citizenship (Sherwin-White 1973: 165). The population statistic is taken from Barraclough 1978: 86.
5. Seneca, *Consolatio ad Helviam*, vii.7: ROMANVM IMPERIVM NEMPE AVCTOREM EXVLEM RESPICIT, QVEM PROFVGVM CAPTA PATRIA, EXIGVAS RELIQVIAS TRAHENTEM, NECESSITAS ET VICTORIS METVS LONGINQVA QVAERENTEM IN ITALIAM DETVLIT. HIC DEINDE POPVLVS QVOT COLONIAS IN OMNEM PROVIN-CIAM MISIT! VBICVMQVE VICIT ROMANVS, HABITAT. AD HANC COMMVTATIO-NEM LOCORVM LIBENTES NOMINA DABANT, ET RELICTIS ARIS SVIS TRANS MARIA SEQVEBATVR COLONOS SENEX.
6. Hopkins 1978: 43–44.
7. Kaimio 1972.
8. Ibid., 133–34.
9. Ibid., 139.
10. The phenomenon characterized by Joshua Fishman as wanting to be "Xmen without Xish" (Fishman 1991: 16–17).

11.   Cicero, *Epistulae ad Familiares*, vii.1 (to M. Marius).
12.   FOEDVS OMNIVM FOEDERVM SANCTISSIMVM ATQVE AEQVISSIMVM (Cicero, *pro L. Cornelio Balbo*, 46).
13.   London, British Museum. Credits: Barbara McManus, 2001.
14.   Kaimio 1972: 13, citing F. G. Mohl 1889: 99–101, 137–39.
15.   Strabo, vi.1.2.

CHAPTER 5: *EXCELSIOR*—LOOKING UP TO GREEK

1.   Plutarch, *Romulus*, vi.1.
2.   Livy, v.1. Roman religious law forbade the consultation of foreign oracles. In fact, Rome's Etruscan neighbor Caere was also in regular touch with the Delphic oracle. Ogilvie 1976: 661.
3.   Pliny, *Naturalis Historia*, xxxiv.26.
4.   Arrian, *Alexander's Campaign*, vii.15.5–6
5.   Feeney 2005: 229–31: Persia, Carthage, as well as the other Italian states of the period, are all citable as well-established, literate societies that had no literature to call their own. It was a radical step for Romans to see their language as capable of sustaining something comparable to Greek.
6.   Ennius, *Hedyphagetica*, cited by Apuleius, *Apologia*, xxxix.2. Classical Latin poetry uses a quantitative meter, based on a pattern of heavy (long) and light (short) syllables, rather than (as most modern European poetry) on a stress rhythm. A syllable is heavy if it has a long vowel, or any vowel followed by two consonants; otherwise it is light. *Hexameter* is Greek for 'six measure', and a line has six measures (feet), each beginning with a heavy syllable, all but the last followed by two light ones. A foot made up of a heavy followed by two lights is called a *dactyl* (Greek for 'finger'). The last foot is a heavy followed by one more syllable, either heavy or light. In practice, any pair of lights can be replaced by a heavy, though this is almost unknown in the fifth foot. Each line therefore ends with a distinctive "tum-ti-ti tum-tum" rhythm.
       Scanning the line we have here, with the usual symbols for heavy and light, it looks like:

   BRŪNDĬSĬ | Ī SĀR | GŪS ‖ BŎNŬS | ĒST; HŪNC, | MĀGNŬS | SĪ ĔRĬT, | SŪMĚ

   The divisions between the feet are marked by |. The ‖ marks the *caesura* 'cut', the point in the line where there is an obligatory word-break (as also at the end of the line); otherwise words can run on arbitrarily across the feet.
       There are, of course, many other refinements, but this is the basic theory. In case the keen reader is perplexed, I should add that this hexameter is in fact a substandard example: the second syllable of ERIT should be heavy, not light, since its vowel I is followed by two consonants; and more oddly, it has seven feet!
7.   *Heauton Timorumenos* (Greek: 'taking it out on himself'), prol. 16–19: NAM QVOD DISTVLERVNT MALEVOLI | MVLTAS CONTAMINASSE GRAECAS, DVM FACIT | PAVCAS LATINAS: FACTVM ID ESSE NON NEGAT | NEQVE SE PIGERE ET DEINDE FACTVRVM AVTVMAT.

8. *Asinaria* 'Donkey Story', prol. II; *Trinummus* 'Three-Dollar Day', prol. 19.

9. Justin, *Epitome of the Philippic Histories of T. Pompeius Trogus*, xx.5.12–13: FACTO SENATVS CONSVLTO, NE QVIS POSTEA KARTHAGINIENSIS AVT LITTERIS GRAECIS AVT SERMONI STVDERET, NE AVT LOQVI CVM HOSTE AVT SCRIBERE SINE INTERPRETE POSSET. This was in the context of a Carthaginian war in Sicily with the Greek colony Syracuse, around 409 BC.

10. Polybius, iii.20.5; Diodorus Siculus, xxvi.4; Cornelius Nepos, *Hannibal*, xiii.3.

11. Livy, xxviii.46 fin.

12. Polybius, v.105.

13. Harris 1979: 69.

14. Pliny, *Naturalis Historia*, xxxiii.57.

15. Tainter 1988: 129, citing Jean-Philippe Lévy, 1967, *The Economic Life of the Ancient World*, tr. V. Biram (Chicago Press).

16. Harris 1979: 70; Livy, xxxix.7.

17. Livy, xxxix.6: LVXVRIAE ENIM PEREGRINAE ORIGO AB EXERCITV ASIATICO INVECTA IN VRBEM EST.

18. Harris 1979: 71. Rome's public works were negotiated through a considerable system of public-private partnerships, as Polybius, a contemporary witness, vi.17, recounts.

19. Cicero, *Cato on Old Age*, 55: CVRIO AD FOCVM SEDENTI MAGNVM AVRI PONDVS SAMNITES CVM ATTVLISSENT, REPVDIATI SVNT; NON ENIM AVRVM HABERE PRAECLARVM SIBI VIDERI DIXIT, SED EIS QVI HABERENT AVRVM IMPERARE. On the battle over Rome's level of intent, see the contributors to Champion 2003: ch. 1.

20. Polybius, xvi.34.3.

21. Ibid., xxxi.24

22. Suetonius, *De Grammaticis*, 2.

23. Quintilian, *Institutio Oratoria*, i.12–14: A SERMONE GRAECO PVERVM INCIPERE MALO, QVIA LATINVM, QVI PLVRIBVS IN VSV EST, VEL NOBIS NOLENTIBVS PERBIBET, SIMVL QVIA DISCIPLINIS QVOQVE GRAECIS PRIVS INSTITVENDVS EST, VNDE ET NOSTRAE FLVXERVNT. NON TAMEN HOC ADEO SVPERSTITIOSE FIERI VELIM VT DIV TANTVM GRAECE LOQVATVR AVT DISCAT, SICVT PLERIS-QVE MORIS EST. HOC ENIM ACCIDVNT ET ORIS PLVRIMA VITIA IN PER-EGRINVM SONVM CORRVPTI ET SERMONIS, CVI CVM GRAECAE FIGVRAE ADSIDVA CONSVETVDINE HAESERVNT, IN DIVERSA QVOQVE LOQVENDI RA-TIONE PERTINACISSIME DVRANT. NON LONGE ITAQVE LATINA SVBSEQVI DEBENT ET CITO PARITER IRE. ITA FIET VT, CVM AEQVALI CVRA LINGVAM VTRAMQVE TVERI COEPERIMVS, NEVTRA ALTERI OFFICIAT.

24. Valerius Maximus, ii.2.3: QVIS ERGO HVIC CONSVETVDINI, QVA NVNC GRAECIS ACTIONIBVS AVRES CVRIAE EXSVRDANTVR, IANVAM PATEFECIT? VT OPINOR, MOLO RHETOR, QVI STVDIA M. CICERONIS ACVIT: EVM NAMQVE ANTE OMNES EXTERARVM GENTIVM IN SENATV SINE INTERPRETE AVDITVM CONSTAT. And Cicero, *Brutus*, 312. As early as 155 BC, an embassy of the three leading philosophers from Athens, Carneades, Critolaus, and Diogenes, had addressed the Senate in Greek. But they had an interpreter, the senator C. Acilius. Plutarch, *Cato the Elder*, 22.5; A. Gellius, vi.14.9; Macrobius, I.v.16.

25. Sallust, *Bellum Iugurthinum*, lxxxv.32: NON SVNT COMPOSITA VERBA MEA: PARVI ID FACIO. IPSA SE VIRTVS SATIS OSTENDIT; ILLIS ARTIFICIO OPVS EST, VT

TVRPIA FACTA ORATIONE TEGANT. NEQVE LITTERAS GRAECAS DIDICI: PARVM
PLACEBAT EAS DISCERE, QVIPPE QVAE AD VIRTVTEM DOCTORIBVS NIHIL
PROFVERANT.

26. Plutarch, *Cato*, xii.5.
27. Cicero, *De Republica*, i.36: SED NEQVE IIS CONTENTVS SVM QVAE DE ISTA
CONSVLTATIONE SCRIPTA NOBIS SVMMI EX GRAECIA SAPIENTISSIMIQVE
HOMINES RELIQVERVNT, NEQVE EA QVAE MIHI VIDENTVR ANTEFERRE ILLIS
AVDEO. QVAM OB REM PETO A VOBIS VT ME SIC AVDIATIS: NEQVE VT OMNINO
EXPERTEM GRAECARVM RERVM, NEQVE VT EAS NOSTRIS IN HOC PRAESERTIM
GENERE ANTEPONENTEM, SED VT VNVM E TOGATIS PATRIS DILIGENTIA NON
INLIBERALITER INSTITVTVM, STVDIOQVE DISCENDI A PVERITIA INCENSVM,
VSV TAMEN ET DOMESTICIS PRAECEPTIS MVLTO MAGIS ERVDITVM QVAM
LITTERIS.
28. Cicero, *Quaestiones Academicae*, i.6–7: . . . ID IAM CORPVS ET QVASI QVALITATEM
QVANDAM NOMINABANT – DABITIS ENIM PROFECTO VT IN REBVS INVSITATIS,
QVOD GRAECI IPSI FACIVNT A QVIBVS HAEC IAM DIV TRACTANTVR, VTAMVR
VERBIS INTERDVM INAVDITIS.'

'NOS VERO' INQVIT ATTICVS; 'QVIN ETIAM GRAECIS LICEBIT VTARE CVM
VOLES, SI TE LATINA FORTE DEFICIENT.' VA. 'BENE SANE FACIS; SED ENITAR
VT LATINE LOQVAR, NISI IN HVIVSCE MODI VERBIS VT PHILOSOPHIAM AVT
RHETORICAM AVT PHYSICAM AVT DIALECTICAM APPELLEM, QVIBVS VT ALIIS
MVLTIS CONSVETVDO IAM VTITVR PRO LATINIS. QVALITATES IGITVR APPEL-
LAVI QVAS ΠΟΙΟΤΗΤΕΣ GRAECI VOCANT, QVOD IPSVM APVD GRACCOS NON EST
VVLGI VERBVM SED PHILOSOPHORVM, ATQVE ID IN MVLTIS; DIALECTICORVM
VERO VERBA NVLLA SVNT PVBLICA, SVIS VTVNTVR.
29. Livy, xxxix.8.2: CVM ARTE EARVM, QVAS MVLTAS AD ANIMORVM CORPORVMQVE
CVLTVM NOBIS ERVDITISSIMA OMNIVM GENS INVEXIT.
30. E.g., Ogilvie 1965.
31. Plutarch (*Camillus*, xxii.3) cites Heraclides Ponticus, who termed Rome a Greek city
when captured by the Gauls; Strabo (v.3.5) mentions Demetrius handing over some
pirates to the Romans, on the strength of their "kinship with the Greeks."
32. Pausanias, *Guide to Greece*, i.12.2, gives Pyrrhus' equation of Rome with Troy (and
himself with Achilles).
33. Plautus, *Rudens*, 583.
34. E.g., Cicero, *De Divinatione*, i.2: GENTEM QVIDEM NVLLAM VIDEO NEQVE TAM
HVMANAM ATQVE DOCTAM NEQVE TAM IMMANEM TAMQVE BARBARAM, QVAE
NON SIGNIFICARI FVTVRA ET A QVIBVSDAM INTELLEGI PRAEDICIQVE POSSE
CENSEAT.
35. Cicero, *In Verrem*, iii.76, and *De Finibus*, v.87; Caesar, *De Bello Gallico*, ii.35.1, iv.21.9,
and *De Bello Civili*, i.75.2.
36. In linguistic contexts, the word continued to have its technical sense of "non-Greek":
Cicero, commenting on the use of Greek words in Latin, wrote that it was absurd to
use a distinctively Greek sound even in a word with a non-Greek case ending
(ETIAM IN BARBARIS CASIBVS GRAECAM LITTERAM ADHIBERE). Cicero, *Orator*,
160.
37. Strabo, vi.1.2.

38. Dionysius of Halicarnassus, *Roman Antiquities*, i.90. The idea that, of all Greek dialects, Latin was closest to Aeolic, is also found in the Roman rhetorician of the first century AD, Quintilian, *Institutio Oratoria*, i.4.8. It is probably based on the valid insight that in the few cases where Greek and Latin share old vocabulary, and these words contain *ā*, Latin and Aeolic will retain this vowel, whereas standard (Attic) Greek will have *ē*: e.g., Latin *fāma*, *māter*, *(t)lātus*, *clāvis*, are Attic *phēmē*, *mētēr*, *tlētos*, *klēis*.

39. Hermeneumata Pseudodositheana, *Colloquium Leidense* 3, *Colloquium Harleanum* 23–24, *Colloquia Monacensia* 10.

40. Cicero, *Brutus*, 205–7.

41. Aulus Gellius, *Noctes Latinae*, v.21.

42. Varro, *De lingua Latina*, viii.3: DECLINATIO INDVCTA IN SERMONES NON SOLVM LATINOS, SED OMNIVM HOMINVM VTILI ET NECESSARIA DE CAVSA: NISI ENIM ITA ESSET FACTVM, NEQVE DISCERE TANTVM NVMERVM VERBORVM POSSEMVS (INFINITAE ENIM SVNT NATVRAE IN QVAS EA DECLINANTVR) NEQVE QVAE DIDICISSEMVS EX HIS, QVAE INTER SE RERVM COGNATIO ESSET, APPARERET.

CHAPTER 6: *FELIX CONIUNCTIO*—A PARTNERSHIP OF PARAGONS

1. Ed. Migne, *Patres Latini*, 172, 667.

2. Cicero, *Letter to Atticus*, xii.52.2: DE LINGVA LATINA SECVRI ES ANIMI, DICES, QVI TALIA CONSCRIBIS. ΑΠΟΓΡΑΦΑ SVNT, MINORE LABORE FIVNT; VERBA TANTVM ADFERO QVIBVS ABVNDO.

3. Cicero, *de Finibus*, i.8.10: SED ITA SENTIO ET SAEPE DISSERVI, LATINAM LINGVAM NON MODO NON INOPEM, VT VVLGO PVTARENT, SED LOCVPLETIO-REM ETIAM ESSE QVAM GRAECAM. QVANDO ENIM NOBIS, VEL DICAM AVT ORA-TORIBVS BONIS AVT POETIS, POSTEA QVIDEM QVAM FVIT QVEM IMITARENTVR, VLLVS ORATIONIS VEL COPIOSAE VEL ELEGANTIS ORNATVS DEFVIT?

4. *La littérature latine a été pendant des siècles le réceptacle universel.* This is a phrase from J. Marouzeau, *Le latin. Dix causeries* (Toulouse-Paris: 1927), 107, heartily approved by Rochette 1997: 257, as he sets out to consider Greek appreciation of Latin literature.

5. Plutarch, *Life of Cicero*, iv.6–7.

6. Plutarch, *Platonic Questions*, 1010D (=x.3): ὡς δοκεῖ μοι ἔχειν ὁ Ῥωμαίων [λόγος], ᾧ νῦν ὁμοῦ τι πάντες ἄνθρωποι χρῶνται.

7. Plutarch, *Demosthenes*, 2 (Dryden's translation).

8. Rochette 1997: 266.

9. Apuleius, *Metamorphoses*, i.i.

10. Rochette 1997: 128.

11. Augustine, *Confessions*, 1.13.20: QVID AVTEM ERAT CAVSAE CVR GRAECAS LITTERAS ODERAM, QVIBVS PVERVLVS IMBVEBAR? NE NVNC QVIDEM MIHI SATIS EXPLORATVM EST. ADAMAVERAM ENIM LATINAS . . . 1.14.23: CREDO ETIAM GRAECIS PVERIS VERGILIVS ITA SIT, CVM EVM SIC DISCERE COGVNTVR VT EGO ILLVM. VIDELICET DIFFICVLTAS, DIFFICVLTAS OMNINO EDISCENDAE LINGVAE PEREGRINAE, QVASI FELLE ASPERGEBAT OMNES SVAVITATES GRAECAS FABVLOSARVM NARRATIONVM.

12. Libanius, *Speeches*, 43.4.

13. Others were Claudian of Alexandria (ca 370–ca 405), who largely wrote epics and panegyrics for the court, and the prolific linguist, philosopher, and miscellanist Macrobius (aka Ambrosius Theodosius, praetorian prefect of Italy in 430).

14. Libanius, *Letters*, 1063.4.

15. Jerome, *Letter to Augustine*, 172 (CSEL 44, p. 639, ll. 6–7): GRANDEM LATINI SERMONIS IN ISTA PROVINCIA . . . PATIMVR PENVRIAM. *Commentarii in iv epistulas Paulinas*, ii.3 (ed. Migne, *Patres Latini*, 26, 382c): SERMONE GRAECO QVO OMNIS ORIENS LOQVITVR . . .

16. Egeria/Aetheria, *Itinerarium Peregrinatio*, xlvii.4: LECTIONES ETIAM, QVECVMQVE IN ECCLESIA LEGVNTVR, QVIA NECESSE EST GRECE LEGI, SEMPER STAT, QVI SIRISTE INTERPRETATVR PROPTER POPVLVM, VT SEMPER DISCANT. SANE QVICVMQVE HIC LATINI SVNT, ID EST QVI NEC SIRISTE NEC GRECE NOVERVNT, NE CONTRISTENTVR, ET IPSIS EXPONITVR EIS, QVIA SVNT ALII FRATRES ET SORORES GRECOLATINI, QVI LATINE EXPONVNT EIS.

17. Valerius Maximus, ii.2.2: MAGISTRATVS VERO PRISCI QVANTOPERE SVAM POPVLIQVE ROMANI MAIESTATEM RETINENTES SE GESSERINT HINC COGNOSCI POTEST, QVOD INTER CETERA OBTINENDAE GRAVITATIS INDICIA ILLVD QVOQVE MAGNA CVM PERSEVERANTIA CVSTODIEBANT, NE GRAECIS VMQVAM NISI LATINE RESPONSA DARENT. QVIN ETIAM IPSOS LINGVAE VOLVBILITATE, QVA PLVRIMVM VALENT, EXCVSSA PER INTERPRETEM LOQVI COGEBANT NON IN VRBE TANTVM NOSTRA, SED ETIAM IN GRAECIA ET ASIA, QVO SCILICET LATINAE VOCIS HONOS PER OMNES GENTES VENERABILIOR DIFFVNDERETVR. NEC ILLIS DEERANT STVDIA DOCTRINAE, SED NVLLA NON IN RE PALLIVM TOGAE SVBICI DEBERE ARBITRABANTVR, INDIGNVM ESSE EXISTIMANTES INLECEBRIS ET SVAVITATI LITTERARVM IMPERII PONDVS ET AVCTORITATEM DONARI.

18. Ammianus Marcellinus, xv.13.1, xviii.5.1.

19. *Novella Constitutio*, xv.preface (in Greek) (I., p.80, von Lingenthal): "and we have written the law not in the paternal voice [Latin], but this common Helladic one [Greek], so that it be known to all for ease of interpretation."

20. Johannes Lydus, *On the Magistracies*, iii.42. The prophecy was transmitted by Fonteius, otherwise unknown. Rochette 1997: 138.

21. Johannes Lydus, *On the Magistracies,* iii.68, interpreted by Kelly 2004: 32–36.

22. Rochette 1997: 143.

23. *De Thematibus, Introduction*, Pertusi, ed., 1952, cited in Horrocks 1997: 150.

24. Nicholas I, *epistula* 88 (to Michael III, AD 865), quoted by Berschin 1980: 39, 53 (1988, ch. 2.2, and n. 29).

25. Herodotus, viii.142–44.

26. Cicero, *ad Familiares*, ix.22.3.

27. Both Attic Greek and Latin based their accentual rules on the pattern of heavy or light syllables starting from the end of the word, but the rules were crucially different. The marking of accent in Greek changed from high tone to stress during the last centuries BC; in Latin, in the historical period, it was always marked by stress.

28. The dictionary used was Thomas 1961. Adding in proper nouns (which were often used for literary effect in Latin poetry, without specific reference to people or places) lifts the Greek percentage to 10 percent.

29. For English, stated by Crystal 2004: 162. For Turkish, calculated from vocabulary lists in Nişanyan 2003, a twelve-thousand-headword etymological dictionary.
30. Aristotle, *Rhetoric*, iii.9.3–4 (1409a-b); iii.8.3. The strung-out style: *léxis eiroménē*; the terminated style: *léxis katestramménē*.
31. Tacitus, *Annales*, i.1.
32. Cato, *Fragments*, 370, 371.
33. A. Gellius, *Noctes Atticae*, xix.8.15: ITE ERGO NVNC ET, QVANDO FORTE ERIT OTIVM, QVAERITE, AN "QVADRIGAM" ET "HARENAS" DIXERIT E COHORTE ILLA DVMTAXAT ANTIQVIORE VEL ORATORVM ALIQVIS VEL POETARVM, ID EST CLASSICVS ADSIDVVSQVE ALIQVIS SCRIPTOR, NON PROLETARIVS. These example words (meaning 'chariot', 'sands') are cited because there was some issue whether they could correctly be used in the singular and plural respectively.
34. Plutarch, *Sertorius*, xiv.3 (translation J. P. V. D. Balsdon).
35. This idea of a felt "secondarity" in cultures that base themselves on a Roman model— looking to somewhere else for inspiration, as Rome looked to Greece—has been developed in Rémi Brague's work *Eccentric Culture* (2002), translated from *Europe, la voie romaine* (1999). But his general idea, that Europe, like Rome, has always found its distinctive culture by aspiring to something exterior to it, is very different from our perception of the self-assured centrality of Latin. It is notable that Brague, when he mentions Latin, always represents it as a language that was given no special status within the religious or the secular culture of Europe—unlike Hebrew, Arabic, or Greek in their own communities. But this is to miss the importance of its continuity as a sustained ideal; ever since the second century BC there has been a conscious pride in mastering Latinity—seen as the hallmark of the highest cultural attainment, even as it remained *nostra lingua latina*, especially for Italians.
36. Thucydides, i.1.
37. Cited by Arrian, *Alexander's Campaigns*, ii.14.

CHAPTER 7: *URBI ET ORBI*—TAKING OVER THE CHURCH

1. The phrase is from Keith Hopkins, the subtitle to his book *A World Full of Gods* (Hopkins 2001). He is also the source of these population estimates (Hopkins 2001: 82).
2. The Sibylline prophecy is attested by the contemporary Lactantius, tutor of Constantine's son Crispus: *On the Deaths of the Persecutors*, xliv.1. It also appears in the anti-Christian historian Zosimus, ii.16. It is Kousoulas 2003: 239 who suggests that the Christian symbol was enlisted specifically to counter the effect on morale of the words from the Sibylline Books. Constantine had not previously publicly espoused Christianity. On the symbol Constantine used, Lactantius writes (xliv.5): FACIT VT IVSSVS EST ET TRANSVERSA X LITTERA, SVMMO CAPITE CIRCVM-FLEXO, CHRISTVM IN SCVTIS NOTAT 'He does as ordered, and with the letter *X* sideways, the top of its head bent round, he marks Christ on the shields.' There is a similar description of it in Eusebius of Caesarea's *Life of Constantine*, xxxi. Evidently it was not the cross itself.
3. Gibbon 1776–88: ch. xv.
4. Palmer 1955: 196, citing Th. Klauser, *Miscellanea Mercati*, i.467ff.
5. Ambrosiaster on Paul, 1 Corinthians xiv.14: MANIFESTVM EST IGNORARE ANIMVM NOSTRVM, SI LINGVA LOQVATVR QVAM NESCIT, SICVT ADSOLENT LATINI

HOMINES GRAECE CANTARE, OBLECTATI SONO VERBORVM NESCIENTES TAMEN QVID DICANT. SPIRITVS AVTEM QVI DATVR IN BAPTISMO SCIT QVID ORET ANIMVS, DVM LOQVITVR, AVT PERORAT LINGVA SIBI IGNOTA: MENS AVTEM QVI EST ANIMVS, SINE FRVCTV EST. QVEM AVTEM POTEST HABERE FRVCTVM, QVI IGNORAT QVAE LOQVATVR?

6. Ambrosiaster on Paul, 1 Corinthians xiv.24–25: EVM ENIM (SC. IDIOTA) INTELLE-GIT ET INTELLEGITVR, AVDIENS LAVDARE DEVM ET ADORARI CHRISTVM PERVIDET VERAM ESSE ET VENERANDAM RELIGIONEM, IN QVA NIHIL FACETVM, NIHIL IN TENEBRIS VIDET GERI, SICVT APVD PAGANOS, QVIBVS VELANTVR OCVLI, NE QVAE SACRA VOCANT PERSPICIENTES, VARIIS SE VANITATIBVS CERNANT ILLVDI. OMNIS ENIM IMPOSTVRA TENEBRAS PETIT, ET FALSA PRO VERIS OSTENDIT: IDEO APVD NOS NIHIL ASTVTE, NIHIL SVB VELAMINE, SED SIMPLICITER VNVS LAVDATVR DEVS.

7. QVI ET IPSIS TRIBVS LINGVIS PLVRES TRACTATVS ET MVLTAE INTERPRETA-TIONES VOLENTIBVS AD VTILITATEM ED AD AEDIFICATIONEM, SIBI AD AETERNAM MEMORIAM ET MERCEDEM POST SE DERELIQVID.

8. Heather 2005: 77–80, based on the Letter of Auxentius, Ulfilas' foster son, from Durostorum.

9. Classical Armenian is also called *grabar* 'written'. The model for the Armenian alphabet, which is highly idiosyncratic, remains obscure, but seems most likely to have been Greek, given the order and forms of the letters, and the peculiarity that the letter for *u* is a combination of *o* + *u*. More remote possibilities include Phoeni-cian or Syriac from Palestine, and Pahlavi from Persia. Armenia was supposedly evangelized by two of the original apostles, St. Bartholomew and St. Thaddeus; and the language is full of borrowings from Persian.

10. Gregory of Nazianzus, *Oration*, iv ("First Invective Against Julian"), 101–5.

CHAPTER 8: *VOX POPVLI VOX DEI*—LATIN AS THE BOND OF UNITY

1. St. Jerome, *Epistulae*, 12, 30.

2. Augustine, *Quaestiones hept.*, vii.56; *De civitate Dei*, x.21.

3. Arnobius Afer, *Adversus gentes*, i.59.5: CVM DE REBVS AGITVR AB OSTENTATIONE SVMMOTIS, QVID DICATVR SPECTANDVM EST, NON QVALI CVM AMOENITATE DICATVR, NEC QVID AVRES COMMVLCEAT, SED QVAS ADFERAT AVDIENTIBVS VTILITATES.

4. Augustine, *De doctrina christiana*, ii.13.19.

5. Augustine, *On Psalm* 36, iii.6. (v. 26): FENERATVR QVIDEM LATINE DICITVR, ET QVI DAT MVTVVM, ET QVI ACCIPIT: PLANIVS HOC AVTEM DICITVR, SI DI-CAMVS FENERAT. QVID AD NOS QVID GRAMMATICI VELINT? MELIVS IN BARBARISMO NOSTRO VOS INTELLEGITIS, QVAM IN NOSTRA DISERTITVDINE VOS DESERTI ERITIS.

6. Tertullian, *Ad Martyras*, xxx.1.9.

7. Palmer 1955: 193–94. Besides this, I am highly indebted to this work for my linguistic characterization of Christian Latin.

8. Lactantius, *On the False Worship of the Gods*, 5.1.fin.

9. Augustine, *De doctrina christiana*, ii.13.20.

10. Augustine, *Confessiones*, vi.3.3: SED CVM LEGEBAT, OCVLI DVCEBANTVR PER

PAGINAS ET COR INTELLECTVM RIMABATVR, VOX AVTEM ET LINGVA QVIESCE-
BANT.

11.   Petronius, *Satyricon*, lx.
12.   Constantine, *Letter to Miltiades* (AD 313); preserved in Eusebius, *Church History*,
      x.5.18–20.
13.   Eusebius, *Life of Constantine*, iii.13.
14.   Matthew xxii.21; Luke xx.25.
15.   Ambrose, *De Fide*, ii.136–40.
16.   Sulpicius Severus, *Chronica*, ii.3: VRBIBVS ATQVE PROVINCIIS PERMIXTAS
      BARBARAS NATIONES; Jerome, *Commentary on Daniel*, i., vision 2.
17.   Athanasius, *Historia Arianorum*, 75.
18.   Cassiodorus, *Varia*, ix.25.5: ORIGINEM GOTHICAM HISTORIAM FECIT ESSE
      ROMANAM, COLLIGENS QVASI IN VNAM CORONAM GERMEN FLORIDVM QVOD
      PER LIBRORVM CAMPOS PASSIM FVERAT ANTE DISPERSVM.

CHAPTER 9: *DIES IRAE*—STAYING ON

1.   *Sermo* xxiv.5.4, *Patrologiae Latinae supplementum*, iii (ed. A . Hamman), col. 606,
      Paris 1963.
2.   Zosimus, *Historia Nova*, vi.5–6. The rather tendentious considerations in dating
      Zosimus can be found in Paschoud 2000: vii–xvi.
3.   Gildas, *On the Ruin of the Britons*, respectively xx, xxiii.
4.   Bede, *Ecclesiastical History*, xiv–xv.
5.   Gildas, *On the Ruin of the Britons*, xxvi.
6.   This non-imperial-sounding term for the Roman Empire first came to be used in
      the fourth century AD, well before its fall in the west. Pirenne 1939: ch. 1, n. 1.
7.   Cassiodorus, *Variae*, ix.14.8: GOTHORVM LAVS EST CIVILITAS CVSTODITA.
8.   Sidonius Apollinaris, *Epistulae*, v.5: IMMANE NARRATV EST, QVANTVM STVPEAM
      SERMONIS TE GERMANICI NOTITIAM TANTA FACILITATE RAPVISSE . . .
      QVANTO MIHI CETERISQVE SIT RISVI, QVOTIENS AVDIO, QVOD TE PRAESENTE
      FORMIDET LINGVAE SVAE FACERE BARBARVS BARBARISMVM. ADSTVPET TIBI
      EPISTVLAS INTERPRETANTI CVRVA GERMANORVM SENECTVS ET NEGOTIIS
      MVTVIS ARBITRVM TE DISCEPTATOREMQVE DESVMIT . . . CVSTODIASQVE HOC,
      PROVT ES ELEGANTISSIMVS, TEMPERAMENTVM, VT ISTA TIBI LINGVA TE-
      NEATVR, NE RIDEARIS, ILLA EXERCEATVR, VT RIDEAS.
9.   Cassiodorus, *Variae*, viii.21.7: PVERI STIRPIS ROMANAE NOSTRA LINGVA LOQV-
      VNTVR, EXIMIE INDICANTES EXHIBERE SE NOBIS FVTVRAM FIDEM, QVORVM
      IAM VIDENTVR AFFECTASSE SERMONEM.
10.   Visigoth numbers estimated in Grant 1996: 126; Vandal and Alan numbers: Procopius,
      De Bello Vandalico, iii.5, and Victor Vitensis, *Historia persecutionis*, i.2—but both thought
      this was a high figure; Procopius adds that their numbers had only shortly before been
      put at fifty thousand; and Victor Vitensis says it included all ages. Estimates for the
      Roman provinces come from McEvedy & Jones 1978: 21–22, 55, 107, 101.
11.   Sidonius Apollinaris, *Epistulae*, vii.14.10: BARBAROS VITAS, QUIA MALI PVTEN-
      TVR; EGO, ETIAMSI BONI.
12.   Orosius, *Historiarum Adversum Paganos*, vii.43.5–6: SE INPRIMIS ARDENTER
      INHIASSE, VT OBLITTERATO ROMANO NOMINE ROMANVM OMNE SOLVM

GOTHORVM IMPERIVM ET FACERET ET VOCARET ESSETQVE, VT VVLGARITER
LOQVAR, GOTHIA QVOD ROMANIA FVISSET ET FIERET NVNC ATHAVLFVS QVOD
QVONDAM CAESAR AVGVSTVS, AT VBI MVLTA EXPERIENTIA PROBAVISSET
NEQVE GOTHOS VLLO MODO PARERE LEGIBVS POSSE PROPTER EFFRENATAM
BARBARIEM NEQVE REIPVBLICAE INTERDICI LEGES OPORTERE, SINE QVIBVS
RESPVBLICA NON EST RESPVBLICA, ELEGISSE SALTIM, VT GLORIAM SIBI DE
RESTITVENDO IN INTEGRVM AVGENDOQVE ROMANO NOMINE GOTHORVM
VIRIBVS QVAERERET HABERETVRQVE APVD POSTEROS ROMANAE RESTITVTIO-
NIS AVCTOR, POSTQVAM ESSE NON POTVERAT IMMVTATOR.

13. Grant 1996: 134.
14. Ramsay 1987: 224.
15. Victor Vitensis, *Historia persecutionis Africanae provinciae sub Geiserico et Hunirico regibus Wandalorum*, iii.3, ii.8.
16. Fulford 1980; Hodges and Whitehouse 1983: 27–28.
17. Paul the Deacon, *Historia Langobardorum*, iv.42.6: HIC ROTHARI REX LANGOBAR-
DORVM LEGES, QVAS SOLA MEMORIA ET VSV RETINEBANT, SCRIPTORVM SERIE
CONPOSVIT CODICEMQVE IPSVM EDICTVM APPELLARI PRAECEPIT. *Historia
Langobardorum Codicis*, vii: ROTHARI REGNAVIT ANNOS SEDECIM; PER QVEM
LEGES ET IVSTICIAM LANGOBARDIS EST INCHOATA; ET PER CONSCRIPTIONEM
PRIMIS IVDICES PERCVRRERVNT; NAM ANTEA PER CADARFADA ET ARBITRIO
SEV RITVS FIERVNT CAVSATIONES. (Ed. Georg Waitz, MGH SS rerum Lan-
gobardicarum, Hannover, 1878.)
18. Orosius, *Historiarum Adversum Paganos*, iii.20.5–7: CVM TAMEN, SI QVANDO DE ME
IPSO REFERO, VT IGNOTOS PRIMVM BARBAROS VIDERIM, VT INFESTOS
DECLINAVERIM, VT DOMINANTIBVS BLANDITVS SIM, VT INFIDELES PRAE-
CAVERIM, VT INSIDIANTES SVBTERFVGERIM, 7 POSTREMO VT PERSEQVENTES
IN MARI AC SAXIS SPICVLISQVE ADPETENTES, MANIBVS ETIAM PAENE IAM
ADPREHENDENTES REPENTINA NEBVLA CIRCVMFVSVS EVASERIM, CVNCTOS
AVDIENTES ME IN LACRIMAS COMMOVERI VELIM ET TACITVS DE NON DO-
LENTIBVS DOLEAM, REPVTANS DVRITIAE EORVM, QVI QVOD NON SVSTINVERE
NON CREDVNT.
19. Gildas, *De Excidio Britonum*, 6: ITA VT IN PROVERBIVM ET DERISVM LONGE
LATEQVE EFFERRETVR QVOD BRITANNI NEC IN BELLO FORTES NEC IN PACE
FIDELES. Jerome, *Ad Ctesiphontem*, xliii: FERTILIS TYRANNORVM PROVINCIA. The
breadbasket status of Britain is implied in Ammianus Marcellinus, xiv.5.6:HORREA
QVIN ETIAM EXSTRVERET PRO INCENSIS, VBI CONDI POSSIT ANNONA A
BRITTANNIS SVETA TRANSFERRI '[Julian in Gaul] also built barns to replace those
burned, for storage of the usual grain supply from Britain'.
20. Inscription from Uley 72 (Hassall and Tomlin 1992): DEO SANCTO MERCVRIO
HONORATVS. CONQVEROR NVMINI TVO ME PERDIDISSE ROTAS DVAS ET VACCAS
QVATTVOR ET RESCVLAS PLVRIMAS DE HOSPITIOLO MEO. ROGAVERIM GENIVM
NVMINIS TVV VT EI QVI MIHI FRAVDEM FECERIT SANITATEM EI NON PERMIT-
TAS NEC IACERE NEC SEDERE NEC BIBERE NEC MANDVCARE SI BARO SI
MVLIER SI PVER SI PVELLA SI SERVVS SI LIBER NISSI MEAM REM AD ME
PERTVLERIT ET MEAM CONCORDIAM HABVERIT. ITERATIS PRAECIBVS ROGO
NVMEN TVVM VT PETITIO MEA STATIM PAREAT ME VINDICATVM ESSE A
MAIESTATE TVA.

21.   Gildas, *Ruin of Britain*, xxiii.1: SAXONES FEROCISSIMI ILLI NEFANDI NOMINIS SAXONES DEO HOMINIBVSQVE INVISI.

22.   For traditional population estimates, see McEvedy and Jones 1978: 22,41. Recent archaeology is summarized in Hills 2003: 91–92.

23.   Weale et al. 2002 and Capelli et al. 2003, comparing sites throughout the British Isles with a "North Germany/Denmark" genetic composite, find average continental (presumed Anglo-Saxon) intrusion in England at 37 percent, but with peaks of over 70 percent in Norfolk and York.

24.   The evidence is marshaled in Keys 1999: chs. 13–16. The *Annales Cambriae* also date the battle of Camlann, King Arthur's final encounter with his son Medraut, to 537; in this year too, they say, MORTALITAS IN BRITTANNIA ET IN HIBERNIA FVIT 'there was a plague in Britain and Ireland'.

25.   Forster et al. 2006 presents evidence from the basic vocabularies of Germanic languages that English had had a period of development separate from Frisian and all other continental Germanic languages. Oppenheimer 2006 points out that the genetic evidence is consistent with Germanic migration from northwestern Europe into Britain at any time between the end of the seventh millennium BC and the Roman invasion.

26.   Caesar, *de Bello Gallico*, v.12.

27.   Ibid., ii.4.

28.   Tacitus, *Agricola*, xi.

29.   Glick 1979: 171. Although Mozarabic women could marry Muslim husbands, there was also a pattern in the Mozarabic (Christian) community of husbands taking Arab names, presumably for cultural convenience, while their wives' names remained Romance: Aiza and Argentea; Yahea and Filoria; Abuhab and Vistrildi; Zuleiman and Loba etc. (Glick 1979: 177).

30.   Ibid., 186. Glick adds, "If language is used as an indicator, Romance/Arabic bilingualism, common in the early centuries, wanes with the fortunes of Christianity."

31.   Corriente 1992, page 34, claims that Muslim Spain was largely monolingual in Arabic by the eleventh century, and completely so by the thirteenth.

32.   McEvedy and Jones 1978: 99.

33.   Procopius, *Secret History*, xviii, 20–21.

34.   Bourciez 1967: 30, 135–37.

35.   Haarmann 1999: 563, 569.

36.   On Karaim, Armenian Poles, see Wicherkiewicz 2005.

37.   See, for example, Tanner 2002: 269: "In Wales the Nonconformist preachers kept the Welsh language alive in spite of the efforts of the Established clergy and the schools. The Catholic Church under Cullen took no stand on Irish."

CHAPTER 10: *ULTRA VIRES*—BEYOND THE LIMITS OF EMPIRE

1.   Prosper of Aquitaine, *Epitoma Chronicon*, entry for 431: "Palladius was sent by Pope Celestine to the Scots [i.e., Irish] who believed in Christ and was ordained as their first bishop."

2.   The Roman was uncial, essentially based on capital letters; and the Irish "half-uncial," with distinctively cursive forms for *a*, *d*, *e*, and *m* (Ullman 1932: 74–75, 83).

3.   The following review of the progress of Christianity into Germany, and the lands to

its north and east, depend heavily on Schaff 1997 (1910), §§ 28–36, which gives references to many medieval sources.

4. Widukind of Corvey, *Res Gestae Saxonicae*.

5. *Regesta Pontificum Romanorum* 3319 (*Industriae tuae*), 3407 (*Quia te zelo*).

6. *Monumenta Poloniae Historica* 1864 (1960): 323: *Quis in laudem Dei totidem coadunavit linguas? Cum in propria et in latina deum digne venerari posses, in hoc tibi non satis Graecam superaddere maluisti?*; *Regesta Pontificum Romanorum* 5151, vii.11.

7. Plezia 1981. Vienna was the next to be founded in the Holy Roman Empire (1365); and then thick and fast came Erfurt (1379), Heidelberg (1385), Cologne (1388), Buda (1389–1460), Würzburg (1402–ca 1415), Leipzig (1409), Rostock (1419); a short break, and then Trier (1454), Greifswald (1456), Freiburg (1457), Basel (1459), Ingolstadt (1459), Pozsony (1465–ca 1500), Mainz, Tübingen (1476). Clearly, universities could close as well as open. Twenty-nine more were added over the next three centuries, thirteen of them in German-speaking countries. (More details in Burke 2004: 53.)

CHAPTER II: *LAPSUS LINGUAE*—INCURABLE ROMANTICS: FRACTURED LATIN

1. Our account, rushing through changes that occurred over a millennium from Portugal to Romania, will naturally be rough and ready. A fuller, and more reasoned, explanation of the general features of what happened can be found in Vincent 1988.

2. More exactly, there is a universal tendency for most final consonants, never very frequent in Latin, to be dropped altogether. Of those that are not lost, *r* and *l* were protected by the addition of an extra unstressed vowel, as is still heard in an Italian accent: hence Italian *miele*, *cuore* as against classical Latin *mel*, *cor* 'honey, heart'. In the west, -n and -s tend to survive, important as markers of the plural in verbs and nouns respectively, but they largely disappear in the east (Italy and Romania).

   In addition, in the lands northwest of the line from La Spezia to Rimini, consonants later in the word tended to be weakened. Internal stop consonants after a stressed vowel tend to be reduced in force, on a scale from voiceless stop consonant (p,t,k) to voiced stop (b,d,g) to voiced fricative (v,ð,γ) to zero. (E.g., *amíca cápra* 'friend nanny-goat' is unchanged in Italian, but becomes *amiga cabra* in Spanish, *amie chèvre* in French.) At the same time, double consonants get reduced to singles.

3. Dante Alighieri, *De vulgari eloquentia*, i.9.10–11: *si ergo per eandem gentem sermo variatur, ut dictum est, successive per tempora, nec stare ullo modo potest, necesse est, ut disiunctim abmotimque morantibus varie varietur, ceu varie variantur mores et habitus, qui nec natura nec consortio confirmantur, sed humanis beneplacitis localique congruitate nascuntur. hinc moti sunt inventores grammaticae facultatis: quae quidem grammatica nihil aliud est quam quaedam inalterabilis locutionis identitas diversibus temporibus atque locis.*

4. This is cited in Wright 1982: 109, as at Vienna Nationalbibliothek 795. I have followed Migne (also cited by Wright) in correcting *sene* to *sine*.

5. This is the thesis established by Wright 1982. The alternative would be to suppose that the pronunciation of Latin had been kept constant for the preceding four centuries, without any special pleading or teaching. The experience in England since the Great Vowel Shift (fifteenth to sixteenth centuries) shows that scholars

even of a written language that is quite distinct from their own do not, without copious urging and dispute, exert themselves to keep its sound system separate from that used in their daily speech.

6. *... et ut easdem omelias quisque aperte transferre studeat in rusticam romanam linguam aut thiotiscam, quo facilius cuncti possint intellegere quae dicuntur.* Cited in Wright 1982: 120, 122, from *Monumenta Germaniae Historica, Legum,* iii.2.1.

7. Verhulst 1995: 481–84; Fossier 1999: 30.

8. Menéndez Pidal 1972: 24–25; also cited in Wright 1982: 173.

9. Wolff 1971: ch. 5, "Crystallisation." I am highly indebted to this work for its wide-ranging summaries of the beginnings of written Romance.

10. Alfonso X of Castile, *Cantigas de Santa Maria,* no. 181, last stanza.

11. Francis of Assisi, *Cantico delle Creature,* 25–29.

12. Dante Alighieri, *De vulgari eloquentia,* i.19.1: *istud, quod totius Ytaliae est, Latium vulgare vocatur. hoc enim usi sunt doctores illustres, qui lingua vulgari poetati sunt in Italia, ut Siculi, Apuli, Tusci, Romandioli, Lombardi et utriusque Marchiae viri.*

13. Wolff 1971, page 151, denies him the palm even here, noting that the learned Spaniard Rodrigo Ximénez de Rada, archbishop of Toledo, writing his *De rebus Hispaniae,* before 1243, had distinguished in addition Bulgarians, Hungarians, various tribes of Slavs and Germans, and even Gaelic and Basque.

14. Dante Alighieri, *De vulgari eloquentia,* i.11.7: *Sardos etiam, qui non Latii sunt sed Latiis associandi videntur, eiiciamus, quoniam soli sine proprio vulgari esse videntur, grammaticam tamquam simiae homines imitantes: nam domus nova et dominus meus locuntur.*

CHAPTER 12: *AMOR VINCIT OMNIA*—LATIN LOVERS

1. *Chanson de Roland,* l. 1093.

2. From the *dīwān* 'collected poems' of Ibn Quzmān; translated from the French version of Dermenghem 1951: 152.

3. Quoted in Stuart 1995: 54.

4. "Cambridge Songs," xxvii, *Invitatio amicae* 'invitation to the girlfriend', last four verses. "Cambridge Songs" is a compilation of eleventh-century verse, a manuscript preserved in the Cambridge University library.

5. "Cambridge Songs," xxiii, *Carmen estivum* 'summer song', last two verses.

6. Cicero, *de Officiis,* iii.75. IN FORO SALTARE seems to be the classical Latin equivalent of "selling your granny."

7. Polybius, ii.19; Strabo, iv.4.5; Diodorus Siculus, v.32; Ostler 2005: 284, 287.

8. Paul, *Ephesians* v.4.

9. Rule of St. Benedict, ch. 4: *Verba vana aut risui apta non loqui. Risum multum aut excussum non amare.* Ch. 6: *Scurrilitates vero vel verba otiosa et risum moventia aeterna clusura in omnibus locis damnamus et ad talia eloquia aperire os non permittimus . . .* Ch. 7: *Decimus humilitatis gradus est, si non sit facilis ac promptus in risu, qui scriptum est: Stultus in risu exaltat vocem suam.*

10. *Titulus Sancti Juliani Monacharum* (the convent of St. Mary and St. Julian at Auxerre). The verse was included in the *rotulus mortuorum* of the daughter of William the Conqueror, Matilda, who died around 1113. This *rotulus* 'roll' was a collection of tributes and prayers for the departed, gathered from monasteries in Norman France and England.

11.   Bernard of Clairvaux (d. 1153), *Sermones super Cantica canticorum*, i.6.11, translation from Piltz 1982: 37.

12.   Walther von der Vogelweide, *Elegie*, lied 124, ll. 26–29.

CHAPTER 13: *LITTERAE HUMANIORES*—THE FRUITS OF A LATIN EDUCATION

1.   Gregory of Tours, *Historia Francorum*, preface: PHILOSOPHANTEM RHETOREM INTELLEGUNT PAUCI, LOQUENTEM RUSTICUM MULTI. *Monumenta Germaniae Historica, Scriptorum*, i, l.31.14.

2.   *Ille qui frequentat magis scholas, et diligentius magistrum audit, debet melior clericus reputari.*

3.   Hrothsvitha, *Dulcitius*, iv:

   C. Quid sibi vult collisio ollarum, caccaborum et sartaginum?

   H. Lustrabo. Accedite, quaeso, per rimulas perspicite!

   A. Quid est?

   H. Ecce, iste stultus mente alienatus aestimat se nostris uti amplexibus.

   A. Quid facit?

   H. Nunc ollas molli fovet gremio, nunc sartagines et caccabos amplectitur, mitia libans oscula.

   C. Ridiculum.

   H. Nam facies, manus ac vestimenta adeo sordidata, adeo coinquinata, ut nigredo quae inhaesit similitudinem Aethiopis exprimit.

   A. Decet ut talis appareat corpore, qualis a diabolo possidetur in mente.

4.   Dante Alighieri, *De vulgari eloquentia*, i.9.11: *quedam inalterabilis locutionis ydemptitas diversis temporibus atque locis.*

5.   This is a telling point in Curtius 1953, especially section 3.5, which lists authors on the medieval syllabus. Keen 1973, assessing the standpoint of medieval history-writing, is in full agreement.

6.   Cicero, *Orator*, 29: IS IGITVR ERIT ELOQVENS, QVI POTERIT PARVA SVMMISSE, MODICA TEMPERATE, MAGNA GRANDITER DICERE.

7.   Cassiodorus, *Institutiones*, ii.16: SIC INSTRVCTVS IN OPERE SANCTO REDDITVR, QVAMVIS ALIQVANTVLVM LIBRIS SAECVLARIBVS OCCVPETVR.

8.   Curtius 1953: 76.

9.   Rule of St. Benedict, ch. 48.

10.   Cassiodorus, *Institutiones*, i.30: FELIX INTENTIO, LAUDANDA SEDŬLITAS, MANŬ HOMINIBUS PRAEDICARE, DIGITIS LINGŬAS APERIRE, SALŬTEM MORTALIBŬS TACITŬM DARE, ET CONTRA DIABOLI SUBREPTIONES ILLICITAS CALAMO ATRAMENTOQUE PUGNARE. TOT ENIM ŬŬLNERA SATANAS ACCIPIT, QŬOT ANTIQŬARIUS DOMINI ŬERBA DESCRIBIT.

11.   The roll is cited by Farfa of Italy, according to Southern 1953: ch. 4, n. 15, which refers it to B. Albers, *Consuetudines Monasticae* (1900), vol. 1.

12.   Alberic, *Flores rhetorici*, ed. D. M. Inguáñez and H. M. Willard (Monte Cassino, 1938) (Miscellanea cassinese 14), 36: *Currat ergo sententia suis membris contenta, nec alienae copulationis foeditas laceret, quam decor in se penitus illustrare sufficiet . . . Quare simplicitatem noli deserere.*

13.   Ibid., 45: *Suum autem est metaphorae modum locutionis a proprietate sui quasi detorquere, detorquendo quodammodo innovare, innovando quasi nuptiali amictu tegere, tegendo quasi praecio dignitatis vendere.*

14. Curtius 1953: 153 gives a variety of ways that the old simple word POETA was paraphased (*versificus metricae artis peritia praeditus, dictor, positor, compositor*) and even more for poetic composition (e.g., *metrica facundia, versibus digerere, poetico cothurno gesta comere*).

15. *Der Libellus scolasticus des Walther von Speyer*, ed. P. Vossen (Berlin, 1962), 234–36: *lusibus abiectis et iuvenum nucibusque relictis | curramus sacrae celeres ad fercula mensae | quae superant omnem devicto melle saporem.*

16. Hrabanus Maurus (ca 780–856), *Enarrationes in epistulas Pauli*, xv.4, cited by Piltz 1981: 30.

17. John of Salisbury (ca 1115–80), *Metalogicon*, I §11 (838a–b).

18. Isidore, *Etymologiae*, iii.1: MATHEMATICA LATINE DICITUR DOCTRINALIS SCIENTIA, QUAE ABSTRACTAM CONSIDERAT QUANTITATEM . . . CUIUS SPECIES SUNT QUATTUOR: ID EST ARITHMETICA, MUSICA, GEOMETRIA ET ASTRONOMIA.

19. Curtius 1953: 37.

20. Augustine, *De Doctrina Christiana*, ii.60.

21. Conrad of Hirsau (d. 1150), *Dialogus super auctores*, cited by Piltz 1981: 34.

22. B. Bischoff, "Eine verschollene Einteilung der Wissenschaften in Archives," *Archives d'histoire doctrinale et littéraire du Moyen-Âge* (1958), 16, cited in Rüegg 1992: 26.

23. Rüegg 1992: 26–27.

24. Ibn Khaldūn (1332–1406), *Muqaddimah*, vi.44 (trans. Rosenthal, ed. Dawood, p. 434); Searle 1969: 39.

CHAPTER 14: *EX ORIENTE LUX*—SOURCES OF HIGHER LEARNING

1. John of Salisbury, *Metalogicon*, ii.20 (869a–b): *Sic fere duodecennium mihi elapsum est, diversis studiis occupato. Jucundum itaque visum est, veteres quos reliqueram, et quos adhuc dialectica detinebat in Monte, revisere socios, conferre cum eis super ambiguitatibus pristinis; ut nostrum invicem, ex collatione mutua, commetiremur profectum. Inventi sunt qui fuerant, et ubi; neque enim ad palmam visi sunt processisse ad quaestiones pristinas dirimendas, neque propositiunculam unam adjecerant. Quibus urgebant stimulis, eisdem et ipsi urgebantur, profecerant in uno duntaxat, dedidicerant modum, modestiam nesciebant; adeo quidem ut de reparatione eorum posset desperari. Expertus itaque sum quod liquido colligi potest, quia sicut dialectica alias expedit disciplinas, sic, si sola fuerit, jacet exsanguis et sterilis, nec ad fructum philosophiae fecundat animam, si aliunde non concipit.*

2. Lévi-Provençal 1934: 248.

3. d'Alverny 1982: 444–45 dismisses the story and argues that the flourishing period was a generation after Raimundus, from around 1150.

4. Burnett 1995: 22–23.

5. Charles Homer Haskins made this conjecture; d'Alverny 1982: 441–42 marshals the evidence.

6. E.g., d'Alverny 1982: 446 n. 104.

7. Black: 725.

8. The first quote comes via d'Alverny 1982: 453. The second runs: *Sed quoniam doctrina Arabum, que in quadruvio fere tota existit, maxime his diebus apud Tholetum celebratur, illuc, ut sapientiores mundi philosophos audirem, featinanter properavi. Vocatus vero tandem ab amicis et invitatus, ut ab Hyspania redirem, cum pretiosa multitudine librorum*

in Angliam veni. The full source of both is in Daniel of Morley, preface to *Philoso-phia, Mittellateinisches Jahrbuch* 14 (1979): 212–45.

9. John of Salisbury, *Metalogicon,* i.15 (844d): . . . *a Graeco interprete et qui Latinam linguam commode noverat, dum in Apulia morarer accepi. Nam et ipsi volo referre gratiam, et si non utilitatis, qua tamen in his aliqua est, saltem bonae voluntatis qua auditoribus prodesse cupiebat.*

10. John Sarracenus's dedicatory epistle to Bishop Odo of St. Denis, p. 459 (in Grab-mann, *Mittelalterliches Geistesleben* [Munich, 1926], i.454–60). John is citing the opinion of Anastasius Bibliothecarius, on John Scot Eriugena: *interpres minus quam oportuisset . . . eruditus.* Anastasius was another commentator on Dionysius the Areopagite.

11. E.g., Rüegg 1992: 14: "A conclusive explanation of why there was no university in London and why universities were founded later in Rome (1303), Cologne (1388), and Mainz (1476) than in Bologna, Oxford, Montpellier, and Salamanca (1218–19) can only be given—if it ever can be given—after further source materials have been discovered and analyzed."

12. *Patrologia Latina* (Migne), cxcix, col. 143: *Fateor tamen elegantias me dictionum eruditissimi et disertissimi viri oratione Latina exprimere nequivisse. Nam apud Graecos quaedam compositiones inveniuntur, quibus eleganter et prorie res significantur; apud Latinos autem eadem res a duabus aut pluribus dictionibus ineleganter et improprie et quandoque insufficienter designantur. Ad commendationem enim alicujus personae vel alterius rei pulchre articuli apud eos repetuntur, et per eosdem articulos multae orationes sibi invicem perpolite connectuntur. Taceo de insigni constructione participiorum et infinitorum articulorum conjunctorum. Hujusmodi autem elegantiae apud Latinos ne quiverunt inveniri.*

13. The change that came about at the Renaissance is discussed in Hankins 2003: 177–92: "Translation Practice in the Renaissance: The Case of Leonardo Bruni."

14. Beaujouan 1981: 348 offers some clear examples of scholastic Latin terminology invented to match Arabic: *experientia-experimentum, elementans-elementatum, naturans-naturatum,* with references to further discussion.

15. Jacquart and Troupeau 1981: 368–70.

16. Thomas Aquinas, *Summa Contra Gentiles,* lib. 2, cap. 54 n. 6.

17. Thomas Aquinas, *Summa Theologica,* q. 1. 42.2.

18. Hugh of St. Victor (1096–1141), *Eruditio didascalia* (PL 176:769d).

19. Curtius 1953: 56.

20. Kelly 2002: 1.

21. Peter Lombard, *Sententiarum Libri IV, Prologus* 5: *brevi volumine complicans Patrum sententias, appositis eorum testimoniis, ut non sit necesse quaerenti librorum numerosita-tem evolvere, cui brevitas collecta quod quaeritur offert sine labore. In hoc autem tractatu non solum pium lectorem, sed etiam liberum correctorem desidero, maxime ubi profunda versatur veritatis quaestio: quae utinam tot haberet inventores, quot habet contradictores!*

22. Thomas Aquinas, *Super Boethium de Trinitate,* pars 3, q. 5 a. 1 ad 3.

CHAPTER 15: *ALTER EGO*—HUMANISM AND THE RETURN OF THE CLASSICS

1. Francesco Petrarca, *Invectiva contra eum qui maledixit Italiae,* 93, 94, 98 (ed. Marsh 2003): *per Grecos ad Latinos, deinde ad Romanos, qui ipsi Latini sunt, temporum seriem deduxerunt . . . Et preterea docti viri, in omni sermone et scriptura, Romanam facundiam*

Latinam vocant, atque e converso, ut duo sint nomina, sed res una . . . Sumus enim non Greci, non barbari, sed Itali et Latini.

2. Francesco de Sanctis, *Storia de la letterature italiana*, ch. 1.

3. This did not mean that Italians yet realized that Latin had actually once been the spoken vernacular, as well as the written language, of Rome. For their views on the actual status of Cicero's Latin in the first century BC, see the footnote to page 237.

4. Leonardo Bruni, *Historia Populi Florentini*, preface (ed. Hankins 2001).

5. D'Amico 1983: 126.

6. O'Malley 1979 discusses this oratory at length, picking on Aurelio Brandolini's *De ratione scribendi libri tres* (ca 1490, first printed in Basel in 1549) as its main theoretical description. Its emphasis was epideictic ("display") oratory, the *genus demonstrativum*, which was about expressing praise and blame rather than giving information. In this it represented a return to the norms of classical rhetoric, after the Middle Ages' deviation into *dictamen* specialized for business use.

   On the debate about the language as spoken in Cicero's day, the main text is Flavio Biondo's *De verbis Romanae locutionis*, in Nogara 1927: 115–30. The import is discussed in Tavoni 1982 and Rizzo 1986, 1990. Reeve 1996: 39, 45, also refers.

7. D'Amico 1983: 34.

8. This is the self-description of the humanists of the Roman academy in 1524, due to Giovanni Battista Cassali, *In Desiderium Erasmum Rotterdamnum Invectiva*, as cited by D'Amico 1983: 139.

9. D'Amico 1983: 128–34

10. Lorenzo Valla, *De elegantiis linguae Latinae*, preface, fol. 8 (Garin 1952: 596).

11. Hankins 2003: 502; more examples can be found at D'Amico 1983: 157–58.

12. Blosio Palladio, *Oratio totam fere romanam historiam complectans . . .* , 48. 'But already Livy had proclaimed as with a trumpet that no State ever had been bigger or holier or better provided with good examples.' *Jam vero T. Livius quasi tuba proclamarat, nullam umquam Rem publicam, aut majorem, aut sanctiorem, bonisque exemplis ditiorem fuisse.* Cited in D'Amico 1983: 289.

13. Erasmus, *Dialogus Ciceronianus* (Welzig 1972: 7:176): *Et in tabulis magis capit oculos nostros Iupiter per impluvium illapsus in gremium Danaes quam Gabriel sacrae Virgini nuntians caelestem conceptum, vehementius delectat raptus ab aquila Ganymedes quam Christus ascendens in caelum, iucundius morantur oculos nostros expressa Bacchanalia Terminaliave turpitudinis et obscoenitatis plena quam Lazarus in vitam revocatus aut Christus a Ioanne baptizatus. Haec sunt mysteria, quae sub Ciceroniani nominis velo teguntur. Mihi crede, per speciosi tituli praetextum insidiae tenduntur simplicibus et ad fraudem idoneis adulescentibus. Paganitatem profiteri non audemus. Ciceroniani cognomen obtendimus. At quanto satius esset vel mutos esse nos quam in hunc affecdtum venire?*

14. This is the accusation of the great classical scholar Eduard Norden: "The Latin language was put in its grave by humanism" (Norden 1898: 773).

15. Francesco Petrarca, *Epistulae de rebus familiaribus*, xxiv.4 (cited from Harrington 1962 [1925]: 560–64).

16. Poliziano, *Silvae, Nutricia*, 67–74.

17. Kristeller 1964: 34. The intent to subordinate dialectic, i.e., logic, to rhetoric became characteristic of the humanists, part of their general impatience with

formal studies. They liked to emphasize one of the traditional definitions of logic, *ars bene disserendi*, conveniently ambiguous between 'art of good reasoning' and 'art of good discourse'. (*Dialektikē* too, in Greek, is ambiguous between 'reasoning' and 'conversation'.) In the *De inventione dialectica* (1479) of the Frisian Roelof Huisman (better known as Rudolphus Agricola—see, e.g., van der Poel 1997), logic is seen as the art of finding arguments to support a point of view; and the highly influential approach of the Parisian Petrus Ramus (1515–72) was similar. In general, modern logicians (e.g., Kneale & Kneale 1962: 300ff) see this as a serious mistake, and fundamental to why no further progress would be made in logic until the nineteenth century, with George Boole and Gottlob Frege.

18. Jensen 1996: 64.

19. Lorenzo Valla, *De elegantiis linguae Latinae*, ii.58 (cited by Reeve 1996: 40).

20. Ibid., preface, foll. 6–8 (Garin 1952: pp. 594–96): *Nostri maiores rebus bellicis, pluribusque laudibus caeteros homines superarunt, linguae vero suae ampliatione seipsis superiores fuerunt . . . linguam Latinam nationibus distribuisse minus erit, optimam frugem, et vere divinam, nec corporis sed animi cibum? . . . ex sermone autem Latino non suum imminui, sed condiri quodammodo intelligebant: ut uinum posterius inuentum, aquae usum non excussit: nec sericum, lanam linumque; nec aurum caetera metalla de possessione eiecit . . . Magnum ergo Latini sermonis sacramentum est, magnum profecto numen, quod apud peregrinos, apud barbaros, apud hostes, sancte, ac religiose per secula custoditur . . . per hunc splendidiorem dominatum in magna adhuc orbis parte regnamus. Nostra est Italia, nostra Gallia, nostra Hispania, Germania, Pannonia, Dalmatia, Illyricum, multaeque aliae nationes.*

21. Reeve 1996: 40.

22. Guillaume Tardif, *Eloquencie benedicendique sciencie compendium* (cited by Levi 2002: 110, 393).

23. Erasmus in a letter to Cornelius Gerard (P. S. Allen, ed., 1906–58: vol. 1, no. 26, p. 115): *Valla qui . . . tanta industria, tanto studio tantis sudoribus barbarorum ineptias refellit, literas pene sepultas ab interitu vindicavit, prisco eloquentiae splendori reddidit Italiam.* For resonance, my translation has reorganized the syntax of this last clause, without affecting the sense.

24. See, e.g., Black 1995: esp. p. 54.

25. Levi 2002: 109.

26. Hankins 2001: 275–77.

27. Francesco Petrarca, *Invectiva de sui ipsius et multorum ignorantia*, 124: *Barlaam Calabrum, modernum graie specimen sophie, qui me latinarum inscium docere grecas literas adortus, forsitan profecisset, nisi michi inuidisset mors, honestisque principiis obstitisset, ut solita est.*

28. Battista Guarino, *De ordine docendi et studendi*, 16, 17: *Scio enim plerosque esse qui eam (sc. litterarum graecarum scientiam) latinis litteris necessariam esse negent, qui, quoniam ignari ipsi sunt, optarent reliquos inscitiae suae pares esse, ut inter ceteros si non superiores saltem nec inferiores iudicarentur. Mihi vero, dum vivam, nemo hunc errorem (si error est) eripiet, ut eam non modo utilem sed pernecessariam litteris nostris esse non credam . . . Nos autem et veterum doctissimorum exempla, quorum nemo graecae linguae expers fuit; et Quintiliani auctoritatem, qui nostras a graecis effluxisse ait* (from Kallendorf 2002: 276–79).

CHAPTER 16: *DEUS EX MACHINA*—PRINTING AND THE PROFUSION OF GRAMMARS

1. Lorenzo Valla, *De elegantiis linguae Latinae*, iii, preface (Garin 1952: 610).

2. Jensen 1996: 65, citing Johannes Santritter's letter to Augustinus Moravus of Olomouc (October 31, 1492), preserved in King Alfonso X, *Tabulae astronomicae* (Venice, 1492), sig. A3 r-v.

3. On Aeneas Sylvius and Gutenberg, see Ing 1988: 67; on the invention of printing, Carter 1925: 211–18; on Latin literature in print, see Reynolds and Wilson 1968: 120, and Davies 1996: 58; on Greek, Hankins 2001: 286; on the spread of printing generally, Febvre and Martin 1958 or 1976.

4. More fully, *cruces interpretum*, from their power to torment the critic. Reynolds and Wilson 1968: 119–20; Grafton 1983: ch. 1–3; Kenney 1974: 76–78, 84–87.

5. Giovanni Sulpizio, *De arte grammatica [opusculum]* (Perugia, ca 1475), fol. 31 v.

6. Erasmus, *De ratione studii*.

7. Quoted in Seebohm 1911: 214. For the origin of Lily's grammar, see page 284.

8. Francesco Priscianese, *Della lingua romana* (Venice, 1540), foll. ii r–iiii v.

9. O'Mahony 1981: 157, 142: *Ad linguas addiscendas . . . duplex hactenus reperta est tantummodo via: regularis, qualis est ad congruitates observandas Grammatica; & irregularis, qualis est communes discentium usus, per lectionem, & loquelam in linguis vulgaribus.*

10. Waquet 2001: 23–26, for the decline of Latin in the eighteenth century.

11. Especially in Febvre and Martin 1958 or 1976, and Anderson 1991.

12. Febvre and Martin 1976: 289–95.

13. Waquet 2001: 8, 19–22.

14. Dixon 1996: 149–51, 156.

15. This word—and the concept—is the invention of Auroux 1994.

CHAPTER 17: *NOVUS ORBIS*—LATIN AMERICA

1. Palladio Blosio, *Oratio totam fere romanam historiam complectans . . .* , 125. Cited in D'Amico 1983: 289.

2. Seneca, *Medea*, 375–79.

3. *la mayor cosa después de la creación del mundo, sacando la encarnación y muerte del que lo creó.*

4. E.g., Robert Hayman, *Quodlibets* (1628), bk. 2, 95. "Great Alexander wept, and made sad mone, because there was but one world to be wonne." This ancient cliché about Alexander—perhaps first recorded by Aelian (AD 170–230)—is probably a vulgarization of Plutarch (*Moralia*, "On Contentment of the Mind"): Alexander cried when he heard Anaxarchus talk about the infinite number of worlds in the universe. One of Alexander's friends asked him what was the matter, and he replied, "There are so many worlds, and I have not yet conquered even one." (See Nick Welman, Lyla Sparks, and Tre at www.pothos.org/alexander.asp?ParaID=96.)

5. History is never quite tidy. First Norway, then Denmark, neither a Roman province, took control of Greenland; and from 1638 to 1655, Sweden maintained a settlement, Ny Sverige, at Delaware Bay, in competition with the Dutch.

6. Inca Garcilaso, according to Gómez 1995: 82.

7. First running along the coast of the American mainland, he noted to his disappointment, "They no more understand one another than we do the Arabs" (Rosenblat 1964: 191).

8. Ibid., 193–95; Quilis 1992: 55.
9. Mendieta 1870 (ca 1595): 134, quoted in Martinell Gifre 1988: 69 (translation mine).
10. Rosenblat 1964: 199.
11. Viñaza 1892. These could be compared with the Summer Institute for Linguistics' estimate of the number of distinct languages in the Americas: 888, with 408 of them in South America (Grimes 1992).
12. These verses are known from an anonymous manuscript, which is otherwise written in Spanish. The composition goes on for 144 lines before breaking off. Lucena Salmoral 1967: 65.
13. Rosenblat 1964: 199, 203.
14. Kerson 1986: 603.
15. Rosenblat 1964: 202–4.
16. See Ricard 1933: bk. 2, ch. 7.
17. Brotherston 1992: 313–14; Ostler 2005: 15–16,
18. Rosenblat 1964: 203.
19. Motolinia 1990 (1541): iii.12.389–90, pp. 170–71. Edmundo O'Gorman, comparing Mendieta 1870 (ca 1595), iv.15, suggests that the disputed phrase was *natus ex Maria Virgine* 'born of the Virgin Mary', which the ignorant Spanish priest had wanted to recite as *nato . . .*
20. *Arte y Grammatica muy copiosa de la lengua Aymara*, Father Ludovico Bertonio, Jesuit (Rome, 1603); *Gramatica de la Lengua general del Nuevo Reino, llamada Mosca*, Father Fray Bernardo de Lugo, Dominican (Madrid, 1619); *Arte y Bocabulario de la lengua guarani*, Father Antonio Ruiz, Jesuit (Madrid, 1640).
21. Alonso de Zorita, *Relación de Nueva España*, xxiii, reported in Rosenblat 1964: 203. Nazáreo's letter can be found in Osorio Romero 1990.
22. The translator was the noted Nahuatl scholar Angel María Garibay K.
23. Kerson 1986: 604.
24. Brotherston 1992: 315–19.
25. See Laurencich-Minelli 2000, and the many references quoted there. The rhetorical analysis was by Luisa López Grigera of the University of Michigan. Hyland 2003: 224–35, argues that Anello, wronged by the Jesuits and possibly with a grudge against Guaman Poma, was the most likely forger.
26. Father Blas Valera's words, quoted by Inca Garcilaso, *Comentarios Reales: la lengua cortesana tiene este don particular . . . que a los indios del Perú les es de tanto provecho como a nosotros la lengua latina.* (Hyland 2003: 124).
27. Garcilaso de la Vega, *Comentarios Reales*, introduction: *como natural del la ciudad de Cuzco, que fue otra Roma en aquel imperio.*
28. Father Blas Valera's words, quoted by Inca Garcilaso, *Comentarios Reales*, pt. 1, vii.3: *porqué la semejanza y conformidad de las palabras casi siempre suelen reconciliar y traer a verdadera unión y amistad a los hombres.*
29. Kerson 1986: passim. Modern editions of the texts can be found in Fernández Valenzuela 1974 and Laird 2006.
30. Rafael Landívar: *Rusticatio Mexicana*, xv, 236–43, 262–73.

CHAPTER 18: *DECUS ET TUTAMEN*—LAST REDOUBTS

1. Olaus Theophilus, *Paraenesis seu praeceptiones sapientes et utiles de vitae ac studiorum honesta formatione . . .* (Copenhagen, 1573). Cited by Jensen 1996: 78, and in

Latinskolens dannelse (Copenhagen, 1982), 13. Theophilus had been a pupil of
   Philipp Melanchthon's.

2. Cited by Hankins 2003: 288, from *Scaligerana* (Cologne, 1595), 299, 308.

3. Ludovicus de Valentia, ed., *Thomas Aquinas, Commentarii in libros octo politicorum
   Aristotelis* (Rome, 1492), sig. a2 r (translated at Kraye 1996: 148).

4. Bots and Waquet 1997: ch. 1.

5. Waquet 2001: 22, citing Max J. Okenfuss, "The Jesuit Origins of Petrine Education," in J. G. Garrard, ed., *The Eighteenth Century in Russia* (Oxford: Clarendon
   Press, 1973), 106–30.

6. Stearn 1983: 42–43.

7. Seebohm 1911: 216. Linacre (ca 1460–1524), a noted perfectionist, had written—in
   four volumes—what he considered a basic Latin grammar (*Progymnasmata Grammatices vulgaria*), which was used to teach the Princess Mary. He also wrote a work
   on Latin composition, *De emendata structura Latini sermonis* (1524), with many
   reprints in continental Europe.

8. William Lily, *Carmen de Moribus*, ll. 1–8, from *A Short Introduction of Grammar*
   (London, 1650).

9. Morison 1935: 333, 84.

10. Butterfield 1961: 363.

11. Kaiser 1984: xvii.

12. Morrell, "Nova Anglia," 64–72, 95-99 (Kaiser 1984: 6–7).

13. Vincent, *Ad lectorem—Authoris carmen eucharisticon de Victoria hac Nov-Anglica*, 7–20
    (Kaiser 1984: 9).

14. E.g., Johnston 1999: 134–36.

15. E.g., Zimmermann 2004.

CHAPTER 19: *EHEU FUGACES*—LATIN'S DECLINE

1. The texts are from the Vatican II–approved Latin translation (Nova Vulgata) of the
   Hebrew Bible, and the World English Bible.

2. This effect of the changing sex ratio in the reading public is emphasized by Burke
   1993: 64.

3. Waquet 2001: 29, 188–89, citing Wladimir Berelowitch, *La soviétisation de l'école
   russe* (Lausanne: L'Âge d'Homme, 1990), 38.

4. Ordonnance de Villers-Cotterêts, art. 111: *Et pour ce que telles choses sont souventes fois
   advenues sur l'intelligence des mots latins contenuz esd. arrestz, nous voulons que
   doresnavant tout arrest, ensemble toutes autres procedures, soient de noz courtz
   souveraines ou autres subalternes et inférieurs, soient des registres, enquestes, contractz,
   commissions, sentences, testamens et autres qielzconques actes et exploictz de justice ou qui
   en deppenden, soient prononcez, enregistrez et delivrez aux parties en langage maternel
   fronçois et non autrement.*

5. Waquet 2001: 96, citing a variety of sources.

6. Kneale and Kneale 1962: 335, citing Carl Immanuel Gerhardt, ed., *Die philoso-
   phischen Schriften von G. W. Leibniz* (1875–90), vii, p. 28.

7. Waquet 2001: 88, citing a variety of sources.

8. Ibid., citing Georges Bonnant, "La librairie genevoise . . . ," *Genava* 31 (special issue)
   (1983): 71.

9. These have been gathered by Waquet 2001: 81–88.

10. Gouthier et al. 2002.
11. Virgil, *Aeneid*, i.279.

CHAPTER 20: *SUB SPECIE AETERNITATIS*—LATIN TODAY

1. Ainger and Wintle 1890 (17th impression, 1963): iii.
2. Another rich source is again Isidore, *Etymologiae*, ix.5–6.21 (*De adfinitatibus et gradibus*).
3. The bias in favor of North American tribes in these names simply reflects the research experience of the anthropologists who named the types. For the anthropology in this section, I am highly (and gratefully) dependent on Brian Schwimmer's Web site, www.umanitoba.ca/anthropology/tutor/kinterms.
4. This is sometimes said to be a remnant of Omaha-type patrilineal kinship in Latin (e.g., Hammel 1968).
5. E.g., la.wiktionary.org/wiki/Fratruelis. Its interpretation is occasionally at issue in interpreting dynastic histories: e.g., in the dispute over the Pictish succession (patrilineal or matrilineal?) where Nennius, *Historia Brittonum* (ninth century), said that king Bridei III of the Picts was King Ecgfrith's *fratruelis*. See Stewart Baldwin at archiver.rootsweb.com/th/read/GEN-MEDIEVAL/1999-11/0943592426. And Jordanes names one Germanus as *fratruelis* of Emperor Justinian (*Iordanes Getarum*, MGH Auct. ant. V.1, p. 77).
6. Berlin and Kay 1969.
7. Lyons 1999.
8. Anderson 2003.
9. A. Gellius, *Noctes Atticae*, ii.26 (*Sermones M. Frontonis et Favorini philosophi de generibus colorum vocabulisque eorum Graecis et Latinis*). In this work of Gellius', *russus* and *ruber* are said to be merely elegant variants of *rufus*, as against a large number of more specific hyponyms, some, e.g., *igneus, flammeus, sanguineus, croceus, ostrinus, aureus*, named after objects: fire, flame, blood, crocus, purple, gold; and others more diffuse—*fulvus, flavus, rubidus, poeniceus, rutilus, luteus, spadix*—which typically give different hues of *rufus*. E.g., *fulvus* is a mixture of *rufus* and *viridis*, which can vary as between the two; *flavus*, a lighter variant of *fulvus* (sometimes so light that it is applied even to water and sea foam); *rubidus* is a darker tone of *rufus*; and *luteus* some paler (*dilutior*) tone of it: it is indeed used by Pliny of egg yolks as well as roses. *Spadix* meant 'chestnut brown'. (Another word, *ferrugineus*, literally 'rusty', meant a darker shade than we should expect, more like puce or purple.) Isidore's *Etymologiae* defines Latin color terms en passant at various points, and xii.1.48–55 is an extended treatment of horse colors; but this is from the seventh century, and there is little else to classify colors explicitly in Latin before it became an artificial book-language.
10. *Meteorologica*, 374b–375b. Theodoric of Freiberg (who died around 1310) wrote an insightful treatise, *De iride et radialibus impressionibus* 'On the rainbow and the effects of light rays', which takes off from Aristotle.
11. Isidore, *Etymologiae*, xii.6.11: *nam caeruleum est viride cum nigro, ut est mare.*
12. *Galb(in)us* from Germanic (cf German *gelb*, English *yellow*), *blavus* from Germanic (*blau, blue*), and *azzurus* or *azzulus* via a Spanish reanalysis of Arabic *al-lāzwardī* (dropping the article *al* and an attached *l*), originally from Persian *lājward* 'lapis

lazuli'. This term contains a Latin borrowing of the same word, and *lazulius* is one word for 'blue' in Medieval Latin—used for example by Theodoric of Freiberg.

13. E.g., recently by Mario Gabriele Giordano, a columnist in the Vatican's quasi-official *Osservatore Romano*, August 13, 2006, 3, www.disvastigo.it/approfondamenti/ approfondamenti_123.htm.

14. Tuomo Pekkanen and Reijo Pitkäranta. *Conspectus rerum Latinus* can be found on www.eu2006.fi/news_and_documents/newsletters/en_GB/newsletters/ (for 2006) and www.presidency.finland.fi/netcomm/news/showarticle650.html (1999). *Nuntii Latini* is at www.yleradio1.fi/nuntii/.

15. Reported by the then English ambassador, Bulstrode Whitelocke, in his *Journal of the Swedish Embassy* (1855), 1: 300, cited in Burke 1993: 52.

16. Edited by Stanislaus Tekieli, at www.ephemeris.alcuinus.net.

17. Data obtained from www.google.co.uk/advanced_search.

18. Anderson 1991: 133–34.

19. Niccolò Machiavelli, *Discourses on the First Decade of Livy*, ii.5.4–7, 17–18.

20. Wittgenstein, *Tractatus Logico-Philosophicus* (1922), § 5.6.

21. This phrase, used during the sanctification of a new pope, is apparently derived from Thomas à Kempis, *De Imitatione Christi*, i.3.6: *o quam cito transit gloria mundi* 'How quickly the glory of the world passes!'

Bibliography

Adams, J. N. 2003. *Bilingualism and the Latin Language.* Cambridge: Cambridge University Press.

Ainger, A. C., and H. G. Wintle. 1890. *An English-Latin Gradus or Verse Dictionary.* London: John Murray.

Allen, P. S., et al., ed. 1906–58. *Opus epistolarum Des. Erasmi Roterodami.* Oxford: Clarendon Press.

Anderson, Benedict. 1991. *Imagined Communities.* London and New York: Verso.

Anderson, Earl. 2003. *Folk-Taxonomies in Early English.* Madison, NJ: Fairleigh Dickinson University Press.

Asor Rosa, A., ed. 1986. *Letteratura italiana, V. Le questioni.* Turin: Einaudi.

Auroux, Sylvain. 1994. *La révolution technologique de la grammatisation.* Liège: Mardaga.

Baldi, Philip. 2002. *The Foundations of Latin.* Berlin and New York: Mouton de Gruyter.

Barraclough, Geoffrey. 1978. *Times Atlas of World History.* London: Times Books.

Beaujouan, Guy. 1981. "Vocabulaire scientifique du latin mediéval." In *Colloques internationaux* CNRS. 589—*La lexicographie du latin mediéval . . .* pp. 345–54.

Benson, Robert L., and Giles Constable, eds. 1982. *Renaissance and Renewal in the Twelfth Century.* Cambridge, MA: Harvard University Press.

Berlin, Brent, and Paul Kay. 1969. *Basic Color Terms: Their universality and evolution.* Berkeley: University of California Press.

Berschin, Walter. 1980. *Griechisch-Lateinisches Mittelalter: Von Hieronymus zu Nikolaus von Kues.* Berne and Munich: Francke.

———. 1988. *Greek Letters and the Latin Middle Ages: From the Middle of the Eleventh Century to the Latin Conquest of Constantinople* (translation of Berschin, 1980). Washington, DC: Catholic University of America Press. www.myriobiblos.gr/texts/english/Walter_Berschin_30.html.

Binns, J. W. 1990. *Intellectual Culture in Elizabethan and Jacobean England: The Latin Writings of the Age.* Leeds: Francis Cairns.

Bischoff, Bernhard. 1990. *Latin Palaeography: Antiquity and the Middle Ages.* Translated by Dáibhí Ó Cróinín and David Ganz. Cambridge: Cambridge University Press.

Black, Deborah L. 1996. "Medieval Translations: Latin and Arabic." In Mantello and Rigg, eds., 723–33.

Black, Robert. 1995. *The Donation of Constantine: A New Source for the Concept of the Renaissance.* In Brown, ed., 51–85.

Bots, Hans, and Françoise Waquet. 1997. *La République des Lettres.* Paris: Belin–De Boeck.

Bourciez, Édouard. 1967. *Éléments de linguistique romane.* Paris: C. Klincksieck.

Bowman, Alan K. 2003. *Life and Letters on the Roman Frontier.* London: British Museum Press.

Brague, Rémi. 2002. *Eccentric Culture: A theory of Western civilization.* South Bend, IN: St. Augustine's Press.

Brotherston, Gordon. 1992. *Book of the fourth world: Reading the Native Americans through their literature.* Cambridge: Cambridge University Press.

Brown, Alison, ed. 1995. *Language and Images of Renaissance Italy.* Oxford: Clarendon Press.

Burke, Peter, 1993. *The Art of Conversation.* Ithaca, NY: Cornell University Press.

———. 2004. *Languages and Communication in Early Modern Europe.* Cambridge: Cambridge University Press.

Burnett, Charles. 1995. "John of Salisbury and Aristotle." *Didascalia* (Tohoku University, Sendai, Japan) 1 (1995): 19–32.

Butterfield, L. H., ed. 1961. *Diary and Autobiography of John Adams: 1, Diary, 1755–1770.* Cambridge, MA: Harvard Belknap Press.

Capelli, C., N. Redhead, J. K. Abernethy, F. Gratrix, et al. 2003. "A Y chromosome census of the British Isles." *Current Biology* 13: 979–84.

Carter, T. F. [1925] 1955. *The Invention of Printing in China and Its Spread Westward.* 2nd ed. Revised by L. C. Goodrich. New York: Ronald Press Co.

Champion, Craige B., ed. 2003. *Roman Imperialism, Readings and Sources.* Oxford: Blackwell.

Coleman, Christopher B. 1922. *The Discourse of Lorenzo Valla on the Forgery of the Alleged Donation of Constantine.* New Haven: Yale University Press.

Corriente, Federico. 1992. *Arabe andalusí y lenguas romances.* Madrid: Mapfre.

Cracco Ruggini, Lellia. 1987. "Intolerance: Equal and Less Equal in the Roman World." *Classical Philology* 82.3: 187–205.

Cribb, Joe, Barrie Cook, and Ian Carradice. 1999. *The Coin Atlas.* London: Little, Brown.

Cristofani, Mauro, ed. 1984. *Etruschi: Una nuova immagine*. Florence: Giunti.

Crystal, David. 2004. *The Stories of English*. London: Allen Lane.

Curtius, Ernst Robert. 1953. *European Literature and the Latin Middle Ages*. Princeton: Princeton University Press/Bollingen Foundation.

Daiches, David, and Anthony Thorlby, eds. 1973. *The Mediaeval World: Literature and Western Civilization*. London: Aldus Books.

Dalby, Andrew. 2002. *Language in Danger*. London: Penguin.

d'Alverny, Marie-Thérèse. 1982. "Translations and Translators." In Benson and Constable, eds., 421–62.

D'Amico, John F. 1983. *Renaissance Humanism in Papal Rome: Humanists and Churchmen on the Eve of the Reformation*. Baltimore and London: John Hopkins University Press.

Davies, Martin. 1996. "Humanism in script and print in the fifteenth century." In Kraye, ed., 47–62.

Dennis, George T. 2001. *Maurice's Strategikon: Handbook of Byzantine Military Strategy*. Philadelphia: University of Pennsylvania.

Dermenghem, Émile. 1951. *Les plus beaux textes arabes*. Paris: La Colombe.

De Simone, Carlo. 1996. *I Tirreni a Lemnos—evidenza linguistica e tradizioni storiche*. Florence: Olschki.

Dickey, Eleanor. 1996. *Greek Forms of Address: From Herodotus to Lucian*. Oxford and New York: Oxford University Press.

———. 2002. *Latin Forms of Address: From Plautus to Apuleius*. Oxford and New York: Oxford University Press.

Dixon, C. Scott. 1996. *The Reformation and Rural Society*. Cambridge: Cambridge University Press.

Dronke, Peter. 1973. "Mediaeval Rhetoric." In Daiches and Thorlby, eds., 315–45.

Dumézil, Georges. 1979. *Idées romaines*. Paris: Gallimard.

Ernout, Alfred. 1930. "Les éléments étrusques du vocabulaire latin." *Bulletin de la société linguistique de Paris* 30: 82–124.

Ernout, Alfred, and Antoine Meillet. 2001. *Dictionnaire étymologique de la language latine: Histoire de mots*. Reprint of the 4th ed. Paris: Klincksieck.

Facchetti, Giulio M. 2000. *L'enigma svelato della lingua etrusca*. Rome: Newton & Compton Editori.

Febvre, Lucien, and Henri-Jean Martin. 1958. *L'apparition du livre*. Paris: Albin Michel.

———. 1976. *The Coming of the Book*. Translation of Febvre and Martin, 1958. London: New Left Books.

Feeney, Denis. 2005. "The Beginnings of a Literature in Latin." *Journal of Roman Studies* 95: 226–40.

Feo, M. 1986. "Tradizione latina." In Asor Rosa, ed., 311–78.

Fernández Valenzuela, Benjamín. 1974. *De Deo, Deoque homine heroica*. Mexico: UNAM.

Fishman, Joshua A. 1991. *Reversing Language Shift*. Clevedon, UK: Multilingual Matters.

Forster, Peter, T. Polzin, and A. Röhl. 2006. "Evolution of English basic vocabulary within the network of Germanic languages." In P. Forster and Colin Renfrew, eds., *Phylogenetic Methods and the Prehistory of Languages*, 131–37. Cambridge: McDonald Institute Monographs.

Fossier, Robert. 1999. "Economic Organisation." In Timothy Reuter, ed., *New Cambridge Medieval History*, 3: 27–63. Cambridge: Cambridge University Press.

Fulford, M. J. 1980. "Carthage: Overseas trade and the political economy, c. AD 400–700." *Reading Medieval Studies* 6: 68–80.

Garin, Ernesto. 1952. *Prosatori latini del Quattrocento*. Milano/Napoli: Ricciardi.

Georgiev, Vladimir I. 1981. *Introduction to the History of the Indo-European Languages*. Sofia: Bulgarian Academy of Sciences.

Gibbon, Edward. 1776–88. *The Decline and Fall of the Roman Empire*. London: W. Strahan; T. Cadell.

Glick, Thomas F. 1979. *Islamic and Christian Spain in the Middle Ages*. Princeton: Princeton University Press.

Golden, Peter. 1992. "The Codex Cumanicus." In H. B. Paksoy, ed., *Central Asian Monuments*. Istanbul: Isis Press. Also at www.unesco.kz/qypchaq/.

Gómez Mango de Carriquiry, Lidice. 1995. *El encuentro de lenguas en el "Nuevo Mundo."* Córdoba: Cajasur.

Gouthier, Daniele, Nico Pitrelli, and Ivan Pupolizo. 2002. "Mathematicians and the perfect language: Giuseppe Peano's case." jekyll.comm.sissa.it/articoli/art01_03_eng.pdf.

Grafton, Anthony. 1983. *Joseph Scaliger: A Study in the History of Classical Scholarship*. Vol. 1. Oxford: Clarendon Press.

Grant, Michael. 1996. *The Fall of the Roman Empire*. London: Phoenix.

Grimes, Barbara. 1992. *Ethnologue*. Dallas: Summer Institute of Linguistics.

Guaman Poma de Ayala, Felipe. [1615] 1980. *Nueva Corónica y Buen Gobierno*. Mexico: Siglo Veintiuno.

Haarmann, Harald. 1999. "Der Einfluss des Lateinischen in Südosteuropa." In Uwe Hinrichs, ed., *Handbuch der Südosteuropa-Linguistik*, 545–84. Wiesbaden: Harassowitz.

———. 2002. *Lexicon der untergangenen Sprachen*. Munich: Beck.

Hammel, E. A. 1968. *Alternative social structures and ritual relations in the Balkans*. Englewood Cliffs, NJ: Prentice-Hall.

Hankins, James, ed. 2001. *Leonardo Bruni: History of the Florentine People*. Vol. 1. Cambridge, MA: Harvard University Press.

———. 2003. *Humanism and Platonism in the Italian Renaissance*. Vol. 1, *Humanism*. Rome: Edizioni di Storia e Letteratura.

Harrington, K. P. [1925] 1962. *Mediaeval Latin*. Chicago and London: Chicago University Press.

Harris, William V. 1979. *War and Imperialism in Republican Rome: 327–70 B.C.* Oxford: Oxford University Press.

———. 1989. *Ancient Literacy*. Cambridge, MA: Harvard University Press.

Hassall, M. W. C., and R. S. O. Tomlin. 1992. "Roman Britain in 1991." *Britannia* 23, no. 5: 310–11.

Heather, Peter. 2005. *The Fall of the Roman Empire*. London: Macmillan.

Hills, Catherine. 2003. *Origins of the English*. London: Duckworth.

Hodges, Richard, and David Whitehouse. 1983. *Mohammed, Charlemagne and the Origins of Europe*. Ithaca: Cornell University Press.

Hopkins, Keith. 1978. "Economic growth and towns." In Philip Abrams and E. A. Wrigley, eds., *Towns in Societies: Essays in economic history and historical sociology*. Cambridge and New York: Cambridge University Press.

———. 2001. *A World Full of Gods: The strange triumph of Christianity*. New York: Penguin Plume.

Horrocks, Geoffrey. 1997. *Greek: A History of the Language and Its Speakers*. Harlow: Longman.

Hyland, Sabine. 2003. *The Jesuit and the Incas*. Ann Arbor: University of Michigan Press.

Ing Freeman, Janet. 1988. *Johann Gutenberg and His Bible*. New York: Typophiles.

Jacquart, Danielle, and Gérard Troupeau. 1981. "Traduction de l'arabe et vocabulaire médical latin: Quelques exemples." In *Colloques internationaux* CNRS. 589—*La lexicographie du latin mediéval* . . . pp. 367–76.

Jensen, Kristian. 1996. "The humanist reform of Latin and Latin teaching." In Kraye, ed., 63–81.

Johnston, David. 1999. *Roman Law in Context (31 BC–AD 235)*. Cambridge: Cambridge University Press.

Kaimio, Jorma. 1972. *The Ousting of Etruscan by Latin in Etruria*. Rome: Aziende tipografiche eredi G. Bardi. (*Acta Instituti Romani Finlandiae* 5; *Studies in the Romanization of Etruria* 3.)

Kaiser, Leo M. ed. 1984. *Early American Latin Verse, 1625–1825: An anthology*. Chicago: Bolchazy-Carducci.

Kallendorf, Craig W., ed. and tr. 2002. *Humanist Educational Treatises*. Cambridge, MA: Harvard University Press.

Keen, Maurice. 1973. "Mediaeval Ideas of History." In Daiches and Thorlby, eds., 285–313.

Kelly, Christopher. 2004. *Ruling the Later Roman Empire*. Cambridge, MA: Harvard University Press.

Kelly, L. J. 2002. *The Mirror of Grammar: Theology, philosophy and the modistae*. Amsterdam and Philadelphia: John Benjamins.

Kenney, E. J. 1974. *The Classical Text: Aspects of Editing in the Age of the Printed Book*. Berkeley: University of California.

Kenny, Anthony. 1985. *A Path from Rome*. London: Sidgwick & Jackson.

Kerson, Arnold L. 1986. "*Los latinistas mexicanos del siglo XVIII.*" *Asociación Internacional de Hispanistas, Actas* 9: 603–7.

Keys, David. 1999. *Catastrophe: An Investigation into the Origins of the Modern World*. London: Century.

Kneale, William, and Martha Kneale. 1962. *The Development of Logic*. Oxford: Oxford University Press.

Kousoulas, D. G. 2003. *The Life and Times of Constantine the Great: The First Christian Emperor*. 2nd ed. Bethesda, MD: Provost Books.

Kraye, Jill, ed. 1996. *The Cambridge Companion to Renaissance Humanism*. Cambridge: Cambridge University Press.

Kristeller, Paul Oskar. 1964. *Eight Philosophers of the Italian Renaissance*. Stanford, CA: Stanford University Press.

Laird, Andrew. 2006. *The Epic of America: An Introduction to Rafael Landívar and the Rusticatio Mexicana*. London: Duckworth.

Lancel, Serge. 1997. *Carthage: A history*. Oxford: Blackwell.

Laurencich-Minelli. 2000. "Breve reseña de los documentos Miccinelli en el ámbito del simposio: 'Guamán Poma de Ayala y Blas Valera. Tradición andina e historia colonial.'" *Espéculo: Revista de Estudios Literarios* (Universitorio Complutense de Madrid) 16. www.ucm.es/info/especulo/numero16/guaman.html.

Levi, Anthony. 2002. *Renaissance and Reformation: The intellectual genesis*. New Haven and London: Yale University Press.

Lévy-Provençal, Évariste, ed. 1934. "Un document sur la vie urbaine et les corps de métiers à Séville au début du XIIᵉ siècle: Le traité d'Ibn 'Abdūn avec une introduction et un glossaire." *Journal asiatique* 224: 177–299.

Lucena Salmoral, Manuel, ed. 1967, 1971. "Gramática Chibcha del siglo XVII." *Revista Colombiana de Antropología* 13: 31–90; 14: 201–20.

Lyons, John. 1999. "The vocabulary of colour with particular reference to Ancient Greek and Classical Latin." In Alexander Borg, ed., *The Language of Colour in the Mediterranean*, 76–90. Wiesbaden: Otto Harrassowitz.

Mallory, J. P. 1989. *In Search of the Indo-Europeans*. London: Thames and Hudson.

Malone, Kemp. 1924. "Artorius." *Journal of English and Germanic Philology* 23: 372.

Mancini, Alberto. 1980. "Le iscrizioni della Valcamonica," *Studi urbinati di storia, filosofia, letteratura* (Università degli studi di Urbino). *Supplemento linguistico* 2/1: 75–166.

Mantello, Frank A. C., and A. G. Rigg, eds. 1996. *Medieval Latin: An Introduction and Bibliographical Guide*. Washington, DC: Catholic University of America Press.

Marsh, David, ed. 2003. *Francesco Petrarca: Invectives*. Cambridge, MA: Harvard University Press.

Martinell Gifre, Emma. 1988. *Aspectos lingüísticos del descubrimento y de la conquista*. Madrid: Consejo superior de investigaciones científicas.

McEvedy, Colin, and Richard Jones. 1978. *Atlas of World Population History*. Harmondsworth: Penguin.

Mellink, Machteld, ed. 1984. *Troy and the Trojan War*. Bryn Mawr, PA: Bryn Mawr College.

Mendieta, Gerónimo de. [ca 1595] 1870. *Historia eclesiástica indiana, escrita a fines del siglo XVI por Gerónimo de Mendieta de la Orden de San Francisco*. Edited by Joaquin García Icazbalceta. México: Díaz de León y White.

Menéndez Pidal, R. 1972. *Origenes del español*. 7th ed. Madrid: Espasa Calpe.

Mohl, F. Georges. 1889. *Introduction à la chronologie du latin vulgaire*. Paris: Bouillon.

Mohrmann, Christine. 1951. Saint Jérôme et Saint Augustin sur Tertullien. In *Vigiliae Christianae* 5: 111–12. Brill Academic Publishers.

———. 1959. *Liturgical Latin: Its origins and character*. London: Burns & Oates.

Morison, Samuel Eliot. 1935. *The Founding of Harvard College*. Cambridge, MA: Harvard University Press.

Motolinia, Fray Toribio. [1541] 1990. *Historia de los Indios de la Nueva España*. Edited by Edmundo O'Gorman. Mexico: Porrua.

Niedermann, Max. 1953. *Phonétique historique du latin*. Paris: C. Klincksieck.

Nişanyan, Sevan. 2003. *Sözlerin Soyağacı 'Family-Tree of Words'*. 2nd ed. Istanbul: Adam.

Nogara, B., ed. 1927. *Flavio Biondo: Scritti inediti e rari*. Rome: Tipografia Poliglotta Vaticana.

Norden, Eduard. 1898. *Die antike Kunstprosa vom VI. Jahrhundert v. Chr. bis in die Zeit der Renaissance*. Leipzig: Teubner.

Ogilvie, Robert M. 1965. *A Commentary on Livy: Books I–V*. Oxford: Oxford University Press.

———. 1976. *Early Rome and the Etruscans*. Glasgow: Collins.

O'Mahony, Sean F. 1981. "The Preface to William Bathe's Ianua Linguarum (1611)." *Historiographia Linguistica* 8, n. 1: 131–64.

O'Malley, John W. S. J. 1979. *Praise and Blame in Renaissance Rome: Rhetoric, Doctrine and Reform in the Sacred Orators of the Papal Court, c. 1450–1521*. Durham, NC: Duke University Press.

Ong, W. J. 1959. "Latin Language Study as a Renaissance Puberty Rite." *Studies in Philology* 56: 103–24.

Oppenheimer, Stephen. 2006. *The Origins of the British.* London: Constable.

Osorio Romero, Ignacio. 1990. *La enseñanza del latín a los indios.* Mexico: UNAM, Instituto de Investigaciones Filológicas, Centro de Estudios Clásicos.

Ostler, Nicholas. 2005. *Empires of the Word: A Language History of the World.* London and New York: HarperCollins.

Palmer, Leonard R. 1955. *The Latin Language.* London: Faber.

Paschoud, François. 2000. *Zosime: Histoire nouvelle, tome I.* Paris: Les Belles Lettres.

Peano, Giuseppe. 1903. "De Latino sine flexione." *La Revue de mathématique* 8.

Pellecchia, Marco, et al. 2006, "The mystery of Etruscan origins: Novel clues from Bos Taurus mitochondrial DNA." *Proceedings of the Royal Society B: Biological Sciences.*

Pertusi, A. 1976. *La caduta di Constantinopoli: Le testimonianze dei contemporanei.* Milan: Fondazione Lorenzo Valla/A. Montadori.

Peruzzi, E. 1973. "Romolo e le lettere greche." In *Origini di Roma* (Bologna) 2: 9–53

Piltz, Anders. 1981. *The World of Medieval Learning.* Translated by David Jones from *Medeltidens lärda värld* (Stockholm, 1978). Oxford: Basil Blackwell.

Pirenne, Henri. 1939. *Mohammed and Charlemagne.* New York: W. W. Norton.

Pisani, V. 1960. Manuale storico della lingua latina. Vol. 3, *Testi latini, arcaici e volgari.* Turin, Rosenberg and Sellier.

Plezia, Marian. 1981. "Le latin dans les pays slaves." In *Colloques internationaux CNRS. 589—La lexicographie du latin mediéval . . .* pp. 131–36.

Pollock, Sheldon. 2006. *The Language of the Gods in the World of Men: Sanskrit, Culture and Power in Premodern India.* Berkeley: University of California.

Quilis, Antonio. 1992. *La lengua española en cuatro mundos.* Madrid: Editorial Mapfre.

Ramsay, S. Robert. 1987. *The Languages of China.* Princeton: Princeton University Press.

Reeve, Michael D. 1996. "Classical scholarship." In Kraye, ed., 20–46.

Reynolds, L. D., and N. G. Wilson. 1968. *Scribes and Scholars.* Oxford: Oxford University Press.

Ricard, Robert. [1933] tr. 1966. *The Spiritual Conquest of Mexico.* Translated by Lesley Bird Simpson. Berkeley: University of California Press.

Rix, Helmut. 1984. "Etr. meχ rasnal=lat. res publica." In *Studi di antichità in onore Di Guglielmo Maetzke,* 455–68. Roma: Brettschneider.

———. 1998. *Rätisch und Etruskisch.* Innsbruck: Innsbrucker Beiträge zur Sprachwissenschaft.

Rizzo, Silvia. 1986. "Il latino nell'umanesimo." In Asor Rosa, ed., 379–408.

———. 1990. "Petrarca, il latino e il volgare." *Quaderni Petrarcheschi* 7 (1990): 7–40.

Rochette, Bruno. 1997. *Le latin dans le monde grec*. Vol. 233. Brussels: Latomus.

Rosenblat, Angel. 1964. "La Hispanización de América: El castellano y las lenguas indígenas desde 1492." In *Presente y futuro de la lengua española: Actas de la Asamblea de Filología del I Congreso de Instituciones Hispánicas* (Madrid), 189–216.

Rossi, V. 1937. *Francesco Petrarca: Le Familiari*. Florence: G. C. Sansoni.

Rüegg, Walter. 1992. "Themes." In Hilde de Ridder-Symoens, ed., *Universities in the Middle Ages*, 3–34. Cambridge: Cambridge University Press.

Salá-Solé, J. M. 1973. *Corpus de poesía mozárabe*. Barcelona.

Schaff, Philip. [1910] 1997. *History of the Christian Church*, Vol. 4, *History of Medieval Christianity from A.D. 590 to 1517*. Oak Harbor, WA: Logos Research Systems Inc. (Charles Scribner's Sons).

Schumacher, Stefan. 1998. "Sprachliche Gemeinsamkeiten zwischen Rätisch und Etruskisch." *Schlern* 72: 90–114.

Searle, John R. 1969. *Speech Acts*. Cambridge: Cambridge University Press.

Seebohm, Frederic. 1911. *The Oxford Reformers: John Colet, Erasmus, and Thomas More*. London: Longmans, Green & Co.

Sherwin-White, A. N. 1973. *The Roman Citizenship*. Oxford: Oxford University Press.

Solin, Heikki. 1999. "Names, personal, Roman." In *Oxford Classical Dictionary*, 1024–26.

Southern, Richard W. 1953. *The Making of the Middle Ages*. London: Hutchinson.

Spitzer, Leo. 1959. *Romanische Literaturstudien*. Tübingen.

Stearn, William T. 1983. *Botanical Latin: History, Grammar, Syntax, Terminology and Vocabulary*. Newton Abbot, London, and North Pomfret, VT: David & Charles.

Steinbauer, Dieter H. 1999. *Neues Handbuch des Etruskischen*. St. Katharinen: Scripta Mercaturae Verlag.

Streckenbach, Gerhard. 1970, 1972. "Paul Niavis, 'Latinum ydeoma pro novellis studentibus'—ein Gesprächsbüchlein aus dem letzten Viertel del 15. Jahrhunderts I, II." *Mittellateinisches Jahrbuch* 6: 152–91; 7: 187–251.

Stuart, Denis. 1995. *Latin for Local and Family Historians*. Chichester: Phillimore.

Tainter, Joseph A. 1988. *The Collapse of Complex Societies*. Cambridge: Cambridge University Press.

Tanner, Marcus. 2002. *Ireland's Holy Wars*. New Haven and London: Yale University Press.

Tavoni, M. 1982. "The 15th-century controversy on the language spoken by the ancient Romans." *Historiographia Linguistica* 9, no. 3:237–64.

Thomas, Millicent Inglis. 1961. *Cassell's Compact Latin-English English-Latin Dictionary*. London: Cassell.

Ullman, Berthold Louis. [1932] 1969. *Ancient Writing and Its Influence*. Cambridge, MA: MIT Press.

van der Poel, Marc. 1997. *Rodolphe Agricola: Écrits sur la dialectique et l'humanisme*. Paris: Honoré Champion / Éditions Slatkine.

Verhulst, Adriaan. 1995, "Economic Organisation." In Rosamond McKitterick, ed., *New Cambridge Medieval History*, 4:481–509. Cambridge, Cambridge University Press.

Viñaza, Conde de la. 1892. *Bibliografía de Lenguas Indígenas de América*. Madrid: Ediciones Atlas.

Vincent, Nigel. 1988. "Latin." Chapter 2 in Martin Harris and Nigel Vincent, ed., *The Romance Languages*. Beckenham and New York: Croome Helm and Oxford University Press.

von Arnim, H. 1892. "Ineditum Vaticanum." *Hermes* 27: 118–30.

Waquet, Françoise. 2001. *Latin, or the Empire of a Sign*. London and New York: Verso.

Ward-Perkins, Bryan. 2005. *The Fall of Rome and the End of Civilization*. Oxford: Oxford University Press.

Watkins, Calvert. 1984. "The Language of the Trojans." In Mellink, ed., 45–62.

Watmough, Margaret M. T. 1997. *Studies in the Etruscan loanwords in Latin*. Florence: L. S. Olschki.

Weale, M. E., D. A. Weiss, R. F. Jager, N. Bradman, and M. Thomas. 2002, "Y chromosome evidence for Anglo-Saxon mass migration." *Molecular Biology and Evolution* 19:1008–21.

Welch, Robert, ed. 1996. *The Oxford Companion to Irish Literature*. Oxford: Clarendon Press.

Welzig, Werner, ed. 1972. *Erasmus von Rotterdam: Ausgewählte Schriften, Ausgabe in acht Bänden*. Darmstadt: Wissenschaftliche Buchgesellschaft.

Wicherkiewicz, Tomasz. 2005. "Diaspora Languages at the Edge of Extinction: Karaim, Tatar and Armenian . . ." In Nigel Crawhall and Nicholas Ostler, eds., *Creating Outsiders*. Bath: Foundation for Endangered Languages.

Wolff, Philippe. 1971. *Western Languages, AD 100–1500*. London: Weidenfeld.

Wright, Roger. 1982. *Late Latin and Early Romance in Spain and Carolingian France*. Liverpool: Francis Cairns.

Zimmermann, Reinhard. 2004. "Roman Law and the Harmonisation of Private Law in Europe." In A. S. Hartkamp et al., eds, *Towards a European Civil Code*. Nijmegen: Kluwer.

Index

Note: European regions and cities (except Rome) are listed under modern countries. There are joint entries for: battles, councils, gods and heroes, grammatical terms, rivers and seas. Numbers in italics indicate a map or illustration.